Navigating Nationalism in Global Enterprise

Navigating Nationalism in Global Enterprise analyzes the role of nationalism in global business strategy, showing how multinationals act not just as drivers of globalization but also as sophisticated operators in a world of nations. Using the case study of German companies in colonial and post-colonial India, Christina Lubinski traces how nationalism's influence on business competitive strategies changed over the twentieth century and across major political turning points, such as two world wars and India's transition to independence. She highlights how national imaginings are both relational because they derive from comparisons with other nations, and historical because they mobilize the past to legitimize future aspirations. Lubinski stresses that learning from the past is how multinationals engage strategically with the content of nationalism – that is, a nation's history, aspirations, and relationships with other nations. In India, German companies' competitiveness was continuously dependent on navigating nationalism and on understanding that nationalism and globalization are inextricably linked.

Christina Lubinski is Professor of Business History at Copenhagen Business School. Her previous publications include *The Routledge Companion to the Makers of Global Business* (2020) and *Family Multinationals: Entrepreneurship, Governance, and Pathways to Internationalization* (2013). She was awarded The Henrietta Larson Article Award (2015) and Oxford Journals Article Prize (2013).

CAMBRIDGE STUDIES IN THE EMERGENCE
OF GLOBAL ENTERPRISE

Editors
Louis Galambos, *The Johns Hopkins University*
Geoffrey Jones, *Harvard Business School*
Susie J. Pak, *St. John's University*

The world economy has experienced a series of globalizations in the past two centuries, and each has been accompanied and shaped by business enterprises, their national political contexts, and new sets of international institutions. *Cambridge Studies in the Emergence of Global Enterprise* focuses on those business firms that have given the global economy many of its most salient characteristics, particularly regarding how they have fostered new technology, new corporate cultures, new networks of communication, and new strategies and structures designed to meet global competition. All the while, they have accommodated changes in national and international regulations, environmental standards, and cultural norms. This is a history that needs to be understood because we all have a stake in the performance and problems of global enterprise.

A complete list of titles in the series can be found at: www.cambridge.org/globalenterprise

Navigating Nationalism in Global Enterprise

A Century of Indo-German Business Relations

Christina Lubinski

Copenhagen Business School

CAMBRIDGE
UNIVERSITY PRESS

University Printing House, Cambridge CB2 8BS, United Kingdom

One Liberty Plaza, 20th Floor, New York, NY 10006, USA

477 Williamstown Road, Port Melbourne, VIC 3207, Australia

314–321, 3rd Floor, Plot 3, Splendor Forum, Jasola District Centre, New Delhi – 110025, India

103 Penang Road, #05–06/07, Visioncrest Commercial, Singapore 238467

Cambridge University Press is part of the University of Cambridge.

It furthers the University's mission by disseminating knowledge in the pursuit of education, learning, and research at the highest international levels of excellence.

www.cambridge.org
Information on this title: www.cambridge.org/9781316511282
DOI: 10.1017/9781009049795

First published 2023

A catalogue record for this publication is available from the British Library.

ISBN 978-1-316-51128-2 Hardback

To Sylvia
who believes as many as six impossible things before
breakfast ... and taught me to always try

Contents

Figures

Tables

Acknowledgments

With so many dear friends and colleagues deserving acknowledgment, starting with an anonymous chance encounter may seem odd. However, this book would not exist had it not been for a conversation between strangers. Across two tables in an Indo-Chinese restaurant in Kolkata, I first heard the life story of an elderly gentleman who not only worked for German multinationals in India all his life but carried forward a family legacy of doing so. His evocative depictions of continuity and change in Indo-German relations accompanied me into different archives and remain a source of fascination to this day.

Many wonderful professionals helped me to find answers to my questions sparked by this dinner conversation, even after the COVID pandemic had imposed severe restrictions on all of us. A heartfelt thank you must go to the archivists at Siemens, Bayer, Krupp, Daimler-Benz, Unilever, EMI, the German Federal and Foreign Office Archives, the City Archive Solingen, the British Library, the Indian National Archives, the Bengal State Archives, the Library of Congress, and the US National Archives. I owe a special debt to Rüdiger Borstel of Bayer Heritage Communications who not only helped me to unearth new material but was also an exceptionally knowledgeable and delightful sparring partner for arguments and ideas.

The editors of the Cambridge Studies in the Emergence of Global Enterprise series, Geoffrey Jones, Susie Pak, and Lou Galambos, read and skillfully commented on the book. The team at Cambridge University Press, especially Michael Watson and Emily Plater, were wonderful in preparing the text for production and guiding me through this process.

I am fortunate to have mentors and friends who challenge and support me. Hartmut Berghoff has advised me well since the days of my PhD and listens even to the less obvious ideas. Geoffrey Jones spent uncountable hours – usually between 4 and 6 am – commenting and helping me clarify my argument. Per Hansen gives the best feedback and delivers it with warm croissants. And Dan Wadhwani is not only an infinite source of energy, motivation, and good ideas but has also taught me the value of fighting for historical reasoning even in adverse environments. I owe all of them an outstanding debt of gratitude and many dinner invitations. Please remind me of them any chance you get!

My colleagues at the Business History Conference were the most constructive critics of this project as it evolved over (probably too) many years. Special thanks go to Mira Wilkins, Rory Miller, Marcelo Bucheli, Stephanie Decker, Teresa da Silva Lopes, Mary Yeager, Heidi Tworek, Jeff Fear, Takafumi Kurosawa, Matthias Kipping, and many more for the thoughtful comments and excellent suggestions during and in between sessions. I learned a lot from Suresh Bhagavatula and Manjunath A N of the Indian Institute of Management Bangalore and from the participants of the conference "Informal and Everyday Markets: Histories of Business and Entrepreneurship in India since the 19th century." Thank you also to the colleagues at the Centre for Studies in Social Sciences in Kolkata for always having an open door and a warm lunch.

My colleagues at the University of Southern California don't just talk about interdisciplinarity; they live it! Thank you to the late Helena Yli-Renko, Elissa Grossman, Noam Wasserman, Violina Rindova, Nandini Rajagopalan, Cheryl Wakslak, Michael Rivera, Susan Harmeling, Jill Kickul, Adlai Wertman, Pai-Ling Yin, Jackie Yu, Sunny Ku, Hovig Tchalian, Paul Adler, and Tom Cummings for making it fun to be a historian in a business school environment. A special thanks to Dan Horowitz for many inspiring conversations.

The Centre for Business History and the Department of Management, Politics, and Philosophy at Copenhagen Business School have become an academic home to me. All my colleagues there have contributed substantively to this book by critiquing my arguments and offering up fresh ideas. Alfred Reckendrees, Chris Viebig, and Morten Tinning got me to the finish line with their critical readings and Mads Mordhorst and Andrew Popp supported the project over many years with thoughtful edits and an always open door. The participants of the departmental Writing Seminar, especially Christian Garmann Johnsen, Ida Lunde Jørgensen, and Daniel Hjorth, challenged me with interdisciplinary perspectives. And Irem Dönmez was the most dedicated research assistant who would make roadblocks disappear and can be counted on to handle any crisis – or flat tire – with a smile. Thank you also to Henrik Hermansen for his genuine curiosity for academic research, Head of Department Mitchell Dean, Vice-Head Lena Olaison, and the dream team of Lucie Alexanian, Karina Ravn Nielsen, Anja Vega Frederiksen, and Anje Schmidt who create the environment that makes it possible to think of business education beyond short-termism and spreadsheets.

For the many late evenings of questions, advice, and laughter, a special thanks to my former colleagues at the University of Göttingen and the German Historical Institute in Washington DC. My friends Jan Logemann, Corinna Ludwig, Jessica Csoma, Laura Rischbieter, Ingo Köhler, Stefan Hördler, and Christine Strotmann accompanied me on both sides of the Atlantic. Thank you all for wasting your time with me at Larry's Lounge.

We did not need a global pandemic to realize that home is a shelter from storms, no matter what kind of storm is blowing. To Sylvia, Hubert, Patricia, Tanja, Thorsten, Tobi, Edina, Kasper, Arni, and the rest of the gang – you are my favorite place in the world, anywhere! And to Oma, who knows a good marzipan cake when she sees it: We miss you.

Introduction

> In conversations with educated Indians of the North, it is particularly apparent that they think more as political speculators than as economic men of realities. ... [T]he fact that Indians' national sentiment is in the process of growing and that Indians move with increasingly greater force into political and economic posts previously dominated by the English, is an important opportunity for us. ... [T]he English themselves told us that the Congress governments in the provinces desire a collaboration with Germany and enthusiastically welcome German participation in industrialization.[1] (Anton Reithinger, I. G. Farben, 1938)

Anton Reithinger worked for one of the most infamous global multinationals of his time, the chemical conglomerate I. G. Farben. Dispatched on a fact-finding mission to India in 1938, he reported on the strategic opportunity that the rise of Indian nationalism seemed to offer his German employer. While he had his doubts about Indian "political speculators," he was not going to let this opportunity pass him by. Working for a company that was active all over the world, Reithinger knew that successful international business meant not just competing on economic terms but also capitalizing strategically on rising nationalist sentiments.

As Reithinger's report suggests, globalization and nationalism have long been intertwined forces shaping how multinational enterprises compete internationally. It is thus puzzling to note how they capture our attention in very different ways. While the forces of globalization have been described as crucial drivers of firm internationalization,[2] nationalism is usually perceived as globalization's antagonist – a fundamental threat to cross-border integration. At best, nationalist sentiments might be "mitigated"

---

[1] Anton Reithinger, "East Asia Travel Reports 1937/38: Politics and Economics," report #1: 13–15, 191/1/3, BA. This and all German sources translated by the author.

[2] Wilkins, *The Growth of Multinationals*. Jones, *Multinationals and Global Capitalism*. Fitzgerald, *Rise of the Global Company*. From a strategy perspective, see also Henisz, *Corporate Diplomacy*. Ghemawat, *Redefining Global Strategy*. Dunning and Lundan, *Multinational Enterprises*. Bartlett and Ghoshal, *Managing across Borders*.

1

by multinationals, but nationalism's essence is assumed to be isolation-ist and fundamentally opposed to deepening global business exchange. Such a view fails to account for the kind of multinational strategy making reflected in Reithinger's report, in which rising nationalism creates oppor-tunities to forge new and deeper business relationships. What we are left with is a historiography moving at two speeds. Whereas our understanding of globalization and business has become increasingly more sophisticated over the past thirty years, research on the many ways in which nationalism plays into global business strategy remains comparatively underdeveloped.

One reason for this neglect may be that economic nationalism once appeared as an antiquated and declining phenomenon. Optimistic visions of a globally integrated world characterized by multiethnic, multicultural cosmopolitanism often treated nations and nationalism as reactionary and backward looking.[3] However, recent years should leave little doubt that we have in no way passed the age of nationalism and that it will continue to influence our societies, economies, and firms – maybe in new forms but certainly not with less penetrating power.

In fact, the very dynamics of globalization seem to have reinforced nation-alist sentiments around the globe. At the exact same time that the costs of bridging geographical distances shrunk and new technologies projected sounds and images around the world, policy regimes increasingly turned against foreigners and foreign firms. Business historian Geoffrey Jones argues that "as technology facilitated human beings to travel and observe one another as never before, so they disliked what they saw. Nationalism and racism proliferated."[4] In response, the need and ambition to manage governments and their national politics rose up corporate agendas.[5]

A closer and more historically sensitive look may also consider nationalism's outward-facing and relational aspects in addition to its inward-focused protectionism. Indeed, nationalism inherently entails an international and comparative dimension as nations form their identities and define their interests in relation to other nations that are perceived as allies or adversaries. As historian Manu Goswami argues, nationhood is forged through "an institutional intermediation between the global (the world economy and the interstate system) and the local (the internal lines of difference) in both a structural and discursive sense."[6] "Indeed," also argues economic historian Christof Dejung, "the immense importance

---

[3] Reich, *The Work of Nations.* Hobsbawm, *Nations and Nationalism*: 163–183.
[4] Jones, "Origins and Development": 22.
[5] Jones and Lubinski, "Managing Political Risk." Kurosawa, Forbes, and Wubs, "Political Risks."
[6] Goswami, *Producing India*: 17.

of the nation can often be better understood, or at least grasped in a different manner, from a global or transnational perspective."[7] Thus, rather than pulling in opposite directions, globalization and nationalism have historically evolved in tandem, mutually reinforcing one another. By necessity, multinational enterprises acted not just as drivers of globalization but also as sophisticated operators in a world of nations, with more diverse and more refined approaches to nationalism than the literature in business history or strategy has so far acknowledged.

Navigating Nationalism in Global Enterprise analyzes the historical role of nationalism in global business to shed light on how the forces of nationalism and globalization might be balanced in multinational strategy in our own time. It explores the evolving ways in which multinational enterprises engaged with nationalism, based on the salient example of German business in India. I opted for India because there are few countries in the world where the impact of economic nationalism was as obvious and as long-lasting as in India. The slowly unfolding process of Indian decolonization provides a context in which it is possible to study the emergence and consequences of businesses' engagement with nationalism over many decades. It allows us to examine how managers and firms learned about economic nationalism and how strategies emerged to respond to and then capitalize on nationalistic thinking. For long stretches of the twentieth century, India was essentially a free-trade zone and thus an arena for competition between multinationals. It thus provides an especially good context in which to consider how multinationals competed and strategized in a world increasingly comprised of nations and nationalism.

In looking at international business in India from the perspective of German firms, the book diverges from existing scholarship and its primary interest in Indo-British relations. While the great interest in British business in India is understandable, shifting the focus to German firms brings to the fore the strategic opportunities created by nationalism and the shifting relationships between nations during the long history of decolonization. In this sense, it reflects the kind of political strategizing by several "catch-up countries" (including Germany but also the US, Japan, Switzerland, and others) which industrialized later than Great Britain and competed with it on world markets.[8] It also reframes some of the questions of Indo-British business history by rethinking India's role

---

[7] Dejung, *Commodity Trading*: 14.
[8] On economic thinking in catch-up countries see also Reinert, "German Economics as Development Economics": 48–49. On Japan's rise in competitiveness see also Da Silva Lopes and Tomita, "Trademarks as 'Global Merchants of Skill.'"

not just in the economy of the British Empire but also in its relationship to the broader world, which held the potential for extra imperial alliances that have thus far garnered less scholarly attention.

Finally, the resilience of German multinationals in India also serves as a compelling puzzle that cannot be solved without careful consideration of the strategic role of nationalism. From a conventional viewpoint, German companies should not have been competitive in the Indian market. The institutional environment offered them no advantages, and in fact many disadvantages compared with their British competitors. They had no political backing in the British Empire, spoke a different language, were unfamiliar with local customs and legal practices, and struggled to obtain necessary information – in short, they were more exposed than their British rivals to what international business scholars refer to as the "liabilities of foreignness."[9] To understand their operations against these odds, it is necessary to look beyond the conventional strategic wisdom to consider the role of nationalism.

As this book will show, the forging of affinities between Germans and Indians against the perceived international domination of the British world fundamentally shaped business relationships, laying the foundations for the success of German multinationals in what in theory should have been an inhospitable foreign market. While German trade with India never surpassed that of their British rivals in the national aggregate, it showed impressive growth beginning in the last third of the nineteenth century and several German firms were fiercely competitive with their British counterparts in their sectors. Yet they strategized differently, not least based on their perception of Indian nationalism and its role in global business. Historically exploring this process on the firm level allows us to untangle the strategies businesspeople employed to compete with their rivals in a world of nations.

Business Strategy in a World of Nations

For companies that expanded globally in the wake of the Industrial Revolution, a world of nations provided the terrain on which their identities as global players were formed. Nationalism first became strategically relevant for global business on a larger scale in the mid-nineteenth century; a moment that global historians have marked as transformational. "The crucial watershed inaugurating twentieth-century world history consisted in a series of parallel, simultaneous crises in the organization of power,

---

[9] Zaheer, "Overcoming the Liability of Foreignness."

production, and culture – that is, in the autonomous reproduction – of virtually every region of the world."[10] With remarkable synchronicity, nationhood became a rallying cry in a number of late developing industrializers (Germany, the US, Japan) as well as many colonial and semicolonial countries (India, China, Thailand). While each of these movements was idiosyncratic and shaped by local developments, their similar structure and competitive logic was also part of a larger transformation of the world. The very notion of companies and products having a nationality emerged not inside one country, where this question would not arise, but in the highly integrated world economy of the late nineteenth century, in which competitive nation-states exchanged goods, services, and ideas.[11]

The bourgeoning literature on the history of nationalism has not failed to capture this transformation and its many consequences.[12] Nationalism scholars date the seeds of modern nationalism to the last quarter of the eighteenth century, focusing on the American and French Revolution, and then trace their spread to other parts of Europe and Latin America. The 1848 revolutions in Europe, leading most prominently to the unification of Germany and Italy, were the culmination of this first wave of nationalism. This was the time when many European nations were formed and developed their national identity. According to historian Eric Hobsbawm, these European nations were driven by their size, economic strength, and alleged cultural dominance to engage in a form of nationalism that was inherently expansionist. Henceforth, nationalism went together with the successes of Western industrialization and the relentless search for resources, territory, and markets abroad.[13]

While nationalism during this first wave can be interpreted as a phenomenon of the modernizing West, it increasingly started to leave its mark on other countries of the world as well. Since the last third of the nineteenth century, the highly industrialized nation-states of Europe encountered a second wave of nationalism, which took place in Eastern and Northern Europe as well as in several places outside of Europe, including India.[14] Political scientist Benedict Anderson notes that "a 'model' of 'the' independent national state was available for pirating," which established an ideal type of nationalist imaginings.[15] While this standard became enacted locally and in very different ways, it entailed

[10] Geyer and Bright, "World History in a Global Age": 1045.
[11] Jones, "End of Nationality?"
[12] Smith, *Nationalism*.
[13] Hobsbawm, *Nations and Nationalism*: 32–36.
[14] Osterhammel, "Nationalism and Globalization."
[15] Anderson, *Imagined Communities*: 81.

several universal elements. It was imagined with a unified national interest (or in Anderson's words "deep, horizontal comradeship"), a delim-
ited national space, and the ideal of national self-determination.[16] These
elements connected and mobilized different nationalizing states within a
global grid of nations. The resulting nationalist movements, while deeply
local, were also the outcome of a global historical process of imitation
and competition between nations.[17] National identities were fundamentally forged in relation to other nations.

This relational nature of nation formation was clearly on display in
the cultural, intellectual, and political entanglements between Germany
and India. As Kris Manjapra elegantly argues about the Indo-German
intellectual relations of the time, the two countries found themselves at
a particular juncture in history, when their interests happened to align.
Together they rebelled against what they perceived as an Anglocentric
world order, reflected in the colonizing of Indian subjects, the "dictated
peace" of the Versailles Treaty after World War I, and Britain's push
for hegemony in Europe and in the Empire. "The entanglement of Germans and Indians thus produced the strongest inflection of intellectual
revolt against the nineteenth-century global status quo – a status quo
constellated by discourses about Enlightenment, Europe, and Empire,
and organized around the star of British world power."[18]

Incorporating the Nation in Multinational Strategy

While the cultural and political history of nationalism as interconnected
movements is well understood, nationalism's role in firm-level strategy
remains rather obscure to date. Too often, "economic nationalism" is
used synonymously with protectionism, despite widespread critiques of
this simplification.[19] The unfortunate practice of limiting nationalism to
a small set of isolationist policies is exacerbated by the ideological bag-
gage that the term carries, focusing primarily on fascist and conservative
versions of economic nationalism.[20] Another common misconception

---

[16] Ibid., 7.
[17] Goswami, "Rethinking the Modular Nation Form."
[18] Manjapra, *Age of Entanglement*: 5.
[19] For examples of economic nationalism as protectionism, see Hodgson, *Economic
Nationalism*: 3. Yarbrough and Yarbrough, *The World Economy*. Recent scholarship has
insisted that economic nationalism can incorporate a variety of ideologies. See in particular, Abdelal, *National Purpose*. Helleiner, "Economic Nationalism as a Challenge
to Economic Liberalism?" Pickel, "Economic Nationalism." Shulman, "Nationalist
Sources." Krampf, *The Israeli Path to Neoliberalism*. Tamir, *Liberal Nationalism*. Helleiner
and Pickel, *Economic Nationalism*.
[20] For this justified critique see, Levi-Faur, "Friedrich List": 156.

about economic nationalism is that it describes economic activities that are subordinated to the interest of the state.[21] This view triggered a second important critique, namely that scholarship so far has described an economic nationalism "without nationalism" and needed ways for "bringing the nation back in."[22] Nationalism is neither confined to official state policy nor adequately described as protectionism.

These critiques do not just occupy political scientists but also pose important questions for firm-level strategy, which have remained largely unanswered. Sociologist Sam Pryke points out that in economic nationalism research "there is very little coverage of the role of private capital. The assumption is that states continue to be the key economic actors and states promulgate national identity."[23] While economic policy is no doubt a worthy object of study, it is focused on state-to-state interactions and the intentions of political leaders but rarely incorporates firm-level analysis. Shifting attention from the state to business reveals a different set of insights and complements the macro-level discussion of economic policy with insights on firm-level strategic decisions and processes.

In recent years, strategy research has advanced a dynamic understanding of capabilities, described as a unique bundle of assets, routines, and processes that firms develop over time and that make them competitive.[24] This perspective embraces earlier explanations for the existence of multinational firms, such as John Dunning's "eclectic paradigm," which argues that multinationals exploit their ownership advantages, benefit from location advantages in host economies, and make a choice for internalization, that is controlling activities through hierarchy rather than having them take place on markets.[25] Yet, while internalization focuses primarily on explaining entry modes of multinationals, the idea of ownership advantages and its extension in the capabilities framework foreground competitive advantages and include processes of learning, entrepreneurship, and market creation. Such a heightened attention to firm capabilities, rather than transaction costs and relative factor prices, may open the door to how multinational firms learned to deal with and even shape nationalism in competing abroad.

---

[21] Gilpin, *The Political Economy*: 31. Gilpin, *Global Political Economy*.

[22] Crane, "Economic Nationalism": 55. For the critique see also Nakano, "Alfred Marshall's Economic Nationalism." Abdelal, *National Purpose*: 33.

[23] Pryke, "Economic Nationalism": 284.

[24] Teece, "A Dynamic Capabilities-Based Entrepreneurial Theory of the Multinational Enterprise." Suddaby et al., "History and the Micro-Foundations of Dynamic Capabilities."

[25] Dunning, "Reappraising the Eclectic Paradigm." For a recent critical discussion of internalization theory see Da Silva Lopes, Casson, and Jones, "Organizational Innovation."

Yet these firm capabilities are understood as internal to business organizations and are rarely connected to national identities, national histories, or the aspirations of nations. While the field of nonmarket strategy is devoted to understanding the relationship of multinationals to their specific home and host countries, it sees nations primarily as territories and less as aspirational communities.[26] One exception is the recent scholarship on the role of legitimacy in strategy formation, which opened up the field to questions of long-term objectives;[27] however, the role of nationalism in generating, challenging, or undermining business legitimacy remains largely unaccounted for. In sum, multinational strategy research typically depicts nations as territories or governments, but largely ignores the identities, aspirations, and histories that hold them together as "imagined communities."[28] The relative neglect of these ideational aspects of nationalism and nationhood limits our ability to grasp its role in business strategy.

The intertwined evolution of business and nationalism plays a bigger role in the business history literature, where scholars have extensively dealt with business responding to political and nationalist challenges at different points in time. Geoffrey Jones, Mira Wilkins, Robert Fitzgerald, and Takafumi Kurosawa and colleagues have established periodizations of global business, which are carefully embedded in the political economy, reflecting how economic nationalism waxes and wanes. Some of the turning points these historians have identified include the emergence of a sharp definition of the "nationality of the company" in World War I, the first efforts at systematic political risk management by global business, the Great Depression of 1929 as the end of laissez-faire economic systems and the rise of state-led protectionism, and a second wave of globalization since the 1970s that took the integration of global markets much deeper.[29] Their research leaves no doubt that nationalism fundamentally shaped global business but also shows how its concrete

---

[26] Boddewyn and Brewer, "International-Business Political Behavior." Ghemawat, *Redefining Global Strategy*. Ghemawat, *The Laws of Globalization*. Henisz and Zelner, "Strategy and Competition in the Market and Nonmarket Arenas." Oberholzer-Gee and Yao, "Integrated Strategy." Luo, "Toward a Cooperative View."

[27] Stevens, Xie, and Peng, "Toward a Legitimacy-Based View of Political Risk"; Sidki Darendeli and Hill, "Uncovering the Complex Relationship"; Stevens and Shenkar, "The Liability of Home."

[28] Anderson, *Imagined Communities*. See also Abdelal, *National Purpose*. Breuilly, "Introduction: Concepts, Approaches, Theories."

[29] Jones, "Origins and Development." Jones, *Multinationals and Global Capitalism*. Ghemawat and Jones, "Globalization in Historical Perspective." Wilkins, *The Growth of Multinationals*. Wilkins, The History of Foreign Investment in the United States, 1914–1945. Fitzgerald, *Rise of the Global Company*. With a specific focus on nationalism and political risk, Kurosawa, Forbes, and Wubs, "Political Risks."

relevance for business was heavily context-dependent, thus requiring more sophisticated approaches for exploring it.

Moreover, these accounts of long-run patterns of multinational strategizing see nationalism primarily as a political risk and highlight how companies cope with it as a threat. The portfolio of management strategies for political risks is one of the core areas of business history research.[30] A few clusters of research emerged around expressions of political risk at specific moments in time, namely political risks triggered by the Nazi regime in Germany,[31] those related to decolonization,[32] war as a source of political risks,[33] risks associated with consumer nationalism,[34] and the risk of (excessive or discriminatory) taxation.[35] This literature excels at shedding light on multinationals' diverse and creative strategies to mitigate the challenges of nationalism, for example by actively localizing, by cloaking origins of people and capital, or by establishing decentralized organizational structures which provided greater flexibility in moments of crisis.[36]

---

[30] Casson and Lopes, "Foreign Direct Investment in High-Risk Environments."

[31] Kobrak and Wüstenhagen, "International Investment and Nazi Politics." Boon and Wubs, "Property, Control and Room for Manoeuvre." Forbes, *Doing Business.* Forbes, "Multinational Enterprise." Kobrak, "Politics, Corporate Governance, and the Dynamics of German Managerial Innovation." For business under German occupation see also Wubs, "Unilever's Struggle for Control." For "aryanization," i.e. the (formal or informal) expropriation of Jewish property, see Köhler, *Aryanization.* Bajohr, *Aryanisation.* Kobrak and Hansen expand on the focus on Nazi Germany by exploring the broader interactions of business and dictatorship. See Kobrak and Hansen, *Business.* In particular, Wilkins, "Multinationals and Dictatorship."

[32] Decker, "Building up Goodwill." Decker, "Corporate Legitimacy and Advertising." Sluyterman, "Decolonisation and the Organisation of the International Workforce." Smith, "Winds of Change." Donzé, "The Advantage of Being Swiss." On the difficulty of managing hostile transition periods see also White, "Surviving Sukarno."

[33] Wubs, *International Business and National War Interests.* van der Eng, "Managing Political Imperatives in War Time." Dejung and Zangger, "British Wartime Protectionism." Andersen, "Escape from 'safehaven'." Panayi, "German Business Interests." van der Eng, "Turning Adversity into Opportunity." Kurosawa, "Breaking through the Double Blockade." Specifically on internment see also Panayi, *Prisoners of Britain.* Lubinski, Giacomin, and Schnitzer, "Internment."

[34] Mordhorst, "Arla and Danish National Identity." Hansen, *Danish Modern.* Hansen, "Networks, Narratives, and New Markets." Higgins, *Brands, Geographical Origin, and the Global Economy.* Jones and Mowatt, "National Image as a Competitive Disadvantage." Rius-Ulldemolins, "Barcelona and SEAT."

[35] Mollan and Tennent, "International Taxation and Corporate Strategy." Izawa, "Municipalisation, War, Tax and Nationalisation."

[36] Jones, "Learning to Live with Governments." Bucheli and Kim, "Attacked from Both Sides." Andersen, "Building for the Shah." Sluyterman, "Decolonisation and the Organisation of the International Workforce." Smith, "Winds of Change." Donzé and Kurosawa, "Nestlé Coping with Japanese Nationalism." Da Silva Lopes et al., "The Disguised Foreign Investor." Forbes, Kurosawa, and Wubs, *Multinational Enterprise.* Jones and Lubinski, "Managing Political Risk."

Engaging in a dialogue with strategy, historians have also shown how companies not just established but continuously maintained legitimacy in changing political environments.[37] Because of a process of "obsolescing political legitimacy" in times of change, which Marcelo Bucheli and Erica Salvaj define as "the gradual loss of legitimacy before the local society, resulting from the identification of this firm with a previous social and/or political regime," multinationals ought to continuously invest in their legitimacy.[38] Yet research has also shown that this investment often paid off. Long-term presence in a market benefited multinationals' political risk management and competitive positioning.[39]

Despite these significant achievements, the literature still leaves us with a truncated conceptualization of nationalism in business strategy. Most contributions focus on the risks of nationalism and ignore both business opportunities and the effects that nationalism can have on the competitive dynamics between multinationals.[40] Moreover, both business historians, such as Mira Wilkins and Stephanie Decker, and international business scholars, such as Pankaj Ghemawat and Charles Stevens, have stressed that not the host country in isolation but the bilateral relationship between host and home country is decisive for the strategy and success of multinationals abroad.[41] However, studies rarely explore this relationship in depth or compare how multinationals from different home countries strategize differently. The impact of historical or aspirational relationships between nations (beyond the direct home–host country link) and in groups of nations, such as colonial nations or catch-up countries, has seldom figured at all.

Yet, if nationalistic goals mobilize and connect different nations, then scholarship must engage more fully with national aspirations and the alliances or conflicts they foster.[42] To understand competitive dynamics based on economic nationalism – between local and foreign companies

[37] Jones and Comunale, "Business, Governments and Political Risk." Bucheli and Salvaj, "Political Connections." Gao et al., "Overcoming Institutional Voids." Bucheli and Kim, "Political Institutional Change." Smith and Simeone, "Learning to Use the Past." On reputation, see also van der Eng, "Turning Adversity into Opportunity."
[38] Bucheli and Salvaj, "Reputation and Political Legitimacy": 730.
[39] Jones, "Learning to Live with Governments." Donzé and Kurosawa, "Nestlé Coping with Japanese Nationalism." Gao et al., "Overcoming Institutional Voids."
[40] For two rare exceptions see Reckendrees, "Business as a Means of Foreign Policy or Politics as a Means of Production?" Donzé, "The Advantage of Being Swiss."
[41] Wilkins, "European and North American Multinationals." Decker, "Corporate Political Activity in Less Developed Countries." Ghemawat, *Redefining Global Strategy*. Stevens, Xie, and Peng, "Toward a Legitimacy-Based View of Political Risk."
[42] On the interplay between nationalism and political alliances in expropriations see Bucheli and Decker, "Expropriations of Foreign Property and Political Alliances."

but also between multinationals from different home countries – it is necessary to study the history and dynamics of such economic and political relationships. In fact, nationalist aspirations may help us better understand rivalries and alliances as well as conflicting and complementary interests between nation-states, which remain hidden in accounts that focus exclusively on material exchanges. To grapple with these relational and historical aspects of nationalism, it is insightful to revisit the thoughts of nineteenth-century political economist Friedrich List (1789–1846) who advanced a view of the world economy as composed of nations.

Productive Powers and Aspirational Communities

Friedrich List was one of the pioneers of a truly nationalist study of the economy.[43] He made the nation and nationality the distinguishing feature of his school of thought and argued that a nation is much more than the aggregation of individuals. In sharp contrast to economic liberals, such as his nemesis Adam Smith, he claimed that liberals in their "boundless [bodenlosen] cosmopolitanism" only see individuals as producers and consumers, but not as citizens and members of nations. His choice of the term "bodenlos," literally translated as "void of grounding" or "territory-less," was not coincidental and accused British liberals of failing to account for the value of a national territory and a national economy, which List introduced as inseparable. Polemically, List quarreled that Smith's book *The Wealth of Nations* in fact ignores the nation and instead assumes a society "not separated by nations, but united by a general law and by an equal culture of mind."[44] List conceded that in this "more perfect but entirely imaginary state of the human race, free trade would be beneficial to mankind"[45]; but he considered it far from being a realistic premise for studying economic and business relations. To complete and correct the scholarship advanced by Smith and his disciples, List set out to explore the principles of national economy, which to him arose historically with the idea of nations.

While nations are the result of political agreement, they are also fundamentally economic units because they are crucial to the development of what List called "productive powers." The productive powers of a nation are defined not only by their access to resources and technologies, but also by "capital of the mind," a category in which List included

[43] Henderson, *Friedrich List*. Hodgson, *How Economics Forgot History*: 58–59.
[44] List, *Outlines of American Political Economy*: letter 1: 7.
[45] Ibid.

"skills, training, industry, enterprise, armies, naval power and government."[46] The cultivation of the capital of the mind is crucial for nations
because it performs a higher-level coordinating role essential for the pro-
ductivity of other resources and gives substantive meaning to the idea of
national community. Writing up against Ricardo and Smith and their
idea that expanding trade resulted in benefits for all parties, List stressed
the inequalities in the development of productive powers. A nation, he
argued, "may well sacrifice much 'exchange value' for the moment, if
its new workshops produce expensive goods of poor quality. But it will
greatly increase its productive powers of the future."[47]

Countries with strong national identities, therefore, evaluate trading
relationships not simply based on their short-term economic benefits
and costs, but also based on notions of long-term national wellbeing.
Nations learn "to sacrifice the advantages of the present moment to the
hopes of a distant future."[48] A nation-state that is interested in expanding its productive powers goes through a process of reevaluating time. To
develop new and higher-ranked productive powers in the future requires
sacrifice in the present. In this sense, List's concept of the nation was
essentially that of an aspirational economic community, fundamentally
geared toward the development of national capabilities. However, List
was also a pragmatist and knew that the long-term interests of a nation
were sometimes at odds with others. He thus emphasized not only the
national community, but also the "other" – those who do not belong or
may even oppose the project of the nation.

As a historical scholar, List understood nations and their productive powers as evolutionary in that he saw nations as developing as they
gained more advanced capabilities. This is the reason for his idea of protecting infant industry from free market forces, which made him popular
with nationalist activists in many developing nations, including India.
List himself did not intend this use of his work. Writing in the early-
to mid-nineteenth century, he was shaped by the historical experience
of imperialism and made a case for emulating the strength and structure of the British imperial economy, not abandoning it.[49] Instead, he
was fearful that Britain could become so powerful that rival Western
nations would inevitably be reduced to dependent territories. "It would
not require many centuries before people in this English world would
think and speak of the Germans and French in the same tone as we speak

[46] Ibid., 193–194.
[47] List, *The Natural System of Political Economy*: 36.
[48] Ibid., 370.
[49] Ince, "Friedrich List."

at present of the Asiatic nations."[50] But to List this was a dystopia that could be avoided by developing productive powers.

Yet the very fact that List mobilized colonial rhetoric to make his case for resisting the powerful British economy allowed Indian nationalists to appropriate him for their struggle against colonialism. Among them were the first visionaries of an Indian national economy in the late nineteenth century, such as Mahadev Govind Ranade (1842–1901) and Gopal Krishna Gokhale (1866–1915), as well as the next generation of nationalists such as Benoy Kumar Sarkar (1887–1949) and Radhakamal Mukherjee (1889–1968).[51] Engaging with List, Ranade argued that it was his writings that clarified that the interest of the nation was not necessarily identical with the interest of the individual. National wellbeing, to Ranade, was "the full and many-sided development of all productive powers. The Nation's Economic education is of far more importance than the present gain of its individual members, as represented by the quantity of wealth measured by its value in exchange."[52] Similarly, Benoy Kumar Sarkar summarized List's teachings in the words: "Wealth is according to him not so important as wealth-making power."[53] Based on this argument, Sarkar saw in List's work "the Bible of a people seeking a rapid transformation of the country from the agricultural to the industrial stage."[54] Ranade, Sarkar, and other Indian nationalists used List to develop their own arguments for a national Indian economy, characterized by a bounded economic space and a strong state that could orchestrate the development of productive powers to achieve industrial prowess.[55]

List's view of the nation, which so inspired Indian nationalists, has a number of implications for studying economic nationalism even today. First, it forces us to explore business strategies and business practices that involve not only calculations of short-term interests based on material gains to trade and investment, but also incorporate the long-term political and social aspirations of a nation. Business historians are uniquely placed to do this because they can study nationalist business

[50] List, *The National System of Political Economy*: 131.
[51] Goswami, *Producing India*: 215, 221–224.
[52] "Indian Political Economy," Lecture delivered in the Deccan College, Poona, in 1892, in: Ranade, *Essays on Indian Economics*: 1–42, here: 20–21.
[53] Sarkar, *The Political Philosophies since 1905*: 43.
[54] Sarkar, "Influence of German Civilization on Modern India," *Amrita Bazar Patrika*, September 25, 1932.
[55] See for example the arguments in Sarkar, "The Hitler-State (part I)." On List's influence on Ranade see also Dasgupta, *A History of Indian Economic Thought*: 87–119. On the emergence of India's colonial economy as an idea see Goswami, *Producing India*: 73–102.

strategy at one moment in time together with its long-term consequences at another. Second, it means broadening the analysis from government and state policy, which is the domain of political scientist, to a much larger and more diverse set of actors and actions that are best explored in empirically rich, historical analysis. Third, it highlights the importance of understanding a nation's history and its aspirations to explore strategic business decisions over time. This means paying attention to the development of the capital of the mind as well as understanding the most significant "other," the selected object of comparison, that is sometimes implicitly, sometimes explicitly inherent in an economic nationalist agenda.

Exploring the impact of nationalism on business strategy in a List'ian framework opens a research agenda that asks how businesspeople engage with and make sense of nations. It explores the impact of nationalist aspirations for competitive positioning, for example when nationalists seek out allies or boycott certain nations to foster a political agenda. It also poses the question how businesspeople make sense of the relationship between nations, how they perceive similarities and differences. Such a constructed cognitive landscape of nationalisms is important as a resource to identify similarities and differences between nations, stress common goals, or find points of complementarity. As this book shows through analysis of historical archival material, German businesspeople simplified the complexity of their experiences with nationalisms around the world in what I call mental maps of nationalism.

Mental Maps of Nationalism

Navigating Nationalism in Global Enterprise explores German business in India over the century spanning the 1880s to the 1980s. By showing how these firms engaged with and perceived Indian nationalism over time, I trace the learning processes in the Indian market and unearth the relevance and evolution of mental maps of nationalism. The concept of mental maps was used by geographers as early as the 1960s to distinguish so-called objective maps from maps focused on people's perceptions of the world around them. Increasingly, though, there was a recognition that all maps are perceptual to some extent. Still, geographers stressed the difference between maps that emphasize physical features and those that focus more on connotations and relationships between elements.[56]

---

[56] Lynch, *The Image of the City*. Gould and White, *Mental Maps*. Musolino, "The Mental Maps of Italian Entrepreneurs."

These relational maps have usually little in common with the colorful renderings of topography that we associate with historical maps and globes. People experience the world long before they know how to depict it. I follow Henrikson's definition of mental maps as "an ordered but continually adapting structure of the mind ... by reference to which a person acquires, codes, stores, recalls, reorganizes, and applies, in thought or action, information about his or her large-scale geographical environment."[57] Rather than being framed on the wall, the mental maps of nationalism I trace in this book become visible as underlying assumptions in speech and action by business professionals, as they set out to explore the strategic landscape that nationalism created. They illustrate and foreground the List'ian insight that national imaginings are both relational and historical. Yet, they only become perceptible in the long view because they are often implicit, become taken for granted, and change only gradually over time. Therefore, it is only in the long run that we can detect changes in these mental maps and explore how they shape business strategy.

No discussion of mental maps in a colonial context can possibly ignore Edward Said's pathbreaking work *Orientalism*. In it, Said engages with the idea of "imaginative geographies" as a perception of space created by discourse. He argues that Western and American imaginations of "the Orient" created an enduring link between knowledge and geography. Said introduces Orientalism as a powerful collection of knowledge – constructed in the West – with a specific history and an established imagery and vocabulary. In admirable clarity, Said shows how Orientalism became an "accepted grid for filtering through the Orient into Western consciousness," while simultaneously confirming the Westerners' position of power and not least providing a justification for their colonial rule.[58]

Yet, Said is also very clear that Orientalism is essentially a British and French phenomenon because "the French and the British – less so the Germans, Russians, Spanish, Portuguese, Italians, and Swiss – have had a long tradition of what I shall be calling *Orientalism*, a way of coming to terms with the Orient." Said explains this with the fact that Orientalism "derives from a particular closeness experienced between Britain and France and the Orient."[59] This may at first seem counter-intuitive because Germany has unquestionably a long tradition of Oriental scholarship. Yet, according to Said, it lacked a "sustained national interest"

---

[57] Henrikson, "The Geographical 'Mental Maps' of American Foreign Policy Makers."
[58] Said, *Orientalism*: 6–7, 39.
[59] Ibid., 1, 4.

and was therefore too removed from colonial practice to develop Orientalism of the same quality as the French and the British. "There was nothing in Germany to correspond to the Anglo-French presence in India."[60] While scholars critically debate this claim, it may be worthwhile thinking about the differences in the imaginative geographies of Britain/France and Germany. There is today little doubt that Germany's colonial aspirations and practices are important to understanding German history and Germany's role in the world economy. They ought to be incorporated more systematically in the historiography.[61]

This book explores how German business engaged with economic nationalism and which role this played for business strategy in India. Like the patterns and processes described by Said, I explore how German businesspeople connected their limited and filtered knowledge about nations – constructed in the West – to the world around them, which during the twentieth century increasingly became perceived as a world of nations. I consciously opt for the term mental map of nationalism, rather than Said's imaginative geographies, to highlight the different goal of this exploration. The literature on Said's Orientalism has focused very specifically on defining "the other" and understanding how the knowledge system of Orientalism established and confirmed political power. It departs from the binary distinction of "us" versus "them." Yet, the world of nations that List described created – in addition to this binary – a space for dynamically evolving alliances. Mental maps of nationalism foreground these changing perceptions of the relationship between different nations. Some relationships remained firmly embedded in an East–West binary and can best be explained in this way. But others were casted in new ways to highlight joint aspirations or complementary interests. "The other" may still be perceived as strange and there was a power differential shaping the relationship. Yet, there were also degrees of strangeness, with some nations being more likely allies or more likely enemies than others. Practical ambitions could bring out the advantage of alliances even with what many perceived as strange bedfellows.

Rather than limiting the view to a binary "us" versus "them," I use the example of German business in India to explore the relationship between two nations that do not think of themselves as "us" by any means but for a variety of reasons experimented with temporary alignments and

---

[60] Ibid., 19.
[61] Conrad, *Globalisation and the Nation.* Zantop, *Colonial Fantasies.* Germana, *The Orient of Europe.* Grimmer-Solem, *Learning Empire.*

entanglement.[62] Mental maps of nationalism, I posit, were able to translate the mass of information about nations and nationalisms into a manageable guiding vision and provided a basic spatial patterning of the world. In global business, they evolved into powerful abstractions, which helped strategically cluster and categorize different nations within the world economy.

Yet, at the same time, mental maps of nationalism are also shortcuts with major flaws and undeniably ideological. They did not replicate the world of nations; they distilled and packaged the various experiences with nations into actionable principles. Depending on their purpose, mental maps varied in content, scale, and usability. And, as the longer historical view taken in this book will show, they changed over time as the world of nations evolved. While geographers have mostly used the concept of mental map to explore how people orient themselves within their environment and perceive the world; historians engage with them to show how context developments change mental maps.[63] For the topic of nationalism in business strategy, understanding how mental maps evolved exposes in particular the fragilities of nationalist strategy. As Lewis and Wigen argue, "[i]t is no coincidence that sea changes in ideology are generally accompanied by a questioning of metageographical categories."[64] Over time, as actors perceived the world of nations in new ways, older mental maps were being amended, replaced, or given a new spin.

The Argument in Brief

The historical narrative in this book unfolds chronologically, starting in the 1880s, when German nationalism first became a noticeable force in business, and ending in the 1980s, when the previous mental map populated by colonial and noncolonial nations eventually became replaced in the context of the Cold War and new understandings of development policy. The book builds on the existing scholarship on Indo-German relations in the context of global and transnational history. Historians have admirably explored the political and intellectual links between India and Germany.[65] However, commercial and business relations have

---

[62] Manjapra, *Age of Entanglement.*
[63] Holmén, "Changing Mental Maps of the Baltic Sea and Mediterranean Regions": 232.
[64] Lewis and Wigen, *The Myth of Continents:* xi.
[65] Manjapra, *Age of Entanglement.* Manjapra, "Transnational Approaches." Panayi, *The Germans in India.* Barooah, *India and the Official Germany.* Barooah, *Germany and the Indians.* Framke, *Delhi - Rom - Berlin.* Osterheld, "British Policy." Ahuja, "Lost Engagements?." Liebau, "Berlin Indian Independence Committee."

received comparatively little attention so far.[66] Instead, the book takes inspiration from a set of otherwise diverse studies converging in the critique that Indian historiography has fixated too narrowly on the Indo-British relationship. Rather than focusing on Indo-British trade alone, this body of work reflects the interconnectedness of the Indian economy with other parts of the world. Historian Christof Dejung and others stress the need to "look beyond the formal empire."[67] Without doubting the importance of the imperial framework, these scholars criticize the exclusive focus on it, which isolates the British–Indian relationship from the larger global economy and either ignores other competitors or subsumes them into overgeneralized concepts, such as the category "Western" or "European."

Instead, comparing different imperial and extraimperial experiences, their encounters and rivalries, allows for a more nuanced multipolar analysis of the Indian business context. The perspective of German competitors in India not only adds an untold story to the historiography but actually reframes it. Rather than understanding India as a secluded territory under British control, it is reinterpreted as a heavily contested market on a world stage – with frequent struggles over commercial control and various parallel sensemaking offers, heavily influenced by national imaginings. This makes it a particularly interesting context for exploring the impact of nationalism on business strategy.

Another factor explaining the choice for a German perspective on doing business in India is the availability of historical sources. To explore strategy formation on the firm-level, detailed and accessible archival collections are needed, which offer insights into general global strategy as well as the specific approach to India. Throughout the book, I take an empirical deep dive into the global business history of the electrical giant Siemens and the chemical juggernaut Bayer (which was part of the I. G. Farben conglomerate from 1925 to 1945) because they were two pioneers in the India business and the two largest German employers in India in the interwar period (see Table 5.2, page 142, for details). Both have outstanding historical archives which allow a detailed analysis of their emergent strategy. This strategy is not always focused on foreign

---

[66] For the post-Independence period, some pioneering work was done by Unger, "Export und Entwicklung"; Unger, "Rourkela"; Faust, *Spannungsfelder der Internationalisierung*. The author of this book has written articles on the German participation in selected industries in pre-Independence India: Lubinski, "Global Trade"; Lubinski, "Liability of Foreignness."

[67] Dejung, *Commodity Trading*: 1. See also, Arnold, *Everyday Technology*. Ramnath, *Birth of an Indian Profession*. Bassett, *Technological Indian*. Akita and White, *The International Order of Asia*. Akita, "Introduction: From Imperial History to Global History."

direct investment, or FDI, per se. As previous scholarship has shown, Germany was a major source of FDI pre-World War I but after losing its foreign assets during the war focused more on exports and substitutes for FDI, such as business collaborations, cartels, and other tailored contractual arrangement for engaging in foreign markets, which I will detail in the book. A major continuity in German engagement abroad is its focus on exploiting ownership advantages in specific sectors, including the chemical and electrical industry, which I study in the two cases.[68]

In addition to these large multinationals, I explore two sectors of the bazaar business – cutlery and gramophones/records – which were heavily influenced by German exporters prior to World War I but then diminish in relevance over time. Business records on them come from the City Archive of Solingen, the regional center of the German cutlery industry, and from the archive of the British EMI, which acquired many of its competitors in the music industry. I complement the records of these companies with trade journals and government reports on these two industries. To counter the survival bias of business archives and multiply the perspectives on historical processes, I triangulate the material pertaining directly to these firms with archival sources from the Indian, German, British, and American Governments, from the archives of German (Krupp, Daimler-Benz) and British (Unilever, EMI) competitors, and from journalists and other observers of the Indian market (for details on the archival collections see the Bibliography.)[69]

The first part of the book, Nationalism and Competitive Dynamics, explores the Anglo-German competition in India from the 1880s to the 1920s. The first two chapters show the market entry and operations of German firms in the shadow of Britain's dominance and frequently also by British mediation. Chapter 1 focuses on the multinationals Siemens and Bayer that built their India business on existing links to Great Britain, while Chapter 2 compares their experience with the small- and midsized German manufacturers active in the bazaar trade. The dominant understanding of nations in this period was derived from colonialisms and rooted in the claim that nations were an exclusive domain of Western, "civilized" people. This provided a justification of colonialism as a "civilizing mission" with an educational agenda,[70] which also permeated Western views of foreign business operations in India. The dominant

---

[68] For the distinctive pattern of German FDI, see Schröter, "Continuity and Change." On alternatives to FDI see also, Pedersen, *Internationalisation and Strategic Control*.

[69] For this process see Kipping, Wadhwani, and Bucheli, "Analyzing and Interpreting Historical Sources."

[70] Mann, "Touchbearers Upon the Path of Progress."

mental map of nationalism perceived nations through a colonial lens, clustering them by their history of political dependence and their role within existing colonial empires.

While this mental map persisted into the interwar period, and some may argue even beyond, German businesspeople in the decade leading up to World War I encountered first signs of a gradual introduction of a competing mental map. The new view of the world of nations highlighted historical and aspirational relationships between India and other nations in East and West. This mental map first emerged briefly in the bazaar business during a period of anticolonial unrest, which German firms experienced as an unexpected but welcome opportunity, as Chapter 2 shows. The idea of an alliance based on animosity to Great Britain became reinforced during World War I, which brought with it a much sharper definition of corporate nationality – distinguishing clearly between German and British endeavors – but also provided a space for experimentations with Indo-German alliances (Chapter 3). Both of these explorations sharpened the outlines of the new mental map and fed into an alignment of interests between India and Germany in the post-war period. After World War I, German business struggled to recuperate its foreign markets and its national pride, while Indian nationalists were looking for new options in their battle for independence, because the sacrifices they had made during the war failed to bring the expected political rewards. At this crucial historical juncture, explained in Chapter 4, German firms started to explore the merits of a still cautious but increasingly more explicit nationalist strategy in collaboration with their Indian partners. Their mental map of nationalism became reconfigured around the doctrine of national self-determination, which mobilized nations around the world.[71] It channeled German businesspeople's attention to new opportunities derived from anti-colonial and nationalist thought, inaugurating an era of explorative jockeying between nations based on their histories (for example, as joint victims of British dominance after World War I and in the context of colonialism) and their aspirations (for political independence and economic strengths). It turned nationalism from an accidental input for strategy into an important lever of business competition.

The second part of the book, Emergent Strategy in a World of Nations, shows the evolving nature of this nationalist strategy, and the continuous adjustments to it that were triggered by severe political turmoil. Because the perceptions of the relationship between nations are dynamic

[71] Manela, *The Wilsonian Moment.*

in nature, strategy must be too. Both global events and Indian nationalist developments reshaped the way the Indo-German business relationship fit – or was made to fit – into nationalist objectives. Chapters 5 and 6 show German business operations in India during the Great Depression and World War II, foregrounding the need for proactive maintenance of a brittle political positioning while simultaneously engaging forward-looking "imagined futures."[72] Importantly, many of the activities of German businesspeople developed as an "emergent strategy" as intentions conflicted with a changing reality, and businesspeople were pressured to engage in continuous creative adjustments.[73] In an inconsistent and unpredictable environment, strategic planning was an ambition that oftentimes did not translate into reality.

By the time of World War II, leading managers of German multinationals synthesized their patterns of past decision-making into a deliberate strategy rooted in a clear mental map of nationalism, which stressed the similarities between what was then labeled "countries with strong nationalist movements," as Chapter 6 explores. Strategies and capabilities developed in India were henceforth applied to other people striving for independence, and insights from nations with similar aspirations shaped the India strategy. German businesspeople learned from their concrete experiences with doing business in India about the needs and sensibilities of nations striving for independence; a thought that survived World War II and Indian Independence in 1947.

Chapters 7 and 8 explore the application of these insights in the post-war and post-Independence period. Chapter 7 shows that business relations between India and West Germany in the immediate post-war period were characterized by remarkable continuities, rather than the historic change one may expect from the transition to Independence.[74] Continuities characterized the business practices and social relationships as well as the perceptions of the relationship between nations. It was not until the 1960s that the sprawling ideology of the Cold War eventually led to a fundamental reconfiguration of the world of nations. Politicians and businesspeople took inspiration from newly available global abstractions (Rostow's stage model, national income accounts) to make sense of a changing world. Grappling with the relationship between nations became less a matter of interpreting nationalist ideas derived from politics, history, and ideology and instead more an exercise of mastering seemingly objective development economics.

[72] Beckert, *Imagined Futures*.
[73] Mintzberg and Waters, "Of Strategies, Deliberate and Emergent."
[74] For details on the relationship between India and East Germany which are beyond the scope of this book, see Voigt, *Die Indienpolitik der DDR*.

Ironically though, as Chapter 8 shows, while top-level strategy turned towards abstract and universal models of the world, strategy on the ground in India was shaped not by repeatable patterns or ideologies of development but by highly specific one-off negotiations with Indian officials, heavily shaped by nationalistic thinking. India's policy of continuously radicalizing enforcement of its licensing regime both disciplined and restricted multinationals. More importantly though, it led to covert haggling between individual firms and Indian officials, raising the unpredictability of doing business in India.

As the specific Cold War interpretation of developing countries found acceptance, politicians and businesspeople alike interpreted development as the statistically measurable economic strength of a nation relative to others. However, they did so at the cost of other characteristics, which had previously been meaningful, such as a nation's history, its concrete relationship to other nations, or qualitative national aspirations. For better or worse, the past of what were now called developing economies was reinterpreted as a stage on the route to prosperity. German companies that managed to make a claim for assisting India on this path bargained for advantages. Yet, the concrete bilateral relationship between India and Germany, which had shaped German business strategy in India for decades, became sidelined. Even the German rhetoric of allegedly being an outsider of colonialism, which German businesspeople in India had celebrated and actively fueled since the turn of the twentieth century, no longer fit the new mental map of nationalism, and eventually dissipated.

Over the course of the entire century, from the 1880s to the 1980s, German multinationals engaged in various and diverse negotiations with Indian officials and stakeholders, as strategy research would predict. However, strategy scholars often claim that governments and multinational companies bargain with each other based on rational and realist self-interest. Even if we accept the rationality focus of this literature, the historical analysis of German multinationals in India shows that the terms on which they bargained were constructed and reconstructed based on underlying assumptions about the relationship between nations, in short: based on mental maps of nationalism. These mental maps govern the epistemology and ideology that determines "what counts" in a negotiation. What the history of German multinationals in India reveals is that business strategy is never void of politics and nationalism; but it leans on underlying mental maps that determine the lens by which we see it.

Part I

Nationalism and Competitive Dynamics

1   The Invention of Nationality

> Once England governed the overseas world business almost exclusively,
> and the economies of other countries, namely Germany, could only
> participate by English mediation. ... Now, the world looks completely
> different! ... [T]he English industry has to fiercely compete with foreign
> industries all over the world.[1]   (Werner Siemens, 1884)

German multinationals, such as the electrical company Siemens and the
chemical firm Bayer, showed an interest in the Indian market dating
back to the late nineteenth century. However, entering India was not
an easy task. As a British colony, India's institutional environment was
favorable to British entrepreneurs, and it was them who had the lon-
gest track record of trading with India. Their contacts, knowledge, and
strategies were valuable to anyone doing business with India. Moreover,
British expansion overseas was accompanied by "a radical re-imagining
of space."[2] The British Empire was also a worldview and an evolving
and often contested identity. Surely, conceptions of empire differed, but
they all took their departure in grandiose visions of unity.[3] In the West,
India and what was described as the "Orient" were perceived through
the lenses of imperialism. Even Friedrich List, the nineteenth-century
pioneer of the study of a nationalist economy, looked enviously at the
breadth and width of the British Empire economy and saw in it a model
to be emulated.[4] Empire was a powerful sensemaking offer in a world of
diverse peoples, politics, and philosophies.

In this context and until at least the late 1880s, German big business
relied heavily on British intermediaries and agencies and piggybacked
on already-established trading routes to India. Capitalizing on the well-
integrated world economy prior to World War I, German businesspeople

[1] Siemens brothers' letters [Brüderbriefe], Werner Siemens, "Letter to L. Löffler," December
21, 1884, SAA.
[2] Magee and Thompson, *Empire and Globalisation*: 22.
[3] Bell, *The Idea of Greater Britain*.
[4] For the perceptions of the Orient see Said, *Orientalism*. On List, Ince, "Friedrich List."

25

imitated British strategies for the Indian market and collaborated with British India experts. The idea of goods and companies having a nationality was extraneous to the cosmopolitan traders of the time – both in Europe, where the newly emerging nation states only began to slowly develop a national identity that stretched into trade, and in India, where the European traders considered themselves an elite group of White Westerners in contrast to the local population.

Yet, as the century came to a close, European national identities started to rival one another. Trade became increasingly interpreted as an extension of national prowess, and businesspeople perceived their goods and companies as having a nationality and reflected on trading patterns as being in the service of a national agenda. Based on the example of two pioneers in the German India trade, Siemens and Bayer, this chapter shows how Germany as an industrial late developer grew into the role of a rival to Great Britain, the motherland of industrialization. In this context of competing nation-states, the community of European businesspeople in India splintered into clusters of nationalist entrepreneurs.

From Cosmopolitanism to Nationalist Entrepreneurs

On April 9, 1868, Werner Siemens tempted potential investors with a high-risk business pitch. The Prussian entrepreneur suggested building a direct telegraph line between Great Britain and India.[5] He had good reasons for requesting investment to the figure of £425,000. In a preparatory note he declared, "One of the most important tasks of the present, of tremendous mercantile and political importance, is the safe and swift telegraphic connection of Europe with India."[6] The proposal left little doubt about the merits of the line. India "with its enormous population and growing production," argued Siemens, was not only "one of the most important export markets in the world" but also "a gateway" for European trade to the markets of China, Japan, and Australia, which "will take on glaring dimensions" in the future.[7] A clever comparison gave Siemens' argument punch. He explained that connecting Europe

[5] Prospectus, reprinted in: Dr. Hans Pieper "In 28 minutes from London to Calcutta" (2 volumes), 1976, 340–342, 35.LK 232, SAA.
[6] Promemoria "The Indo-European Telegraph Line," reprinted in: Ibid., 306–311, here: 306.
[7] Ibid., 306. For the same argument in the 1880s, see also "Report about Foreign Territories: British East-India: Foreign Trade in the years 1886, 1887, and 1888," *Deutsches Handels-Archiv* (hereafter, *DHA*), October 1889, 620.

with India was more important than even the connection with New York because India's population was more than four times larger and the communication challenges more severe. It took thirty days to deliver letters from London to Calcutta,[8] compared to only eleven from London to New York.

Siemens was not the first to see this potential. Several failed attempts preceding his proposal led the editor of the daily *Times of India* to say, "we dare not anticipate much benefit from Mr. Siemens' line."[9] Yet, Werner Siemens was excited "to show what telegraphy can achieve."[10] Indeed, the Siemens family business built "the Indo" in the years 1867 to 1870, and the line remained in use for over sixty years, until 1931.[11] At the same time, competitors also invested in new telegraphic links, so that Britain and India had reliable coverage to transmit messages in about five hours by the late 1870s – an essential prerequisite for successful trade.[12]

Many of the arguments meant to entice investors about this venture, such as India's size, relevance, and future potential, still echo today. However, the participation of Prussian entrepreneurs and investors in connecting Europe with the Indian subcontinent seems less than obvious. In the context of an imperialist world order, one would expect India to be under firm control by its British overseers. The literature of India's trading relations before Independence is heavily dominated by accounts of Indo-British relations, the collaborations between British traders and local Indian businesspeople, as well as their conflicts in the struggle for self-determination. Britain's dominance is so self-evident that the terms "European" and "British" are largely synonymous in the historiography of India.

However, at closer scrutiny, the argument of British dominance and control is less obvious than it first seems. Trade statistics show Great Britain responsible for between 48 and 73 percent of all overseas imports to India between 1850 and 1914.[13] Since the last third of the nineteenth

---

[8] Prior to 2001, the city of Kolkata was known as Calcutta. Like many Indian cities (including Bombay, known as Mumbai and Bangalore, now Bengaluru), the name was changed to reflect the Indigenous pronunciation of its original moniker. Throughout the book, I follow the official name usage, e.g., employing Calcutta when speaking about the city prior to 2001 and Kolkata thereafter.

[9] "Editorial Article," *Times of India*, November 26, 1869: 2.

[10] Siemens brothers' letters, Werner Siemens, "Letter to Carl," January 1867, SAA.

[11] Bühlmann, *Ligne*.

[12] Headrick, *Tools*: 160.

[13] Great Britain. India Office, "Statistical Abstract Relating to British India" (several volumes).

century, around the same time that the telegraph connections were established and provided reliable service for commercial communication, competitors from around the world started doing business on the Indian subcontinent. German entrepreneurs were among the fiercest rivals for British businesspeople before World War I and developed targeted strategies for entering and exploring the Indian market.

This was certainly a sea change. Previously, Great Britain's supremacy in world trade had been uncontested for decades and it exercised an unconcealed institutional stronghold on India, in particular. In the late nineteenth century, India covered an area of c. 1.8 million square miles (4.6 million square kilometers), with about 1.1 million under direct British rule and 0.7 million belonging to autonomous princely states. By population, the British territory held about 60 percent of the population and the princely states accommodated about 40 percent. British India was concentrated in the coastal areas, whereas the princely states made up the largest portion of the inner parts of the country (For a map see, Figure 1.1).

Within this political setup, Britain exercised control over the country. The Government of India Act of 1858 transferred the power over India from the East India Company to the so-called India Office, a department of state, and made the Queen of England the highest political authority in India.[14] The British Cabinet in London had a Secretary of State for India, who headed the council for Indian affairs. In India, the authority of the British monarch was represented by the Governor General and Viceroy. British India, that is, the portion under direct British control, consisted of fifteen provinces, of which two – Bombay and Madras – were known as presidencies. Each province had a governor appointed by the British monarch whose work was assisted by a council. While the Government of India was responsible for the customs and financial system as well as specific infrastructure elements, such as the post, telegraph, and (to some extent) railway system, the provinces dealt with the day-to-day administrative work, including the collection of revenues and the organization of local public works. In addition to these British-Indian territories, there were approximately 900 princely states in India. The biggest ones by population were Hyderabad, Kashmir, Mysore, Gwalior, and Baroda. They had their own custom houses at the respective borders and collected import duties for goods moving into the state. The British Government exercised some control over the princely states through political officers called "residents" because they resided in the respective states. While

---

[14] Webster, *Twilight*.

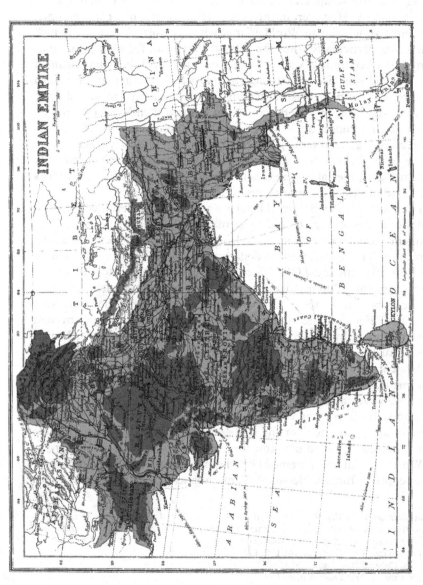

Figure 1.1   Map of India, 1912. *Author's depiction based on "The Indian Empire," from an atlas by John Bartholomew and Co., 1912, published by the Edinburgh Geographical Institute. (Public Domain).*

formally politically autonomous, the princely states were prevented from having diplomatic or political relations with other countries.[15]

Based on this setup, Great Britain exercised political and military control over India. However, in the commercial sphere, India was an open economic zone prior to World War I, with few formal barriers. British politicians particularly from the Liberal Party had for long been committed to a free trade doctrine.[16] Consequently, tariffs in India remained low and did not discriminate against imports from outside the British Empire. Up to the 1860s, tariffs amounted to 10 percent ad valorem. In the mid-1870s, they were reduced to 7.5 and then 5 percent; and by 1882, general import duties were abolished all together.[17] In 1894, Britain revived a general tariff of 5 percent, however with some exceptions. While other British possessions, such as Canada, Australia, and New Zealand, gave special preferences to imports from Great Britain, India's tariffs did not exhibit any such discriminatory effects.[18]

The most substantial formal barrier was that the Government of India and the various local governments were officially obliged to conduct government purchases either in Great Britain or in India. Practically all the purchases for the government departments and railways in India were made through the India Office Stores Department in London. However, competitors of different origins frequently circumvented such regulation by pre-importing goods to Great Britain or India where they were kept in stock.[19] For example, a report of 1897 revealed that all government departments in India used pencils made by Faber (Germany) or Hardtmuth (Austria-Hungary) rather than British makes.[20]

As a consequence, a German trade report of 1912 proclaimed, "India is a free trade country" and "custom duties ... are so low that they cannot have any protective impact."[21] Similarly, the US consul in Bombay described India as "one of the few large countries of the world where there is an 'open door' for the trade of all countries."[22] This openness was mirrored in, and at the same time reinforced, the fact that the group of Westerners in India seemed fairly homogeneous. Most Western businesspeople in India understood themselves as part of a White Western

---

[15] In addition to the British territories, India also consisted of a French area, Pondicherry, on the southeast coast (and some smaller French settlements up the coast) and of the Portuguese colony Goa on the southwest coast.

[16] Trentmann, *Free Trade Nation*: 169–171.

[17] Jebb, *Colonial Nationalism*: 313.

[18] Trentmann, *Free Trade Nation*: 169.

[19] Department of Commerce and Baker, *British India*: 13.

[20] Government of Great Britain, *Trade of the British Empire*: 577.

[21] Trade report 1912, R/901/13404, BArch-B.

[22] Department of Commerce and Baker, *British India*: 9.

elite. They lived together in the same areas of town, mingled in social clubs, and formed a community that was defined by an identity as "cosmopolitan bourgeoisie."[23]

However, political and economic hostilities increased during the last third of the nineteenth century with the rise of the nation-state and the development of industrial prowess in countries hitherto less developed, especially Germany and the US. As historian Charles Jones argues, not without judgment, "this progressive class [the cosmopolitan bourgeoisie, CL] resolved itself into reactionary nationalist fragments."[24] In tandem with this nationalist rivalry, companies and goods started to be perceived as having a nationality. Entrepreneurs and policy makers made sense of the world around them in increasingly more nationalist terms.[25] They developed a mental map of nationalism which went beyond a binary of East and West and guided their thinking about trade rivalry and competitiveness.

This mental map ran counter to contemporaneous imperial imaginations and challenged British supremacy. Roughly since the depression of 1873, Britain experienced a new anxiety over rivals that played catch up with the motherland of industrialization. And Germany seemed the most dangerous of these late movers.[26] While in 1871 *The Times* was still able to report about "a development of English Trade without parallel in our commercial history,"[27] in the new era British politicians anxiously evaluated their rivals' export dealings. To engage in such comparative evaluations, decision-makers initiated new forms of statistics, classifying exports by country of origin. To closely observe rival nation-states, British export statistics were extended by special reports about foreign competition. For example, one of Joseph Chamberlain's first acts when joining the Colonial Office in 1895 was researching the influence of foreign rivals in the different territories of the British Empire. The results, published in 1897, documented that in India, non-British imports had increased from £1.7 to 4.2 million between 1884 and 1894. In percentages, these "foreign" imports rose from 23.2 percent (1884) to 36.6 percent (1894).[28] As Britain's keenest competitors the report identified Germany, the US, and Japan, as well as (in some sectors) Belgium.[29]

[23] Jones, *International Business in the Nineteenth Century*.
[24] Ibid., 1.
[25] Jones, "End of Nationality?".
[26] Hoffman, *Great Britain and the German Trade Rivalry*.
[27] "The last Report of the Commissioners of Customs," *The Times*, September 26, 1871: 7.
[28] Research was done only for those articles for which foreign imports exceeded 5 percent of total imports Government of Great Britain, *Trade of the British Empire*: 2.
[29] Ibid., 5.

Interestingly, the more detailed numbers in the official British trade statistics seem to indicate that the German "threat" was vastly overstated. For most products, German imports did not rise to more than 20 percent of total imports. Only for spirits (40.6 percent), chemicals (33.5 percent), different wool products (23–24 percent), and copper (23 percent) were they higher.[30] However, concerned observers, particularly the proponents of a discriminatory tax, pointed to the growth rate rather than absolute numbers.[31] Moreover, because comparative statistics of this type were new territory, there were grave doubts about the reliability of existing trade statistics for the specific purpose of evaluating competition. As one analyst posited, based on qualitative intelligence from several British colonies, "the importation of foreign-made goods has increased in a much larger ratio than is shown by the returns,"[32] due to shortcomings in the reporting of country of origin, which previously had never been a major concern.

Trade statistics already had a long history. They had been collected with the intention of governing the economy as early as the seventeenth century. They also had for long served politicians and businesspeople in their efforts to make sense of a complex reality.[33] In the specific context of colonialism, trade statistics were frequently seen through a political lens. Most colonial powers sought to increase trade links to their colonies, often using political means, both formal and informal ones, and Britain was no exception.[34] By giving a quantitative overview of inflows and outflows, trade statistics marked needs, shed light on changes, and helped to identify new opportunities. Most importantly, it was trade statistics that could prove a strong commercial grip over a territory, which might be interpreted as a proxy for political power.

With the rise of nation-state competition, politicians and business leaders became increasingly keener on clearly classifying imports by nationality. However, the question what determines the nationality of goods is anything but trivial, and trade statistics mirror this challenge.[35] Both historians and contemporaneous observers highlighted the deficiencies of British Indian trade statistics (for details see, Appendix 2). One central point of concern was that the statistics did no distinguish "country of origin" from "last port of shipment," which meant that "[s]tatistics

---

[30] Ibid., 579–599.
[31] Lethbridge, *India*: 21.
[32] Government of Great Britain, *Trade of the British Empire*: 4.
[33] Tooze, *Statistics*: 3.
[34] Gallagher and Robinson, "Imperialism."
[35] Jones, "End of Nationality?"

show the course of trade, not the origin ... of produce."[36] This irritated German observers because the statistics systematically miscounted those goods manufactured in Germany but shipped to India indirectly, via ports in Belgium (Antwerp),[37] Austria-Hungary (Trieste),[38] Italy,[39] and importantly Great Britain.[40] All of these were frequent choices for shipments to India. Almost every year, and with increasing intensity, observers remarked that the statistics were unreliable and that determining the percentage that individual countries imported to India was impossible based on the available data.[41] In the Statement of Trade 1886/87, even the statistician of the Indian Government remarked that "[d]irect imports from Germany are still quite trifling ... Most of the small and cheap German wares so often seen in India must come through England still."[42]

It was not unusual for German goods to make their way to India via British ports because shipments via Great Britain were generally faster than the alternatives.[43] Manufacturers could exploit "the splendid export organizations in London, either by selling goods to such organizations for reexport to India or by working the business with them on a commission basis."[44] In addition to the well-established trade via Great Britain, there were other alternative routes available to German entrepreneurs. Before World War I, one such route went through the port of Antwerp in Belgium. By 1905, the trade report by the Imperial Consulate in Bombay

---

[36] Government of Great Britain, *Trade of the British Empire*: 5.

[37] "British East-India: Foreign Trade and Shipping in 1901/02, Report by the Imperial Consulate in Calcutta, October 20, 1902," *DHA*, May 1903, 477.

[38] There was a direct steamer line from Trieste to Bombay. See, "British East-India: Foreign Trade in the years 1886, 1887, and 1888," *DHA*, October 1889, 612.

[39] "Bombay: British East-India: Trade Report by the Imperial Consulate in Bombay about Trade and Shipping in the Bombay Presidency for the year ending March 31, 1904, October 1904," *DHA*, March 1905, 237.

[40] "British East-India: Foreign Trade in the years 1886, 1887, and 1888," *DHA*, October 1889, 615.

[41] "British East-India: Foreign Trade and Shipping in the accounting year 1903/04. Report by the Imperial Consulate in Calcutta, April 1905," *DHA*, August 1905, 687; "Bombay (British East-India): Trade Report by the Imperial Consulate in Bombay for the year 1909," *DHA*, March 1911, 209.

[42] Statement of Trade 1886/87, quoted in "British East-India: Foreign Trade in the years 1886, 1887, and 1888," *DHA*, October 1889, 625.

[43] "British East-India: Foreign Trade in the years 1886, 1887, and 1888," *DHA*, October 1889, 615.

[44] Department of Commerce and Baker, *British India*: 10. The report by Consul Henry Dunster Baker was initiated by the US Departments of Commerce and State with the goal to explore business opportunities for American firms. Baker (1873–1939) was a career diplomat who served in Tasmania prior to becoming the American consul in Bombay in the years 1913–1914; he then moved on to a position as commercial attaché in Petrograd, Russia.

estimated that at least half of the goods officially coming from Belgium were actually from Germany;[45] only a few years later, in 1907–1908, that estimate even increased to 75 percent.[46] While reliable data was hard to come by, evidence for a fast-growing German trade with India mounted.

Contemporaneous observers explained the alleged success of German business in India as two-pronged. In his *Handbook of Commercial Information for India* (published in 1919), British civil servant C. W. E. Cotton attributed the pre-World War I increase in German exports "partly to the special skill which that country developped [sic] in certain lines," and "partly to the displacement of expensive British goods by cheaper substitutes more readily absorbed in the bazaar."[47] The former was achieved by German manufacturers mainly in the electrical and chemical industries, which mostly sold business-to-business. The latter was the result of a plethora of smaller companies exporting their manufactured products to India to engage in the bazaar trade. The distinction between both lines of business is not clear-cut. The business by large German multinationals and the one by bazaar exporters were connected in many ways and some companies served both. The chemical company Bayer, for example, sold its dyes to Indian factories business-to-business but also engaged in the bazaar trade through its dealers. Moreover, British observers were often concerned that the bazaar trade could serve as a stepping stone for German firms capturing market share in India.[48]

The German multinationals that pioneered the business with India sold primarily to corporate buyers and public authorities. To explore their business on the level of the company, the remainder of this chapter will focus on two first mover companies in this segment: the electrical company Siemens and the chemical company Bayer. These two were selected because they started to trade with India early – 1865 and 1892 respectively – paid close attention to this market, and eventually became the two largest German employers in India prior to World War II.[49] As business with Indian bazaars followed different rules, this aspect will be explored in more detail in Chapter 2.

---

[45] "Bombay: British East-India: Trade Report by the Imperial Consulate in Bombay about Trade and Shipping in the Bombay Presidency for the year ending March 31, 1904, October 1904," *DHA*, March 1905, 237.

[46] "Bombay (British India): Report by the Imperial Consulate in Bombay about Trade and Shipping of the Bombay Presidency during the accounting year 1908," *DHA*, February 1910, 227.

[47] Cotton, *Handbook*: 94.

[48] Department of Overseas Trade and Ainscough, *Conditions and Prospects 1919*: 10.

[49] See Chapter 5 and Table 5.2 for details and the numbers of employees of these two companies in India.

Accessing India with British Mediation: Siemens

Initially, German multinationals that engaged in trade with India did so in collaboration with British businesspeople and trade experts. The case of Siemens is a fairly representative microcosm for the earliest collaborative ventures. The electrical company Siemens, founded in Berlin, was a pioneer of German-Indian business. It started by engaging in occasional exports to India, usually delivered via Great Britain, before developing a more systematic trading relationship via a stable partnership with an import–export trading house. Siemens' business centered on the exploitation of telegraphic communication technologies. Co-founder Werner Siemens (1816–1892) received an education in the Prussian Army and studied mathematics, physics, and chemistry.[50] He started commercializing some of his inventions via the firm Telegraphenanstalt Siemens & Halske, which he co-founded with the engineer Johann Georg Halske in 1847. His younger brother Wilhelm (1823–1883) had moved to Great Britain a few years earlier and exploited some of their patents there.[51] Over time, Werner Siemens expanded the business internationally and to that end relied on his brothers Wilhelm (renamed William) in Great Britain and Carl, who had earlier relocated to Russia.[52] In the business environment of the late nineteenth century, family provided an important resource for the emerging multinational company. Trust, loyalty, and the frequent correspondence between the brothers helped to tackle the challenge of managing across borders.

The beginnings of Siemens' business with India date back to 1856, when William Siemens delivered equipment for the telegraph line from Bombay to Calcutta to the Anglo-Indian Telegraph. In 1858, Siemens' London business was turned into an independent subsidiary with William as a partner and a British cable company, R. S. Newall & Co., as an investor.[53] Pre-dating the German Empire (founded in 1871), national ideologies had little impact on the business organization at this time. Kinship, on the other hand, did. The Siemens family members, who had strategically relocated to different commercially important countries, collaborated on developing what they perceived as a global family business. William Siemens immersed himself well in British society, married a Scottish woman, took British citizenship, and joined various

---

[50] Feldenkirchen, *Werner von Siemens*: 28–29.
[51] British patent No. 9741, May 29, 1843. Weiher, *Siemens-Werke*: 18. König, *Sir William Siemens*.
[52] Kocka, "Entrepreneur."
[53] Siemens brothers' letters, Werner, "Letter to Carl," November 22, 1854 and May 12, 1858, SAA.

clubs and associations. Yet, throughout his life, he never stopped communicating with his German family, fostered close social relationships with German expats in Great Britain, and took great pride in speaking German.[54] Yet, nationality and citizenship took a back seat to his identity as an entrepreneur keen on completing large-scale cross-border projects in a well-integrated global economy. In autumn 1859, investor Newall, Werner Siemens and twelve additional Siemens employees went to India to extend a cable from Aden to Karachi.[55] However, this early cable connection was beset with technical difficulties and eventually led to the dissolution of the Siemens–Newall partnership.

Leading up to the unification of Germany in 1871, founder Werner Siemens' outlook on the global organization of his business slowly started to change. His brother William frequently lobbied for completely separating the London and Berlin businesses. One point of disagreement was whether the German Siemens would subsequently be allowed to openly compete with Siemens products from Britain, which it had not done previously. "Not even in India, despite articulated requests, have we made offers because we did not want to damage the London business," argued Werner in a letter of 1864.[56] While Werner Siemens' co-founder in Germany, Johan Georg Halske, was keen on spinning out the British Siemens because he considered the business too risky, Werner wanted to keep the unity of the global family empire. He suggested to start a new firm, composed of three relatively independent branches located in Berlin, St Petersburg, and London. The three brothers would each manage the day-to-day business of one affiliate and only consult the others on big and risky ventures. Consequently, in 1865, the British Siemens was renamed "Siemens Brothers" with William at the helm.[57]

From 1867 to 1870, Siemens built the prestigious telegraph line (described at the beginning of the chapter) from Great Britain via Russia and Persia to the British submarine cable in the Persian Gulf, and on to India. It was completed in April 1870 and remained in use for over sixty years.[58] The venture was financed by a newly created joint-stock company, registered in London, but with half of the capital raised on the European continent, giving evidence of the global flow of capital. The Siemens brothers transferred all their concession rights to the new

---

[54] König, *Sir William Siemens*.
[55] Dr. Hans Pieper "In 28 Minuten von London nach Kalkutta" (2 volumes), 1976, 64–65, 35.LK 232, SAA.
[56] Siemens brothers' letters, Werner, "Letter to Carl," December 7, 1864, SAA.
[57] Scott, *Siemens Brothers*: 65–68.
[58] Bühlmann, *Ligne*.

British company, and in return Siemens & Halske and Siemens Brothers collectively received the order to construct the line, for a payment of £400,000 and the contract for its maintenance valued at £34,000.[59] The project being managed by Siemens was not without its critics. In a controversy between William Siemens and several opponents in *The Times*, one foreshadowed the increasing importance of national ideology. "It is indeed an imperial necessity that there should be an English line from end to end, in English hands alone, and worked throughout by Englishmen."[60] Yet his pleas remained unheard.

The completion of the project depended as much on diplomatic skills as on technical knowhow because a significant number of different authorities had to grant permissions for the line. For this task, an international business family was well positioned. The brothers Carl (in Russia), William (in Great Britain), and Werner (in Prussia/Germany) used their respective contacts to bring this mega-project to completion.[61] In December 1880, at the peak of its success, Siemens Brothers was transformed into a limited company, and one of the leading managers, Ludwig Löffler, became a minority equity partner. Three years later, William died unexpectedly leaving the unresolved question whether the British and the German Siemens should eventually be separated.

William's death came just at the moment in time when new commercial rivals questioned Britain's economic supremacy. The Anglocentric world order of the previous period slowly began to dissolve in the 1880s. Interestingly, historians often present the period of "high imperialism" – roughly from the 1880s to the outbreak of World War I – as the climax of the process of imperialistic expansion. However, intellectual historian Kris Manjapra argues convincingly that "the ideal of Empire (with a capital E) fell apart beginning in the 1880s because the concept of a unified European identity sustaining it was quickly crumbling away."[62] Consequently, imperialism did not dissolve, but the phenomenon became more diverse and gave rise to widespread intra-European competition over imperial projects, fueled by growing nationalistic sentiments. In line with this change in context, Werner Siemens increasingly pushed for expanding the German business to overseas territories, including those of the British Empire, which he had previously left to his brother. Commercial considerations certainly played a role in his agenda; however,

[59] Scott, *Siemens Brothers*: 53.
[60] Quoted in: König, *Sir William Siemens*: 73 and 73n114.
[61] Feldenkirchen, *Werner von Siemens*: 95.
[62] Manjapra, *Age of Entanglement*: 3.

he also tapped into the emerging German nationalism. "Once England governed the overseas world business almost exclusively, and the economies of other countries, namely Germany, could only participate by English mediation. ... Now, the world looks completely different! ... [T]he English industry has to fiercely compete with foreign industries all over the world"[63], he argued in a letter to Löffler. Löffler, on the other hand, insisted that the British Siemens had exclusive rights to the British territories overseas, based on established practices of the past. "It is the old English arrogance that Bismarck will hopefully manage to break," Werner commented to his brother Carl on this position.[64] The continuous conflict with Löffler over their respective spheres of influence led Werner to buy back Löffler's shares in 1888. Werner's cousin Alexander Siemens was appointed the new manager of the British business, which now cooperated closely with the German partner. This opened the door for new business in India.

The British Siemens Brothers started working with John Fleming & Co. in Bombay in 1889 and then made Turner, Hoare & Co. the firm's sole agent in India. They frequently advertised with the catchphrase, "The name of Siemens is a guarantee of excellence."[65] However, Siemens Brothers was not the only company holding the name that guaranteed excellence. The German Siemens, simultaneously, initiated a joint venture with the agency Schroeder, Smidt & Co. (SSC) in Calcutta on April 1, 1903.[66] SSC was an import–export agency founded by Johannes Schröder (1837–1916) and Johann Smidt (1839–1910), both members of the trading community in Bremen, Germany. Johannes Schröder had worked in Calcutta since 1859, as employee of the company J. B. Rentiers, a Hamburg-based agency. Johann Smidt began his career with the Johann Philipp Schneider agency in Calcutta in 1860. In 1862, they founded SSC, which they strove to make the best German agency in East India.[67]

Together Siemens and SSC created an Indian agency with independent accounting, for which SSC provided office space and human resources. Profits and costs were split evenly, and Siemens gave SSC the exclusive rights to distribute its products in British India, excluding Burma and Ceylon. For its part, SSC committed to running the

[63] Siemens brothers' letters, Werner, "Letter to Ludwig Löffler," December 21, 1884, SAA.
[64] Ibid., Werner, "Letter to Carl," October 20, 1884, SAA.
[65] Frequent ads, e.g. *Times of India*, September 5, 1906: 6.
[66] "Contract with Schroeder, Smidt & Co," July 14, 1903, 13092, SAA.
[67] Hoffmann, *Auswandern*: 93–96.

day-to-day business and to sending detailed reports back to Germany, which allowed Siemens to familiarize itself with Indian market conditions. The contract also explicitly stated that SSC was responsible "for the careful selection of customers and the evaluation of their credit." To minimize risks, Siemens and SSC agreed not to have a large consignment warehouse in India but deliver upon request. Goods held in India were supposed not to exceed a value of 20,000 Mark.[68] Siemens and SSC advertised as "manufacturers of electrical machinery and material of highest standard" and gave free technical advice to anyone requesting it – an important proposition in the business-to-business sector, in which pre- and post-sales activities mattered a great deal.[69] However, financial success eluded the partners. While sales increased steadily indicating demand, the accounting years 1903–1904 to 1906–1907 each ended with an operating loss.[70]

In 1908, Carl Friedrich Siemens (1872–1941), the youngest son of Werner Siemens and his second wife Antonie, traveled to British India. Carl had joined the family business in 1899, and from 1901 to 1908 was director of the British business. In the years 1908 to 1912, he restructured Siemens' international business and in preparation visited India as well as China and Japan in the spring of 1908.[71] Shortly thereafter, Siemens held a conference in Berlin with German and British business representatives to reorganize the overseas business based on Carl's observations. The Central Verwaltung Übersee [Central Administration Overseas] was founded, establishing close cooperation between the German and the British Siemens, and avoiding any direct competition as best as possible.

With this new organization, Siemens continued to do most of its Indian business via London prior to World War I. Among the largest contracts of the time was the delivery of four generators for the famous Tata organization, specifically for the Tata Hydro Electric Supply Company in Khopoli; the costs for which amounted to 569,000 Mark.[72] While the idea of a "German" or "British" product was only slowly starting to take hold, the large shiny generators proudly displayed Siemens as the name that guaranteed excellence (see Figure 1.2.)

---

[68] "Contract with Schroeder, Smidt & Co, July 14, 1903," 13092, SAA.
[69] Advertisement in: *Times of India*, June 5, 1905: 12.
[70] "Accounting statements by SSC," 1905–1907, 2910–2912, SAA.
[71] "Historical Development of the Overseas Trade and its Organization," 8188, SAA.
[72] "Remarkable contracts of SSW in India," 68.LI/156, SAA. "Hydro-Electric Scheme," *Times of India*, October 20, 1911: 5. On Tata's hydroelectric venture see, Raianu, *Tata*: 29–31.

Figure 1.2 Siemens turbo-generator at Tata, c. 1910. © *Siemens Historical Institute.*

Colorful Customers: Bayer

Comparable to Siemens, a pioneer in the business with electrical equipment, Bayer was one of the first movers in the business with synthesized colorants of natural dyes. Aniline dyes derived from coal tar first became available in the late 1850s. In the 1890s, German firms started offering synthesized indigo from aromatic hydrocarbons.[73] Dyes were a crucial import article for India with its large and continuously growing textile industry. It is particularly in this industry that German companies left a very clear footprint on the Indian market. Bayer, founded in 1863, was one of the leading players. Its dyes first came to India in the 1870s and 1880s through occasional deliveries by London-based import–export houses, such as Ullmann Hirschhorn & Co., Bell Brandenburg & Co., and the long-established trading company Graham & Co.

Like Siemens, Bayer initially made no effort to avoid British mediation in the globalized economy before World War I. Instead, it capitalized on the long-established links that Britain sustained with India and the availability of knowledgeable traders. It was through their business in Great Britain that Bayer's managers first became acquainted with Lancashire businessman James Kerr in the 1880s. Kerr had spent many years as a partner in the import firm Kerr, Tarruck & Co. in Calcutta, which was founded in February 1873 by Tarruck Chunder Sircar, a Bengali merchant, in conjunction with William Barlas Jameson and Kerr. Together with the latter, Bayer established its first consignment warehouse in India in 1888.[74]

Shortly thereafter, in December 1888, the company sent Henry Theodor Böttinger (1848–1920) on a trip to India to study the opportunities for a more systematic business. Böttinger had been a managing director of Bayer since 1882 and was married to one of the founder's five daughters. Manager Carl Rumpff (1839–1889), the in-house expert on India who oversaw much of the India business, could not join the trip due to health issues. However, as co-owner of the company and another of the founder's sons-in-law, Rumpff wrote an extensive memorandum on the potential of the Indian market and how to best approach it.[75] While there is no evidence of him having previously traveled to India, his analysis dated December 10, 1888, is one of the first detailed reports by a German businessman about India. Comparable to Siemens, Bayer's leading managers were also connected to the founder through kinship, again

---

[73] Travis, *The Rainbow Makers*. Engel, *Farben der Globalisierung*. Abelshauser et al., *German Industry and Global Enterprise*. Bäumler, *Farben, Formeln, Forscher*.

[74] Bayer, *Geschichte und Entwicklung*: 400–402.

[75] C. Rumpff, "India/Memorandum," December 10, 1888, 82/1, BA.

stressing the high value placed on trust in international business, which could at times be established through family connections.

Rumpff's memo was remarkable in its clearly articulated thoughts on distribution challenges; a topic otherwise often underappreciated (see Chapter 2). He proposed first to intensify the study of the current import conditions for dyes, distinguishing between the practices of three groups of importers – British agency houses, German trading companies, and the Indian Parsees – and understanding how each distributed dyestuffs around the country.[76] The latter group, the Parsees, were an ethnic community that for long had provided services to Europeans. With the rise of Bombay as an important trading city, the Parsees excelled as middlemen between European trading houses and Indian dealers. As a minority group in Bombay, characterized by their Zoroastrian religion and Persian origin, they had the advantages of possessing local knowledge and being able to mediate between different local interest groups.[77] As Jamsetjee N. Tata, a prominent Parsee, described in 1894, "Our small community, to my thinking, is peculiarly suited as interpreters and intermediaries between the rulers and the ruled in this country."[78] As a consequence, many Parsees at the time were not opposed to British rule but rather generally in favor of it. "Now it is acknowledged on all bands, and by Parsees themselves most of all, that any change in the rulers of this country is sure to affect most seriously the welfare and prosperity of their community."[79] The Parsees were highly successful in their business endeavors and served many European companies in their India business.

However, for Bayer's manager Rumpff, collaborating with one of the large Parsee traders came with drawbacks. He labeled them "the seducers of direct trade," and feared that a partnership with these influential players would create a lock-in effect and prevent collaboration with other importers or wholesalers. Instead, he envisioned a more decentralized system with various offices and suitable middlemen in the cities of Bombay, Calcutta, Karachi, Delhi, Madras, and possibly Rangoon. This would allow for better coverage of the vast Indian market, in which he predicted a profitable business not just for Bayer's dyestuffs but also, in the future, for its pharmaceutical products. On the other hand, Rumpff did not doubt that a savvy Parsee was needed to market to Indians. He envisioned the development of an easily recognizable trademark

[76] Ibid., no page numbers [p. 2], 82/1, BA.
[77] Kulke, *Parsees*.
[78] Jamsetjee N. Tata, "Mr. Tata's Finance: To the Editors of the Times of India," *Times of India*, April 12, 1894: 5.
[79] Ibid.

accompanied by the company name translated into Hindi. Indeed, he had already met with a Mr. Dady, a Parsee and one of the agents of the cotton yarn company Coats of Paisley, Glasgow, who had approached him as a potential agent. His impression of Dady was positive. He stressed his "intelligence, vitality and resilience" and was stunned by his extensive research of Bayer and its dye business.[80] Rumpff gave detailed instructions to the Bayer representatives embarking on their journey to India. He counseled that it was generally advisable to remain calm and short with Indian buyers, implying they would otherwise take advantage of the visitors. He also asked his colleagues to set up a showroom in a local hotel, including at least three rooms for, respectively, a chemical laboratory, a coloring studio, and a printing chamber to boast what Bayer's products could achieve. Any visitor should feel, as he phrased it, that "the Maharaja of Elberfeld [location of Bayer's headquarters] is here."[81]

For the future business with pharmaceuticals, Rumpff distinguished between English and Indian customers, highlighting that the former was a small group, while the latter was composed of 250 million potential buyers. For the English, he proposed introducing Phenacetin, a pain medication, which "can neutralize the effects of alcohol consumption, which is a larger illness among the English in India than cholera or fever." He also wanted to explore if there could be a market for Sulfonal, a sleeping aid.[82] To introduce these products, he suggested approaching doctors and giving free samples to hospitals. For the business with Indian consumers, he insisted on working with Indian-born health professionals and suggested approaching renowned doctors in the Parsee community. He calculated that if a mere 20 percent of the Indian population was to choose Bayer products, it would equal the entire population of the United States of America.

Finally, Rumpff engaged in the question of pricing and product quality. He criticized that some European competitors delivered second-rate dyes ["Schundqualitäten"] to India, simply because they could not sell them in Europe. He suggested to study how exactly dyes were used in India and whether it may be advisable to deliver a secondary quality; not because it was unsellable in Europe but because it could fill a void in the market. However, he was critical towards the generalized argument – often heard by dyestuff experts – that Indian consumers were exclusively interested in the lowest available qualities and heavily diluted colors. He suggested that it might actually be the wholesalers who deliberately choose to sell heavily diluted dyes because they hoped to increase their

---

[80] C. Rumpff, "India/Memorandum," December 10, 1888, [p. 21], 82/1, BA.
[81] Ibid., [p. 26].
[82] Ibid., [p. 33].

Figure 1.3   (a) Charles J. Vernon, (b) Kaba Virchand, and (c) Bayer Offices in Bombay, 1902. *Pictures 17788 (a) 17787 (b), 00156 (c), © Bayer AG, Archives Leverkusen.*

margins. His suspicion was based on the fact that with newly introduced types of dyes, he was unable to determine an explicit preference for low quality.[83]

Because Rumpff's health did not allow him to travel, his brother-in-law Henry Böttinger went on the trip from December 11, 1888, to June 1, 1889, accompanied by two colleagues.[84] He studied the market conditions and, in addition, initiated collaboration with an Indian chemist and a "School of Dyeing and Chemical Technology" in the princely state of Baroda (see the text that follows). About three years later, in 1892, Bayer massively expanded its organization in India. It hired Charles J. Vernon (Figure 1.3a), a former employee of the British Graham & Co., as its managing director in Bombay. In line with Rumpff's suggestions, Kaba Virchand (Figure 1.3b), a Parsee and former employee of an Indian dyestuff company, was engaged to organize the local sales activities. Böttinger came to India a second time, in 1896, and transformed the agency formerly called Vernon into the Bayer & Co. Ltd., which was registered under the Indian Companies Act of 1882. It was Bayer's first wholly owned subsidiary in Asia (for a picture of the office building, see Figure 1.3c).[85]

The company sold a variety of different colors: alizarin-red, congo-red, benzo-purpurine, delta-purpurine, benzo-azurine, resazurine, and chrysamine.[86] Like all larger German dye manufacturers, Bayer had its main

[83] Ibid., [p. 17].
[84] Böttinger, *Tagebuchblätter*. About Böttinger's India trips, see also Knoke, *Zwischen Weltwirtschaft und Wissenschaft*: 108–109.
[85] Bayer Group, "Bayer Group in India," (undated), www.ibef.org/download/bayer.pdf.
[86] Bayer ad, *Times of India*, November 19, 1889: 9.

Figure 1.4   Bayer advertisements for dyes, 1880s. *(a) 0-35600 c. 1885;*
(b) 0-33814, c. 1882, both BA, © Bayer AG, Archives Leverkusen.

depots with laboratories and technical staff in Bombay supplemented
by smaller depots in the important dyestuff-selling cities. The dyestuffs
were shipped in bulk and then diluted to the required strengths in Bombay. They were sold to dyeing and printing factories but also, in small
quantities, to bazaar dealers. Depending on quantity and usage, dyes
were provided in capsules, bottles, tins, kegs, and casks.[87] Packaging
decisions were important due to the climatic conditions in India. In particular, during the Monsoon, from the end of May to December, clouds
and thunderstorms were frequent. The mix of extreme heat, and then
extreme moisture, required suitable packaging, often best achieved in
tins.[88] As for the business with pharmaceuticals, by 1900, Bayer offered
a variety of remedies in India, including the abovementioned pain killer
Phenacetine and sleeping aid Sulfonal, but also the nutrition supplement
for typhoid patients Somatose, the diarrhea medicine Tannigen, the sed-
ative/antidepressant Trional, and the pain killers Aspirin and Salophen.[89]

With the input of their Parsee employee, Bayer developed graphic
localized advertisements to sell its dyes. The ads included colorful depictions of Indian deities and exotic animals, as well as the indication "Ger-
man-Make" or "Made in Germany" (see, Figure 1.4.)

Finally, Bayer also invested in training and developed local salespeople and demonstrators.[90] To educate potential future employees, Bayer's
Böttinger established a relationship with the Indian chemist Tribhuvandas Kalyandas Gajjar. Gajjar had a chemistry degree from Elphinstone

[87] Bayer ad, *Times of India*, February 20, 1895: 8.
[88] Department of Commerce and Baker, *British India*: 31.
[89] Bayer ad, *Times of India*, March 10, 1900: 11
[90] This organization inspired US and British competition during and after World War I;
see Department of Overseas Trade and Ainscough, *Conditions and Prospects 1919*: 54.

College in Bombay and had studied the Indigenous dyeing and printing industry in much detail. In 1890, he was asked by the local ruler of the princely state of Baroda, Sayyaji Rao Gaekwar, to establish an industrial school to train students for the development of local industry. The "Kala Bhavan" was composed of six schools, including the "School of Dyeing and Chemical Technology," and was focused on applied sciences and the creation of intimate links to industry. Training in chemical technology included dyeing and bleaching, calico printing, organic chemistry, and the chemistry of coal tar.[91] It was Gajjar who first suggested to Bayer "to train students and instruct native dyers in the use of their [German] dyes if they desired India to become one of their great customers."[92] Bayer financially supported the establishment of a laboratory in Surat and appointed Gajjar the firm's consulting chemist. The German firm also sent (and funded) several experts to the school, such as a technician named Schuhmacher and a professor of chemical technology, Dr. Ehrhard. Training centers for dyers were opened in Ahmedabad, Delhi, Cawnpore, and Amritsar under Gajjar's supervision. Many of the students were later employed by Bayer in its India business.[93]

Between 1900 and 1913 Bayer's sales in India increased more than sevenfold, from 320,199 to 2,451,647 Mark, generated in a total of sixteen offices.[94] The firm employed five Germans and 68 Indians.[95] The business success of Bayer and other German dyestuff manufacturers, notably Hoechst and BASF, was the result of their near-monopolistic position. Just before World War I, three-quarters of all synthetic dyes came from Germany; another eighth was dependent on German intermediates.[96] India was Germany's fourth largest market by value, after China, Great Britain, and the US.[97] Having used British mediation as an entry strategy, German dyestuff makers established their own organization by the 1890s, nevertheless relying on the support of British India experts, British infrastructure, and Indian middlemen, notably the Parsees, who were also the preferred partners of their British rivals.

[91] Raina and Habib, "Technical Institutes in Colonial India": 2619–2620, appendix 2611; Kochhar, "Tribhuvandas Kalyandas Gajjar."
[92] Gajjar, "Welcome Address": 9–10.
[93] Mehta, "Science versus Technology": 157; Bayer, *Geschichte und Entwicklung*: 400.
[94] Based on "Report to the Bayer Advisory Board," April 1902, 5, 5/E.a./16; "Peace Negotiations World War I," March 1918, 202/16; both BA.
[95] "Peace Negotiations World War I," March 1918, 202/16, BA.
[96] United States Tariff Commission, *Census of Dyes 1921*: 124.
[97] Ibid., 125, table 121.

It would be misleading to interpret the Indian market as Britain's backyard. Over the course of the late nineteenth and early twentieth century, it became a stage for intense economic rivalry, in particular between Germany and Great Britain. Although British businesspeople found some support in the formal and informal institutional environment of British India, these factors triggered targeted strategies by their competitors but did not amount to insurmountable barriers to entry. The large German manufacturers selling business-to-business started their India business facilitated by British mediation. They made no effort to avoid the British in the context of a globally integrated economy. Instead, they benefited from the advantage of the late mover and capitalized on the long-established links that Britain had built with India.

A closer look at the details of German business in India reveals that the concepts of firm and nationality sit uneasily with the realities of these early endeavors. Nationality of the company only first emerged as a topic of discussion in the period discussed here. Much of the early trade with India is better described by kinship and social networks – concepts that were central to the realities of the trading community. Additionally, it was a battle for market knowledge, using local intermediaries and experts. While the German entrepreneurs thought about their companies as an organizational unit challenged by long-distance trade with all its obstacles, they only slowly started interpreting it in a nationalist framework as a "German" entity as well.

2   Bazaar Goods "Made in Germany"

While the larger German multinationals initially entered the Indian market by imitating their British rivals or by collaborating with them (see Chapter 1), the smaller German firms that penetrated the bazaar trade followed different rules. The everyday products in the bazaar had much higher visibility for both travelers and residents, and many testified to the universal availability of goods that were "Made in Germany." From the 1870s to World War I, German exporters competed intensely with their British counterparts, mostly by leveraging their advantages as late movers, that is, learning from the first mover and making small adjustments to well-established processes. There were of course areas of overlap between the business conducted by the larger multinationals and the retail trade of the bazaar. Chemical companies, such as Bayer, sold their dyes to both large factories and in smaller amounts to end consumers in the bazaar. However, for the most part, the trade in specialized chemicals, technical products, and mechanical equipment required before- and after-sales services and thus a longer relationship with government or corporate buyers, as seen in Chapter 1. The bazaar, by contrast, invited on-the-spot purchases by end consumers, who responded to prices, advertisements, and the sights, sounds, and smells that emanated from the rows of stalls and mats.

It was in the bazaar trade where consumers and traders first showed an explicit interest in the national identity of foreign products and producers. As German companies negotiated with Indian intermediaries and dealt with the bazaar market, they gradually became aware that Indian customers saw value in their identities as non-British. The rise of Indian nationalism, in particular through the Swadeshi movement, heightened not only Indian consumers' and businesspeople's sense of their own identity, but also reconfigured the meaning of products in the bazaar. Distinctions emerged among "foreign goods," as Indian nationalists avoided British wares and actively sought out noncolonial alternatives in ways that shaped the politics of purchasing. German traders did not trigger this development, and neither did they foresee it. But with the help of Indian interlocutors, they learned to capitalize on the opportunity of the political moment.

Stuff and Wares in Indian Streets

After having traveled through Bengal, the English writer Robert Ernest Vernede described the hustle and bustle of the bazaar in a city near the Nepalese border in 1911:

There was a main street through the town where the stuccoed buildings and the mud huts stood side by side. The open fronts of the bazaar shops half revealed and half concealed the goods that were for sale and the private life of the shop-keeper. There were few good things to be bought, and the bulk of them did not look to be Indian but German or Brummagem [from Birmingham]. Still, the bazaar too, poor as were the goods sold there, was full of animation, and the people exchanging pice [Indian coin] for rubbish were keen enough on their transactions.[1]

From a different up-country place Vernede continued, "though there were some local industries represented, 'Made in Birmingham' or 'Made in Germany' stared at one from most of the stuffs and wares."[2] US consul Henry Baker, reporting from Bombay, confirmed not without envy that in the bazaar "American goods ... are not sold in nearly the same volume and value as the goods of the United Kingdom and Germany."[3]

The Indian bazaar trade was deemed to be of great importance by foreign manufacturers due to the large number of Indian consumers who could potentially be reached. However, Indian consumers also posed daunting challenges. First, they were huge in numbers and diverse in background. In 1901, the Indian population was about 287 million, in comparison to 32 million in Great Britain, 56 million in Germany, and 77 million in the United States. Language and religious variety added to the diversity.[4]

Second, disposable income was limited, leading to small individual purchases. It was estimated that Indian consumers spent an average of US$1.91 (or Rs 5.2) annually per person on bazaar goods. However, in aggregate the market was still appealing to importers.[5] The average

---

[1] Vernede, *An Ignorant*: 34–35.
[2] Ibid., 147.
[3] Department of Commerce and Baker, *British India*: 10.
[4] Great Britain India Office, *Statistical Abstract Relating to British India from 1892/3 to 1901/02*: 1. United States Census Bureau, *Statistical Abstract 1901*. Census of England and Wales 1901. Preliminary Report, presented to both Houses of Parliament by Command of His Majesty, London 1901, V, www.histpop.org. Statistisches Bundesamt, *Statistisches Jahrbuch 2011*, 34, www.destatis.de. Department of Commerce and Baker, *British India*.
[5] Department of Commerce and Baker, *British India*: 13.

bazaar buyer was interested in food, clothing, and a few everyday luxuries. The Indian diet at the time was vegetarian and heavy on sugar.
As for clothing, Indian buyers typically purchased simple cotton cloth.
Other items available at the bazaar included paper, cutlery and hardware, matches, glassware, cooking utensils, and a variety of containers
for carrying water and food, as US consul Baker found in his market
research. As living standards gradually rose, Indian customers began
purchasing increasing quantities of soaps, shoes, watches, and clocks
as well as occasionally small-scale technological items, such as sewing
machines, typewriters, and gramophones.[6]

Not unlike today's portrayals of "emerging markets," expectations for
a growing middle-class and concerns over price-conscious consumers
were often-discussed features of India's bazaar trade at the time. Contemporaries identified price as the chief competitive factor, and perceived
it as more important than product quality. "Many articles meeting with
enormous sales in India are so poor in quality that many American manufacturers would be ashamed to have their names attached to them,"
judged Baker.[7] Higher-priced articles could reportedly only be sold to a
very specific section of society, which Baker estimated at approximately
1 million people. Among them were the Europeans and Americans in
India, in particular businesspeople and their families, missionaries, persons connected with the civil administration, and officers and soldiers of
the British Army. However, he also counted upper-class Indians, princes
and nobility, large landowners and merchants, and the so-called Anglo-
Indians (people of mixed British and Indian descent, or people of British
descent born in India) who mostly worked in offices and for the railways.[8]
Although the market for higher-class products was considered limited
because many of these articles were "far beyond the purchasing ability of
the great masses of the country,"[9] entrepreneurs still engaged heavily in
this trade explaining it with their great expectations for the future. As the
Indian standard of living increased, they reasoned, a growing upper and
middle class would be interested in purchasing more valuable products.

The Anglo-German competition that many travelers saw when visiting the Indian bazaar dominated a series of industries. The next sections
explore two of them as exemplars for the competitive dynamics: cutlery

---

[6] Ibid., 13–14. In his excellent monograph David Arnold studies the most important work-
related everyday technological items but also acknowledges the role of recreational technologies, see Arnold, *Everyday Technology*: 11–12.
[7] Compare Department of Commerce and Baker, *British India*: 10, 13.
[8] Ibid., 14.
[9] Ibid., 15.

and gramophones/recorded music. While the former represented a relatively frequent purchase, the latter was a more sophisticated technological item of higher value that was primarily bought by the wealthy. The last section then looks at the influence of politics on these competitive dynamics, exploring the changing perceptions of what was considered a "foreign" good in the Indian bazaar.

Cut-Throat Competition

Cutlery products were typical bazaar goods, available in the streets of India throughout the country. The category "cutlery" in Indian trade statistics describes a diverse set of hardware products, such as penknives, scissors, and razors, which were principally available from many Western manufacturers as well as from Indian producers. In India, the town of Shahjahanpur, located in today's Uttar Pradesh in northern India, had about thirty families working in cutlery. The city of Meerut, in the same region, was a well-known center for scissor manufacturing with about twenty small factories and 200 employees around the turn of the twentieth century.[10] While local Indian products were thus widely available, imports from Europe increased rapidly in the decades before World War I. Among the many manufacturers, a handful of German and British firms dominated the market.

British Indian import and German export statistics both attest to the overall growth in cutlery imports to India. The values provided in German and Indian statistics, respectively, do not match because the underlying trade year was defined differently, and the German statistics frequently showed higher values because they included (some) exports via third countries that were missing in the Indian statistics. The numbers reflect an intense Anglo-German competition: Germany provided between 30 and 43 percent of cutlery imports, while Great Britain accounted for between 41 and 57 percent in the years leading up to World War I (see, Table 2.1 and Table 2.2; however, bearing in mind the shortcomings of these statistics, as described in Appendix 2.)

In Britain, the main exporters for cutlery came from either Birmingham or Sheffield, the latter of which emerged as Britain's leading cutlery and tool center. In Germany, the manufacturers of cutlery clustered around the city of Solingen.[11] In both countries, the industry was dominated by small- and medium-sized companies.

---

[10] Chatterjee, *Industries of the United Provinces*: 130–131.
[11] For Sheffield, see Higgins and Tweedale, "Asset or Liability?" For a general overview see, United States Tariff Commission, *Cutlery Products*: 27.

Table 2.1 *British Indian trade statistics on cutlery exports to British India, 1908–1914*

Year	Cutlery Total (in £1,000)	Cutlery from Ger. (in £1,000)	% of Total	Cutlery from GB (in £1,000)	% of Total
1908–1909	117	41	35.0	61	52.1
1909–1910	98	29	29.6	56	57.1
1910–1911	142	45	31.7	74	52.1
1911–1912	146	50	34.2	73	50.0
1912–1913	150	59	39.3	70	46.7
1913–1914	189	82	43.4	78	41.3

Annual Statements (several volumes).

Table 2.2 *German trade statistics on cutlery exports to British India, 1906–1913*

Year	Value (in 1,000 Mark)	Value (in £1,000)[12]
1906	652	31.9
1907	1,053	51.5
1908	1,143	55.9
1909	970	47.5
1910	1,078	52.8
1911	1,138	55.7
1912	1,180	57.8
1913	1,601	78.4

Statistisches Jahrbuch für das Deutsche Reich, Berlin (several volumes).

The German town of Solingen had a long and storied history in cut-lery production. Its manufacturers exported their products overseas as early as the seventeenth century. Solingen's manufacturers first used the European trade centers of Antwerp, London, and Lisbon to distribute their products to the world, including to India.[13] Antwerp – located at a distance of 229 kilometers (142 miles) from Solingen, compared to the closest German harbor, Hamburg, which was 396 kilometers (246 miles) away – provided the most important trade link to India. "Those knives, which were needed … in East and West India … are called good of the sea [*Seegut*] because they were sent to Antwerp and from there out to the sea," reported an expert of the Solingen trade as early as 1802.[14]

---

[12] £1 = 20.429 Mark. See, Bidwell, *Currency Conversion*: 22–24.
[13] Lohmann, *Die Ausfuhr Solinger Stahlwaren*: 13–15. Available at BSB.
[14] von Daniels, *Abschilderung*: 39–40.

Table 2.3 *Kaufmann's sales in British India, 1906–1913*

	Sales (in 1,000 Mark)	Sales (in £1,000)	Total German Imports (in £1,000)	% of Total German Imports
1906	302	14.78	31.9	46.3
1909	296	14.49	47.5	30.5
1911	480	23.50	55.7	42.2
1912	508	24.87	57.8	43.0
1913	528	25.85	78.4	33.0

Lohmann, Die Ausfuhr Solinger Stahlwaren, 21–2; Statistisches Jahrbuch für das deutsche Reich, Berlin (several volumes).

There was no reason to prioritize a German harbor in the highly integrated world economy.

Since the late nineteenth century, businessmen from Solingen relocated to India to promote trade. In 1875, Otto Tesche went to Calcutta as a representative of the company J. E. Bleckmann, Solingen, and was placed with the trading company Fornaro Bros. to promote Bleckmann's products. However, initially, the low quality of the German products made his task difficult. According to his memoirs, written retrospectively in the 1920s, a trader in a Calcutta bazaar told him bluntly, "We don't want your damned german [sic] rubbish!"[15] About a decade later, in 1884, Alfred Kaufmann followed Tesche's example and promoted goods for his company Henry Kaufmann & Sons, India-Works Solingen. The Solingen-based company, which was founded in 1856, became famous in India for its "Old No. 55 India Brand."[16] Kaufmann's export trade with India turned into one of the most successful of all German cutlery manufacturers prior to World War I. His sales increased steadily until the outbreak of the war accounting for 30–46 percent of total German imports (see Table 2.3.) Next to Carl Schlieper, one of his main competitors, he was market leader among the German manufacturers in India.[17]

After arriving in British India, cutlery imports went primarily to the provinces of Bengal (32.1 percent) and Bombay (34.1 percent), with smaller quantities going to Burma (15.9 percent), Sind (10.5 percent), and Madras

[15] Otto Tesche, "Letter to Heinrich Lohmann," December 12, 1931, no page numbers [4], NA/15/48, CASol.
[16] "Advertisement with short historical sketch," NA/15/2, CASol.
[17] Lohmann, *Die Ausfuhr Solinger Stahlwaren*: 22. The author refers to these numbers as the sales of one leading Solingen cutlery firm. The author's personal connection to Kaufmann and Kaufmann's leading position in India make it likely that these numbers refer to Kaufmann. See also, Department of Commerce and Baker, *British India*: 216.

(7.4 percent).[18] Once shipped to the port, a system of import agents, wholesalers, dealers, and hawkers distributed the products to the end consumers.[19] The import agent usually had an office in the European quarters of the respective port city but no direct sales facilities. If the import agent was European, he frequently used an Indian agent for the bazaar business. This so-called guaranty broker received a commission for his services, which included guaranteeing payments of the goods, which were delivered to wholesalers and dealers in the bazaar. As insurance, he had to provide a security for the goods he took, often in the form of gold or silver barrens. These brokers also organized orders for future deliveries.[20] Wholesalers and dealers then took the products from the Indian broker or directly from the import agent. The boundaries between the wholesaler and dealer function were fluid. Both owned stores or stands in the bazaar areas, and the wholesalers often engaged in direct sales activities as well. Finally, products not sold directly by the wholesales/dealers went to hawkers, who sold from a small stand or often a piece of cloth on the floor (see Figure 2.1).[21]

Neither the hawkers nor the dealers and wholesalers engaged in much advertising but rather expected the manufacturers to do so. Many especially small and mid-sized companies faced the challenge of acquiring market knowledge and organizing ad campaigns. Traveling salesmen and pictographic advertising were frequently used forms of promoting bazaar goods. According to the Indian Census Report of 1901, the literacy rate in India was 5.3 percent; with male literacy at 10 percent and female literacy at 0.7 percent.[22] Thus, newspaper advertisements could only reach the highly educated part of the population. Instead, manufacturers of bazaar goods often relied on enamel signs displaying easily recognizable labels. Frequent images included Indian deities and animal labels, as also seen in Chapter 1, Figure 1.4, for Bayer's business.[23]

Cutlery included a variety of different products, of which the most important for the Indian bazaar were penknives, scissors, and razors. Kaufmann's most popular penknives cost US$0.49 per dozen and were usually sold in sets of six in paper wrappers. Rival makes were available at prices between US$0.40 and US$0.70.[24] Kaufmann scissors came in

---

[18] *Annual Statements*, total cutlery imports for the year 1908 to 1914 by province. Also Lohmann, *Die Ausfuhr Solinger Stahlwaren*: 27.

[19] Ibid., 29.

[20] Dejung, *Commodity Trading*: 41. Ray, "Bazaar."

[21] Lohmann, *Die Ausfuhr Solinger Stahlwaren*: 29.

[22] India Census Commissioner, *General Report of the Census of India, 1901*: 158.

[23] Department of Commerce and Baker, *British India*: 17. Specifically for cutlery see also, Otto Tesche, "Letter to Heinrich Lohmann," December 12, 1931, NA/15/48, CASol.

[24] Department of Commerce and Baker, British India: 217.

Figure 2.1 Hawkers in a bazaar in Darjeeling, 1899. Universitätsbib-
liothek Heidelberg, Kurt Boeck, "Indische Gletscherfahrten: Reisen und
Erlebnisse im Himalaja" (Stuttgart 1900): between 50 and 51, http://
digi.ub.uni-heidelberg.de/diglit/boeck1900/0071. (Public domain).

boxes of six in assorted sizes, priced at US$0.60, but they could also
be acquired separately. For individual scissors, "Kaufmann's No 11344
(pointed)" competed with a Birmingham-made pair called "Popular."
The former cost US$1, and the equivalent from Birmingham US$1.02.[25]
Small price differences could be decisive and, consequently, fraud was a
common evil, especially those types of deception that reduced the quality
of the product but were hard to spot at first sight. Some products were
advertised as made of one raw material when they were really made of a
cheaper alternative. For scissors, which were often sold strung to post-
cards, the visible front side of the scissors was often nicely polished while
the backside remained untreated.[26]
   The main British competitors for Solingen's entrepreneurs came from
the British city of Sheffield. For decades, Sheffield and Solingen went

[25] Ibid.
[26] Otto Tesche, "Letter to Heinrich Lohmann," December 12, 1931, no page numbers
[4], NA/15/48, CASol.

head to head for India's cutlery markets. The British firms frequently complained that the German late movers imitated their trademarks and provided low-cost goods, which resembled the original products so closely that Indian consumers confused the German imitations for the British original. Some of these complaints made it into court records. In 1889, the renowned British manufacturer Joseph Rodgers & Sons Ltd. complained about the Solingen entrepreneur Röttgen. The German was said to take advantage of the resemblance of his family name with Rodgers and of the well-established trademark. The British judge agreed that these practices led to confusion abroad.

[I]t was in India, where the plaintiffs had a large trade, that the defendant Röttgen intended to compete with them; and the evidence was irresistible that the defendant ... had copied the plaintiffs' label slavishly ... in the hope that the eyes of persons not familiar with the English language would not detect the difference in the labels. The thing was quite transparent. It was an intended fraud.[27]

He thus ordered Röttgen to immediately stop sending cutlery marked with his name to Great Britain for sale or shipment to India. The *Sheffield Daily Telegraph* commented on the fraud:

In India, English cutlery is bought to great extent on sight. Buyers who can read a little English, and those who can not read English at all, trust to their eyes to recognize the outlines of the popular name Rodgers, the shape of their mark, and the color of the label. How are these unsophisticated natives to distinguish Röttgen with a double cross, from Rodgers with a Maltese cross and star, in both cases labels in the same color and arrangement being used. The difficulty of distinguishing between the two appears to be too much for the Indian buyers.[28]

The *Sheffield and Rotherham Independent*, moreover, expressed the hope that the case would act as "a deterrent to those who have acted as if the laboriously-attained reputation of English firms is fair game for greedy competitors." However, the journalist also criticized that there is no way to prevent German manufacturers from supplying their goods directly to India, where they "may even mislead colonial salesmen!"[29] For that reason, they pled for a swift adoption of a law, the Merchandise Marks Act, in India. The British variety of the Merchandise Marks Act had been passed in 1887, only two years prior to this case.[30]

---

[27] United States, *United States Congressional Serial Set, No. 2685*: 47. Copy in: NA/15/48, CASol.

[28] *Sheffield Daily Telegraph*, July 19, 1889, NA/15/48, CASol.

[29] *Sheffield and Rotherham Independent*, July 19, 1889. Copy in: NA/15/48, CASol.

[30] Payn, *Merchandise Marks Act 1887*. For context on the debates, see also Higgins, *Brands, Geographical Origin, and the Global Economy*: 29–56.

While there is a resemblance between the names and trademarks, it seems overstated to assume that they could not be told apart, especially by professional salesmen. However, in the mid-nineteenth century Sheffield was a "metropolis of trade marks" and deeply involved in the political process of protecting them. It may not have been of immediate relevance to establish a high-quality trademark for cutlery in India. After all, given the prices of the products – US$0.40 to 0.70 for penknives and at least US$1 for scissors – and the annual spending of bazaar buyers of, on average, less than US$2, it is unlikely that a very large number of buyers were repeat customers and developed great brand loyalty. However, Sheffield's manufacturers were known to invest in the long-term building of a high-quality trademark and may have thought more about future bazaar exchanges, assuming, as so many exporters did, that purchasing power would increase.[31]

The legal battle over trademark infringement was also a way for British producers to compete by shaping the institutional environment in their favor. Toward that end, British businessmen and the courts together developed a racially framed trope of the easily duped Indian consumer and used it to legitimize the extension of the Merchandise Marks Act to India. There is, in fact, little evidence that Indian consumers were regularly confused about the products they bought, and it is more likely that price and product specification were the decisive factors for buying decisions. While German manufacturers knowingly imitated existing British trademarks, British competitors, for their part, exaggerated the effects of this fraud with the aim of using this argument to lobby for supportive legislation.

In 1889, shortly after the cutlery scandal, the British Indian government implemented the Indian Merchandise Marks Act, modeled after the British antecedent. The act was designed to distinguish high-quality British goods from inferior German alternatives. It stipulated that goods had to be marked with their country of manufacture "to protect the consumer from being induced to purchase inferior foreign goods under the impression that they were manufactured in England."[32] In instructions for customs officers, the British Indian government requested that goods manufactured on the European continent should be detained if the name and trade description were in English (which they usually were), unless they were accompanied by the name of the country of origin "in conspicuous letters." The same rule applied for products marked with British

[31] Higgins and Tweedale, "Asset or Liability?": 2 for the direct quote.
[32] Government of India, *Dispatch No. 91, dated March 14, 1901, reprinted in: Report of the Bombay Chamber of Commerce for the year 1901*: 220.

or British Indian names or trademarks. Therefore, the label "Made in Germany" was de facto obligatory for all German products arriving in India.[33]

Based on the new law, Rodgers was able to take legal action against other Solingen-based manufacturers. In 1895, the German firm Kaufmann, and its Sheffield-based agent, were sued by Rodgers in a British court for trademark infringement. The judge concluded that Kaufmann's trademark was indeed intended to deceive and an article in the trade journal *Hardware and Metal* commented that surely if the knives were placed side by side "no Englishman of average intelligence would be likely to be misled"; however, these "goods were for the Indian, and not for the English, market," where "the natives ... cannot read English."[34] With similar claims, Rodgers was also successful in a lawsuit against Otto Henckels & Company.[35] As a pre-emptive step, Rodgers announced on the front page of the *Times of India* that it would take immediate legal action against any future offender.[36] These legal battles had in common the prejudice that Indian buyers were too unsophisticated to distinguish between different-quality products or countries of origin. At the same time, they portrayed bazaar consumers as repeat customers and sophisticated enough to be motivated by trademarks rather than other markers of quality. The arguments were inconsistent at best.

In addition, the actual business decisions of the manufacturers suggested that local adaptations played an important role for competition in the Indian market. Lohmann, himself an entrepreneur from Solingen, reported that manufacturers were very attentive to the influence of religion, for example, and understood that their Hindu customers rejected knives and other tools with grips made of cow bones and instead demanded the variety made of cocoa wood. By contrast, Islamic customers preferred the bone variety, which was considered higher quality.[37] For product adaptation, there were advantages to being a late mover. German manufacturers were seen as eager to respond to local needs, not

---

[33] Government of India, "Instructions (Executive) for the guidance of Customs Officers in the administration of the India Merchandise Marks Act, IV. of 1889," reprinted in: Kerly, *The Law of Merchandise Marks and the Criminal Law of False Marking*: 178–179.
[34] "Piracy of Trade Marks," *Hardware and Metal* [Toronto and Montreal] 7, no. 18, May 4, 1895: 3.
[35] "Joseph Rodgers & Sons Win Again," *Hardware and Metal* [Toronto and Montreal], vol. 7, no. 31, August 3, 1895: 25.
[36] "In the Matter of the Trade Mark of Joseph Rodgers & Sons, Limited," *Times of India*, December 24, 1895: 1.
[37] Lohmann, *Die Ausfuhr Solinger Stahlwaren*: 30.

just by providing lower-priced alternatives in India but also by carefully studying customer needs to compete with the long-established British first movers. Japanese observers found that "Germany's influence has penetrated India's heart," and that this strategy was even institutionally embedded. To them, one reason for the success was the support of the German government, which was helping to scout local conditions and employed Indians to help understand local customs and norms, collect samples, and translate Indian trade journals.[38] The US consul in Bombay Henry Baker confirmed, "German manufacturers have gone to considerable trouble to keep themselves well informed as to Indian conditions and have shown enterprise and perseverance in their campaign for trade."[39] With a similar goal in mind, the US departments of Commerce and State together had appointed the consul in 1913 to systematically explore business opportunities for American firms in India.[40] By contrast, an often-repeated British worry was that "the long uncontested superiority" may have installed in British entrepreneurs "a feeling of self-sufficiency, and one may almost say of indolence,"[41] suggesting that hubris may have prevented the formerly uncontested British manufacturers from adjusting their offerings to meet the highly diverse and dynamic desires of the Indian bazaar.

Selling Sounds

Next to common items, like cutlery, the bazaar was also where consumers bought higher value technological items. Gramophones were exported to India beginning at the turn of the century, along with sewing machines, typewriters, bicycles, and other everyday technologies.[42] Just like cutlery, the industry showed a fierce Anglo-German rivalry, namely the competition between the first mover, the Anglo-American Gramophone Company, and the German rivals Beka and Odeon, with other competitors coming from France, Switzerland, and the US. While local adaptation was important for success in the cutlery business, it became even more relevant in the trade with gramophones and musical recordings. Moreover, and in contrast to cutlery, these more sophisticated and culturally specific products required close attention to distribution

[38] Translated article in *Kokumin*, October 3, 1908, R/901/5432, BArch-B.
[39] Department of Commerce and Baker, *British India*: 10.
[40] Ibid., 17.
[41] Consular report No. 1977. Germany. Berlin. Consul-General Schwabach to the Marquees of Salisbury, received at Foreign Office June 30, 1897, 14; excerpts reprinted in: "British and German Trade," *Times of India*, August 30, 1897: 6.
[42] Domosh, *American Commodities*; Arnold, *Everyday Technology*.

channels and local partnerships, which were crucial competitive factors in this industry.

At the turn of the twentieth century, the gramophone came to India as a novelty item, with several events held to celebrate its arrival.[43] The technology had been invented in 1878 by American inventor Thomas Edison but it was not before the 1890s that technological improvements turned it into a commodity.[44] In 1897, the Massachusetts-born William Barry Owen quit his position with a US gramophone company and went to Britain, where he founded the Gramophone Company Ltd. (hereafter, Gramophone Co.) together with the British investor Trevor Williams. In 1899, the partners incorporated the Gramophone Co. and bought the European and British Empire rights for the manufacture of sound recordings. Since 1901, the Gramophone Co. and its primary US competitor Victor's Talking Machine Company had a wide-ranging partnership, including joint research, a record licensing royalty arrangement, and price fixing, and divided the world market between them: Gramophone Co. was to sell in Europe, the British Empire, and Russia, while Victor covered the rest of the world.[45]

Having acquired the British Empire rights, it was Gramophone Co. that first engaged in a more systematic business with India. In July 1901, after ending a partnership with a British trading company, Gramophone Co. sent its own agent, John Watson Hawd, to Calcutta to explore business opportunities.[46] Hawd opened a branch in Calcutta in November 1901 but criticized the company's choice of recorded music on offer. Its initial strategy of selling English music in India had failed because local consumers showed little interest in Western music. Hawd shared his concerns that "until we get native records we shall only be able to sell to Europeans and they are only 1 per 100 natives."[47] Therefore, his most urgent task was to amass a larger selection of country-specific sounds. "You must however send one man to make records," he insisted.[48]

The business practice of going on recording tours was well established in the industry. The Gramophone Co. had previously sent

[43] Ray Choudhury, *Calcutta*: 16.
[44] United States Patent Office, Thomas A. Edison, Phonograph or Speaking Machine, Patent No. 200, 521, dated February 19, 1878, application filed December 24, 1877, http://edison.rutgers.edu/patents/00200521.PDF; Kittler, *Gramophone*.
[45] Martland, *Recording History*: 132–133. Jones, "Gramophone": 81.
[46] London Office, "Letter to Hawd," January 13, 1900 and August 23, 1901, EMI.
[47] Hawd, "Letter to London Office," November 21, 1901, EMI.
[48] Hawd, "Letter to London Office," October 3, 1901, EMI.

recording engineers to different European markets to spot new talent and expand the repertoire of available recordings.[49] In 1898, American Fred Gaisberg moved from Washington DC to London, where he was responsible for the company's first recording studio and several recording tours. He was selected to go to Calcutta as well as Singapore, Hong Kong, Shanghai, Tokyo, Bangkok, and Rangoon. According to Gaisberg, the aim of this trip was "to open up new markets, establish agencies, and acquire a catalogue of native records."[50] Gaisberg detailed his experiences in India in his travelogue.[51] His descriptions and interpretations resembled travel reports by other recording engineers working in Asia and Africa, which were frequently published in trade journals.[52] As typical for the genre, Gaisberg stressed his self-understanding as a pioneer: "[A]s we steamed down the channel into the unknown I felt like Marco Polo starting out on his journeys."[53] Emphasizing their identities as cultural explorers, the recording tours were called "expeditions" among trade experts and internally at the gramophone companies.[54]

The Gramophone Co. was the first mover in the Indian market and organized two more recording expeditions prior to World War I. However, it faced fierce global competition. Its rivals came from the US, Switzerland, France, and most importantly Germany. The industry had an increasingly international outlook, and recording crews crisscrossed the subcontinent to record local artists (see Table 2.4 and Figure 2.2).

For all these traveling engineers, local intermediaries were indispensable. The recording crews usually arrived in either Bombay or Calcutta, the largest Indian trading ports. The German Beka, founded in 1904 in Berlin, went on its first recording tour in 1905–1906. Heinrich Bumb, co-founder and owner, remarked that arriving in Bombay was a great disappointment. "Bombay has nothing Indian about itself when you arrive by water: European houses, churches as in our cities, clean streets,

---

[49] Martland, *Records*: 44. Martland, "Gaisberg."
[50] Gaisberg, *Music*: 52.
[51] The original is at the EMI archives. It was published as a book in an edited form as ibid. All page numbers in the following refer to this version published in Great Britain. An almost identical edition was published in the US as Gaisberg, *The Music Goes Round*. About Gaisberg, see also Martland, "Gaisberg"; Moore, *Voice*.
[52] For examples, see "The Talking Machine in China," *Talking Machine World* (1905), June 15, 1905: 11; "The Talking Machine in Alaska," *Talking Machine World* (1905), March 15, 1905: 3. For a German example, see "Das Grammophon in Britisch-Ostafrika," *Die Sprechmaschine* 9 (1907), March 2, 1907: 206.
[53] Gaisberg, *Music*: 52.
[54] Farrell, *Indian Music*: 114.

Table 2.4 *Principal recording sessions of Western gramophone firms in India, 1902–1908*

Date	Company	Recording Engineer (Assistants in Brackets)
1902 (November–December)	Gramophone Co.	Frederick William Gaisberg (George Dillnutt, Thomas Dowe Addis)
1904–1905 (March)	Gramophone Co.	William Sinklar Darby (Max Hampe)
1904–05 (July 04–September 05)	Nicole Frère	John Watson Hawd and Stephen Carl Porter
1905–1906	Beka	Heinrich Bumb (Wilhelm Hadert, Willy Bielefeld)
1907	Beka	
1906–1907	Gramophone Co.	William Conrad Gaisberg (George Dillnutt)
1906–1907	Talking Machine Co. m.b.H. (Odeon)	Alexander Nagel
1907–1908	Beka	Heinrich Bumb
1908	Pathé Frères	Henri Lachappelle and M. M. Saife
1910	Odeon	*Unknown*

On Gramophone Co., see Kinnear, Gramophone; Martland, Recording History; on Beka, see Heinrich Bumb "Unsere Reise um die Erde: Skizzen von der großen 'Beka'-Aufnahmen-Expedition," *Phonographische Zeitschrift* 7 (1906), article series; on Odeon, see Kinnear, Sangeet Ratna; on Nicole, see Kinnear, Nicole Records.

Figure 2.2 The Beka expedition in Rangoon, 1905. Heinrich Bumb, "Unsere Reise um die Erde. Skizzen von der großen 'Beka'-Aufnahmen-Expedition," *Phonographische Zeitschrift* 7 (1906), 29: 602–604, here: 604. (Public domain).

a boulevard, shadowy alleyways with broadleaf trees. Only the life and flurry in the streets of the native quarters and in the bazaars let us recognize that we were in India."[55] Gaisberg similarly remarked that the British agents he worked with "dwelt in an Anglo-Saxon compound of their own creation, isolated from India. … The native bazaars never saw them, and even the Eurasiens aped them to the extent of tabooing all Indian society."[56]

The first contact upon arrival was usually the respective company's agent in India, who awaited the crews. When Gaisberg and his fellow travelers reached Calcutta in October 1902, agent Hawd arranged for a location for the recording sessions and got them in touch with local entertainment experts.[57] Similarly, the Beka crew was met by representatives of its agent Valabhdas, Lakhmidas and Co. upon arrival in Bombay in 1905, and through them became acquainted with Indian traders.[58]

Another group of local middlemen were well-off inhabitants of the city who showed a personal interest in a richer selection of popular music. Hawd reported in November 1902 that "[w]e have several wealthy rajas who are interested in the gramophone that have volunteered to help us in every way possible."[59] Both Beka's Bumb and Gramophone Co.'s Gaisberg were invited to wedding ceremonies, where they met popular local performers. At the house of a wealthy Indian clerk, Gaisberg was introduced to Gauhar Jan, a female singer and dancer, who would become one of the most popular Indian recording artists.[60] Gauhar Jan belonged to the group of so-called "nautch girls," female musicians who, accompanied by male instrumentalists, sang and danced at public events (see Figure 2.3.)

Women who performed publicly had a low social status in India, and Gaisberg commented on how difficult it was to recruit them for recordings. "[I]n those days it was practically impossible to record the voice of a respectable woman."[61] In the bigger cities, they could be found in entertainment quarters and therefore, as one recording engineer remarked, "are looked upon as prostitutes."[62] Dance and music were

[55] Heinrich Bumb, "Unsere Reise um die Erde: Skizzen von der großen 'Beka'-Aufnahmen-Expedition," Phonographische Zeitschrift 7 (1906), 28: 582–602, here: 582.

[56] Gaisberg, Music: 54.

[57] Kinnear, Gramophone: 15–16.

[58] Heinrich Bumb, "Unsere Reise um die Erde: Skizzen von der großen 'Beka'-Aufnahmen-Expedition," Phonographische Zeitschrift 7 (1906), 28: 582–602, here: 582.

[59] Hawd, "Letter to London Office," November 16, 1902, EMI.

[60] Gaisberg, Music: 55.

[61] Ibid., 57.

[62] T. J. Theobald Noble, "Recording Artists of all Castes in India," Talking Machine World 9(4), April 15, 1913, 32–33, here: 33.

Figure 2.3 Nautch girls performing, c. 1900 and c. 1914. (a) Nautch girl dancing with musicians, Calcutta, India, c. 1900, LC-USZ62-35125, www.loc.gov/item/2001705518/. (b) Nautch girl dancing on rug, c. 1914, LC-USZ62-133133, https://lccn.loc.gov/2003675560; both: Library of Congress, Prints and Photographs Division, Washington, DC. (No known copyright restrictions).

closely intertwined, which may have been one of the reasons for the one-sided depiction of the performers. However, the increasing number of presentations in bigger cities was also part of a changing music scene at that time. At the turn of the twentieth century, previously common forms of artistic patronage by princes or local rulers had largely been replaced. This went hand in hand with larger parts of the population moving into urban areas, where the nautch girls were part of a group of professional urban musicians.[63] Gauhar Jan's success with gramophone recordings is partly attributable to her musical talent and the popularity of her style. At the same time, she was also well suited to serve as a cultural intermediary for the Western recording crews. Her family was ethnically and religiously diverse, which meant she was familiar with different cultures.[64]

The expectation that Indian artists could be recorded "on the cheap" quickly turned out to be incorrect. In the case of Gauhar Jan, Gaisberg noted that she was savvy in business matters. "She knew her own market value as we found to our costs when we negotiated with her."[65] While she was said to earn Rs 300 or US$97, for an evening soiree, she charged

---

[63] Farrell, *Indian Music*: 111–112. Neuman, *Life*: 100–102. Sampath, *Name*.

[64] Her father, William Robert Yeoward, was Jewish and Armenian, her mother, Allen Victoria Hemming, daughter of an Indian Hindu mother and an English father. She grew up in Benares with her mother, who after a divorce converted to Islam.

[65] Gaisberg, *Music*.

Rs 1,000, or US$325, for her recording session. In comparison, the average wage of a skilled blacksmith in Calcutta was less than Rs 22, or approximately US$7, per month that same year.[66] Beka's crew had similar experiences on their recording tour. In Burma, they mostly recorded entire theatre performances. Bumb stressed that the artists charged up to Rs 3,000, or US$975, for such a recording session, which filled fifty to sixty records.[67] Artists also increased their fees when prior recordings had been proven successful. In 1913, Gauhar Jan increased her rates to US$2,000 per recording session, a more than sixfold increase over the course of a decade.[68]

Despite market expansion, the recording professionals remained outsiders in terms of Indian music and mostly relied on easily observable proxies to categorize the music, most importantly language. In the summer of 1903 Thomas Addis took over from Hawd as the agent of the Gramophone Co. in Calcutta. He echoed his predecessor's concern about record variety. In response, his superiors instructed him to extend the catalog by 2,500 records to cover the twelve languages that were considered most popular; without further specifications for musical genre or style.[69] Advertisements also emphasized language variety, stressing records in "all Indian dialects";[70] and Gauhar Jan's recording fees were partly justified by the argument that she could sing in several languages, increasing the languages covered in the company's catalogs.[71] Differences in Indian musical styles, by contrast, were initially ignored by Western gramophone companies, not least because their understanding of Indian music was limited. Gaisberg critically remarked that the company's agents in India "might be living on another planet for all the interest they took in Indian music."[72] Educated as a classical pianist, he himself had a hard time evaluating the sounds. "One had to erase all memories of the music of European opera houses and concert halls: the very foundations of my musical training were undermined."[73]

---

[66] Commercial Intelligence Department, *Prices and Wages*: 236.
[67] Heinrich Bumb, "Unsere Reise um die Erde: Skizzen von der großen 'Beka'-Aufnahmen-Expedition," Phonographische Zeitschrift 7 (1906), 28: 582–602, here: 603.
[68] T. J. Theobald Noble, "Recording Artists of all Castes in India," *Talking Machine World* 9(4), April 15, 1913, 32–33, here: 32.
[69] Addis, "Letter to London Office," December 23, 1903; London Office, "Letter to Addis," December 6, 1904, both EMI.
[70] Ad, *Times of India*, May 2, 1905: 8.
[71] T. J. Theobald Noble, "Recording Artists of all Castes in India," *Talking Machine World* 9(4), April 15, 1913, 32–33, here: 32.
[72] Gaisberg, *Music*: 54.
[73] Ibid.

As the business with native records by far outnumbered the business with English recordings, the services of local partners were not just indispensable but also costly. The rivalry between the Gramophone Co. and the German Beka intensified in 1906, when Beka engaged in a more formal relationship with a prominent local partner. Valabhdas Lakhmidas and Co. (VLC) was the company that had arranged recordings for Beka in Bombay on its first tour. It was founded by Valabhdas Runchordas (1875–1945) and Lakhmidas Rowji Tairsee (1876–) and had been active in the gramophone business for several years, as an agent for Edison, Columbia, and Pathé before becoming Beka's representative.[74] Both partners were members of the Bhatia community of Bombay, and their expertise in the gramophone trade was beyond reproach. One of the Gramophone Co.'s directors, Norbert Rodkinson, reported that Lakhmidas was "the most intelligent and thorough Merchant I have ever met" and "fully informed of all that was going on in the trade."[75] With VLC's support, Beka challenged Gramophone Co. in the three most important areas of competition: product (here: record) variety, distribution channels, and price.

The VLC partnership rapidly generated a great variety of recorded Indian music for Beka's catalog. After only two years, Beka had approximately 1,000 titles to offer.[76] Both Beka and VLC made sure these facts were known to customers and competitors. "Their [Beka records] popularity is second to none in our territory," reported Valabhdas in a US trade journal and with the typical focus on language variety announced that, "800 to 1,000 records in all the principal dialects of our country" were to be made.[77] Internally, the Gramophone Co. considered the new competition inferior. However, as a countermeasure, managers debated the option of temporarily reissuing records that had been withdrawn from the catalog at a cheaper price "as a measure for the destruction of the Beka Agency."[78]

Given the great importance of the relationship with VLC for Beka's competitive positioning, the Germans offered rather favorable contract conditions; much to the disapproval of Gramophone Co. Beka guaranteed VLC the sole and exclusive rights to sell Beka products throughout India, while VLC was free to take on other business. The German manufacturer sent large quantities of goods on consignment,

---

[74] Kinnear, *Gramophone*: 9.

[75] Rodkinson (Calcutta), "Letter to London Office," December 18, 1906, EMI. Rodkinson went to India in late 1906 and stayed four months reorganizing the India branch.

[76] *Talking Machine News* 6, June 1908; *Talking Machine World* 3, February 15, 1907: 25–29.

[77] *Talking Machine World* 3, March 1907: 37.

[78] London Office, "Letter to Rodkinson," November 28, 1906, EMI.

allowed the Indian agent to pay for them only when they were sold, and did not expect a minimum quantity of sales in a fixed period.[79] Despite its costs, the relationship proved advantageous for both partners. Beka profited from VLC's knowledge of local market conditions, while VLC gained access to Beka's technological and organizational skills.

VLC was such a trade expert that the German and British companies competed over its services. VLC temporarily acted as wholesaler for the Gramophone Co. in the Bombay presidency and promised Gramophone's representative Rodkinson that "everything will be done to keep the business of the Beka Co. down to the very lowest minimum."[80] This led Rodkinson to predict a slow death for the German rival. However, the arrangement with VLC proved to be short lived because Gramophone Co. did not receive the preferential treatment it had hoped for. As competition increased, the Gramophone Co. struggled with its own agents to assure the exclusive sale of their products. One of its agents was caught selling Beka records in two of their retail shops in 1907 and was very reluctant to give up this business.[81] By 1908, Gramophone Co. abolished its system of territorial wholesale agents and instead dealt directly with the retail trade through a large number of English and Indian dealerships.[82] They found that working with wholesalers, they "lost control of the Trade" and that "our selling organization has been practically placed at the disposal of our competitors, Odeon, Beka, and Nicole."[83]

In August 1910, Beka was acquired by the Berlin-based company Carl Lindström, which also owned the International Talking Machine GmbH of Berlin with its label Odeon. Odeon products had entered the Indian market in late 1906 under the agency of The Talking Machine Co. of India founded by E. H. Christensen. Christensen was another important middleman. India-born, he was the son of a Swedish sailing captain and an Indian woman. He had previously worked for the Gramophone Co., and then established his own retail outlet.[84] During the Gramophone Co.'s second excursion (1906–1907), Christensen expertly "engineered all the dealings with Natives regarding Artists."[85] After Odeon's first recording tour in 1910, the company quickly released

[79] Rodkinson, "Letter to London Office," December 18, 1906, EMI.
[80] Ibid.
[81] Calcutta Office, "Letter to London Office (Birnbaum)," July 2, 1907, EMI.
[82] Kinnear, *Gramophone*: 33.
[83] Muir (Calcutta), "Letter to London Office (Birnbaum)," August 28, 1907, EMI.
[84] Kinnear, "Odeon in India."
[85] Calcutta Office, "Letter to London Office," June 28, 1906, EMI.

a catalog tailored to South India, and became a big importer of both machines and discs.[86] With the merger, VLC represented both Beka and Odeon and, moreover, the Indian agency introduced its own brand of gramophones, which were manufactured by Carl Lindström and sold as "Grand-o-Phone."

Eventually, the fierce competition led to an outright price war. Overall, the Indian market had a large demand for low-end gramophones, whereas the high-end machines sold infrequently. However, the Gramophone Co. made little attempt to penetrate the mass market and left the machine business to German competitors. The bestselling gramophones in the two decades before World War I cost about Rs 40, or roughly US$13, which equaled two months' wages for a skilled blacksmith or carpenter. The high-end models, in which the Gramophone Co. specialized, cost between Rs 225 and Rs 800, that is, between US$72 and US$260. The cheapest machines from Germany were available for Rs 9.25 or US$3.[87] German manufacturers were able to sell significantly cheaper machines because many inventions targeted at decreasing the price of production originated in Germany.[88]

The more lucrative business was in the complementary product – records. The availability of cheap machines expanded the market for records for all manufacturers. Records by the Gramophone Co. sold for between Rs 3 and Rs 6 (US$1–2). Beka and Odeon records were slightly cheaper, selling for Rs 3–4 (US$1–1.30). Record dealers were usually granted up to 25 percent discount; wholesalers up to 40 percent.[89] Faced with this competition Gramophone Co. decreased the price of its records twice in January 1907 and again in January 1908.[90]

Eventually and pressured by the competition, the Gramophone Co. took the significant step to invest in a manufacturing facility in India. The site was found by the end of 1906, about a mile east of the commercial center of Calcutta.[91] The first Indian discs were pressed there in June 1908. The company also established permanent recording studios in Calcutta, Bombay, and Madras. By December 1908, the factory was pressing 1,000 discs per day. The record storerooms held stocks of over 150,000 discs, of which some 100,000 were recordings in the vernacular

[86] Kinnear, "Odeon in India": 2262.
[87] Department of Commerce and Labor, *Foreign Trade*. Ads in *Times of India* (several issues).
[88] *Phonographische Zeitschrift* 7/44, 1906: 1.
[89] London Office, "Letter to Gilpin (Calcutta)," November 23, 1906, EMI.
[90] *Die Sprechmaschine* 4/2, 1908: 36; Gramophone Co. ad in *Times of India* February 4, 1908: 2; Odeon ad in *Times of India* October 3, 1907: 2.
[91] Hodkinson Calcutta, "Letter to London Office (Birnbaum)," December 27, 1906, EMI.

languages of India.[92] The Indian factory gave Gramophone Co. a clear advantage on the Indian market, not least because the company could now advertise that it was producing in India, rather than just importing products. Local production not only helped to be closer to the customer and speed up the production cycle but also developed into a political argument in the context of rising economic nationalism in India, as the next section shows.

Playing the National Card

German and British businesses went head to head in the Indian market, fiercely competing for market share and future business opportunities. The institutional setup of the British colony provided British business-people with many advantages over their competitors: they had access to well-established trading houses, ports and shipping lines to India, an established banking system, laws closely mirroring British equivalents, established partnerships with local intermediaries, and English as the predominant foreign language. For German businesspeople, many of these important areas of international trade initially required British mediation or created obstacles that needed to be overcome.

By contrast, the Indian movement for independence was one of the few developments providing German firms with a competitive advantage over their British counterparts. The nationalist "Swadeshi" movement – swadeshi meaning "of/from one's own country" – called on Indians to consume indigenous goods, rather than imported ones, claiming that foreign imports stalled India's economic development. Swadeshi ideas had been circulating for quite some time. For example, Bholanath Chandra in his famous article "A Voice for the Commerce and Manufactures of India," published in the nationalist *Mookerjee's Journal* in 1873, vilified imported British goods:

With regard to the so-much talked about Imports, to view them as proof of our prosperity is at variance with common sense and with the acknowledged truths of economic science. They are exotics which yield no fruit to India, but to Manchester, Birmingham, and Cheshire. To regard them in their true light, is to regard them not as a blessing but as a curse which has culminated in the ruin of our national industry and home-made manufactures.[93]

As in the above quote, Swadeshi ideas were closely linked to the perceived deterioration of the Indian economy that Indian nationalists

---

[92] Kinnear, *Gramophone*: 30.
[93] Chandra, "Voice": 90.

frequently stressed. Many of India's traditional handicraft industries had declined during the nineteenth century. Some nationalists even considered it a deliberate British policy to exploit India and prevent its economic development. Romesh Chandra Dutt's *The Economic History of India*, published at the turn of the twentieth century, highlighted the "political injustice" and "unfair jealousy" of the British rule in India. In the typical language of the Swadeshi movement, he described the "perpetual Economic Drain from India," which "continues to this day in an ever-swelling current, and makes India a land of poverty and famine."[94] The call for industrialization dominated the Indian nationalist press in the last quarter of the nineteenth century.[95] To achieve economic autarky and boost industrialization, Swadeshi activists advocated for a combination of boycotting foreign, primarily British, goods and growing the indigenous industry.

The Swadeshi movement experienced a major push in the wake of the anti-partition campaign of the province Bengal after 1903.[96] The Viceroy of India, Lord Curzon, had decided to partition Bengal, which he allegedly considered too large for effective governance. Lord Curzon's plans were met with deep resentment by the Bengali population because they were seen as restraining the growing power of Bengali Hindus.[97] In the surge of Indian nationalism accompanying the partition, activists' calls for a boycott of foreign goods grew louder. "Terrible oppression has commenced ... the remedy for this state of things lies in giving up entirely the use of foreign goods and in using country-made goods," argued a nationalist newspaper in 1906.[98] The impact of Swadeshi was greatest in the province of Bengal and triggered the founding of a number of Bengali enterprises but the sentiment also spread to other regions of the country.[99]

With the anti-Partition campaign, nationalistic Swadeshi ads appeared everywhere. "How can we patronize Swadeshi – it is only by making a sincere attempt at promoting indigenous goods," read an ad by P. M. Bagchi & Co.[100] Although Swadeshi theory condemned all foreign

[94] Dutt, *Economic History of India*: preface and 51.
[95] Chandra, *Nationalism and Colonialism in Modern India*.
[96] "R. W. Carlyle's Report on the Agitation Against the Partition (1905)," Pol. (Pol.) F. No.86(J)/1905, WBSA. For the impact of Swadeshi on foreign business see also Cox, *Global Cigarette*: 207–208.
[97] Sarkar, *Swadeshi*: 8–12.
[98] *Bande Mataram*, September 10, 1906.
[99] Bhattacharyya, *Swadeshi Enterprise*.
[100] Quoted in: Bhattacharyya, *Swadeshi Enterprise (vol. 2)*: 209. Bagchi was founded in 1883 and became a household name for almanacs, though it also produced many other articles.

products because they delayed India's industrial development, early activists argued that while India was dependent on imports, they should come from countries *other than Britain*. Their arguments started to create a simple order in the world of nations, rooted in national history and national aspirations and in clear rejection of the geopolitical identity of the British Empire.

While the Swadeshi movement rejected British goods, it was a matter of pragmatism to cooperate with foreigners from other countries to obtain certain products and know-how. It led to politically motivated differentiation between British and other foreign products, which remained an important sales argument for years to come. The nationalist Sri Aurobindo (1872–1950) distinguished between economic and political boycott with the latter following the political agenda of India's self-determination. "Why should we take revenge upon America or Germany for the oppression caused to us by the people of Britain?," he asked in speech on January 30, 1908, and explained that "[t]here is a political reason ... for the boycott of British goods; it is to make the brethren of our oppressors feel the pinch."[101] Bal Gangadhar Tilak (1856–1920) prompted his followers to investigate, "whether we can import them [goods] from non-English places. We must win the sympathy of traders in Germany, France, America, Japan, etc."[102] Historian Amit Bhattacharyya, in his work on Swadeshi business, observed in hindsight that, "many Swadeshi entrepreneurs did not seek any technical knowledge or import machinery from Britain, and that was an expression of the national spirit of the time. There were, however, many among them who sought assistance from other western countries such as Germany, France or the USA."[103]

The political tensions put British firms and goods at a distinct disadvantage. Moreover, it was especially German competitors that could seize the moment because of the existing German–British trade rivalry and the association of the German nationality with hostility towards Britain. Evolving perceptions of the relationship between nations reconfigured the mental map of nationalism. Indian nationalists looked at the world of nations through a lens of anticolonialism. For that reason, the Swadeshi movement created a unique opportunity for non-British business in general, and German companies in particular. Charles Stevenson-Moore, Inspector-General of the Police of Bengal, observed in 1905: "A distinction is being made between English and Continental goods,

---

[101] Aurobindo, "The Aims of the Nationalist Party": 852.
[102] Quoted in: Wolpert, *Tilak and Gokhale*: 167n126.
[103] Bhattacharyya, *Swadeshi Enterprise (vol. 2)*: 213.

adverse to the former."[104] A commentator from Lahore confirmed with dismay that such a distinction was becoming widespread and tried to push back on the idea that "the people should buy, even at some pecuniary sacrifice, goods made in America, Germany and France"[105]. Several commentators pointed out that the targeted boycott of British goods would inevitably have a positive effect on other Western imports, especially the inexpensive products from Germany. "By boycotting English goods only, we will have to throw ourselves on [sic] the mercy of foreign nations, who will not be slow to take advantage of their opportunity, and dump the country with cheap worthless goods."[106] A newspaper article on the boycott in *The Scotsman* argued, "it is impossible at once to dispossess European articles by Indian-made goods. Therefore, German, American, and Japanese goods will come in."[107] The perceived nationality of a product turned into a political statement.

In Bengal, even a case of fraud was reported, in which English goods were being sold successfully as "Made in Germany."[108] Ironically, the label had been forcefully introduced by Great Britain in the Merchandise Marks Act of 1887 and the Indian Merchandise Marks Act of 1889 (see earlier) to stigmatize low-quality German products. It was initially perceived as an additional administrative hurdle because each product had to be visibly marked with its country of origin or they would be rejected upon arrival in India.[109] However, in the new political context, that same "Made in Germany"-label now turned into an advantage because it allowed German manufacturers to publicly display the non-British origin of their products. This also affected chosen trade routes. A German manager in the cutlery industry reported that a particular trader had explicitly asked for a shipment of goods to the harbor of Okha in the princely state of Baroda, which the ruler of Baroda had established as an alternative to British Indian harbors on the west coast to support India's struggle for autonomy from Britain.[110]

It was the bazaar trade in Bengal that was most affected by the boycott. *The Statesman* found that at Calcutta's main bazaar, shoppers no longer

---

[104] "Report on the Agitation Against the Partition of Bengal by C. J. Stevenson-Moore, Inspector-Genl. of Police," POL. (Pol.) F. No. (J)/1905, WBSA.

[105] From our own correspondent, "Opinion in the Punjab," *Times of India*, October 31, 1905: 5.

[106] Lalubhai Samaldas, "Swadeshism: A Native View," *Times of India*, October 20, 1905: 6.

[107] From our Calcutta Correspondent, "The Swadeshi Movement," *The Scotsman*, September 11, 1905: 7.

[108] "Report on the Agitation Against the Partition of Bengal by C. J. Stevenson-Moore, Inspector-Genl. of Police," POL. (Pol.) F. No. (J)/1905, WBSA.

[109] Otto Tesche, "Letter to Heinrich Lohmann," December 12, 1931, NA/15/48, CASol.

[110] Lohmann, *Die Ausfuhr Solinger Stahlwaren*: 27–28.

bought English clothing items and minor luxuries. "The Swadeshi idea has touched every class. It has captured the homes of the people; it has inspired the women; it finds its missionaries, not in youthful enthusiasts alone, but in mature and sober persons."[111] Even buyers who would have liked to buy British goods were prevented by activists from doing so, sometimes violently.[112] In the gramophone industry, the British Gramophone Co. found that, "Bengali Trade (i.e., in Bengali Records) is practically at a standstill. The Bengalis are boycotting us as much as possible."[113] The movement favored not just local but all non-British alternatives. "We are boycotted practically, and our trade is entirely done by Mohommedans [sic] and a few Europeans," reported the market leader in June 1906.[114]

While the Gramophone Co. struggled, Indian competitors, such as entrepreneur Bose, adjusted their business to political currents. As a Bengali businessman, Bose advertised his records as "the only real swadeshi records." He also specialized in nationalist music and speeches, which sold increasingly well in the heated political environment. Stirring Swadeshi sentiments among his clientele, Bose called on his customers, "Don't send your money beyond the seas, be a true Swadeshi by using Genuine Swadeshi records."[115]

The German competitor Beka leveraged its collaboration with VLC and released titles with a clear political focus, such as "Bande Mataram – Swadeshism" and "Partition of Bengal," actively capitalizing on the political context of anti-colonial unrest.[116] The fact that Germany was a colonial power itself did not prevent the German companies from exploiting the opportunity in India, where Germany had no record of colonialism and where they could present themselves as politically neutral outsiders. Positioning towards the issue of self-determination was the most powerful force in the experimental reshaping of the mental map of nationalism of that time; it determined the divide between allies and enemies. The Gramophone Co., by contrast, could not believably signal support for the nationalists. Instead, it highlighted its local Indian production site, which had been opened in 1908. Its advertisements explicitly stressed that its "Indian, Burmese and Ceylonese records are

---

[111] *The Statesman,* September 7, 1905, reprinted in: "The Bengal Boycott," *Manchester Guardian,* September 29, 1905: 7.
[112] "Swadeshi Movement," *Times of India,* November 9, 1905: 7; "The Swadeshi Movement: Calcutta Police Assaulted," *Times of India,* October 5, 1905: 5.
[113] Calcutta Office, "Letter to London Office," June 28, 1906, EMI.
[114] Ibid.
[115] Bose ad, quoted in: Kinnear, *Gramophone:* 43.
[116] Ibid., 46.

now made at our Calcutta factory – using Indian materials – by Indian workmen,"[117] thus presenting itself as a Swadeshi-conscious business by highlighting local production.

On the brink of World War I, Anglo-German rivalry in India had reached a peak (for an overview of German imports at this point, see Appendix 3). A variety of sectors, both business-to-business and bazaar goods trade, were fiercely contested among competitors from different origin countries, and Germany and Great Britain went head-to-head in many of them. To enter the market, the German late movers depended crucially on a diverse group of local partners and existing trading and social networks. Rivalry often crystallized in a hard-to-unpack amalgamation of price, control over distribution channels, and local adaptation. Contemporary observers, in particular those of British origin, frequently focused on price as a main criterion for success in Indian bazaars. At the firm level, however, other competitive factors were market knowledge, access to distribution channels, with local Indian intermediaries becoming increasingly more powerful, and the local adaptation of goods to the demands of consumers.

These demands also included political interests. Swadeshi-conscious customers looked for alternative exporting countries other than Great Britain. This rather unexpected competitive edge revealed itself to German entrepreneurs during the Swadeshi protests of 1905. While short-lived and with limited immediate impact on business, the nationalist upheaval taught German competitors that presenting themselves as "outsiders" of the British–Indian colonial economy could come with advantages. A potentially fertile alliance of interests revealed itself: Indians were looking for alternative manufacturers in the West, which would allow them to continue importing manufactured goods as needed without having to rely on their colonial overseers. German firms were after accessible markets and an opportunity to celebrate and showcase their still-forming national pride in the field of international trade. Both took on the role of challengers of a world economy dominated by Britain, and thus found themselves with an adversary in common.

---

[117] Quoted in: ibid., 30.

3 Mapping Enemies in World War I

World War I interrupted the explorations of the Indian market described in Chapters 1 and 2 and changed the lives and self-perceptions of Germans in India. World War I was a global war, even if it was not necessarily perceived as such by all contemporaries.[1] However, the globally integrated world economy before 1914 and the fact that all the Entente powers were also colonial powers led to a situation in which the war affected not just Europe but also much of the world. India played a prominent role in the war. When Britain entered the conflict, all countries in its colonial empire legally turned into Germany's enemies. India became a central source of material resources and manpower for Great Britain and its allies. An estimated 1.3 million Indians served as soldiers during the war, mostly outside of their home country.[2] And Indian nationalists by and large supported the British during the war. Scholars of Indian history have interpreted World War I as a transition period from Indians' imperial identity, which became increasingly tested, to an emerging nationalist consciousness. "With one singing its death-aria and the other waiting to find a clear voice, it was a moment in parenthesis."[3]

For German business in India, the war was a turning point. For them as newly declared "enemy aliens," it led to asset expropriations, a reconfiguration of trade, and an important loss of trust with Indian business partners. Yet, the war also brought with it an opportunity for closer collaboration with a group of nationalist activists in India or in diaspora, with Berlin becoming one of the centers of anti-imperial protest. While these Indo-German conspiracies were unsuccessful in the short term, they had long-term consequences of significance. They triggered publications dedicated to telling an entangled Indo-German history, created a social community of Indian activists in Germany, and started a process of reflection on mutual goals and aspirations that shaped the war and post-war interactions.

---

[1] For this argument see, Strachan, "First World War." Morrow, *The Great War*.
[2] Great Britain War Office, *Statistics of the Military Effort*: 29.
[3] Das, *India, Empire, and First World War Culture*: 42.

The Outbreak of the War

The day when Britain declared war – Tuesday, August 4, 1914 – created immediate turmoil in India. The *Times of India* issued several special editions during the day, struggling to stay on top of the latest news coming in by continuously arriving telegraphs. German businesspeople observed the news particularly closely. "[A]mongst the German and Austrian communities was excitement evident and in some commercial and shipping circles the war generally overshadowed business."[4] The German Consulate in Bombay had been closed one day earlier, and the German Consul Friedrich August Heyer and his wife left India on one of the last ships on Tuesday. The representation of German interests in India fell temporarily into the hands of US consul Henry Baker.[5] On Wednesday, August 5, the Governor General of India, Charles Baron Hardinge of Penshurst, officially proclaimed that "war has broken out between His Majesty and Germany."[6] Immediately afterwards, a Royal Proclamation prohibited residents to do business with Britain's enemies.[7] Enemy ships were granted a one-week grace period to unload and depart from India.[8] And with them departed the belief in future business with Germany.

Many European and Indian traders initially had their doubts about the details of the enemy trading rules. The stark contrast between the highly integrated world economy before World War I and this new form of intense protectionism left many protagonists confused about the implementation of the new legal framework. To clarify enemy trading, the British Treasury issued a memorandum at the end of August, allowing British firms to trade with German and Austrian firms if they were established in neutral or British territory. Existing commercial contracts with firms *on enemy territory* were not to be honored anymore.[9]

In Britain, it was the "Trading with the Enemy Proclamation, No. 2," issued on September 9, 1914, which eventually established a definition

---

[4] "The Position in Bombay: The German Consul to Leave," *Times of India*, August 4, 1914: 7.

[5] "Commercial and Industrial Review of Bombay," August 4, 1914, Record Group 84: Records of the Foreign Service Posts of the Department of State, United States Consular Records for Bombay, India, Correspondence 340/621, 194, vol. 96, NARA.

[6] Proclamation No. 503, August 5, 1914, Gazette of India 1914, Part I: 1294; reprinted in: Government of India Legislative Department, *Legislation and Orders Relating to the War*: 37.

[7] "By the King. A Proclamation Relating to Trading with the Enemy," Supplement to the London Gazette, August 5, 1914; see also "Outlook in India: Trade with the Enemy," *Times of India*, August 11, 1914: 7.

[8] Government of India Legislative Department, *Legislation and Orders Relating to the War*: 39–42.

[9] Bentwich, "International Law": 356–357.

of enemy and enemy firm. It was released as a substitute for all previous proclamations and defined the enemy as "any person ... resident or carrying on business in the enemy country."[10] This residency-based definition confirmed that business with an enemy firm was considered legal, as long as the branch was situated or incorporated in non-enemy territory. This British proclamation was reprinted in the *Gazette of India* for general information. While it technically did not apply to British India, it was used as a guideline in the uncertain situation.[11]

In India, the British legislation was eventually enacted in the ordinances of October 14, 1914.[12] Even stricter than British laws, the Viceroy and Governor General of India forbade all commercial dealings with enemy subjects and the "Hostile Foreigners (Trading) Order" of November 14, 1914, unmistakably defined enemies as all subjects of the German Empire, Austria-Hungary (which had been at war with the UK since August 13) and the Ottoman Empire (since November 1). It also specified enemy firms as any company of which any member was a hostile foreigner.[13] This caused some confusion among Indian businesspeople, as the *Times of India* reported in December. While British legislation made residency the decisive factor for determining enemy character, the Government of India based its determination also on nationality, declaring all German, Austrian and Turkish nationals, even if residing in neutral or allied territory, enemy aliens.[14] The Bombay Chamber of Commerce quibbled that "the numerous proclamations and notifications, etc., which in some cases modify, amend, or cancel each other have proved very confusing."[15] Still in 1916, a trader in Madras was initially fined Rs 2,500 but later acquitted because he was allegedly unaware of his trading with enemies and because of what the judge perceived as "the novelty of the law."[16] Defining the enemy was hard legislative work.

And the consequences of this definition were significant. The Hostile Foreigners (Trading) Order was the law that created the legal framework

[10] Trading with the Enemy Proclamation No. 2, September 9, 1914 [1914, no. 1376], in: Huberich, *Law*: 357–360. See also, Bentwich, "International Law": 358–361.
[11] Gazette of India, 1914, Part I: 1743.
[12] Huberich, *Law*: 22. Government of India Legislative Department, *Legislation and Orders Relating to the War*: 27–30.
[13] The Hostile Foreigners (Trading) Order, November 14, 1914, reprinted in: Government of India Legislative Department, *Legislation and Orders Relating to the War*: 138–141, quote: 138.
[14] "India and the War: Determining Factors," *Times of India*, December 2, 1914: 7.
[15] "The War and Trade," *Times of India*, January 7, 1915: 3.
[16] "India and the War: The Hooper Case," *Times of India*, March 25, 1916: 9; "India and the War: Impressions of India," March 29, 1916: 7; "Mr. Hooper Acquitted," April 29, 1916: 9.

for expropriations. It stipulated that enemies must deposit all their assets, business and personal, with a person appointed by the local government and that it was the British-Indian Government that decided how to employ those assets.[17] To organize this process, a Trading with the Enemy Department was created on November 30, 1914. Only six months later, in May 1915, reports indicated that the custodian had taken control of enemy property in the amount of £84.6 million and received income of approximately £700,000.[18] Income was possible because some enemy firms managed to receive licenses from the Government of India to continue their business. The most common form of license was a temporary permission to trade under the supervision of the controller to liquidate assets before closing. A second, much smaller set of companies, was allowed to continue trading during the war; however only under the supervision of an officer nominated by the Government of India. A third group was classified as crucial to British interests and allowed to continue doing business without restrictions. In January 1916, 114 enemy firms (47 percent) were in the process of liquidation, seventy-nine (33 percent) were trading under supervision, and fifty firms (20 percent) had been granted a license for unrestricted trading.[19]

Neither Siemens nor Bayer were that lucky. Bayer had had a wholly owned subsidiary in India since 1896 (see Chapter 1), which was fully expropriated by the British Indian Government.[20] While Bayer's German agents were interned as enemies, their Indian and British employees liquidated the business under the supervision of a British auditor.[21] Siemens had conducted most of its business with India from Great Britain, where all its manufacturing facilities were equally seized. Both companies also lost important patents and trademarks. For the plethora of German exporters that had delivered to Indian bazaars, all trade officially ended. "[A]t present import of any goods from Germany or Austria-Hungary is absolutely shut off," reported US Consul Baker already in late August 1914.[22] Since December 1914, the British Government

---

[17] The Hostile Foreigners (Trading) Order, November 14, 1914, reprinted in: Government of India Legislative Department, *Legislation and Orders Relating to the War:* 139.

[18] "Public Trustee: Year's New Business," *Times of India*, May 4, 1915: 11.

[19] Hansard 1803–2005, Bill Enemy Trading in India HL Deb January 27, 1916 vol 20 cc1092-9. Available online: http://hansard.millbanksystems.com/lords/1916/jan/27/enemy-trading-in-india. For the different licenses issued, see also "India and the War: Bengal and Enemy Traders," *Times of India*, November 30, 1914: 8

[20] "Peace Negotiations World War I," 1918, 202/16, BA.

[21] "Report by Heinrich Müller," accompanying letter to Wesendonk, May 20, 1915, 200–202, R/21083, PA.

[22] Henry Baker, "German and Austro-Hungarian Trade with India," August 27, 1914, Record Group 84: Records of the Foreign Service Posts of the Department of State, United States Consular Records for Bombay, India, Correspondence 340/621, 194, vol. 96, NARA.

placed companies on blacklists if they were believed to stand under any kind of enemy influence.

Consequently, German businesspeople were forced to disappoint their Indian buyers, with whom they had built relationships before the war. "The name 'Germany' makes Indian merchants swear in Karachi," observed the US consul in Karachi, James Oliver Laing.[23] Laing compiled a report on the US trade opportunities during the war, in which he detailed that Indian merchants had "lost faith in German and Austrian shippers" and that the fact that German commercial travelers had stopped coming to India was reason enough for local merchants to seek new partners. "The better informed native importers here are keen business men and perfectly able to understand what is going on and how to take advantage of it."[24] He also predicted that even the end of the war would not change the locals' attitude. "The native mind goes in for results in business and a shock to confidence lasts a long time [underlining in the original]."[25] Much goodwill had already been destroyed.

However, despite the official policy, not all German business ceased to operate immediately. In many cases it proved difficult to determine if a company was indeed of enemy character.[26] Some enemy companies engaged in "cloaking" and continued their business through middlemen of non-enemy character.[27] The chemical company Agfa (which belonged to the group of chemical companies consolidating in Germany into what would eventually become I. G. Farben[28]) continued selling goods via its Swiss agent Volkart Brothers, which had served as Agfa's representative since the 1890s.[29] The tire company Continental ordered their employee Rosenthal, who happened to hold British citizenship, to move from Colombo to Bombay to continue their business there. However, in February 1915, the British authorities pressured him to leave India because he was rightly seen as representing German interests.[30]

---

[23] James Laing, "Letter to James A. Smith, American Consul General Calcutta," August 20, 1914, Correspondence 610–621, 1914, Dep. of State, U.S. Consulate Calcutta India (1855–1947), US Consular Records for Calcutta, India, compiled 1856–1935, NARA.

[24] Ibid.

[25] Ibid.

[26] Dejung and Zangger, "British Wartime Protectionism." Dejung, *Commodity Trading*: 118.

[27] This was a common strategy in both world wars. The literature on cloaking has focused primarily on World War II. For some conceptual considerations see, Aalders and Wiebes, *Art*. For a case study spanning both world wars, see Jones and Lubinski, "Managing Political Risk."

[28] Plumpe, *I.G. Farbenindustrie AG*: 47.

[29] File "India" [for Advisory Board meeting on November 14, 1914], R/8128/16228, BArch-B. See also, Dejung, *Commodity Trading*: 258.

[30] Continental, "Letter to Foreign Office," April 22, 1915, 47 and 55–57, R/21082, PA.

Not just German businesspeople but also their Indian trading partners tried creative solutions to uphold their business relationships. The
Indian firm Ganpat Roy and Co. was charged with enemy trading in
December 1914, when it used a middleman from Genoa to sell to German firms. The scheme was revealed through censored correspondence
between the business partners; British Indian officials used the case as a
cautionary tale for others.[31] The responsible parties were fined Rs 1,000
and sentenced to eighteen months' imprisonment.[32] While similar cases
occurred from time to time,[33] the warning by the pro-British Calcutta-
based periodical *The Englishman* that there was continuous secret trade
between Indians and Germans elevated selected anecdotes to a pattern
that did not exist.[34]

Instead, expropriation proved to be a complicated and often lengthy
process. Those companies licensed by the Indian Government to liquidate their assets frequently took their time doing so. In Calcutta, the
Bengal Chamber of Commerce lobbied the Government of Bengal
because it felt that liquidation processes were unduly delayed. Although
liquidators had been appointed in many firms, they often turned out to
be former members of the respective company that was to be wound up.
Supporting the original owners and anticipating renewed employment
after the war, these liquidators were accused of prolonging the proceedings in the hope that the war would come to an end before they could
fully complete the task.[35] Most of these efforts were fruitless in the long
run. By July 1918, orders to wind up or prohibit were made in 507 cases,
and in ninety-five additional cases a forced sale to British subjects had
already been initiated.[36]

Besides expropriations, communication was another major challenge,
not just for the struggling German business community but for all business in India. "A great, an impenetrable fog has hid India from Europe,"
reported the *Times of India* one day after the outbreak of the war. The
newspaper warned its readers of the "absence of news" owing to the
pressure on the cables and the necessity of time-consuming censorship.[37]
Censors in Bombay and Calcutta scrutinized all incoming foreign mail

---

[31] "Trading with the Enemy," *Times of India*, December 5, 1914: 6.
[32] "The Trading Ordinance," *Times of India*, January 5, 1915: 6.
[33] "Trading with the Enemy," *Times of India*, May 14, 1915: 10. For a detailed legal discussion of trading with the enemy cases in India, see also Campbell, *The Law of Trading
with the Enemy in British India*.
[34] December 10, 1914, in German translation: R/21078: 91, PA.
[35] "Government and Enemy Firms," *Times of India*, August 6, 1915: 7.
[36] "German Trade Tricks," *Times of India*, July 13, 1918: 11.
[37] "The Situation," *Times of India*, August 5, 1914: 6

to look for violations of the trading with the enemy act. Innocent mail was resealed and marked with the stamp of the censor.[38] Frequent complaints by interested parties in Germany indicated that censorship was indeed strict and the news from India remained scarce throughout the war.[39] An employee of the Swiss trading company Volkart complained in November 1914, "We have been thrown back to the times of our forefathers who had to make do without telegram correspondence at a time when the Indian mail took four weeks."[40] Moreover, the British cut several of Germany's undersea cables, which later became interpreted as a great disadvantage for Germany because it limited the ability to influence hearts and minds abroad.[41] Intelligence efforts and communication infrastructure were more important than ever.

Resolving these communication challenges was a constant struggle. Several German businessmen proposed their "German-friendly" Indian business partners to the government because they were supposedly able to deliver up-to-date information.[42] The chemical firms vorm. Weiler-ter Meer and Buckau pleaded with the Foreign Office to allow the Indian B. B. Eranee of the company Pragjee Soorjee & Co. to return to India so that he could investigate what happened to their business assets, of which they had no news since the war broke out. Eranee had lived in Germany for many years but now desired to return home.[43] Foreign Office employees, for their part, explored creative ways to receive intelligence about India. They relied on neutral, most notably Swiss, informants and naturalized British citizens. For example, the British citizen Oscar Schmidt-Ernsthausen, a previous German Consul in Calcutta and member of the trading firm Ernsthausen & Co., went to England to collect more details about the development of the Indian situation. He promised to deliver his reports written in secret ink in his private correspondence.[44] By and large, however, information flows dried up and incoming news was patchy and unreliable – which was one of the biggest challenges for continuous business relations in those rare cases in which licenses had been granted, or German firms found trustworthy middlemen to manage their affairs.

[38] "The Post Office Censor," *Times of India*, December 16, 1914: 7.
[39] Heinrich Müller, "Letter to Wesendonk," May 20, 1915, 200–202, R/21083, PA.
[40] "Volkart to J. H.Reitz, Chemnitz, November 18, 1914"; quoted in: Dejung, *Commodity Trading*: 116.
[41] Tworek, *News from Germany*: 52, 69.
[42] Otto Roehm, "Letter to Grossherzogliches Staatsministerium," December 4, 1914, 6, R/21076, PA.
[43] Eranee, "Letter to German Foreign Office," 13 February 1915, with support letter by vorm. Weiler-ter Meer and Buckau, 18–24, R/21079, PA.
[44] "Note October 7, 1914," R/21073, PA. About Schmidt-Ernsthausen see, "Lebensumriss und Personalien," July 11, 1915, 139–143, R/21085, PA.

Behind Barbed Wire

While business assets changed hands slowly, the war brought immediate turmoil to the day-to-day life of German nationals in India. German businesspeople were not only abruptly excluded from market exchanges but also rounded up in internment camps.[45] The internment camp system of the British Empire operated at both the national and imperial level, with prisoners frequently being transferred between different locations and across national borders.[46] India hosted one of the largest internment camps in the British Empire: Ahmednagar.[47] It was situated in the state of Maharashtra, about 120 kilometers (75 miles) northeast of Pune and 250 kilometers (155 miles) east of Bombay. Camp Ahmednagar had a history as a prisoner-of-war camp. During the Boer War in South Africa, the British shipped around 9,000 prisoners from Africa to Ahmednagar.[48] In World War I, it was once again used as internment camp for enemy aliens.

Between the outbreak of the war and March 1917, about 1,621 men, primarily Germans and Austrians, were rounded up in Ahmednagar. Of those, 452 (28 percent) were prisoners of war, predominantly captured on German ships. The remaining 1,169 (72 percent) were civilians, mostly businesspeople and missionaries. Only very few Germans with good social networks in India received special permission to continue working during the war and escaped internment. For example, fifty-one Germans had been working at Tata's Iron and Steel Works at Kalimati when the war broke out. They went to Bombay to board a ship for Germany but were unable to do so in time. However, rather than being interned, the Government of India gave them special permission to continue working at Kalimati, and the Government Inspector of Railways was responsible for watching over them.[49]

The prisoners at Ahmednagar were accommodated in old stone barracks and newly constructed huts made of corrugated iron. The camp was surrounded by barbed wire fences and British and Indian soldiers kept guard. Internees were not forced to do physical labor, but some worked

---

[45] American Consulate "Letter to Secretary of States, November 19, 1915, Detention and Internment of German and Austrian Subjects," Record Group 59, M367, NARA. For detailed descriptions see also, Murphy, *Colonial Captivity during the First World War*. Ganachari, *Indians in the First World War*: 164–215. Lubinski, Giacomin, and Schnitzer, "Internment."

[46] Panayi, *Germans as Minorities*: 15.

[47] Proctor, *Civilians in a World at War*: 79n13.

[48] Great Britain War Office, Maurice, and Grant, *History of the War in South Africa*: vol. 4, appendix 20.

[49] "Position in Bombay: The Tata Iron Works," *Times of India*, August 25, 1914: 5.

in the kitchen for pay. Most spent their time learning foreign languages or engaged in theatre, sports, or studies at the camp library.[50] In retrospect, the internees argued that the desire for meaningful occupation was most essential to fight the boredom, for the "fresh young men" who had taken on qualified positions overseas to broaden their horizons. However, the longer the internment lasted, the more infrequent these activities became.[51]

When a Red Cross Committee visited the camp in early 1917, they too commented specifically on the great divergence between the previous life-style of the internees and their current predicament: "Most of them had been several years in India, engaged in business, managing prosperous commercial firms or enjoying well-paid employment. They had become used to the free, comfortable Indian life …. To have to leave their pretty bungalows for the internment camp, give up business, see their future com-promised and their interests endangered, was truly hard to endure."[52] They also reported that the British Government had initially allowed the firm liq-uidators of German and Austrian businesses to pay the former employees Rs 80 to Rs 120, equaling about £5.3 to £8 per month.[53] This permission was withdrawn in August 1916, leading to a sudden decline of liquidity in the camp.[54] Wives and children were held at a different internment location in Belgaum, 400 kilometers (248 miles) south of Ahmednagar. Initially, the families were allowed to visit the Ahmednagar camp once a month.[55] In March 1916, after several petitions, the British authorities turned Belgaum into a family camp and held couples and families together.[56]

With internment came a perceived loss of status for the German busi-ness community. While most Germans had previously felt themselves part of the "White Western elite" in India,[57] many struggled with the new line of distinction based on nationality rather than race. "Before the war," one internee remembered, "the British in India only recognized the difference between Europeans and natives and always stressed that no matter what the whites would have to stick together against the Indi-ans."[58] This changed with the war. In his report, N. O. Tera, who had

---

[50] International Committee of the Red Cross and Thormeyer, *Reports*: 32–33. Probst, *Unter indischer Sonne*: 59.

[51] Probst, *Unter indischer Sonne*: 92–93.

[52] International Committee of the Red Cross and Thormeyer, *Reports*: 12.

[53] Rs 1 equaled 16 pence or £1/15th. For details see, Roy, *Economic History of India*.

[54] International Committee of the Red Cross and Thormeyer, *Reports*: 33.

[55] Heinrich Müller, "Letter to Wesendonk," May 20, 1915, 200–202, R/21083, PA.

[56] International Committee of the Red Cross and Thormeyer, *Reports*: 35–39.

[57] For the emergence of this self-understanding of the "community of White people," see also Ganachari, *Indians in the First World War*: 35.

[58] Report March 1917, quoted in: Murphy, *Colonial Captivity during the First World War*: 106.

come for a Hamburg-based rubber company to India, argued that the day of the internment was when "the British destroyed the 'Schicksalsge-meinschaft' [community of fate] of the Europeans vis-à-vis the colored races of the world. Here is when for the first time the British destroyed the fiction of the superiority of the White race."[59] Similarly, the mission-ary Hans Georg Probst remembered the good old times when "there still was a feeling of community between the Europeans vis-à-vis the Blacks."[60] Among Western businesspeople in India, nationality had often been perceived as secondary to race in attributing privilege and status. Before the war, German businessmen had shared with their British peers European clubs, which one historian describes as vehicles for a "political mobilization of whiteness." These clubs consolidated the racially exclu-sive colonial elite in India and at the same time served important busi-ness functions, such as information exchange, conflict mediation, and networking.[61]

With the outbreak of the war, Germans and Austrians were expelled from these clubs and the doors remained closed to them even after the war.[62] While the internment conditions in India were overall acceptable in terms of nutrition, health, and control over personal time, the German internees' major affliction was their exclusion from what had once been a social community of Western businesspeople in India.

Reconfiguring Trade

With German businessmen interned and their assets expropriated, Ger-man imports became suddenly unavailable in India. "Before the war, ... the trade of Germany and Austria with this market [India] was consid-erable and growing rapidly" reported Thomas Ainscough, the British Senior Trade Commissioner in India and Ceylon.[63] With the outbreak of the war, however, the situation changed dramatically, giving rise to three new trends: (i) shortages of goods and increasing prices, (ii) new players in the import trade, notably the United States and Japan, and (iii) grow-ing Indian competition.

The sudden outbreak of the war led to shortages and price increases throughout the Indian economy. In Bombay, the US consul reported

---

[59] N. O. Tera, "Report," attachment to letter Kuehns to Waibel, December 6, 1939, 330/596, BA.
[60] Probst, *Unter indischer Sonne*: 11.
[61] Sinha, "Britishness": quote: 505.
[62] Consulate Calcutta, "Letter to Foreign Office Berlin," July 29, 1930, R/3101/02664, BArch-B.
[63] Department of Overseas Trade and Ainscough, *Conditions and Prospects 1919*: 12.

that prices for agricultural produce and all imported articles increased between 10 and 100 percent.[64] In the most important industry in India, the cotton textile industry, prices for cotton cloth were also on the rise. However, the industry developed rather positively in the new environment, which was now protected from foreign competition. With imports decreasing from a pre-war annual average of 2.1 billion yards in 1906–1908 to a war-time average of 1.4 billion yards in 1916–1918, Indian textile mills stepped up to fill the gap. Centered in Bombay and Ahmedabad, the local factories enlarged their production from 0.6 billion to 1.3 billion yards during the same period. However, the overall availability of cloth still receded slightly, and the diminishing supply pushed up prices.[65] Costs of shipments to London also multiplied by a factor of three to four.[66]

In the complementary business with dyestuffs, which before the war had come primarily from Germany, the availability contracted even more drastically. Imports fell abruptly to one-third of pre-war amounts.[67] While in many other industries British, American, and Japanese competitors quickly filled in the voids that the Germans had left, none of them had the production capacity to meet the demand for dyes immediately.[68] Those dyes remaining in India, or making their way there during the war, were sold at auction. By 1916, the scarcity was so acute that prices increased sharply. The *Times of India* reported on a Madras-based auction in July 1916: "Never there was such a large crowd of industrialists, not even in any of the Industrial Conferences in India … as there was yesterday at the auction."[69] The price of one keg of Alizarine (diluted to 16 percent), which had cost Rs 35 (or US$11) before the war, went for Rs 1,000 (or US$314) on average, with the highest price of the day reaching Rs 1,400 (or US$440), or forty times the original price.[70] In Cawnpore, the shortage of dyes was obvious to even the casual observer "by the remarkable absence during the recent Holi festival of colour throwing," a custom for which dry powder and colored water were traditionally used.[71] Over the following years, Germany's competitors supplied increasingly greater

[64] "Commercial and Industrial Review of Bombay," August 4, 1914, Record Group 84: Records of the Foreign Service Posts of the Department of State, United States Consular Records for Bombay, India, Correspondence 340–621, 194, vol. 96, NARA.
[65] Rothermund, *Economic History of India*: 67.
[66] Heinrich Müller, "Letter to Wesendonk," May 20, 1915, 200–202, R/21083, PA.
[67] Department of Overseas Trade and Ainscough, *Conditions and Prospects 1919*: 53.
[68] Ibid., 12.
[69] "Auction Sale of Dyes: High Prices Realised in Madras," *Times of India*, July 12, 1916: 5.
[70] Ibid.
[71] "Shortage of Dyes," *Times of India*, March 23, 1916: 8.

quantities of dyestuff. While the German manufacturers had provided their dyes to both textile mills and bazaars, the late movers followed a division of labor. British dyes were sold primarily to factories, while American and Japanese dyes went to the bazaar segment.[72]

Besides pushing up prices, the war also opened a window of opportunity for new foreign competitors. The US consul in Bombay reported that, "[t]he sudden outbreak of war ... has caused local merchants in India to hastily consider the possibility of being able to secure goods ordinarily imported from Germany and Austria-Hungary."[73] His office was flooded with urgent inquiries regarding the possibility of establishing trade connections with the US to replace missing goods.[74] Indeed, US shipments to India almost doubled between 1913/1914 and 1917/1918, with loads coming from both the Atlantic and Pacific coasts.[75] Jumping on the opportunity, US import houses advertised in India as early as August 1914 with the slogan: "If it is made in the United States, we can get it for you."[76]

Even more remarkable was the swift increase of Japanese imports. From the outbreak of the war until its end, Japanese imports increased eightfold in value.[77] The British trade commissioner for India observed that both Japanese overseas banks and export–import houses opened branches in Calcutta and Bombay, direct steamer lines between Japan and India were established, and Japanese commercial travelers crisscrossed the country.[78] Especially in the bazaar trade, Japanese goods captured significant market shares.

Finally, the war gave a strong impetus to the development of local industries, not least because British policies in India underwent a considerable transformation. The war highlighted that India's industrial capability was important for securing and stabilizing India, and for its ability to contribute to the war effort. The Government of India established the "Indian Industrial Commission" to investigate the status quo

[72] Department of Overseas Trade and Ainscough, *Conditions and Prospects 1919*: 54.
[73] "Commercial and Industrial Review of Bombay," August 4, 1914, Record Group 84: Records of the Foreign Service Posts of the Department of State, United States Consular Records for Bombay, India, Correspondence 340–621, 194, vol. 96, NARA.
[74] American Consulate Bombay, "Letter to US Secretary of State," September 12, 1914, Record Group 84: Records of the Foreign Service Posts of the Department of State, United States Consular Records for Bombay, India, Correspondence 340–621, 194, vol. 96, NARA.
[75] Department of Overseas Trade and Ainscough, *Conditions and Prospects 1919*: 12.
[76] "Letter [signature illegible] to American Consul General Calcutta," August 28, 1914, Correspondence 610–621, 1914, Dep. of State, U.S. Consulate Calcutta India (1855–1947), US Consular Records for Calcutta, India, compiled 1856–1935, NARA.
[77] Department of Overseas Trade and Ainscough, *Conditions and Prospects 1919*: 14.
[78] Ibid., 15.

of industrial development in India and suggest ways to promote industry.[79] It was during the war that many Indian industries first developed their competitiveness, as foreign goods stopped being available or supplies were heavily reduced. As mentioned before, the Indian textile mills stepped up their production as soon as imports dwindled. Similarly, Indian coal mining was able to capture larger shares of the home market.[80] Most importantly, the war was decisive for the Indian steel industry, which could now develop in a protected sellers' market, after imports from Germany and Belgium had been cut off and British imports became increasingly scarce. Before the war, over 1 million tons of steel were shipped to India; in 1917/1918 this number decreased by 84 percent to 165,000 tons.[81] During the same time, the steel manufacturer Tata increased its domestic production nearly sixfold from 31,000 tons to 181,000 tons of steel.[82] While the contributions to the war effort gained Tata much goodwill with the colonial government, one effect of the war was a renewed focus on Swadeshi, reflected in an "earnest desire among both Indians and Europeans, industrialists, merchants and officials alike, to render India as far as possible self-supporting," as the British trade commissioner diplomatically put it.[83] While the Swadeshi ("from one's own country") movement looked back at a longer history (see Chapter 2), the war served as a catalyst for the nationalistic agenda of economic self-reliance, and Indian industrialists and merchants were confident that economic autarky could be achieved in a reasonable timeframe.

Swadeshi Conspiracies

The spirit of Swadeshi also captured the imagination of German politicians, who saw in India not just a large market but also a possible tool for war against Great Britain. Already before the outbreak of the war, individual voices close to the German Foreign Office stressed that mobilizing Indian nationalist activists may give Germany an advantage over Great Britain. Specifically, they observed two groups of insurgents, namely Islamic and Bengali protesters. The goal was to turn the colony India, which was seen as being of great strategic relevance to Great Britain, into a liability for its colonial overseer. From inception, these plans for conspiracies had not only a strategic-military component, but also a

---

[79] Indian Industrial Commission, *Indian Industrial Commission Report 1916–1918.*
[80] Rothermund, *Economic History of India*: 67–68.
[81] Headrick, *Tentacles*: 291.
[82] Rothermund, *Economic History of India*: 69.
[83] Department of Overseas Trade and Ainscough, *Conditions and Prospects 1919*: 19. See also, Raianu, *Tata*: 34–36.

business and economic one, designed to support German export business and render it more competitive with Britain. However, the business angle of the plans became increasingly sidelined as the war intensified and has largely been forgotten in the historiography of the Indo-German World War I conspiracies.[84]

The discussion of the idea that uprisings in India could work to Germany's advantage pre-dated the outbreak of the war by several years. One of the earliest systematic analyses of the situation came from the Prussian general and military writer Friedrich A. J. von Bernhardi (1849 –1930) in his book *Germany and the Next War*, first completed in October 1911 and published in 1912, two years before the outbreak of the war.[85] Bernhardi advocated strongly for war and saw in the nationalist movements in India and also Egypt a threat to England which Germany could exploit. "[T]he danger is imminent that Pan-Islamism, thoroughly roused, should unite with the revolutionary elements of Bengal. The co-operation of these elements might create a very grave danger, capable of shaking the foundations of England's high position in the world."[86] The two groups identified by Bernhardi – Islamic insurgents and Bengali revolutionaries – were to remain the focus of Germany's efforts throughout the war years.

Bernhardi was also the first to merge economic and military arguments for fueling uprisings in India. He argued that England's sovereignty so far had depended as much on military power as it had on economic prowess. "England, doubtless, would not shrink from a war to the knife ... if any attack threatened her Indian market, the control of which is the foundation of her world sovereignty."[87] Not least for this reason, a war between Germany and England was as much commercial as it was militaristic, and England aimed at "crippling the German oversea commerce."[88] To counter such efforts, Bernhardi proposed preparations for commercial activities during a possible war, which he summarized as "commercial mobilization."[89] However, ultimately, only a defeat of the enemy would protect Germany's business long-term.[90] Bernhardi did not hold an official position at the German Foreign Office, however his

---

[84] Fraser, "Germany and Indian Revolution, 1914–18." Fraser, "Intrigues of German Government"; Hanisch, *Der Orient der Deutschen*. Loth and Hanisch, *Erster Weltkrieg*. Oberhaus, *Propagandastrategie*. Gossman, *The Passion of Max von Oppenheim*: 81–105.

[85] Bernhardi, *Deutschland*. Available online: https://catalog.hathitrust.org/Record/10235 7195. In English translation: Bernhardi, *Germany and the Next War*.

[86] Bernhardi, *Germany and the Next War*: 96.

[87] Ibid., 24.

[88] Ibid., 97.

[89] Ibid., 159.

[90] Ibid., 228.

views circulated broadly and foreshadowed many of the efforts undertaken during the war.

Not least because of studies like Bernhardi's, the general interest in India was widely shared among German political and economic elites. On July 30, 1914, the German Kaiser called it most succinctly when he said, "our consuls in Turkey and India, agents, etc., must get a conflagration going throughout the whole Mohammedan world against this hated, unscrupulous, dishonest nation of shopkeepers – since if we are going to bleed to death, England must at least lose India."[91] It is thus not surprising that at the outbreak of the war, German authorities were quick to formulate a policy towards Indian revolutionaries. To that end, the detailed report by Max von Oppenheim titled "Memorandum on revolutionizing the Islamic territories of our enemies" was an important milestone.[92] The report was written in mid-October and early November 1914.[93]

Oppenheim's analysis reorganized the nations of the world on a heavily political mental map, spotlighting those that shared anti-British sentiments. It called most urgently for fomenting insurrections in Egypt and India, the two countries that Bernhardi had also highlighted, and which Oppenheim singled out as "the Achilles heels of ... the British giant."[94] For the outcome of the war, Oppenheim argued, the success of the strategy in India was particularly decisive. "Among the countries to revolutionize, India is by far the most important with regards to the final success of the war."[95] Observing the Indian National Congress (the primary nationalist political party in India) and some of its leaders, Oppenheim was confident that the Indian intelligentsia was by and large anti-British and strove for self-governance and economic autarky.[96] In the case of an uprising supported by Germany, he predicted that India would make great strides towards these goals.[97] At the same time, Oppenheim expected a general decline of colonialism in the future that would strengthen Germany economically; again merging military and commercial arguments. In a different publication, Oppenheim laid out

[91] Kautsky, *Die Deutschen Dokumente*: Vol. 2, Nr. 401, 133.
[92] Max von Oppenheim, "*Denkschrift betreffend die Revolutionierung der islamischen Gebiete unserer Feinde, 1914*"; hereafter: Oppenheim, *Denkschrift*, R/20938, PA. The full text was made available in: Epkenhans, "Geld." For context see also Oberhaus, *Propagandastrategie*; Hanisch, "Max Freiherr von Oppenheim." Broad outlines in English are available in: Gossman, *The Passion of Max von Oppenheim*: 81–105.
[93] For details on dating the report, see Hanisch, "Max Freiherr von Oppenheim": 16–17.
[94] Oppenheim, *Denkschrift*: 3 and 125, quote: 125.
[95] Ibid., 78.
[96] Ibid., 81–82.
[97] Ibid., 136.

his detailed plans for an intelligence agency, which after the war could be at the disposal of German business to reinforce export activities. He wanted to present Germany not just as the primary political and military power but also as an economic and industrial giant, proving that "one can buy everything, best and cheapest, in Germany."[98]

By the time Oppenheim wrote his memorandum, his campaign for unrest in India and Egypt had already been officially sanctioned by the German Government.[99] Oppenheim himself had started to realize some of his plans. "In greatest silence, I have instituted a committee of Indians living here [in Germany] and in Switzerland. It has 18 members."[100] The committee, later called Indian Independence Committee (IIC), was composed of Indian students, journalists, and writers, and would become the organizational base for the revolutionary conspiracies that Germany supported.[101] The number of anticolonial activists in Germany, most notably in Berlin, grew during World War I. "Berlin was the Mecca of Oriental patriots of all shades and opinions. Their common bond was hatred of England and France," reported Har Dayal, one of the Indian freedom fighters in Berlin.[102] The Indian community clustered in Charlottenburg, one of Berlin's western boroughs, where the Foreign Office set up its Committee for the Orient and "Nachrichtenstelle für den Orient" [Intelligence Bureau for the Orient], of which Max von Oppenheim was the first director.[103]

The different members of the IIC held various roles within the group. With most of them being students, they were strong writers and published a series of pro-Indian articles and pamphlets. They were less well prepared to do the more practical tasks, such as smuggling arms, training activists in combat or the clandestine movement of money across borders. Many of the publications by the IIC members included attempts to recast the history of India, often with an eye to a German audience. One prominent author was A. Raman Pillai who had come to Europe in 1909 to pursue a degree in Forestry at Edinburgh University. He moved to

---

[98] Max von Oppenheim, *Die Nachrichtenstelle der Kaiserlichen Botschaft in Konstantinopel und die deutsche Propaganda in der Türkei*. Berlin 1916, quoted in: Hanisch, "Curt Prüfer – Orientalist, Dragoman und Oppenheims 'man on the spot'": 183.

[99] In a telegram by Bethmann Hollweg dated September 4, 1914, quoted in: Fraser, "Intrigues of German Government": 173.

[100] Oppenheim, *Denkschrift*: 90.

[101] The committee included among others Chempakaraman Pillai, Har Dayal, Tarakanath Das, Chandra K. Chakrabarti, Heramba Lal Gupta, Virendranath Chattopadhyaya, Bhupendranath Dutta, A. Raman Pillai, Maulavi Barkatullah, M. Prabhakar, Birendra Sarkar.

[102] Har Dayal, *Forty-Four Months*: 55.

[103] Manjapra, "The Anticolonial Laboratory": 153.

Germany in 1913 to work on a project in the Black Forest. In April 1914, he joined the University of Göttingen. When the war broke out, he was unable to return to Edinburgh and instead registered for a PhD at Göttingen's Philosophical Department. He regularly published pro-Indian articles, condemning British imperialism and foregrounding commonalities in the history of Indians and Germans, thus clustering different national histories and national aspirations in an exercise of compare and contrast.[104] "It is entirely incorrect to pretend that the English nation conquered India; India is herself to blame for its ruin. In the same way as Italy and Germany were easy prey for Napoleon, because there was no stable Italian or German feeling of nationality, India fell as prey in the hands of the English."[105] The IIC also had ties to Switzerland, especially to Chempakaraman Pillai (1891–1934), the president and founder of the International Pro-India Committee in Zurich, who also agitated for India. Pillai had studied engineering at the Eidgenössische Technische Hochschule (Swiss Federal Institute of Technology, ETH) Zurich from 1910 to 1914. Since June 1914, Pillai issued the journal *Pro India*[106] and in October, he relocated to Berlin and joined the IIC.

Hopes for the Indo-German schemes were high in the Indian expat community. Har Dayal described how, "[u]nbounded optimism and sincere faith in the power and professions of Germany were common to all these Oriental 'Nationalists' [quotation marks in the original, CL]."[107] The French police reported in November 1914 that "it was generally believed among revolutionary Indians in Europe that a rebellion would break out in India in a short time and that Germany would support the movement with all her power."[108] Von Oppenheim remained influential in the workings of the IIC until early 1915, when he departed for an assignment in Constantinople. Replacing Oppenheim, the Foreign Office put the twenty-nine-year-old lawyer Otto Günther von Wesendonck in charge of managing the committee.

Together the IIC and the German Government initiated a series of revolutionary schemes. They orchestrated activities in the United States and the Far East with the goal of providing weapons and money to the revolutionaries and inflaming unrest in India. By the end of 1914, the IIC described some of its plans in a document for the German Foreign Office. Among the suggestions of the committee was a campaign to

---

[104] Pillai, *Deutschland-Indiens Hoffnung*; Pillai, "B. T. und Indien." Both SUB.
[105] Pillai, "Indien." SUB.
[106] J. C. Pro India, "Our Aims and Objects," *Pro India* 1(1) June 1914: 4, 1914, 37, R/21072, PA.
[107] Har Dayal, *Forty-Four Months*: 57.
[108] Reported in: East India (Sedition Committee), *Revolutionary Conspiracies*: 52.

influence Indian soldiers in German captivity.[109] A similar argument, but with an economic bent, came from Oscar Schmidt-Ernsthausen, who argued that Indian prisoners of war in German camps "could guarantee German trade in the future uncountable successes."[110] The second and more immediately relevant suggestion of the committee was to provide arms and ammunition to activists in India. Several IIC members had departed for India to establish links with secret and revolutionary organizations. They had previously received training by the German Government in dealing with explosives, which they were keen to pass on to crusaders in India. Jnanendra Chandra Dasgupta, for example, had lived in Berlin since 1909, where he studied chemistry and received his PhD in May 1913.[111] He was one of the activists providing their services for smuggling arms to India in November 1914.[112]

To bring arms to India despite war-related restrictions on travel and shipments, the committee joined hands with another revolutionary organization, the Ghadar Party, a predominantly Sikh organization of Indian immigrants to the US. The Ghadar Party ("Ghadar" meaning revolt or rebellion in Urdu) was founded in 1913 and headquartered in San Francisco. The leaders of the Ghadar Party identified World War I as a great opportunity for a rebellion against the British Raj, supported by the German Government. An article in their weekly newspaper *The Ghadar* of November 15, 1913, stated that, "[t]he Germans have great sympathy with our movement, because they and ourselves have a common enemy (the English). In the future Germany can draw assistance from us, and they can render us great assistance also."[113] Just before the outbreak of the war, the party's weekly confirmed that, "[a]ll intelligent people know that Germany is an enemy of England. So the enemy of our enemy is our friend."[114] However, the timing of the collaboration with the Ghadar Party proved ill conceived. Immediately at the outbreak of the war, several hundred party members had returned to India to agitate for a rebellion, which eventually took place in February 1915. By the time the German consul in San Francisco had contacted the remaining party members, this uprising had already come to a rather unsuccessful close.

---

[109] "A short summary of the plans of the Indian committee in Berlin," undated [end of 1914], R/21075, PA.
[110] Oscar Schmidt-Ernsthausen, "Lebensumriss und Personalien," July 11, 1915, 139–143, here: 142, R/21085, PA.
[111] CV in his dissertation, see Dasgupta, Studien über 2-Chloranthrachinon-3-carbonsäure.
[112] On Dasgupta see, "Note October 28, 1914," 126, R/21073, PA; "Telegram November 2, 1914," 8, R/21074, PA.
[113] Quoted in: Strother, *Fighting*: 227.
[114] *The Ghadar*, July 21, 1914, quoted in: ibid.

However, two of the most prominent Ghadar leaders, Har Dayal and Barkatullah, relocated to Berlin in January 1915 to support the work of the IIC.

To provide both the Ghadar activists and Bengali revolutionaries with weapons and ammunition, Franz von Papen, the German military attaché to the United States (and later German Chancellor) was selected to secure them in the United States. In his memoirs, he reflected in hindsight that "[w]e did not go so far as to suppose that there was any hope of India achieving her independence through our assistance, but if there was any chance of fomenting local disorders we felt it might limit the number of Indian troops who could be sent to France and other theaters of war."[115] The plan was for the Ghadar Party members to invade Burma with arms provided by the Germans, while for the Bengali revolutionaries, money and weapons should come via the Dutch East Indies, allowing them to start a second revolutionary outbreak.

From the inception of these plans, German Government officials relied heavily on the German business community for support. Gathering arms, von Papen sought the help of Hans Tauscher, a representative of the German steel manufacturer Krupp in the US. However, two attempts to ship them failed; not least because the American authorities, although officially neutral at this point, identified and stopped the cargo.[116] The non-arrival of the promised weapons was a great disappointment for the Indian activists.

Similarly, the German business community in the Dutch East Indies supported different schemes, led by the brothers Emil and Theodor Helfferich. For example, they intended to use long-standing trading routes between Sumatra and Calcutta to move arms and money into India but were exposed by an anonymous whistleblower who informed the British consul-general in Batavia of the underground activities. Based on this information, the police not only destroyed the revolutionary organization in Calcutta but also killed its leader in September 1914.[117]

Finally, the Ghadar Party took an interest in Thailand as an area of operations. The German Government supported these activities with another attempt at shipping weapons, which failed yet again because American customs refused clearance. In Thailand, the Ghadar supporters were trained by Peking embassy guards, which the Germans paid for, and received arms from the German Government, which were smuggled by an

---

[115] von Papen, *Memoirs*: 40.
[116] For details on the logistical challenges, see Fraser, "Intrigues of German Government."
[117] Fraser, "Germany and Indian Revolution, 1914–18."

officer on a Norwegian ship. By July 1914, a sizeable group of armed Ghadar Party members was positioned near the Burmese border. However, British police officers in Thailand uncovered the scheme and several leading revolutionaries were arrested. On March 19, 1915, the Governor General of India passed "The Defence of India Act," an emergency law with wide-ranging executive powers, such as preventive detention, imprisonment without trial, and restrictions on freedom of speech and movement, designed to curtail revolutionary activities. The act was first applied in the trial against the Ghadar conspirators, which took place in Lahore in 1915.

In hindsight, all the conspiracy schemes were failures. However, they were not inconsequential. While historians have speculated on the reasons for the failed attempts, including lack of leadership, lack of experience, and the superiority of British intelligence work,[118] few have studied the conspiracies' long-term consequences. First, they were one trigger for the passing of extraordinary legislation in India (i.e., the Defence of India Act in 1915) and the growth of a British intelligence system in several countries of the East. These laws continued to exist in modified form even after the end of the war and became a focal point of political protest and nationalist agitation. Second, the conspiracies started reflections in both Germany and India on their joint interests and their position vis-à-vis the common enemy Great Britain. This process was supported by the flurry of publications in Germany highlighting the joint plight and parallel histories of Germany and India, mostly written by the small group of diaspora Indians who supported the IIC. They explored how they could collaborate on the world stage, making way for some of the post-war collaboration strategies. Third, the connections established between selected Indians (mostly living in Germany) and German Government officials remained intact and continued into the post-war period. This Indian diaspora in Germany was to become important in the post-war period. Most of them remained in the neighborhood of Berlin where they started their activities during the war, using the same social spaces first established for the conspiracies.[119] Finally, the heavy involvement of the business community would prove important for the re-establishment of Indo-German commercial relations after the war, with many businesspeople also nurturing their contacts with Indian activists. While all German assets in India were lost, Indo-German collaboration was not at its end but rather was revitalized by the close-knit collaboration during the conspiracy schemes and by the establishment of activist groups and targeted publications in both India and Germany.

---

[118] Fraser, "Intrigues of German Government." Fraser, "Germany and Indian Revolution, 1914–18."

[119] Manjapra, "The Anticolonial Laboratory": 153.

4   The Alliance of the Disillusioned

The conspiracies between Indian nationalists and their German partners that World War I fomented failed in the short term. But Indo-German business and political alliances were reinvented in surprising ways in the post-war period. For both Indians and Germans, this was a time of grave disappointments. The war and the Treaty of Versailles destroyed the German economy domestically and decimated the presence of German firms abroad, leaving the country's multinationals in desperate need of new opportunities. Indian nationalists were also looking for new options in their struggle for independence. Many Indians were bitterly disappointed that the growing rhetoric of national self-determination that the war had generated excluded them and that Indian sacrifices made during the war were not sufficiently rewarded by the British colonial administration. This common sense of loss and unjust treatment set the stage for perceiving the world of nations in new ways and for reconsidering the Indo-German business relationship in it.

The perceived humiliation of Germany at Versailles allowed Indian nationalists to see their German counterparts through what seemed like a familiar lens: as the victims of unjust British aggression. German firms gradually re-entered India not only based on renewed economic strength but also with a new geopolitical identity. In their loss they found new allies as a late-developing nation that confronted the dominance of British supremacy. Seeking self-determination, Indians looked for both the manufactured products and the technical know-how that German firms were keen and increasingly able to provide. This growing sense of economic and political mutualism was bolstered by experiments with a new historical narrative, which claimed that Germans and Indians shared an ancient and lasting "Aryan" identity that anteceded Western colonialism altogether.

In the Shadow of Versailles

Germans and Indians came together as an alliance of the disillusioned in the aftermath of the Peace Treaty of Versailles. As seen in Chapter 3, World War I put a temporary stop to Indo-German business relations. The

British government abolished its blacklists of enemy companies in October 1919.[1] More than a full year passed after the armistice on November 11, 1918, before the German internees were released from the Indian camps in 1919 and 1920.[2] Ending World War I was a process rather than an event.

At the end of the devastating war, the German economy lay in ruins. Nobody, least of all German businesspeople, expected Germany to return to the Indian market soon. Indeed, there were so many obstacles to overcome that many observers were rather pessimistic about their prospects. An entrepreneur in the cutlery trade wrote in a private letter in 1917, "What the situation in India will be after the war is today unpredictable. Incalculable are also the enormous costs that will occur to reintroduce my products there."[3] His anxiety was not unfounded. The German economy had suffered great losses during and after the war. The victorious Allies imposed harsh conditions on Germany, with war debts and reparation payments amounting to a considerable financial obligation for the new German Republic. The immediate losses included large amounts of territory, people, and resources in Germany. But the new Germany was also no longer a global power. It had lost all its overseas colonies, most of its foreign investments, and its allies around the world.[4]

To make matters worse, the status of German multinationals after the war seemed less than ideal for rebuilding an international business. In many industries, economic production had shifted away from civilian to war-related military goods during the war. Moreover, the Treaty of Versailles provided for some production output as reparation payment and for technology transfer in favor of the victors. By the early 1920s, much relevant technology had passed into the hands of global challengers.[5] In addition, jumpstarting German industry was difficult because of the many new barriers to accessing export markets. France, the US, and Britain manufactured more products domestically and established protective barriers, which allowed the home industry to fulfill the lion's share of internal demand. Many markets that had been important to German industry before the war were closed off.

Frustrations also reverberated in post-war India. For Indian independence activists, Versailles and US President Woodrow Wilson's principle

---

[1] "Cables in Brief," *Times of India*, October 15, 1919: 9.
[2] Panayi, *The Germans in India*: 218.
[3] Kaufmann, "Letter to Venn," November 14, 1917, NA/15/2, CASol.
[4] For a contemporaneous discussion of the peace treaty and its results, see Keynes, *The Economic Consequences of the Peace*. For the relevance of the losses for the export economy, see also Gross, *Export Empire*: 48–49. For the impact of the colonies on German nationalism, see Conrad, *Globalisation and the Nation*.
[5] Johnson and Macleod, "The War the Victors Lost."

of national self-determination triggered hopes for a new progressive spirit in world politics. Wilson, in his famed Fourteen Points, had publicly declared the right of all people to self-determination, and around the world hopeful nations saw in him a new ally and advocate.[6] India was one of them. Indian nationalist Bal Gangadhar Tilak even corresponded with Wilson directly, sending him a political pamphlet, which detailed "what the principles of right and justice for all nations may demand in the case of India." The pamphlet made a case for India's claim to be an independent nation.[7]

During the war, the predominant organization of Indian independence activists, the Indian National Congress party, had by and large supported the British. Many prominent Indian politicians had advocated for the drafting of Indians into the British Army, which they saw as an opportunity to prove Indian loyalty to the British Empire and as a step toward equal rights. One argued that the war "has put the clock ... fifty years forward." It was time for Indians "to take their legitimate part in the administration of their own country."[8] Many Indians expected Britain to reward them for their loyalty with a greater voice in their own government, and that Wilson's principle of self-determination be applied to India.[9] A speaker at the 1918 Congress meeting in New Delhi, Ajmal Khan, argued that, "[n]ow when the right of self-determination is being granted to the smallest nationality in Europe, the question is naturally asked, shall India, who has so ungrudgingly and cheerfully made sacrifices in the defence of the principles of liberty and freedom, right and justice, be deprived of the right to determine her own form of Government?"[10]

In the aftermath of Versailles, India became a member of the League of Nations. However, those who hoped for a big step toward Indian self-government were disappointed. Instead, the Government of India Act of 1919 instituted the principle of diarchy. It was based on the Montagu-Chelmsford Report, which suggested a gradual introduction of self-governing institutions to India.[11] Indian ministers were chosen by

---

[6] Manela, *The Wilsonian Moment*.

[7] Tilak, "Letter to Wilson," January 2, 1919, and The Indian Home Rule League Office, "Self-Determination for India," London: Indian Home Rule League [undated 1918], 9, in: Presidential Papers Microfilm Woodrow Wilson Papers, Series 5F and 5G: Peace Conference Correspondence 1918–1919, Reel 446, LOC.

[8] Quoted in: Manela, *The Wilsonian Moment*: 82n25.

[9] Ibid., 95–97.

[10] "National Congress: Proceedings at Delhi Presidential Address," *Times of India*, December 27, 1918: 10

[11] The report was named after Edwin Samuel Montagu, Secretary of State for India during the latter part of World War I and Lord Chelmsford, the Viceroy of India between 1916 and 1921. On the process of researching and writing the report, see Ryland, "Edwin Montagu in India"; For a review of the liberal and educative intent of the reforms, see Woods, "The Montagu-Chelmsford Reforms."

the British governor from the elected members of the provinces' legislature and given responsibility over a few selected areas of government, such as education and public health. This was a significant change from the Morley-Minto reforms of 1909, which had fully rejected such participation. However, and to the disappointment of Indian nationalists, all other government business remained under the control of the British Viceroy, including the key areas of defense, foreign affairs, and communications.[12]

As part of the reform, India obtained for the first time a limited measure of fiscal autonomy. The British Government would not interfere in India's fiscal policy as long as there was complete agreement between the Government of India and the legislature. The Government of India, however, was responsible to the British Government and made sure that British commercial interests were fully considered. Despite these first timid steps towards a greater voice in the government of their country, nationalistic Indians experienced the end of World War I as a major frustration. While nationalists had expected control over their government and self-determination, the reforms "fall far short of that."[13] After having supported Britain during the war, their expectations for a reward were deeply disappointed.

The feeling of having been ill-treated mirrored how many critics in Germany felt about the Versailles Treaty. Termed the Versailles "Diktat," i.e. the dictated peace, public opinion considered it a grave injustice because it allegedly destroyed Germany's political and economic position not just in Europe and in Germany's former colonies but also in many countries overseas, where the German export industry had previously been successful.[14] And trade was more important to Germany than ever, not least to break out of political constraints. Hans Posse, the Under-Secretary of the German Economic Ministry argued, "[f]or a weakened state, like Germany, ... the almost only tool to fight back unjustified interests from abroad is its trade policy."[15] The search for accessible export markets, where German goods could find sympathetic customers, was an economic and political priority.

And seeds for a new beginning existed. The war-related shift in production to military goods had preserved the industrial capacity of Germany and many of the wartime products found peacetime applications.[16]

---

[12] Curtis and Great Britain. Parliament. Joint Select Committee on the Government of India Bill, *Papers Relating to the Application of the Principle of Dyarchy*.

[13] Malaviya, *Criticism*: 28.

[14] Gackenholz, *Diktat*: 39–40.

[15] Hans Posse, Under-Secretary of the Economic Ministry, "Manuscript: Memorandum about the Trade Policy of the Government," 1924/25, N 1303/2, BArch-K.

[16] Johnson and Macleod, "The War the Victors Lost": 222–223. Szöllösi-Janze, "Losing the War."

The pressure of wartime and the fear of expropriation after the war also precipitated industrial cooperation in several industries, leading to cartels and collaborative agreements.[17] Both the German chemical and electrical industries became more organized. As early as 1916, eight German dyestuff firms had entered into a pooling agreement, the so-called community of interest (*Interessengemeinschaft*, or I.G.), which continued after the war, and provided the industry with organizational advantages and economies of scale and scope.[18] Similarly, the German electrical industry was largely controlled by Siemens and its main competitor AEG, which now engaged in a strategic partnership.[19] Coordinated capitalism shaped the postwar corporate landscape.

This newly organized German industry eagerly searched for open markets abroad for its continuously increasing production. Despite all obstacles, India remained a place of latent possibilities. The Deutsche Wirtschaftsdienst, a German economic intelligence service, highlighted not only the huge potential of India but also how politically accessible it was, both in terms of public approval and equal treatment of foreign importers. "For the future, India is one of the few large export markets, where the mass of consumers is sympathetic to German products and where no dangerous protective taxes are to be expected."[20]

While being unlikely allies in many respects, Germans and Indians thus found themselves at a moment of aligned interests. German multinationals eagerly sought markets abroad; while Indian nationalists had an interest in developing their industry, for which selected imports from the West were unavoidable. Already prior to World War I, the idea of non-British foreign goods had been established (see Chapter 2) and the nations that could provide them included Germany, the US, and Japan. The shared identity as victims of British power drew Germany and India even closer together. According to Bengali economist Benoy Kumar Sarkar, India was interested in Germany because of its history and its identity. Historically, as Europe's most advanced late-developing economy, it could serve as a model for India's industrialization. But Sarkar's reasoning was based not only on the practical knowledge that Germany could provide but also on the sense of India's and Germany's common identity as victims of British power. "[T]he treatment that Germany as the halfway house to a dependency or a colony has been receiving

---

[17] Fear, "Cartels": 277–278; Schroeter, "Cartelization."
[18] For details on the I. G., see Plumpe, *I. G. Farbenindustrie AG*: 96–100. Abelshauser et al., *German Industry and Global Enterprise*: 171–173.
[19] Feldenkirchen, "Big Business."
[20] Deutscher Wirtschaftsdienst, *Britisch Indien*: 10–11.

[at the Peace Treaty of Versailles] ... is absolutely identical with what Asians and Africans have been used to obtaining from Eur-Americans ... All this treatment is a corollary to colonialism"[21]. Along similar lines, the nationalist German historian Oswald Spengler pointedly referred to Germany as "a European India," exploited as a "colony of reparation payments" after the peace negotiations.[22] The group of Berlin-based Indian nationalists summarized, "German and Indian people have no doubt to endure presently also politically similar conditions, whereby of itself a certain community of interests is going to be created."[23] Fighting for autonomy, both "Germans and Indians ... must hasten to liberate themselves from their inner and outer economic thralldom."[24] The common plight that they allegedly experienced translated into aligned political goals: weakening British hegemony in Europe after World War I and in Asia in the context of a disintegrating empire. It gave the idea of an Indo-German alliance the appearance of a mutually beneficial opportunity.

Organizing the India Business – Yet Again

Despite the general alignment of interests, Indo-German business had to craft new pathways in the difficult environment of the post-war period. Seen from a German perspective, India was simultaneously one of the few accessible markets for industrialized goods and one of the most competitive places in the world. Germany's efforts to re-enter India were challenged by continuous British competition, powerful Indian rivals, who had built up strengths in steel and many bazaar goods industries, as well as new entrants from the US and Japan, which both had moved forcefully into the Indian market during the war. In light of such competition "[i]t is difficult to see ... how they [Germany and Austria] can even regain their former position" opined the British Trade Commissioner in 1919.[25]

All these competitive pressures were compounded by the fact that German nationals remained expelled from the Indian subcontinent until long after the war had officially ended. German nationals were officially

---

[21] Sarkar, *The Politics of Boundaries*: 35.
[22] Spengler, *Neubau des Deutschen Reiches*: 14.
[23] Article in Indo-German Commercial Review, quoted and critically reviewed in: "Effrontery," *Times of India*, August 22, 1923: 8. See also, Barooah, *Germany and the Indians*: 17.
[24] "Indian Business Morality: A Reply to German Critics," *Industrial Review for India*, 1 (1923), 3: 56–58, quote: 58.
[25] Department of Overseas Trade and Ainscough, *Conditions and Prospects 1919*: 12.

banned from traveling or residing in India until August 31, 1925.[26] The German press interpreted this ban not just as a commercial obstacle but also as an insult based on the ideal of a White, Western elite in Asia; an identity that had been important before the war and that, for many Germans, had been damaged by expropriations and internment (see Chapter 3 for details.) "It is still today possible that the Chinese coolie will be permitted to enter India without further ado but not the German merchant," lamented an article in a German trade journal, explicitly contextualizing the discrimination of White Germans in contrast to non-White Chinese traders.[27] Not to be able to directly work the Indian market and re-establish pre-war relationships put the German export industry at a critical disadvantage.

However, demand was there. India showed an insatiable appetite for industrial products of the type that the German industry could provide. During the war, the Indian commercial classes had accumulated considerable wealth and invested it in industrial enterprises. Jute and cotton mills, iron and steel plants, engineering works and a variety of smaller plants required supplies of machinery, tools, and other articles not yet manufactured in India, thus making India's further industrialization dependent on foreign imports.[28] In the context of the German (hyper-) inflation between 1919 and 1923, German products were often significantly cheaper on export markets than those from competitors.[29]

While the travel ban lasted, the initiative came mostly from India. Selected Indian merchants visited German companies at home to resume cooperation. An entrepreneur from the cutlery trade reported Sikh buyers roaming the country to purchase much-needed goods for sale in India.[30] One of them was Nehal Singh of the company Singh, Sarcar & Co. who connected with a representative of the cutlery company Kaufmann in 1921, and established a trade relationship that lasted until 1927.[31] In the chemical industry, representatives of Bayer met with

---

[26] Government of India Press Communiqué, "Exclusion of former Enemy Nationality from India," November 1919, excerpt printed in: James A. Smith, "German Enemy Subjects Excluded from India," March 12, 1920, *Commerce Reports* 60, March 1920, 1434. The initial plan suggested 1926 but the law was changed prematurely in the summer of 1925.

[27] Paul Felzer, "Ein verlorener Markt," *Industrie- und Handelszeitung* 6/44, February 21, 1925: 1–2.

[28] Chapman and United States. Bureau of Foreign and Domestic Commerce, *India as a Market*: 4.

[29] Department of Overseas Trade and Ainscough, *Conditions and Prospects 1921*: 10.

[30] Lohmann, *Die Ausfuhr Solinger Stahlwaren*: 43.

[31] Heinrich Lohmann, "Letter to Ernst Kaufmann," July 12, 1922; August 5, 1926 and May 16, 1924, Na/15/3; Ernst Kaufmann, "Letter to Heinrich Lohmann," January 19, 1927, Na/15/4; Singh Sarkar & Co, "Letter to Ernst Kaufmann," November 17, 1927, Na/15/5, all CASol.

the chemist J. C. Dasgupta of Calcutta at the company's headquarter in Leverkusen in 1921. Dasgupta had studied chemistry in Berlin and had worked for the Swiss company Hoffmann-La Roche. During World War I, he was involved in the Indo-German conspiracies and delivered 60,000 Marks (US$11,194) from the Foreign Office to Indian revolutionaries.[32] With his experiences during the conspiracies, he served as a middleman between Germany and India and represented several Indian firms eager to establish contact with Bayer. According to the internal memo, Dasgupta tried "to lay the ground for the many Indians who now arrive daily in Hamburg."[33]

While the interest of Indian buyers signaled that there was unfulfilled demand in India, the travel ban forbid Germans from sending their own employees to India or set up shop there. Instead, German firms reverted once again after the war to "cloaking," that is, "the art of concealing the true ownership of a company from authorities."[34] Both Siemens and Bayer first rebuilt their business through a collaboration with the Italian company G. Gorio Ltd., in 1921 and 1922 respectively.[35] Gorio had offices in Bombay and Calcutta as well as initially in Karachi and maintained tight connections with the local colonial administration. Both Siemens and Bayer also hand-selected those engineers among their ranks who held non-German passports and posted them to India to support the new business under Gorio's leadership. Bayer sent Giulio Gut, a native German who had acquired Italian citizenship as resident of Asmara, Eritrea, and Siemens the Austrian national Edmund von Rziha, who had worked in Turkey before the war.[36] Other German multinationals followed. Having a direct representative in India was important for the German business community, which had disappointed so many Indian buyers at the outbreak of the war. "Above all else," urged a cutlery entrepreneur, "we ought to regain the trust in German goods, which has suffered so badly everywhere."[37] However, the lengthy travel ban was

---

[32] "Visit of Das Gupta [Dasgupta], 1921," Sales Representatives of Bayer AG, 9/K/1, BA. About Dasgupta during World War I, see, chapter 3 and Barooah, *Chatto*: 43–44. For a CV of Jnanendra Chandra Dasgupta see his dissertation, Dasgupta, Studien über 2-Chloranthrachinon-3-carbonsäure.

[33] "Visit of Das Gupta [Dasgupta], 1921," Sales Representatives of Bayer AG, 9/K/1, BA.

[34] Aalders and Wiebes, *Art*: 9.

[35] For Bayer see, "Bayer to I.G. Farben firms," October 27, 1921, Sales Dyes, 420, BA. Bayer's collaboration was with the support of the Milan-based firm Iridiscente, which in turn cooperated with G. Gorio Ltd. For Siemens see, "Memorandum of Association," November 8, 1922, 8156, SAA.

[36] Bayer, "Letter to Gorio," March 16, 1921, 420, BA; HR files SAA; Rziha, "Letter to Reyss," April 4, 1923, 8106, SAA.

[37] "Letter unsigned [Kaufmann] to H. C. Lohmann," November 25, 1920, NA/15/2, CASol.

Table 4.1 *Imports to British India by country of origin (in % of imports),*
1913/1914–1924/1925

	1913/ 1914	1918/ 1919	1919/ 1920	1920/ 1921	1921/ 1922	1922/ 1923	1923/ 1924	1924/ 1925
Great Britain	64.1	45.5	50.5	61	56.7	60.2	57.8	54.1
Germany	6.9	0.0	0.02	1.4	2.7	5.1	5.2	6.3
Java	5.8	6.6	9.4	4.7	8.9	5.5	6.2	6.3
USA	2.6	9.5	12.1	10.5	8.1	5.7	5.7	5.7
Japan	2.6	19.8	9.2	7.9	5.1	6.2	6.1	6.9
Belgium	2.3	0.003	0.3	1.6	2	2.7	2.4	2.7

Annual Statements.

felt as "heavy damage,"[38] and the often-raised suspicion in the German press was that Britain tried to keep German rivals out of India for fear of being commercially challenged.[39]

The legal situation improved with the Anglo-German trade agreement, ratified in 1925, which abolished the war-related travel restriction.[40] Shortly thereafter, British India became Germany's fourth largest overseas market, after the US, Argentina, and Japan. As in all previous years, Great Britain clearly dominated the trade to India and accounted for 54.1 percent of all official imports into the country. The three main competitors, Japan, Germany, and the US, held overall shares of 6.9, 6.3, and 5.7 percent, respectively (see Table 4.1). The official statistics still miscounted imports if they came via an intermediary harbor. One estimate concerning Bombay assumed that of all German products arriving in this important harbor, as much as 60 percent came from British ports and were registered as English goods, and another 10 percent from Dutch ports.[41]

As the Germans re-entered India, knowledge about the competitive situation and the Indian consumer was crucial. As before the war, Indian consumers fell roughly into three groups: public authorities, large

[38] "German-Indian Trade Relations: Before and After the War," *Industrial and Trade Review for India* (1925), 4–5: 59–62, quote: 61.
[39] Report in *Industrie- and Handelszeitung*, quoted (without publication details) in: "Review of the Press: Difficulties of Germany's Trade with India," *Industrial and Trade Review for India* (1925), 4–5: 63–64.
[40] Treaty of Commerce and Navigation between the United Kingdom and Germany December 2, 1924, ratified September 8, 1925. Great Britain. Foreign Office, *Handbook of Commercial Treaties*: 299. About the lobbying process leading up to it see McDonough, *Neville Chamberlain*: 135.
[41] *Industrie- und Handelszeitung*, February 21, 1925, quoted in: Schickert, *Die Ausfuhr*: 84.

corporate or private buyers, and bazaar customers. The largest immediate changes occurred in the business with public authorities. Although the India Office Stores Department in London remained in place for government purchases, it was transferred from the authority of the India Office to that of the High Commissioner for India. The Stores Department administered lists of approved manufacturers, called for tenders, placed orders, arranged shipments, and inspected deliveries. It was also the Stores Department that decided if tenders should be open or by invitation, with solicitations usually being limited to the companies preregistered with the Department.[42] Under the pressure of Indian industrialists and the Indian Industrial Commission, appointed to examine the possibilities for India's further industrial development, the percentage of Indian government purchases made in London declined from 93.7 to 76.8 percent between 1922/1923 and 1926/1927.[43] By 1927, the British Trade Commissioner emphasized that, "British and foreign firms are now on an equality in tendering for these Government stores. The foreign firm which has an established organization in India, can quote competitive rates, and give equal service, stands an even chance of securing the business."[44] This was a call to action for the larger German companies. They opened their own agencies in India, both to submit offers to public tenders and to better serve their large customers. The examples of Siemens and Bayer (since 1925, I. G. Farben) give an overview of the India strategies that nearly all large German multinationals pursued.

As early as 1925, Siemens transferred the business facilitated by Gorio to a newly founded company, the Siemens (India) Limited. This British-Indian corporation with a capital of Rs200,000 represented Siemens' interests in India.[45] In line with recommendations by industry experts, it had offices in Calcutta, Bombay, Rangoon, and Lahore and hired agents for Karachi, the United Provinces, Delhi, Madras, and Ceylon.[46] In September 1926, Siemens sent thirty-year-old engineer Eduard Beha, who

---

[42] Department of Overseas Trade and Ainscough, *Conditions and Prospects 1921*: 165–189.
[43] Indian Industrial Commission, *Indian Industrial Commission Report 1916–1918*. Schickert, *Die Ausfuhr*: 100.
[44] Department of Overseas Trade and Ainscough, *Conditions and Prospects 1927*: 27.
[45] "Organization of Siemens (India) Ltd.," and "Memorandum of Agreement," March 25, 1925, 8156, SAA.
[46] Reyss, "Speech about travels and Siemens' export business," 1924, 8185, SAA. Gorio, "Letter to Siemens," December 27, 1923 with attached map, SAA 8156. General Electric Trading Co. acted as agent for United Provinces and Delhi, Chari & Chari Ltd. for Madras, Messrs. Freudenberg & Co. for Ceylon. See, 8156, SAA. Recommended by Chapman and United States. Bureau of Foreign and Domestic Commerce, *India As a Market*: 5; Schickert, *Die Ausfuhr*: 60.

had worked in the Siemens Overseas Department in Berlin since 1921, to head the Calcutta office.[47]

The chemical industry opted for a similar set-up but added a layer of cloaking to the organization. In December 1925, Bayer and five other German chemical firms, including the major players BASF and Hoechst, expanded their war collaboration and formed the "Interessen-Gemein-schaft Farbenindustrie," or I. G. Farben, creating a chemical giant that produced 90 percent of the world's dyes.[48] The massive conglomerate had a total workforce of 100,000 people worldwide.[49] The newly founded I. G. Farben ended its relationship with Gorio in 1926 and signed a sole-importer contract with the Dutch trading company Havero.

Havero was to sell all I. G. Farben products in India, Burma, and Ceylon.[50] In addition to this contract, Havero and I. G. Farben crafted a secret agreement according to which two Dutch companies, Overzee (30 percent) and Unitas (70 percent), held the shares of Havero and promised to oversee Havero's complete compliance with I. G. Farben's wishes.[51] In their correspondence, the top managers explicitly agreed that "our leading managers in Bombay should only know the sole-importer contract; the special agreements, which stipulate our real relationship to Havero, shall remain completely secret."[52] This elaborate cloaking continued to disguise German ownership for two primary reasons: First, the complete loss of assets in World War I had put political risk manage-ment on the company's agenda and a Dutch-owned organization prom-ised some protection against future expropriations.[53] Second, in 1922 Indian tax law first made room for the possibility of taxing foreign man-ufacturers based on their "Manufacturer's Profit," meaning all profits generated worldwide that had a relationship with India; and authorities increasingly applied this law more rigidly.[54] However, an importer such as Havero, registered under Indian law, would usually only be taxed for

---

[47] Eduard Beha (1896–1959) worked in India until 1936, then returned to a post at the Overseas Department in Berlin. Information by Siemens Corporate Archives based on HR files. Special thanks to Dr Frank Wittendorfer for his kind assistance.

[48] For details see Plumpe, *I.G. Farbenindustrie AG*.

[49] Tammen, *Die I. G.*: 195.

[50] "Sole Importer Vertrag zwischen I.G. und Havero Handel My., Rotterdam," 19/A/590-2, BA.

[51] Ibid., "Secret Agreement with Havero," 9/K/1/2, BA.

[52] Seyd, "Letter to I.G. director Mann," January 21, 1926, 9/K/1/2, BA.

[53] Sophisticated cloaking arrangements were common in the interwar period. See Aalders and Wiebes, *Art*; Jones and Lubinski, "Managing Political Risk"; Kobrak and Hansen, *Business*; Reckendrees, *Beiersdorf*.

[54] "Chemicals/Our sales organization until the war," 9/K/1/2; "Tax issues British India" and Havero, "Letter to IG," June 24, 1929, 330/1088, all BA. See also "Income Tax Claim," *Times of India*, March 22, 1928: 15.

the difference between purchase and sales price, with both set by I. G. Farben.[55] "You will see from the special agreement that the Havero, Bombay, dyes departments is in reality us," summarized an I. G. manager.[56] It was not until 1938 that I. G. Farben founded locally incorporated subsidiaries in India.

In Bombay, most German companies had their offices at the Ballard Estate, the city's premier business district.[57] The products that the German multinationals delivered were diverse, but many were higher-value manufactured products of relevance for industrialization. Siemens advertised a variety of different electrical products, such as machinery, instruments and meters, light fittings, motors and engines, medical appliances, and many more.[58] In the context of the new rules for government purchases, it managed to introduce German water meters (in 1926) and insulated cables (in 1930) with the British Indian authorities.[59] More importantly, the company positioned itself as an expert for power generation in spinning and weaving mills, which were plentiful in India.[60] It was also a crucial supplier and provider of resident engineers for electrical plants, for example, for the Amraoti Electric Supply Company, the Madura municipality, or the Sukkur (Sind) Municipal Power Station. These projects frequently made it into the news as signposts for industrial development and were celebrated for bringing light to cities and municipalities.[61]

Like Siemens, Havero (for I. G. Farben) served both public authorities and large corporate buyers with a wide array of dyestuff and chemicals. As before the war, the dyes also continued to go to the Indian bazaars, which required a different organization (see next section). For the public and corporate buyers, the increased production capacity of the newly formed I. G. in combination with its well-functioning organization helped recuperate business swiftly. German dyestuff imports into

[55] Dr Deissmann, "Memorandum about the Founding of Agfa India Ltd.," 1938: 13, 330/1271, BA.
[56] Seyd, "Letter to I.G. director Mann," January 21, 1926, 9/K/1/2, BA.
[57] Times of India, Directory of Bombay 1932.
[58] "The Indian Engineer's Buyers Guide," Times of India, March 25, 1926: 19.
[59] Siemens India Ltd., "Annual Report 1931/32," 1932, 4286, SAA; "Contracts Awarded," Times of India, June 6, 1929: 13; "Indian Engineering Contracts," Times of India, January 23, 1930: 17.
[60] Siemens ad, Times of India, September 9, 1926: 19.
[61] "Amraoti Electric Co.," Times of India, January 1, 1926: 18; "Good Progress in C. P. [Central Provinces]," Times of India, June 10, 1926: 17; "Engineering in the C. P.," Times of India, July 15, 1926: 14; "Power Scheme at Amraoti," Times of India, December 30, 1926: 18; "Sukkur Power House," Times of India, March 16, 1928: 18; "Madura Scheme," Times of India, October 21, 1926: 16.

India overtook British imports as early as 1920, despite leading British companies having invested in their sales organization in India during the war, with hopes of becoming more competitive.[62] The factory business was done in selected large centers, where the majority of the cotton mills were located, namely Bombay, Ahmedabad, Cawnpore, Calcutta, and Bangalore. Mills bought primarily sulphur black for coarse cloth, and the majority operated in-house dyeing departments. In Bombay, they also sometimes outsourced the dyeing process to contractors. Havero sold dyes directly to the mills or their contractors and to that end visited the factories regularly.[63] Just like Siemens, it had branches in Bombay, Calcutta, Karachi, Madras, and Rangoon, where it kept considerable stocks. In Bombay, it also maintained a laboratory and a demonstration office, where a staff of seven highly paid specialists demonstrated to customers the workings of the dyes and responded to questions or concerns. In addition, Havero also staffed 150 smaller depots with sub-agents scattered over the country to serve both their business and bazaar customers.[64] Due to the close contact with their large customers and a good understanding of their needs, Havero managed to successfully introduce even I.G. Farben's more expensive fast colors, a market that was growing quickly.[65]

For all the large German multinationals one of the biggest challenges was finding and managing qualified staff in India after the war. Many of the European employees who had worked in India before the war had returned home after their release from internment. "Only few of the old India experts have found their way back here," reported the German consul in Bombay.[66] Reports about unqualified, unmotivated, or in other ways under-performing Europeans were abundant.[67] The process of hiring Indians was complicated by misinformation and prejudices.[68] European companies still experimented with how to manage Indian employees. Many of their practices were criticized by nationalists advocating for better opportunities for Indians. Siemens' manager Eduard Beha was called out during a visit to the Lahore office in 1931 on not

---

[62] Department of Overseas Trade and Ainscough, *Conditions and Prospects 1921*: 122.
[63] Consul W. Keblinger, Bombay, "Chemical Division Market for Aniline Dyes in India," 5, U.S. Department of Commerce, Special Circular No. 221, R 8128/5484, BArch-B.
[64] Department of Overseas Trade and Ainscough, *Conditions and Prospects 1927*: 63–64.
[65] For this detailed market analysis, see ibid., 4–10; "Havero's Dye Business in British India," February 1, 1938, R/8128/9967, BArch-B.
[66] Karl Kapp, "Report on the question of representatives in British India," June 30, 1927, R/3101/21030, BArch-B.
[67] E. Rziha, "Letter to Reyss," October 4, 1926, 8106, SAA.
[68] Department of Overseas Trade and Ainscough, *Conditions and Prospects 1919*: 19.

having hired more Indian engineers and clerks. He admitted to having been hesitant in the past but stressed that "good engineers and managers, independently if Europeans or Indians, should always have the best prospects in our company."[69] To prove his commitment Beha offered two Indian employees the chance to manage the Lahore office during the general manager's leave of absence. When Beha informed the head office in Berlin about his decision, he explained that he wanted to give clear proof of his openness towards qualified Indians: "You know how sensitive the Indians are in this point."[70]

Formal employment conditions differed markedly for European and Indian employees. European employees had an initial contract for three to five years, similar to what Miller reports about British business in South America in the immediate post-war period.[71] German employers paid for their relocation and travel. For the higher-ranking employees it was standard to grant at least one business trip back to Germany during a five-year period. In contrast to the Europeans, few Indians working for Siemens signed any written contract; they worked based on verbal agreements. Written contracts were actively avoided because of fear that Indians might use them as a basis for litigation against the company, a concern the Germans shared with British businesspeople in India. Even written house rules that were common in other Siemens overseas offices were avoided in India.[72] These challenges were not unique. Miller reports a similar setup for the staffing policy of British multinationals in Latin America,[73] and Dejung's analysis of the Swiss trading company Volkart in India shows similar differences in the working conditions.[74] Equality played a greater role in the rhetoric of multinationals than in their human resources practices.

Back in the Bazaar

For German companies serving the Indian bazaar, experiences changed more slowly. Typical bazaar customers, even in urban areas, continued to have only limited disposable income to spend on bazaar items. According to US analyst Emmett Chapman, net per capita annual income in

---

[69] Siemens (India) Ltd., "Letter to Headquarter," January 24, 1931, HR Calcutta, 1925–36, 9470, SAA.
[70] "Guidelines for overseas staff," 1929, 9424, SAA.
[71] Miller, "Staffing and Management."
[72] "Guidelines for overseas staff," 1929, 9424, SAA. For the fear of litigation see Misra, *Business, Race, and Politics*: 127.
[73] Miller, "Staffing and Management."
[74] Dejung, *Commodity Trading*: 178–179.

the early 1920s was approximately Rs75 (US$25) for rural and Rs100 (US$33.33) for urban inhabitants. Based on an analysis of 2,500 family budgets in Bombay, where one can expect them to have been relatively high, he found that the urbanites spent 57 percent of their money on food, 10 percent on clothing, 7 percent on fuel and light, and another 7 percent on rent. Only the remaining 19 percent could be allocated to other items of daily consumption in the bazaar.[75]

The pre-war system of import agent, wholesaler, dealer, and hawker remained essentially in place. One of the new challenges for German bazaar manufacturers was the fact that the number of export-import companies in India had multiplied compared to before World War I. Before the war, the business was done by a few European or large Indian houses; after the war, the large number of small and relatively inexperienced agencies posed difficulties for the Germans who had limited information on their records of accomplishment, credit worthiness, and skills.[76] Increasingly, Indian wholesalers addressed European manufacturers directly, avoiding the intermediation and service fees of the import agencies.

Compared to the numerous small- and medium-sized exporters, the larger German companies that sold in the bazaar had advantages. After the war, they usually set up their own Indian companies to organize sales activities in India. Small- and medium-sized exporters, by contrast, rarely opted for this investment, for which costs were estimated at approximately 50,000–60,000 Marks annually, excluding travel costs.[77] The large German multinationals also had more resources to incentivize Indian brokers. Havero, for example, marketed its dyes through sixteen Indian distributors. The dyes were delivered on consignment for a cash deposit, on which the distributor received a monthly interest of 6 percent. Sales prices were fixed by Havero, and the sellers received commissions and reported their sales daily. Prior to the collaboration in the I. G., each German manufacturer had employed its own distributors with long-term agreements. This meant that they were and remained unavailable to competitors. However, there was also a significant overlap between the regional responsibilities, and no seller had exclusive rights to any territory. Visiting India, Carl Duisberg, chairman of the supervisory board of I. G. Farben, remarked that "most of them are rich orthodox

---

[75] Chapman and United States. Bureau of Foreign and Domestic Commerce, *India As a Market*: 2.

[76] Deutscher Wirtschaftsdienst, *Britisch Indien*: 10–11.

[77] "The Question of Agents in British India," June 30, 1927, copy as appendix to "Confidential Report: Indian Boycott," July 15, 1930, R/3101/02664: 335–340, BArch-B.

merchants with little knowledge of dyes."[78] However, similar to the pre-war situation, their local knowledge made them valuable and powerful intermediaries.

Controlling these Indian distributors in the bazaar segment was challenging, even for such an elaborate organization as Havero. It created a series of principal-agent conflicts, frequently based on the generous discounts that distributors gave in the competitive market space. The Indian distributors sold the dyes in one- or half-pound tins to both end-consumers and intermediaries, with the latter reselling the product out of open tins in extremely small quantities, often measured in spoons. The colors were diluted so that a minimum purchase of half a pound was affordable. Larger quantities, up to 112 pounds, could be sold to local dye houses. A group of inspectors visited the up-country depots in regular intervals. They evaluated if each depot was getting enough business, investigated complaints, supplied business information, and assisted customers.[79]

Thanks to the long track record in the Indian market, German dye-stuff trademarks were well-introduced and appreciated by both corporate buyers and bazaar customers.[80] Smaller exporters, like the ones in the cutlery trade, also banked on their trademarks and pictorial labels in the multilingual Indian context with its high rates of illiteracy.[81] To own the right of a trademark, manufacturers had to prove that they were the first to use it.[82] While experts recommended registering trademarks with the Register of Assurances in Calcutta or at least with a chamber of commerce, in most cases, manufacturers pragmatically published their trademarks in Indian newspapers and kept a few copies as proof.[83]

The recovery of the German bazaar business was industry specific, and not all exporters rekindled their business successfully. The German gramophone trade, for example, had been a very successful pre-war business (see Chapter 2). After the war, the companies returned to a market that was clearly dominated by the well-established Anglo-American Gramophone Co. as well as a few US-based rivals.[84] Like several German industries, the business with gramophones and music

---

[78] "Critical Notes on the Selling of I.G. Products in East-Asian Countries," April 1929, in: Carl Duisberg's Travel Reports, vol. 6, BA; "Havero's Dye Business in British India," R/8128/9967, BArch-B.

[79] Department of Overseas Trade and Ainscough, *Conditions and Prospects 1927*: 64.

[80] Ibid.

[81] Lohmann, *Die Ausfuhr Solinger Stahlwaren*: 53–54.

[82] Cotton, *Handbook*: 26.

[83] Schickert, *Die Ausfuhr*: 39–40. Lohmann, *Die Ausfuhr Solinger Stahlwaren*: 74.

[84] Department of Overseas Trade and Ainscough, *Conditions and Prospects 1921*: 142.

had been heavily consolidated just before the outbreak of World War I by a wave of mergers and acquisitions. Both Beka and Odeon had been bought out by Carl Lindström, which promoted the trio – Lindström, Beka and Odeon – as its "three world labels."[85] It continued selling them in India until 1926, when Lindström was acquired by US rival Columbia. In 1931, Columbia merged with the Indian market leader Gramophone Co. to form Electric and Musical Industries Ltd (EMI). Having taken over most of its competitors, the new EMI controlled the Indian market almost completely; however, the market was also changing rapidly with the availability of substitutes, such as radio, film, and television.

In the cutlery trade, by contrast, German entrepreneurs swiftly recuperated their market share and by 1922/23 overtook imports from Great Britain in value (see Figure 4.1). By 1927, the Trade Commissioner lamented that the British share of cutlery in the bazaar "has fallen to almost negligible proportions."[86] Price was one reason for this development. However, reports also indicate that the continental European competitors gave better credit terms and were said to be more flexible in adjusting standard types of their products – an argument that persisted from the pre-war period.[87]

To be close to the customer, experts of the cutlery trade recommended to travel across India and personally connect with potential dealers.[88] Commercial travelers were an important element of the marketing mix. These individuals either did business on their own account and had contracts with individual firms; or worked as collective travelers for a consortium of firms that together paid them for their services. There were no discriminatory rules for commercial travelers in India, independent of their country of origin.[89] An experienced exporter from Germany reported, moreover, that, "the appearance of a European traveler sparks delight, in particular if he visits cities in the interior of the country." He was described as "a welcome bearer of news," which the locals were keen to hear.[90]

Over the course of the 1920s, Great Britain's share of the import trade continuously declined. While the pre-war average had been 63 percent in the five years preceding the war and the percentage during the short-lived boom of 1920 was again 61 percent, the 1920s saw a rather swift

---

[85] Gutmann, *25 Jahre Lindstroem*: 21 and 95–100.
[86] Department of Overseas Trade and Ainscough, *Conditions and Prospects 1927*: 65.
[87] Ibid., 67.
[88] Schickert, *Die Ausfuhr*: 61; Lohmann, *Die Ausfuhr Solinger Stahlwaren*: 54.
[89] Warren, *Commercial Travelling*: 277–279.
[90] P. Martell, "Winke für den Export," *Export-Organisation* 3/1924: 6–8, quote: 7, DNBL.

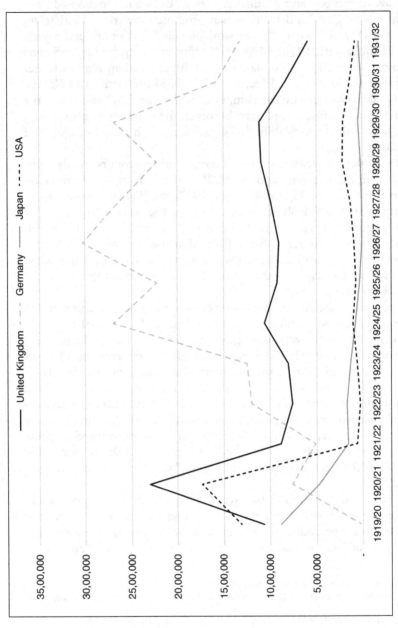

Figure 4.1 Import of cutlery into British India (in rupees), by country, 1919–1932. Annual Statements of the Sea-Borne Trade of British India with the British Empire and Foreign Countries. General Imports/Total Value of Cutlery. See also, Lohmann, 46–7.

United Kingdom — · · — Germany —— Japan - - - - USA

1919/20 1920/21 1921/22 1922/23 1923/24 1924/25 1925/26 1926/27 1927/28 1928/29 1929/30 1930/31 1931/32

35,00,000

30,00,000

25,00,000

20,00,000

15,00,000

10,00,000

5,00,000

Table 4.2 *Imports to British India by country of origin (in % of imports), 1913/1914–1926/1927*

	1913/14	1924/25	1925/26	1926/27
Great Britain	64.1	54.1	51.4	47.8
Germany	6.9	6.3	5.9	7.3
Java	5.8	6.3	6.2	6.2
USA	2.6	5.7	6.7	7.9
Japan	2.6	6.9	8.0	7.1
Belgium	2.3	2.7	2.7	2.9

Annual Statements (several volumes).

fall to 48 percent in 1926/1927 (see Table 4.2). The reduction was "a matter for serious concern," as the British Trade Commissioner in India and Ceylon, Thomas Ainscough, articulated.[91] He saw domestic economic issues as one reason but also voiced trepidation about the fact that the trade balance between Great Britain and India was uneven. "There is a growing tendency all over the world for a country to purchase its imports from those countries which are the most important customers for its own products."[92] In the case of India, these competitors were Germany, the US, and Japan.

Some of the market share was lost due to competitors' cheaper prices, and Trade Commissioner Ainscough suggested investing in British mass manufacturing to counter this trend. He also saw room for improvement in British business organization. While British export agents had for long dominated the trade, Ainscough believed that the new era required the opening of sales offices in India. "The number of efficient, modern selling organizations adequately covering the India market is extraordinarily few. ... British manufacturers have been content to leave the matter in the hands of their mercantile agents in India, who in most instances have too many irons in the fire to give close personal attention to any one agency."[93] Moreover, Ainscough observed one other way for competitors to capture market shares from Britain: by "playing on the political and racial feelings of the dealers."[94] Indeed, political sentiment and national aspirations became increasingly important for business success in the Indian market, and all foreign multinationals critically reviewed and expanded their arsenal of political strategies.

[91] Department of Overseas Trade and Ainscough, *Conditions and Prospects 1927*: 22.
[92] Ibid.
[93] Ibid., 25.
[94] Ibid., 26.

The Business of National Aspirations

The war had elevated nationality to a distinguishing feature within the community of Westerners in India. German businesspeople lamented being excluded from British clubs, which they had previously frequented. The old-established Bengal Club in Calcutta, for example, put a ban on Germans and Austrians in 1916.[95] As late as 1930, English clubs remained closed to German nationals.[96] Von Rziha, who represented Siemens in the early 1920s, explicitly complained to his superiors that he had no access to the British clubs, where he could make valuable business contacts.[97] Heinrich Lohmann, a traveling entrepreneur from Solingen, was allowed to stay overnight in an English club house in Cochin (Kochi) in 1927 but was banned from dining with any of the club members.[98] The few German clubs that had existed before the war only reopened slowly, if at all. In Calcutta and Bombay, a German club was re-established in 1928 and 1930 respectively; the German club of Rangoon remained closed for good.[99]

Claims of unjust exclusion formed the core of a German critique of the British regime in India. Moreover, the Germans saw the importance of the Indian nationalist movement and how it impacted their business. Most were hesitant to threaten the slowly improving Anglo-German relationship over an Indian matter.[100] They nevertheless were keen on showing, if not showcasing, their political neutrality. The German Foreign Office argued, "[t]hat the Indian national movement promotes our goods is known to everybody here. But if we start saying this publicly the Indian Government would reward us with trade restrictions."[101] Thoughtful diplomacy was required.

The idea of a potential Indo-German alliance had initially developed in parallel and sometimes in contradiction to the Congress Party's "Non-Cooperation Resolution," which the Indian organization of independence activists approved in December 1920. The Resolution stipulated among other measures a general boycott of all foreign goods; not just British ones as the pre-war Swadeshi movement had advocated (see Chapter 2). The stance against all foreign goods owed much to Mahatma Gandhi's

---

[95] Sinha, "Britishness": 489n482.
[96] Consulate Calcutta, "Letter to Foreign Office Berlin," July 29, 1930, R/3101/02664, BArch-B.
[97] Von Rziha, "Letter to Reyss," September 25, 1923, 4286, SAA.
[98] Lohmann, *Die Ausfuhr Solinger Stahlwaren*: 43.
[99] *Der Auslandsdeutsche* 19, no. 8 (1936): 593, quoted in: Zöllner, *Birma*: 243n264.
[100] Barooah, *Germany and the Indians*: 2–12.
[101] "Comment dated September 19, 1923," quoted in: Barooah, *Chatto*: 191.

philosophy. It insisted on the inextricable link between indigenous goods and self-government and argued that only a reformed lifestyle, symbolically captured in the wearing of the uncolored homespun khadi, would lead to the necessary radical changes. Swadeshi, in this Gandhian sense, meant the complete rejection of all foreign products.

However, there was never a consensus on this vision within the Congress Party. Gandhi's critics ridiculed him for refusing to embrace industrialism, and he increasingly (not least under the pressure of Indian industrialists who supported the movement financially) softened his position. By 1930, the distinction between handmade and industrial products, central to Gandhi's thinking, was largely set aside within the Congress Party. The one between indigenous and foreign products remained but was lacking in definitional clarity. Goods manufactured in India by foreign companies, and goods from countries other than Great Britain, were never explicitly but often silently excluded from boycotts. "By 1930," historian Lisa Trivedi argues, "swadeshi was a term configured broadly enough to cover a range of economic and political processes."[102]

While the Non-Cooperation movement did not reject all foreign goods, it did add to the general politicizing of business. It foregrounded racial feelings, which according to the British Trade Commissioner, were "more apparent to-day than ever before." For this savvy and experienced observer, "political feeling is entering into every branch of trade and economic life as the 'swadeshi' movement grows in strength."[103] However, these political feelings were targeted very specifically at Britain; "anti-German feeling does not exist among the Indian community. On the contrary," observed the Commissioner. In contrast to his earlier, pessimistic predictions for Germany's participation in Indian trade after the war, he now argued: "It is only to be expected that, in India, Germany will find one of the most promising fields for trade expansion in the near future. It is more than probable that the very strong political feeling which is prevalent among all classes of the Indian community will contribute materially to this result."[104] Anti-colonialism in business produced winners and losers.

Especially the larger German companies with business in India provided products that were seen as indispensable for Indian industrialization

---

[102] Trivedi, *Clothing Gandhi's Nation*: 5–9, quote: 36. See also the analysis of the German consul in Calcutta who observed the shift from a pro-Gandhi attitude to a strong focus on industrialization: Dr Pausch, "Letter to German Foreign Office," December 20, 1938, 330/442, BA.

[103] Department of Overseas Trade and Ainscough, *Conditions and Prospects 1921*: 11.

[104] Ibid., 10–11.

and were therefore of great interest to Indian nationalists. Recognizing the alignment of German capabilities and Indian needs, Siemens (India) made a symbolic move and appointed Lala Harkishen Lal, an outspoken and revered nationalist, to its board of directors.[105] Lal was a well-connected entrepreneur of the Punjab who had studied at Lahore and Cambridge and in the spirit of Swadeshi floated several financial companies that provided capital for indigenous enterprises. In early 1924 Lal travelled to Europe and met with Siemens' representatives in Berlin who agreed to supply machinery and equipment for nearly Rs1.5 million (US$476,191) for his Lahore Electrical Supply Company on flexible terms, after Lal's previous negotiations in London had been unsuccessful. Siemens put up a model power station in Lahore, which became an often-visited advertisement for the German firm.[106]

Lal's competence was beyond doubt. The Germans considered Lal's network with Indian banks and insurances useful, making him an important local intermediary. He was also described as "a spearhead of the fight for India's own industry."[107] Appointing him as director was important for Siemens' legitimacy with nationalists and the social capital to be gained. Looking back at his tenure, however, one Siemens manager reported that Lal seldom attended the board meetings.[108] While Siemens managers lamented Lal's infrequent appearances, they were content with the prestige they gained by having a symbolic figure like him on their board. Political sentiments made striving for legitimacy an important part of the strategy that German companies pursued in India. In 1927, looking back at almost a decade of experience after the war, the British Trade Commissioner concluded that the political feeling, "has probably been of assistance to them [foreign competitors] in strengthening their connections in the market, particularly in the case of Germany since the war."[109]

In this politicized context, it helped when German firms could point to successfully completed "nationalist" projects, such as the Lahore Electrical Supply Company and the collaboration with Lal. They also noticed how nations observed one another in their progress towards self-determination. They started thinking about nations in clusters based on

---

[105] "Sixth Meeting of Board of Directors," December 24, 1924, 8156, SAA. Gauba, *The Rebel Minister*.

[106] Mittal, *Freedom Movement in Punjab*: 203; Gauba, *The Rebel Minister*: 123; Department of Overseas Trade and Ainscough, *Conditions and Prospects 1927*: 74.

[107] Siemens (India), "Letter to Siemens," January 24, 1931, Human Resources Calcutta 1925–39, 9470, SAA.

[108] Siemens India, "Letter to SSW," January 6, 1936, 8156, SAA.

[109] Department of Overseas Trade and Ainscough, *Conditions and Prospects 1927*: 29.

their history and objectives for the future. The completion of major engineering projects in other countries striving for national autarky served to bolster their reputation in India. For example, Siemens profited from the Indian press coverage of the Shannon project in Ireland.[110] "The Shannon" was a large-scale hydroelectric power station in the newly independent state of Ireland, which was built between 1924 and 1929. It was important because it was Siemens' first large project after the war, reaffirming the company's status as one of the principal electrical firms in the world. The scheme was also hotly debated, with British opponents objecting to Siemens being a German company and Irish nationalists countering that German influence was preferable to British. The Irish Colonel Maurice George Moore explained, "England is much nearer and more capable of holding on to that stranglehold. ... They had it, they lost it, and they want to regain it."[111] Choosing a German rather than an English manufacturer, thus, bolstered Ireland's independence. The *Times of India* reported regularly on the Shannon, praising the Irish Government for its economic policy.[112] The fact that the project was completed in a newly independent state and free from British influences, despite Ireland's history as a British dependent territory, increased Siemens' goodwill with other nations striving for self-determination. It played on the idea of politically suppressed countries having a joint identity and being sensitive to the actions of others like them.

As buying in Germany became a definite political statement, the label "Made in Germany" was once again perceived as a tool for publicly declaring one's political affiliation. Initially introduced by the British to highlight low-quality German goods (see Chapter 2), it signaled politically inconspicuous products from a noncolonial country. As early as 1920, a correspondent of the *Times of India* reported that, "in the bazaar, and also in some of the better class shops of Bombay, the shopkeeper appears to be under the impression that to say an article is made in Germany is to give it the hall mark of value" and even suspected that many of the products were actually manufactured elsewhere.[113] Havero, I. G. Farben's Dutch cloaking company, reported that the label "Made in Germany" was recognized and appreciated with both bazaar and

---

[110] "Harnessing the Shannon: The Irish Free State Scheme," *Times of India*, December 30, 1926: 18; "The Shannon Power Scheme," *Times of India*, May 19, 1927: 13; "The Irish Free State," *Times of India*, June 21, 1929: 8.

[111] Railway (Directorate) Bill, 1924 (Second Stage), Seanad Éireann Debate, vol. 3, no. 26, December 17, 1924, available online: www.oireachtas.ie/en/debates/debate/seanad/1924-12-17/4/#spk_12

[112] "Irish Politics," *Times of India*, August 19, 1927: 8.

[113] "Current Topics: Made in Germany," *Times of India*, November 20, 1920: 12.

corporate customers.[114] The German origin of products was also regularly highlighted in advertisements, indicating its marketing value.[115]

However, the Germans had to learn how to make use of this political advantage. A report from Ahmedabad indicated that in the future only goods visibly marked "Made in Germany" would be accepted because the label served as a protection against obtaining "something undesirable."[116] It was not enough to sell German products; they also needed to be marked in bold letters to help others see the political statement. The German Consulate in Bombay, moreover, recommended targeted marketing campaigns and directed German firms that "advertisement in India can be much more efficient than in most other countries and the purely Indian and in particular also the nationalist press can be utilized to support German trade." Ads in Indian rather than British newspapers were recommended because "their readers have a greater interest in German goods than those of the purely English press."[117]

Yet, manufactured goods were not the only input Indian nationalist hoped to receive from Germany. The complementary interests in trade stretched into cooperation in other fields, most importantly technical education. Education was not a new priority of the Indian nationalist movement. In a List'ian understanding of national development, it was considered crucial and had been a pillar of the nationalist agenda since before the turn of the century.[118] However, during and just after World War I, Indian nationalists observed the world of nations around them and identified a cluster of rapidly developing economies that interested them. Their mental map of nationalism had changed to perceive the similarities between Germany, the US, and Japan and to see them as models for their own future development. What these three countries had in common was their "enormous progress in manufacturing industries" since 1870, supported by "a system of general and technical education," as Madan Mohan Malaviya argued.[119] Malaviya was one of ten members of the "Indian Industrial Commission," which had been appointed in 1916 to examine the possibilities of further industrial development in India. In its report, published in 1918, the Commission proposed

---

[114] "Havero's Dye Business in British India," XI, R/8128/9967, BArch-B.
[115] Ad in *Times of India*, for Krupp: April 15, 1926: 17, for Huschke: November 26, 1924: 16.
[116] "Confidential Report on the Indian Boycott," undated [1930], R/3101/02664, BArch-B.
[117] "Confidential Report: Indian Boycott," July 15, 1930, R/3101/02664: 335–340 BArch-B.
[118] Subramanian, *The Caste of Merit*: 58–59.
[119] Indian Industrial Commission, *Indian Industrial Commission Report 1916–1918*: 310.

a series of steps to foster industrialization and state-control of industries, including specific provisions for technical training and education. The nationalist Malaviya, president of the Congress Party in 1909 and again in 1918 wrote in a "note of dissent" that the German technical education would have to be considered superior to the British. In his cross-examination of a British official, Malaviya asked, "Is it a fact that England had been more backward in the matter of systematized technical instruction than Germany?", and received the expected answer, "Very much so. I do not think that people out here realized that."[120] The nationalist critique rejected Britain's claim to a monopoly over industrial expertise and demanded the right to independent collaborations beyond the boundaries of Empire. One of the most frequent points of criticism was that Britain's education privileged humanistic studies but was new to the idea of industrial education and applied sciences, which were supposedly of greater use to India. The attorney B. N. Basu testified that education in India "is far removed from the actual facts of life which young men have to face when they are called upon to do practical work, and the result is generally disappointing."[121] To counter this trend, nationalist India looked to Germany for practical technical education.

The German dual-education system combining factory work with schooling and the options for internships was particularly appealing and the system was well-known among Indian nationalists.[122] Experiencing the difference first-hand, Khwaja Abdul Hamied, an Indian nationalist who studied chemistry in Germany from 1924 to 1927, wondered why "in our educational system in India, we lay so much importance on book knowledge without acquiring sufficient proficiency in experimental chemistry." After receiving his doctorate, Hamied stayed in Berlin for one more year for practical education in several German companies, including the pharmaceutical company Schering-Kahlbaum.[123] Like Hamied, a number of Indians, mostly students, received industrial training in German firms, and German businesspeople hoped they would get acquainted with their business and in the future serve German companies as employees.[124] The long-established German apprenticeship

---

[120] Witness No. 115, Mr. W. W. Hornell, Director of Public Instruction, Calcutta. Indian Industrial Commission, *Minutes of Evidence, Vol. II*: 242.

[121] Witness No. 102, Babu Bhupendra Nath Basu, Attorney at Law, Calcutta. Ibid., 142.

[122] "Technical Education: Training of Apprentices in the German Industry," *Industrial Review for India* 1 (1923), 3: 77–83; "Technical Education: Training of Apprentices in Metal-Casting," ibid. 1 (1923), 4–5: 109–112.

[123] Hamied, *An Autobiography*: 37. See also, Vatsal, *Caring for Life*: 22.

[124] "Review of the Press: Commercial Importance of German-trained Asiatics," *Industrial and Trade Review for Asia* (1925), 24: 365–366.

system made it easy for German companies to admit Indians into their factories. Importantly though, the fact that Indian students could get easily admitted was a major difference to practices in Great Britain, where admissions were rare and costly. As such it was often specifically highlighted as a measure to develop Indian capabilities, in contrast to the lack of development and practical training Indians received in Britain.[125]

University studies were another focus of attention. The German consul in London engaged in facilitating Indian students' travels to Germany and was confident that Germany could provide better education to them than Britain. In 1921, Virendranath Chattopadhyaya (Chatto) established the "Association of Indians of German Europe." By 1923, around 300 Indians were resident in Berlin.[126] It was Jawaharlal Nehru, later Prime Minister of India, who in the late 1920s backed an Indian Students Information Bureau in Berlin, which the Congress financially supported with £30 per month. The Bureau had the mandate to publish information about German educational institutions in the Indian press, answer inquiries, help Indian students upon arrival, and support them in arranging internships in Germany.[127] It was managed by Chatto and his assistant A. C. N. Nambiar, later an Indian ambassador in post-World War II Germany.[128] The largest Indian community in Germany congregated in Berlin. The so-called "Hindustan House" was their residence and social gathering place, with many of them living in close proximity to Uhlandstrasse and the Technical University Berlin in Charlottenburg.[129] They built on the earlier clustering of Indians in this neighborhood during World War I (see Chapter 3). The Indo-German alignment of interests centered on both trade and education, which were seen as inextricably intertwined in the quest for industrialization.

From Civilizing Mission to "Aryan" Community

Complementary economic needs and the perception of joint victimhood created space for experimenting with new narratives. Identifying with suppressed colonized nations had a longer tradition among German intellectuals and pre-dated German colonialism.[130] Indian independence

[125] "Education in Germany," R/77462, PA; for Siemens' activities in this area see also Manjapra, *Age of Entanglement*: 94.
[126] Ibid.
[127] Our own correspondent, "Helping Indian Students: Congress Votes Subsidy," *Times of India*, February 2, 1929: 16.
[128] Nambiar was appointed the second Indian Ambassador to the Federal Republic of Germany in 1955.
[129] Manjapra, "The Anticolonial Laboratory": 155.
[130] Zantop, *Colonial Fantasies*.

activists, for their part, had before and during World War I conjured up the image of an age-old "Aryan" community that pre-dated the British regime in India. In the journal "Pro India," first issued in June 1914 by Chempakaraman Pillai, who a few months later joined the Indian Independence Committee in Berlin (see Chapter 3), Pillai highlighted India's Aryan origin. "India as a country has many claims on the sympathy and good-will of all enlightened Europeans. India is the cradle of Aryan civilization. The people of India are ethnically the elder brethren of the European nations. They belong to the great Caucasian race."[131] These claims fit seamlessly into the earlier history of Indian nationalism with many nationalists having a track record of claiming Aryan origins as a source of pride. The nationalist Sri Aurobindo had argued before World War I that "the history of the country is taught to the students of Bengal in a national context," not by memorizing recent historical events but by teaching the students "how in ancient times the Aryans formed the nation."[132]

Today, the concept of Aryanism is closely associated with the later National Socialist regime in Germany. However, its roots come from Vedic (ancient Indian) tradition. The Rig Veda composed around 1500 BCE talked about tribes that self-identified as "Arya" and were settlers from Central Asia encountering the indigenous population of Northern India. European linguists, who before 1914 started to map out the similarities between Greek, Latin, and Sanskrit, combined their work with the Vedic framework, essentially arguing for a common heritage of these languages. From the early nineteenth century onwards, Aryanism was a prominent concept in many genealogies of newly emerging nation states.[133] German-speaking scholars claimed that the Aryan community was comprised of Germans, Indians, and Iranians, and thus blurred the line between East and West.[134] When taking his position as principal of the University of Munich, Ernst Kuhn encouraged his students to study the influence of Aryan India and learn about the "solidarity of the joint European culture," which "includes the highly developed nations of the East."[135] In the years just before and after World War I, the concept of Aryanism was molded into sense-making and identity offerings to both Germans and Indians. In the context of commercial and political rivalry

---

[131] J. C. Pro India, "Our Aims and Objects," *Pro India: Monatsschrift des Internationalen Komitees "Pro India,"* 1(1) June 1914: 4, copy in: R/21072, 37, PA.
[132] Aurobindo, "National Education [Speech Delivered in Girgaum, Bombay, January 15, 1908]."
[133] Ballantyne, *Orientalism and Race.*
[134] Schroeder, *Mysterium und Mimus im Rigveda.*
[135] Kuhn, *Einfluss des arischen Indiens.*

in Europe and in the British Empire, this new "us" versus "them" line
provided an alternative to groupings based on "East vs. West" or "White
vs. Colored."[136]

While the references to the Aryan community on the German side
came mostly from intellectuals and scholars, not from the business community, nationalistically thinking Indians of all professions flocked to
this "imagined community" (Anderson). It suggested to them a different relationship with Germany than the one with Great Britain. In that
spirit, the Indian Information Bureau in Berlin reported in 1929 that
Indians "are treated here [in Germany] as equals and respected as a
cultured race."[137] Importantly, the promise of belonging to an (however defined) Aryan community was a clear counter-point to the dominant narrative traditionally associated with the British colonizers, the
"civilizing mission." The British had long subscribed to this idea of a
civilizing mission, arguing that their actions in India were aligned with
the project of "confer[ing] upon the natives of India the benefits of ...
European wisdom and benevolence."[138] Bringing civilization to India by
means of "benevolent despotism" was the primary justification for British colonialism.[139]

However, since the beginning of the twentieth century and especially
with the outbreak of the war, the narrative of a British "civilizing mission" came under attack. Indian nationalists argued that not only had
India's industry been destroyed, and its wealth been plundered, but the
British had also "denationalized" Indians and kept them in ignorance,
"with stories of England's greatness and 'mission' in the world, and
systematic efforts ... made to obliterate the race-consciousness."[140] By
contrast, the counter-narrative of an Aryan community allowed India to
"outpast" British colonialism and point to an even more ancient origin
story. The Aryan narrative developed into a targeted critique of the British civilizing mission.[141]

In the decade after World War I, Indian nationalists used the Aryan
claim as a positive sense-making offer towards Germans. Highlighting
their joint ancestry, an Indian journal published in Germany argued

[136] Manjapra, *Age of Entanglement*. Trautmann, *Aryans*.
[137] "Education in Germany" 1929, Political and cultural propaganda (India), R/77462,
PA.
[138] Kaye, *Administration*: 5.
[139] The term "benevolent depotism" appears in Smith, *Early History of India*: 331. For the
civilizing mission and its counter-narrative see also, Mann, "Touchbearers Upon the
Path of Progress"; Fischer-Tiné, *Der Gurukul Kangri*: 270–308.
[140] Indian National Party, *British Rule in India*: 9.
[141] Lubinski, "From History as Told."

that, "mentally we stand nearer to the Germans, for example, than to the Chinese or Japanese or even the Jews and the Egyptians." In this frame of reference, learning the German language, as many Indian students did when joining German universities or factories, was also a way to revive "the spirit of the old Aryan tongue of our common linguistic ancestors."[142] When addressing a German audience in 1921, nationalist A. Raman Pillai stressed in particular "the danger of the destruction of the Aryan civilization, which has contributed so much to elevating the human race to the high level it had achieved before the war"[143]. The narrative threads highlighting an Indo-German community of Aryanism provided Indian nationalists useful arguments for partnership and collaboration.

However, the German business community was slow in responding to the idea of an Aryan community and by and large uncomfortable with supporting it. Instead, they insisted on their neutrality, which they hoped would allow them to collaborate with Indian partners without raising suspicions in Great Britain. This, however, disappointed Indian activists who stressed the contradiction between the rhetoric of the Aryan community and German practices. When a 1925 article in Germany, provocatively titled "Betrayers of the White Man's Cause," once more insinuated that British actions during the war had ruined the trade relations of "the white races with the colored races of this world"[144], Indian nationalist Virendranath Chattopadhyaya (Chatto), at the time located in Berlin, responded that if "the expression 'colored races' is continually used in a provocative manner, the other Continents may retaliate and, by using black as their unit of comparison, carry on a murderous crusade against the 'bleached races' of the world."[145] For Chatto, Germany had appeared as having different aspirations, which is why "we in Asia have hitherto confined our definition of the white man to England."[146] However, Chatto left little doubt about the importance of the race question for future Indo-German relations. If the opinions expressed in this article prevailed, then "the distinctions that Indians and Chinese have invariably made between German and Englishmen ... will be abandoned, and we shall ... add German goods to the list of those that come under a

---

[142] "The Value of German to Educated India," *Industrial and Trade Review for India* (1925), 11: 141–143, quote: 142.

[143] Pillai, *Das Judentum*: 1. SUB.

[144] C. Pillai, "Letter to Prüfer," August 16, 1925, and enclosed articles published in *Export and Import Review*, R/77414, PA.

[145] Anonymous [Virendranath Chattopadhyaya], "Betrayer of the White Man's Cause," *Industrial and Trade Review for India*, 13, July (first half) 1925: 183–184, here: 183.

[146] Ibid.

boycott."[147] For nationalistic Indians, the racially framed argument and the language of betrayal of a however defined "White community" were insulting.

The Aryan narrative was only appealing if it could serve as a counter-point to colonialism, and thus required a clear distinction of the Germans from the British colonizers. Other alliances on a geopolitical stage, however, were easy to integrate into the emerging mental map. In 1925, the *Industrial and Trade Review for India* discussed alliances of Asia "with those European peoples who are naturally not interested in a colonial policy" and referenced the writings by Karl Haushofer. Haushofer was a German professor of "political geography," a field he significantly shaped, and an expert on India. He believed that Germany's lack of a geopolitical strategy in World War I was to blame for its defeat because Germany failed to find the right allies in the world. After the war and the failed conspiracies, he suggested an "Eurasiatic block," which would provide "a defensive union among the States that have suffered most by the World War." Such a union could "constitute a balance against the merciless and unscrupulous exploitation of their present difficulties by the United States of America and the Western Powers, who are the chief propagators of race prejudice and colonialism in the world, and also the principle obstacle to the realization of the self-determination of the peoples."[148] Mental maps of nationalism remained in flux in the 1920s but they found crystallization points in joint victimhood after the war and complementary needs and aspirations, under the broad umbrella of anti-colonialism.

---

[147] Ibid.
[148] "The Pan-European Movement," *Industrial and Trade Review for India* (1925), 9, 109–111, reviewing, Haushofer, "Ost-Eurasiatische Zukunftsblock."

Part II

Emergent Strategy in a World of Nations

5   Refining Political Capabilities

In the period after World War I, Indians and Germans expressed similar frustrations with the British claim for hegemony. Their perception of each other changed based on a new mental map of nationalism, focused on the complementarities between India's aspirations for industrialization and self-determination and Germany's desire to expand its export business. The outlines of an alliance had been established.

The Great Depression brought turmoil to this evolving relationship. Previously, India had often stood out as a particularly accessible export market free of protectionist barriers. The British Empire trading bloc reshuffled this world of nations, creating new clusters of countries inside and outside the Empire free-trade zone and accentuating the dividing line with discriminatory tariffs. It changed how India's trading partners abroad evaluated their opportunities. For Germany, the problem was further compounded by the rise of the Nazi regime, which provoked protests in India with its racialized rhetoric and street violence against ethnic and religious groups in Germany. While Indian Hindus were generally sympathetic to the narrative of Aryanism (see Chapter 4), they were also disappointed in German politicians pushing their own interpretation of what and who it described.

Given the explosive mixture of political challenges in the 1930s, German business could have decided to exit the Indian market. Yet, instead, German multinationals expanded their activities in the country. They tackled the new challenges by intensifying collaborations with other German firms and with German Government institutions in the context of collaborative capitalism. They also devoted resources to expanding and professionalizing their political capabilities. Nurturing their political intelligence services, they went from passively consuming Indian news to actively pushing narratives that harmonized the ideals of the Indian nationalist movement with Nazi Germany. It was no longer enough to be politically neutral and discern the host country's political landscape. Instead, multinationals invested in a broad bundle of political capabilities to manage not only host country politics, but also the perception of Germany abroad and the interpretation of the evolving relationship between home and host country. Political conditions were no longer seen as an externality to endure but rather needed to be actively shaped with an expanding toolbox of corporate diplomacy.

Responses to the Great Depression

The Great Depression triggered a collapse of world trade in the early 1930s. The overall volume of trade in 1932 was nearly 30 percent below the status quo in 1929.[1] The Indo-German trade relationship during this time was reconfigured by several new forces, chief among them (i) the heightened influence and increasing public visibility of the Indian Independence movement, in particular Gandhi's civil disobedience, (ii) Great Britain's decision to depart from the gold standard and its effects on the global monetary system, and (iii) the establishment of the system of imperial preferences for British and Empire products, which created the protectionist British Empire trading bloc.

The Civil Disobedience Movement (1930–1932) and Gandhi's famous salt march triggered a new, intensified wave of anti-imperial boycotts in India. On March 12, 1930, Gandhi and some followers began their march to Dandi, a coastal village in Gujarat, to protest the Salt Law and in doing so brought worldwide attention to the Indian struggle for Independence. Boycotts of foreign products, in particular cotton piece goods, were ubiquitous in those years.[2] British colonial intelligence reports stressed that the Indian nationalists called on consumers to buy products "made in any non-British country" even if they were costlier than British alternatives.[3] German politicians and German businesspeople tried to strike a delicate balance between wanting to capitalize on this opportunity, while not provoking any political reaction by the British.

The challenges for them multiplied when, in the fall of 1931, the British Pound departed from the gold standard and the British Government imposed a Sterling standard on the Rupee against the will of the Government of India.[4] With the German Reichsmark remaining on the gold standard, German goods became more expensive in India. Moreover, the German Government, in desperate need of foreign currency

---

[1] Eichengreen and Irwin, "Trade Blocs."

[2] For context, see Gordon, *Businessmen and Politics*: 210–218; Markovits, *Indian Business*: 72–76.

[3] "Note by Director of Intelligence Bureau," February 16, 1931, Home Dept., Pol. 33/6, NAI.

[4] Tomlinson, "Britain and the Indian Currency Crisis."

Table 5.1 *Value of 100 Indian rupees in German (Reichs-)mark,*
1914–1938

	100 Indian Rupees in German (Reichs-)mark	Change in%
1914	133	
1928–1931	150	+12.8
1931 (January–September)	150	0
1931 (September–December)	123	–18
1932	111	–9.8
1933	105	–5.4
1934	95	–9.5
1935	92	–3.2
1936	93	+1
1937	93	0
1938	92	–1

Based on: "The Situation of the Indian Rupee," 1938, 82/1, BA.

exchange, increased state controls over imports and exports, which further depressed trade.[5]

The instability of the international monetary system was a major problem for German firms in India. Siemens reported 33 percent loss in value on existing liabilities and contracts confirmed prior to the change.[6] But there were also more subtle and indirect effects. For example, European employees in India were paid in Rupees. The depreciation of the Indian currency relative to the Reichsmark (see Table 5.1) meant that overseas employees could no longer accumulate savings, which had been a common incentive for many of the young Germans working in India. Siemens' overseas human resource department noted that this fact discouraged especially the highly qualified and much needed engineers from relocating.[7]

In addition to the tumultuous currency situation, the Great Depression also intensified protectionism. While some protectionist measures disincentivized imports in general, e.g., the 1930 Smoot–Hawley Act in the US, others established discriminatory regimes that favored trade

[5] Tooze, *Wages of Destruction*: 71–86. For the impact of these restriction on goods from India see also, S. N. Gupta, "Quarterly Report by S. N. Gupta, Government of India Trade Commissioner, for the period April-June 1934," Trade Relations between India and Germany, 1934, R/245171, 4–45, PA.
[6] "Siemens India Business Report 1931/32," March 31, 1932, 4286, SAA.
[7] Overseas HR Department, "Annual Report of the Overseas HR Department, 1937/38," 1938, 8110, SAA.

with some countries over others, and thus contributed to a compartmentalization of world trade. The Ottawa Agreement of 1932 and its follow-on deals belonged to the latter group. They were designed to strengthen and stimulate trade within the British Empire. Britain was keen on securing market access for its export products, and in return agreed to admit freely many of the (primarily agricultural) goods from its dominions and colonies.[8]

Debates over protectionist tariffs were certainly not new in India. The first Indian Fiscal Commission, in 1921, had generally recommended a protectionist policy to spur India's industrial development. In some industries, multinational companies bargained with the Indian Tariff Board for better conditions, for example in exchange for Indianization of operations and management, as in the case of the Swedish Match Company.[9] The Fiscal Commission also already discussed the idea of giving preferential treatment to British dyes in India. However, the proposal was ultimately rejected with the argument that limiting where Indian textile mills could buy the best possible products would hinder their competitiveness.[10] Moreover, the Calcutta-based economics professor Pramathanath Banerjea, an expert on fiscal policy, argued that since India had no dyestuff industry of its own, there was little to be gained from protectionism.[11] The Imperial Conferences of 1923, 1926, and 1930 all debated the question of tariff preferences. Moving into the early 1930s, Indian mill owners still insisted that raw materials and machinery, needed for the development of India's own industry, should be allowed into the country without restrictions and from any foreign country.[12]

However, there were exceptions to India's open-door policy. The Steel Industry (Protection) Act of 1927 granted a reduced tariff to British steel products and remained in force until March 1934.[13] Similarly, the Cotton Industry (Protection) Act of 1930 established a discriminatory tariff for cotton piece goods.[14] The Ottawa Agreement generalized these policies from selected product groups to the establishment of an Empire trading bloc and was put into place on January 1, 1933. At the core of

---

[8] Eichengreen and Irwin, "Trade Blocs."

[9] Modig, *Swedish Match Interests in British India*: 95–103, 106–118.

[10] India Fiscal Commission, *Report of the Indian Fiscal Commission*: 137.

[11] Banerjea, *Fiscal Policy in India*: 176.

[12] Manikumar, *A Colonial Economy in the Great Depression*: 100. "New Taxation Not Justified: A Bad Precedent, Ahmedabad Millowners' Protest," *Times of India*, October 12, 1931: 11.

[13] Indian Tariff Board, *Supplementary Protection to the Steel Industry*.

[14] Government of India, *Report of the Indian Delegation*: 338. Copy in: Tariffs in India, 27/12, BA.

the agreement was a long list of preferential tariff rates for British Empire goods over foreign products. For the most part, India gave a 10 percent tariff advantage to British Empire products, mostly manufactured and semi-manufactured goods. In return, Great Britain guaranteed the tax-free import of most Indian goods or a reduced tariff rate.[15]

The consequences of the Ottawa system were fiercely and often polemically debated in India. Not surprisingly, representatives of the British-Indian Government were largely in favor of the system, while Indian nationalists opposed it. The British Trade Commissioner for India stressed how the agreement saved India from "the quagmire in trade in which other countries with equal resources, but without the Ottawa Pact, now find themselves."[16] By contrast, Manu Subedar, the general secretary of the Indian Merchants' Chamber, argued that Ottawa was an "altogether unprovoked discrimination" against German and Italian goods; and "they were not slow to hit back." He found that Germany retaliated against India by restricting exports from India or admitting them only under license, because the German decrees of March and April 1934 imposed a temporary prohibition on Indian exports.[17] While these two extremes marked the opposing ends of the debate, there was little doubt that Britain expanded its market for industrialized goods, while India's market for (primarily) raw materials was redirected to countries within the British Empire, but not significantly expanded in size. Prior to Ottawa, India had been able to sell many of its products to countries that also exported manufactured goods to India, leading to a nearly even balance of payments. It is therefore understandable that observers feared that the preferences "will only contribute to a further worsening of the passive trade balance."[18] German officials considered it their task "to support and strengthen this opposition with adequate educational work [Aufklärungsarbeit]."[19] This strategy seemed to the German observers a suitable yet prudent counterpropaganda to the British

---

[15] "Durchführung der in Ottawa mit Großbritannien vereinbarten Zollmaßnahmen in Britisch-Indien," *Industrie und Handel* 3 (1933), 11, January 13, 1933; copy in: Tariffs in India, 27/12, BA.

[16] See, "Letter German Consulate Bombay to Foreign Office," August 3, 1935, with newspaper clippings of "Two Views on Ottawa," *Times of India*, August 1, 1935 and "The Fruits of Ottawa," *Daily Sun*, August 1, 1935; Trade Relations between India and Germany, 1934–35, R 245171, PA.

[17] Ibid. For the restrictions see also, S. N. Gupta, "Quarterly Report by S. N. Gupta, Government of India Trade Commissioner, for the period April–June 1934," Trade Relations between India and Germany, 1934, 40–45, R/245171, PA.

[18] German Consulate Bombay, "Letter to Foreign Office," April 16, 1935, ibid., 65–69.

[19] German General Consulate Calcutta, "Letter to Foreign Office," May 10, 1935, Trade Relations between India and Germany, 1934, 40–45, R/245171, PA.

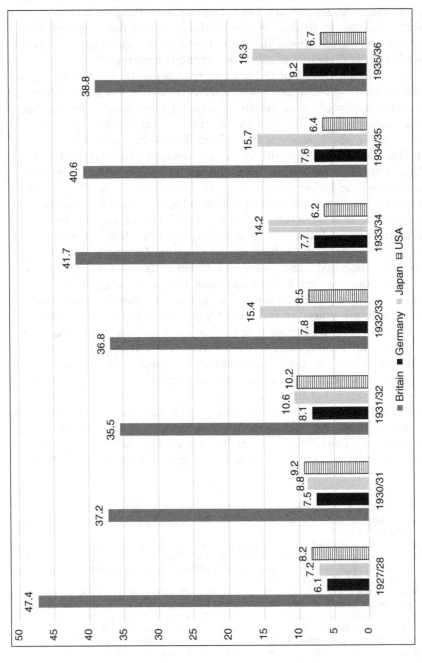

Figure 5.1 Official imports to British India by country (in percentage), 1927–1936. *Annual Statement* (several volumes).
See also: Sen, Deutschland und die indische Wirtschaft, 99.

who "do what they can to continue making the spirit of Ottawa accept-able to Indians."[20]

Evaluating the Ottawa system was anything but straightforward for the contemporaries. The German governments' initial take was: "Ottawa hurt us considerably."[21] Depending on specific products and industries, the effects, however, varied widely. For (luxury) cutlery, the standard rate for German imports was 50 percent; while the preferential rate for Commonwealth countries was 40 percent. For ordinary cutlery, the dif-ference was 30 and 20 percent.[22] In the dyestuff industry, the Taxa-tion Act of 1934 introduced a 10 percent tax on dyes. However, it was applicable to all foreign dyes, both from within and outside the British Empire, and did not change the competitive dynamics between foreign companies.[23]

The concrete impact of the Empire Free-Trade bloc on Indo-German trade was difficult to evaluate because of the series of developments that unfolded simultaneously.[24] The discriminatory tariffs emerged around the same time that the British Pound departed from gold, German food imports from India declined in the context of stricter import controls, and Japanese competitors successfully challenged German manufactur-ers in the Indian bazaar business. Moreover, experts kept stressing that trade statistics had never been precise enough to capture the import-export trade by nationality (for details see Appendix 2). However, even the official statistics, which likely underestimated German trade, showed subtle rather than extreme changes after the establishment of the empire trading bloc (See Figure 5.1 and Appendix 1 for the long-term development).

In the end, the official Ottawa regime was short-lived. The Indian del-egation had only signed off on the deal for three years and kept the right to cancel with a six-month notice. On March 31, 1936, the Indian Legis-lative Assembly voted the agreement down and resolved it by November 13, 1936. However, practically, the system of preferences remained in

---

[20] German Consulate Bombay, "Letter to Foreign Office," April 16, 1935, Trade Relations between India and Germany, 1934, 40–45, R/245171, PA, 65–69.
[21] General Consulate Calcutta (Wachendorf), "Letter to Foreign Office (Pilger)," August 29, 1935, Trade Relations between India and Germany, 1934, 40–45, R/245171, PA, 123 (verso).
[22] Lohmann, *Die Ausfuhr Solinger Stahlwaren*: 73.
[23] Government of India, *Acts of 1934*.
[24] "The Influence of the Ottawa Agreement on the British-Indian and German-Indian Trade: Summary Based on Reports of the German General Consulate in Calcutta and the German Consulate in Bombay," appendix to Foreign Office (Pilger), "Letter to General Consulate Calcutta (Wachendorf)," July 20, 1935, Trade Relations between India and Germany, 85–99, R/245171, PA.

place because there was no new agreement to replace it.[25] In June 1937, January 1938, and May 1938, different attempts were made to negotiate a new trading agreement – to no avail.[26] Eventually, on March 20, 1939, India and Britain agreed on a revised Trade Agreement, just a few months before the outbreak of World War II in September.[27]

The Ottawa Agreement was certainly a watershed moment for British–Indian trade because it first established the principle of preferential treatment for Empire products.[28] While its concrete outcomes are hard to disentangle from parallel developments, economic historian Barry Eichengreen shows that in the Sterling area, which included India and Great Britain, companies did trade more extensively with one another, as one would expect. However, they also expanded their trade with the rest of the world. One explanation for this overall boost of trade is that all Sterling countries departed from the gold standard at an early date. Devaluation of their currency stimulated recovery after the depression and made them more competitive internationally, hence encouraging them to export more to each other and to countries with more conservative monetary policies. By contrast, the currency blocs linked to gold and with strong controls of import and exports, like Germany, did not trade more with one another because the exchange controls generally inhibited trade.[29] But trade barriers were not the only political challenge to tackle.

The Battle over Historical Identities

While the Depression and the protectionist policies in its aftermath compartmentalized trade, the new political regime in Germany impacted the spirit of the Indo-German business relationship. On January 30, 1933, the Nazi Party came to power. Swiftly after the regime change, the Indian press began to report on assaults against Indians in Germany. Over the previous decade, the number of Indians, in particular Indian students, in Germany had continuously increased. Not only did the anticolonial attitude of nationalistic circles lead some students to avoid studying in Britain, but there were also new forms of legal discrimination against Indian students in the US, Canada, and Australia, which previously had been

[25] "Status of the Indo-British Trade Agreement," undated [c. December 1938], 330/422, BA.
[26] Ibid.
[27] "Assembly Criticism of Indo-British Trade Agreement," *Times of India*, March 28, 1939: 4; "Anglo-Indian Trade Agreement," *Times of India*, March 29, 1939: 11.
[28] Markovits, *Indian Business*: 51–55.
[29] Eichengreen and Irwin, "Trade Blocs": 4, 21. See also, Drummond, *Imperial Economic Policy*.

attractive destinations.[30] Both tendencies channeled Indian students to Germany. US steel worker John Keenan, who worked for Tata, remembered that one German engineer

arranged it so that our Technical School graduates went to Germany instead of to America. The United States depression had made it difficult to place our young men in American industry. Now the yearly exodus of boys went to Krupp's, Demag's, and Thyssen's works, and the Germans were careful to treat them royally. When the lads come back to India, they were so many more salesmen for anything German.[31]

To support the Indian students in Germany, Nehru had initiated the Indian Students Information Bureau in Berlin in the late 1920s (see Chapter 4), which was financially supported by the Congress Party.

Shortly after the Nazis came to power, some of these members of the Indian diaspora in Berlin experienced incidents of street violence. As early as February 1933, the journalist A. C. N. Nambiar, later an Indian ambassador to West Germany (see Chapter 7), was placed under arrest and only released after inquiries by the British embassy. After leaving Germany, he reported in the English-speaking press about assaults by German storm troopers. These articles triggered a series of anti-German protests in India.[32] They were further strengthened by the fact that Adolf Hitler, the new German Chancellor, had never made any effort to hide his deep disregard for India's Independence movement. In his book *Mein Kampf* [*My Struggle*], published in 1925, he had criticized Indian nationalists as being 'pompous big-mouths' [*schwatzhafte(r) Wichtigtuer*].[33] These statements and their reception in India were closely observed by the German business community. In July 1933, one German firm addressed the German Foreign Office to report about the negative image consequences of the regime change.[34] Yet, conditions stabilized again after the initial shock. Calls for boycotts of German products emerged briefly in the spring of 1933 but were short-lived.[35]

While the discriminatory and racist regime of the Nazis, in hindsight, seems like it was obviously anti-Indian, many contemporary observers were less certain about Nazi Germany's political positioning towards

[30] Manjapra, "The Anticolonial Laboratory": 152–153.
[31] Keenan and Sorsby, *A Steel Man in India*: 178.
[32] "Mr. Nambiar's Awful Ordeal: How He Was Treated by Nazi Storm Troopers," *Advance*, May 11, 1933; "India's Political Relations to Germany," 1933, R/77416, PA. Kreutzmüller, "Augen im Sturm?" Framke, *Delhi – Rom – Berlin*: 69–70.
[33] Hitler, *Mein Kampf*: 656. For context see also, Voigt, "Hitler und Indien."
[34] Sanitas, "Letter to Foreign Office," July 20, 1933, R/77416, PA.
[35] General Consulate Calcutta "Letter to Foreign Office (Pilger)," August 29, 1935, Trade Relations between India and Germany, 1934, 122, R/245171, PA.

nationalistic India. Paradoxically, the new German regime, steeped in racial ideology, initially did not communicate a clear racial policy beyond its rampant anti-Semitism, but rather worked off a series of ad-hoc, vague, and often conflicting postulates. While Hitler never showed much interest in India, other leading Nazi politicians did. Heinrich Himmler, Reichsführer of the SS, a paramilitary organization under the Nazis, and leading member of the Nazi Party, was known to be an India buff with extensive knowledge of Hinduism and a deep fascination for Indian culture.[36] The uncertainties left many people hoping that Indo-German cooperation was not at its end.

An important symbol of this ambiguity was the term "Aryan," which had been vague and opaque before the regime change and continued to be ill-defined under the Nazis. While Aryan was understood to mean non-Jewish in Nazi Germany, it was less clear if Indians could claim to belong to the group of Aryan nations. In fact, the German "Law for the Restoration of the Professional Civil Service" of April 7, 1933, which called for the early retirement of all "non-Aryans," defined Aryans in an accompanying order as either Western (European) races or "Eastern (Asiatic) races, i.e. Indians (Hindus) and Iranians (Persian, Afghan, Armenian, Georgian and Kurds)," thus explicitly including Indians in the community of Aryans.[37] The alluring narrative of a joint Indo-German Aryan community, which had existed before, was thus contested but not destroyed. An article in the Indian nationalist newspaper *Amrita Bazar Patrika* in 1934 reminded readers that the Germans "have reverence for our race and country as (1) they claim to be belonging to Aryan race; (2) they possess and study vast Sanskrit literature; and (3) they have adopted the 'swastika' as their national symbol, which is a typical Indian emblem."[38]

To ease the escalating home country political challenge, the German business community developed an arsenal of propaganda tools for India. Together with the German Consulate in Calcutta, German business-people coordinated their efforts to influence Indian public opinion in favor of Germany. This, they argued, was crucial because "the Indian has an inferiority complex vis-à-vis the white race."[39] As a first step, German entrepreneurs and consulate officials identified news outlets and addressed them with English-language articles that took a German-friendly stance. Pro-German articles highlighted that, "[t]here is no

[36] Tietke, *Yoga im Nationalsozialismus*.
[37] Sieferle, "Indien und die Arier": 461.
[38] "Indians in Germany," *Amrita Bazar Patrika*, November 24, 1934: 12, NLI.
[39] Consulate Calcutta, "Letter to Foreign Office," June 7, 1933, R/77416, PA.

color prejudice in Germany and an Indian is readily admitted to German society, which makes him feel quite at home."[40] Regular lists showed the growing number of articles in the Indian press supporting the German version of the Indo-German relationship.[41]

German managers not only distributed articles in response to external developments, but also actively created new narratives. Oswald Urchs, a leading manager of the Havero pharmaceutical department (the cloaking company of I. G. Farben) in Bombay, took it upon himself to reharmonize Nazi ideology with the joint Indo-German history.[42] He gave a lengthy speech in September 1933 in India and then had it circulated widely through the consulate and the Indian press. In it, Urchs shifted the focus from questions of race to practical government concerns. He made an argument for a community-based idea of nationalism and against other forms of state governance. Economic liberalism, he argued, led to "materialistic individualism until finally an unlimited selfishness of the economic individual, the duty towards its own nation was forgotten." In his rant against economic liberalism, Urchs took a position against Great Britain, without explicitly mentioning the economic and political rival. But this was not the only way that he appealed to an Indian nationalistic audience. He also highlighted alleged connecting threads between nationalistic India and Nazi Germany, such as support for peasants and workers in both countries. The "neglect and alienation of the lower classes particularly of the peasants and laborers was the sin of the old regime," which the Nazis corrected, argued Urchs. He could expect listeners from India with its large agricultural sector, a strong workers' movement, and a general appreciation for communal forms of living to appreciate this fact.

Aware of the regional diversity of India, Urchs also emphasized Hitler's efforts to unify the German nation, analogue to what many believed to be a chief challenge for India. "It is to be understood that the various German countries: Prussia, Saxony, Bavaria, etc. still remain individuals and retain their cultural perspective and peculiarities ... but the political associations of these tribal names are no more and every inhabitant of the German Reich is now also in the political sense of the term – a German." Much of Urchs' discussion about unification of the nation was

---

[40] "Letters to the Editors," *Advance,* July 20, 1933: 3, copy in: R/77416, PA.

[41] "List of the most important articles in the Indian press, placed by the information committee Hamburg-Bremen in the months June, July, August and September 1934," R/77462, PA.

[42] Oswald Urchs, "The Constructive Work of Hitlerism in Germany," speech to a Rotary Club in India, appendix to Consulate General Calcutta, "Letter to Foreign Office," September 13, 1933, R/77416, PA.

more readily applicable to India than it was to Germany at the time. It certainly intended to create a sense of "sameness."

The arguments presented by Urchs are reminiscent of the writings of the Indian nationalist Benoy Kumar Sarkar (1887–1949), who had strong ties to Germany and often highlighted the parallels between Eastern and Western nations. A two-part article with the title "The Hitler-State," published in October and November 1933, gives a more academic and, in many respects, more accurate elaboration of several of Urchs' arguments.[43] Although unproven, it may very well be that Urchs encountered Sarkar, listened to one of his public speeches or came across a draft version of the article. The economist Sarkar was a committed nationalist and active in both the Swadeshi and the National Education movement in his home state of Bengal. He was also a vocal proponent of Germany as a partner for India's Independence movement. His German-language skills allowed him to both publish and lecture in German. He was appointed lecturer at the Department of Economics at Calcutta University in 1925 and, in 1947, was promoted to professor and head of department. He established several schools and at least nine research institutes in Calcutta, including the Bangiya German Samsad (Bengal German Institute, established in 1933).[44]

Sarkar made many contributions to scholarship, including sophisticated elaborations of nationality and nationalism.[45] In his 1926 book *Politics of Boundaries*, he argued for a distinction between old and new forms of nationalism. "Nationality as interpreted by the political philosophers of the nineteenth century is not the same as the nationalities actually realized in modern times. ... History knows only 'states'. Diplomats and politicians also know only states. But patriots, philosophers and poets talk of nations."[46] His arguments reflect his knowledge of German political scientist Friedrich List, about whom Sarkar said that he tutored Germans into "the solid conviction that under certain circumstances protection was the only effective economic policy of a people."[47]

For Sarkar, the deterministic idea of nationality based on language, culture, or race had no basis and turned more absurd with the advancement of technology, facilitating worldwide interactions and the growth of an increasingly more intertwined global economy. He rejected the idea of systematic cultural or biological differences between people – an

[43] Sarkar, "The Hitler-State (part I)." Sarkar, "The Hitler-State (part II)."
[44] Sinha, "Sarkar."
[45] For a more complete analysis of Sarkar's work see, Bandyopadhyay, *Sarkar*.
[46] Sarkar, *The Politics of Boundaries*: 5.
[47] Sarkar, "The Hitler-State (part I)": 467.

argument used to legitimize, among others, colonialism. Instead, Sarkar identified the state as the basis of nationality. He argued that nationality is the (often temporary) outcome of an agreement between people and their ability to defend it militaristically. "[T]he sole origin and rationale of the state or the nation have to be sought in the will of the people to agree to its formation. ... [T]he might of the sword is the only guarantee of the existence of the nation or state."[48] This is not to say that he did not assign great relevance to nationality, which he understood as the "embodiment of political freedom, maintained by military and economic strength. ... Not unity, but independence is the distinctive feature of a national existence."[49] In this way, Sarkar elevated the task of achieving Indian Independence, while simultaneously providing a framework that incorporated diverse religions and ethnicities into a possible Indian state.[50]

Not least Sarkar's admiration for strong governments triggered his interest in Nazi Germany. While he had previously identified similarities between the treatment of Germany after Versailles and the yoke of the colonized people of India,[51] he approvingly studied the early days of the Hitler regime in 1933. In his article "The Hitler-State," he openly expressed his esteem for the actions of Nazi Germany, which he saw as a model for many of the emerging Asian nations. "Hitler and his followers and advisers are destined to rank among the greatest in the annuals of the world's constructive statesmanship. It is nothing short of a profound societal remaking that is going on among the German people today."[52] Reviewing many of the measures of economic reconstruction, Sarkar stressed that "nobody is likely to derive more profit as well as inspiration from the methods and principles of Hitler's economics than the people of Asia bent as they are on assimilating the technique of a radical transvaluation of life's values."[53] However, it would be overstating it to consider Sarkar a fascist by ideology. He was fascinated by the authoritarian government and the collective will to change the fate of the German people but also rejected racial segregation. There are, however, elements of anti-Semitism in his writings when he expressed understanding for the anti-Jewish laws and actions of the Nazi state.[54]

---

[48] Sarkar, *The Politics of Boundaries*: 12, 14.
[49] Ibid., 21.
[50] While Sarkar frequently rejected racialized notions of nationality, he continued to apply the category of race to his topic and thereby ultimately confirmed the practice of describing nations in racialized terms. See also, Six, "Challenging the Grammar of Difference": 439.
[51] See Sarkar, *The Politics of Boundaries*: 28–35.
[52] Sarkar, "The Hitler-State (part II)": 515.
[53] Ibid.
[54] For a discussion of this issue, see Framke, *Delhi – Rom – Berlin*: 140–141, 188–208. Six, "Challenging the Grammar of Difference." Zachariah, "Transfer."

Despite these voices defending Nazi Germany and foregrounding similarities with India, the rise of the Nazi regime put public pressure on the Indo-German business relationship.[55] The turning point, however, came in January 1936, when Adolf Hitler gave a speech that escalated tensions in the relationship with India. Speaking to over 6,000 students in Germany, Hitler proclaimed that "the white race is destined to rule. This is its unconscious urge, which arises from a heroic conception of life." He also claimed that it was the British who taught Indians "how to walk."[56] With this strong statement, Hitler expressed once again his disdain for the narrative of a joint Aryan heritage and instead sided with the earlier narrative of a "civilizing mission" (see Chapter 4) that the British had for long maintained.[57]

While previous calls by Jewish organizations for a boycott of German products had shown little effect in India, this speech triggered a wave of anti-German protests.[58] Indians demonstrated in front of the German Consulate and even the Mayor of Bombay called for a boycott of German products.[59] An article in the *Jewish Tribune* said, "Indians who before this tirade were not concerned in any way with the treatment of the Jewish people in Germany continued to be one of Hitlerland's best customers. ... However, the Fuhrer has exceeded himself and it is not surprising that self-respecting Indians have paused to think for themselves."[60] In a heated debate in the Indian press, Indians reproduced their own understanding of history as a counterpoint to Hitler's speech. They argued that Hitler "conveniently forgets the glorious history of 'Aryans' from times immemorial, when the white race he speaks of, was in the woods and jungles and had no notion of society and nation-hood. One wonders why he takes pride in calling himself 'Aryan'."[61] It was a battle of historical identities.

By the late 1930s, it had become obvious that the policies in Germany did not support the aims of Indian nationalists and that there was no "Aryan" alliance. There were a few exceptionally extremist voices among the more radical Indian nationalists, such as Padamraj Jain, a leader of

[55] See for example, "Anti-Semitism in Germany." *Advance*, June 11, 1933, in R/77416, PA.
[56] Speech by Adolf Hitler on January 26, 1936, reprinted in: Baynes, *Speeches of Adolf Hitler*: 1258.
[57] Mann, "Touchbearers Upon the Path of Progress."
[58] "Reports on Anti-German Boycotts," 1934–1935, R 98706, PA. See also, Framke, *Delhi – Rom – Berlin*: 127–130.
[59] "Letter Consulate in Bombay to Foreign Office," 6 and 10 February 1936, R 77418, PA.
[60] *Jewish Tribune*, March 1936: 3, quoted in: Egorova, *Jews and India*: 43.
[61] "Hitler's Insult," *Bombay Chronicle*, February 1, 1936: 12.

a Hindu nationalist party. He expressed to the German authorities that "Germany's crusade against the enemies of Aryan culture will bring all Aryan nations of the world to their senses and awaken the India Hindus for the restoration of their lost glory."[62] But the idea of an Indo-German Aryan community had already lost traction in Germany. Nazi ideologues now argued for a community of "Western Aryans" distinct from the allegedly less evolved "Eastern Aryans."[63] The narrative of racial distinction ultimately dominated over the counternarrative of a joint ancient heritage.

Employment between Home- and Host-Country Demands

The ubiquitous debates about race, nationhood, and Aryanism at the time became a (sometimes explicit, sometimes implicit) part of thinking about nationalism's role in business and the mental map of nationalism. German businesspeople reflected on the value of self-determination and their evolving relationship with colonial countries, like India. The issue of race also impacted the employment conditions in German companies and the daily life of the German business community in India.

A clear division between "Western" and "Indian" employees had for long shaped how work was organized in German and other Western companies in India. Most of the higher-qualified managerial staff in Western multinationals was European. The Anglo-Dutch multinational Unilever was seen as a pioneer when it appointed its first Indian manager in 1937.[64] Among the other Indian employees only the much-needed engineers were able to significantly improve their employment conditions in the 1930s, despite a general push for Indianization. For Jewish employees in German companies, even as far away from home as India, the Nazis' rise to power created new challenges and usually led to them leaving under pressure or being fired.

In the business year 1937/1938, the year of highest employment after 1929, the three largest German companies in India employed a total of approximately 128 Europeans and 1,531 Indians (see Table 5.2).

I. G. 's pharmaceutical department, which employed seventeen Europeans and 119 Indians, reported that the total amount paid to the seventeen Europeans was 25 percent higher than the salaries paid to all 119 Indians combined. "This shows that the Indian staff holds positions

---

[62] "Letter with enclosed statement by Jain," March 25, 1939, R/104777, PA.
[63] Manjapra, *Age of Entanglement*: 85.
[64] Jones, *Renewing Unilever*: 158.

Table 5.2 *Number of employees of the three largest German employers in India, 1937/1938*

Year	Siemens		I. G.		Krupp	
	Europeans	Indians	Europeans	Indians	Europeans	Indians
1937/38	31 (5%)	622 (95%)	76 (8%)	833 (92%)	21 (22%)	76 (78%)

Based on, for Siemens: "Übersee-Personal 1938," 8188; "Ergebnisse Übersee," 8150, both SAA; For I. G. Farben: Chemdyes, "letter to Reichswirtschaftsministerium," November 1, 1938, 330/1114 BA; For Krupp: "Development Abroad Krupp India Trading Co.," vol. 1, 1932–1939, 51–5060 WA.

which one could never expect a European to hold."[65] Concretely, Krupp's leading managers in India earned between Rs 800 and Rs 2,000 monthly in 1930, with technical managers often receiving higher salaries than their commercial counterparts. At Siemens, salary levels were similar, but the company made more use of bonuses. The very experienced (commercial) manager Paul Jürges (born 1885), who ran the Calcutta office, earned Rs 1,750 per month before resigning as a manager and joining the board of directors in 1936. In addition to his regular salary, he was granted a performance-based supplement of between Rs 6,000 and Rs 11,000 annually. A younger and less-qualified business manager, Ernst Kunisch (born 1896), earned Rs 900 and a monthly performance-based add-on of Rs 200.[66]

In all multinationals, the ongoing process of "Indianization" gathered momentum in the interwar period. Indianization referred to the replacement of Europeans by Indians in legislative bodies, government administration, and private enterprise. This process advanced in fits and starts. Public services slowly integrated Indians while still maintaining a sizeable number of British officers in the most responsible positions.[67] Private industry – both domestic and foreign – Indianized its staff. The Tata Iron and Steel Company (TISCO), the first major Indian producer of steel, had employed around 175 foreign technical experts in a workforce of roughly 2,000 in 1910. These experts came primarily from the US and Germany, as well as in smaller numbers from Britain, Austria, Italy, Switzerland, and China. Over time, they increasingly replaced these foreigners with local talent, many of whom were trained

[65] Chemdyes, "Letter to Reichswirtschaftsministerium," November 1, 1938, 330/1114, BA.
[66] See, "Report of the CVU HR Department," 1935/36, 8149 and HR files Paul Jürges and Ernst Kunisch, SAA.
[67] For a discussion of Indianization, see Ramnath, *Birth of an Indian Profession*: 27–55.

abroad.[68] In 1926, the number of foreign experts was 161, by 1933 it had decreased to seventy, and by 1937 to approximately fifty.[69] German firms, too, increasingly opened their doors to qualified Indians. This included appointments of Indians to their boards of directors, which Siemens had already initiated in the early 1920s. After the experience with the appointment of Lala Harkishan Lal to their board (see Chapter 4), Siemens expanded the number of posts on its board in March 1933 "because we have an interest in appointing relevant Indian personalities, who can also be commercially advantageous."[70] I. G. Farben took a similar decision five years later, at the occasion of restructuring its business in India (see Chapter 6.)[71]

While the process of Indianization created opportunities, it only improved the working conditions for highly qualified Indian employees. The highest salaries went to engineers who were in short supply throughout the interwar period.[72] In 1930, an Indian engineer at Krupp made approximately Rs 200 per month, which was the highest salary paid to any Indian employee. (At the same time, the lowest-paid German engineer on staff made triple, Rs 600 per month.[73]) But Indian engineers earned not only higher salaries than any other profession but also had better bargaining positions to negotiate working conditions. For example, while all Western employees had employment contracts, only Indian engineers signed any written agreement.[74] On the opposite end of the scale, sweepers, office boys and "coolies" (manual workers who carried loads) earned the lowest salaries. The salary for coolies at Krupp ranged from Rs 15 to Rs 27 per month.[75]

For non-Jewish German nationals in India, the Nazi regime affected first and foremost their day-to-day socializing. Germans residing in India started to meet at dedicated German clubs organized by the Auslandsorganisation [Foreign Organization], or AO, of the Nazi Party since 1931,

[68] Ibid., 182–200.
[69] Sen, *Deutschland und die indische Wirtschaft*: 41.
[70] Siemens CVU, "Letter to Siemens India," March 15, 1933, Siemens Abroad 1913–1940, 8156, SAA.
[71] "Reorganization of our [Havero's] Indian Dye Business" 1938: 7, 9 and 31, 191/1/3, BA.
[72] Overseas HR Department, "Annual Reports," 1934–1938, 8149 and 8110, SAA.
[73] "Development of Krupp India Trading Co., vol. 1, 1932–1939, salary statements," salary lists, WA 51/5060, HAK.
[74] "Rules for Overseas' Employees," 1907–1930, 9424; "Siemens in Middle East," 1937–1972, 8106, both SAA.
[75] "Development of Krupp India Trading Co., vol. 1, 1932–1939, salary statements," WA 51/5060, salary lists March 31, 1933, December 31, 1934, and January 1, 1937, HAK. Between 1927 and 1947, 1 INR equaled approximately 18 pence or 0.075 GBP. For details see, Roy, *Economic History of India*.

two years before the Nazis officially came to power. During the first year of the AO's existence, there were two clubs in India, in the two cities with the largest German population, Calcutta and Bombay.[76] The main activity of the AO group in India was propaganda, most importantly downplaying the persecution of German Jews and stressing the achievements of the Nazi regime. The AO began publishing a propaganda paper *Der Deutsche in Indien* [*The German in India*] in 1936, which circulated among the Germans in India.[77] Smaller AO groups were established in Madras and Tatanagar, which held meetings in the living rooms of individual club members.[78] By 1937, the AO in India had 130 members and was the forty-seventh-largest of approximately 600 Nazi groups outside of Germany.[79]

While the leadership of the AO group in Calcutta changed frequently,[80] in Bombay, the group was headed by the previously mentioned medical doctor Oswald Urchs, who came to India as an employee of the pharmaceutical department of Havero. Urchs, who was born in Plzeň/Pilsen in Austria-Hungary in 1895, was an expert on malaria treatment. He had conducted research in Dutch Guyana between the years 1923 and 1926, and then worked as a medical doctor in Munich before traveling to India in 1927.[81] He became notorious for being one of the leading figures of the Nazi Party in India and was quoted in a newspaper for saying that the Nazi club "must make every German abroad an ambassador of the National Socialist movement."[82] Eventually, by the summer of 1938, several articles in the *Bombay Sentinel* called for Urchs' expulsion from India.[83]

---

[76] Koop, *Hitlers fünfte Kolonne: Die Auslands-Organisation der NSDAP*: 265 and 272. For the fact that these were the two cities with the largest German population, see Table 6.2.

[77] See for this fact the description by Wilhelm Koppers, an Austrian ethnographer on mission in India: Koppers, *Geheimnisse des Dschungels*: 205.

[78] *Der Deutsche in Indien* 1 (July 1936), 3: 15, Stabi.

[79] Jacobsen, *Nationalsozialistische Aussenpolitik*: 663. McKale, *The Swastika Outside Germany*: 33.

[80] The head of the AO group in Calcutta was initially Klaus Haerms, then from 1936 to 1937 Dr Franz Harenberg, and starting in 1937 H. Bischoff. *Der Deutsche in Indien* 1 (July 1936), 3: 21; ibid. 1 (October 1936), 6: 28; ibid. 1 (December 1936), 8: 22, all Stabi.

[81] On Urchs see, 330/114, BA; City Archive Munich, Citizen Files [Einwohnermeldekartei]; University Archive Munich, Student Files [Studentenkartei].

[82] Oswald Urchs, directly quoted in "Spreading Nazism Abroad," *The Singapore Free Press and Mercantile Advertiser*, September 8, 1937: 2.

[83] "Clear up Nazi Cob-Webs in India," *Bombay Sentinel*, July 9, 1938: 4–5; "Ambitious Nazi Scheme for 'German House' in Bombay," *Bombay Sentinel*, July 15, 1938: 6–7; "Challenge to Come Out in the Open," *Bombay Sentinel*, July 15, 1938: 7. See also the opposing article by Paul Leszczyński in *Der Deutsche in Indien* 3 (August 1938), 28: 4, Stabi.

With the increasing influence of the Nazi club in India, German businesspeople started to get together more frequently. As seen in previous chapters, prior to World War I, German businessmen had striven
to assimilate into the group of Europeans and socialized with the much
larger group of British businesspeople. World War I had ended many
of these attempts and started the practice of groups getting together by
nationality. A German-Jewish emigrant, Ernest Schaffer, who relocated
to India in 1933, remembered that "[t]he Europeans in Bombay mainly
came together by nation, which one could also note in the clubs. When
I expressed regret for the fact that we [Europeans] were not closer this
far away from home, an Englishman with whom I became friends told
me: 'You know, you are not part of our tribe [Sippe]'."[84] The Nazi club
activities were thus the predominant social context for most Germans in
India.

Being an official member of the Nazi Party was comparatively less
crucial to the German businesspeople in India than it would have been at
home. By December 1938 even the heavily politically engaged I. G. Farben employed only seven official party members out of a total of seventy
German employees in its chemical division.[85] It was up to Oswald Urchs
to report that all of the employees, party members or not, were nevertheless "politically reliable" – which he did.[86] Several of the German companies in India also had employees with supposedly "neutral" nationalities
(or no nationality at all) on staff, who acted as an insurance policy in case
of any discrimination against Germans. I. G. Farben employed thirty-
seven Europeans in its dye business, of whom twenty-four were German,
four Swiss, two Italian, two Czech, and one each British, Dutch, Norwegian, Danish, and "stateless." The carefully crafted diversity of the
workforce was by design. The focus was on nationalities that historically
had been unsuspicious; a fact that could be mobilized to circumvent
potential nationality-based restrictions.[87]

The biggest burden after the regime change was on German-Jewish
employees. At I. G. Farben, several Jewish or half-Jewish employees
were replaced, for example, Stephen Popper (manager for chemicals)
and Albrecht von Leyden (at Agfa). Both Popper and von Leyden had

[84] Shaffer, *Ein Emigrant*: 20.
[85] Chemdyes, "Letter Wipo to Seyd," December 1, 1938, 330/1114, BA. Namely: Dr
   Oswald Urchs, Kurt Schumacher, I. B. Acklin, Dr Franz Harenberg, Heinz Nebeling,
   Josef Wilde, I. Goessling.
[86] Chemdyes, "Letter Urchs to Kuepper," December 9, 1938, 330/1114, BA.
[87] "Reorganization of our [Havero's] Indian Dye Business" 1938, 33, 330/1124, BA. The
   stateless Geo Kreczmer owned a Nansen passport, an official document issued by the
   "Nansen International Office for Refugees," which allowed him to travel.

been with their respective companies for many years.[88] Yet, this treatment of Jewish employees hurt the image of the German companies in India. When the Nazi Foreign Organization back in Germany requested the firing of all Jewish employees and proof of "Aryan" descent for all others, I. G. Farben's manager hesitated, knowing this policy would have consequences for the company's image in India.[89] There was a significant Jewish population in the country, largely concentrated in the Bombay Presidency, where I. G. conducted most of its business.[90] The call for firing non-Aryan employees posed not only a human resources but also a significant public relations quandary. For that reason, I. G. Farben's top managers agreed on a public statement arguing that it was in the interest of the Jewish employees to stop working for I. G. Farben so that they could avoid business trips to Germany in the new political context. The stateless manager Geo Kreczmer advised all employees to adopt this explanation given that "it would be stupid to try and deny the resignation of all non-Aryans or its reason."[91] A few months later, when I. G. Farben was pressed once again for "proof of Aryanization" of all its employees, Oswald Urchs replied that Indian press coverage of Germany's latest laws against Jews had been so negative that an official request for any such proof would only make the position of German firms more difficult.[92] Bargaining with home-country institutions and politicians about the rules of engagement was part of the growing portfolio of political tasks.

Political Strategizing and Political Capabilities

The 1930s undoubtedly raised many new host-country challenges, including a discriminatory tariff regime and expectations for Indianization, which German companies had to manage. It also added home country trials to the agenda, such as the perception of the Nazi regime in India, the negative press coverage of discriminatory laws against Jews, and street violence against ethnic and religious groups. Managing political home- and host-country challenges rose up on corporate agendas.

Yet, there were also some promising developments for German business in India. The Congress Party, while encompassing diverse and

---

[88] "A Walking Ticket?", *Filmindia* 4 (1938), November: 67.
[89] Series of letters and "Confidential Note," December 1938, Chemdyes Ltd., Correspondence I, 1938–42, Legal Department, 330/1114, BA.
[90] Roland, *The Jewish Communities of India.*
[91] "Letter Havero to IG," August 15, 1938, Reorganization British India, 330/1111, BA.
[92] "Letter Urchs to Kuepper," December 9, 1938, Chemdyes Ltd., Bombay, Correspondence I, 1938–42, 330/1114, BA.

conflicting interest groups, evolved into a more organized party after the mid-1930s and gained greater concessions from the British Government. The 1935 constitution introduced a larger measure of autonomy to the provinces of British India, direct elections, and more elected Indian representatives, while retaining the British right to suspend government, among other restraints. Due to these limitations and to the fact that it was drafted without Indian participation, the law was met with little enthusiasm. The Congress nevertheless participated in the provincial elections and scored impressive victories, including an absolute majority in six of the eleven provinces in 1937. The majority of the Indian business elite showed some support for the Congress, despite pockets of resistance and fear that Gandhi's hostility toward modern industry might be reflected in policy.[93] Despite diverging opinions within the Congress, it was obvious to the German observers that greater Indian participation in both politics and economics was not only inevitable but also potentially beneficial to Germany. At Siemens, managers reported that there were a growing number of business opportunities for non-British firms in India. "The precondition for a stronger participation of Siemens is given."[94]

To exploit these opportunities more systematically, German companies reflected the value of political capabilities in their organizational structures. Since World War I, Siemens had a Wirtschaftspolitische Abteilung [Political Economic Department], dedicated to studying political environments for Siemens' business around the globe.[95] Starting in 1929, I. G. similarly developed a complex of offices in Germany, known collectively as "Berlin NW 7," after their postal code. NW 7 included two offices: the Volkswirtschaftliche Abteilung [Economic Department, founded in 1929], which focused on overseas investment opportunities; and the Wirtschaftspolitische Abteilung [Political Economic Department, founded in 1932], which had the task of surveying relevant legal, foreign policy, and taxation issues. Both were dedicated to political strategizing and monitoring the development of the political economic context abroad and increasingly also in the home market, where the politics of the Nazi regime required attention.

Both I. G. departments had close personal ties to the German Government. The staff of the Economic Department, including its chief Anton Reithinger, came primarily from the German Statistical Office. The Political Economic Department was formed as a specialized unit

---

[93] For a detailed analysis of the election results and the relationship of the Congress Party to the Indian business class, see Markovits, "Indian Business."
[94] "Siemens in the Middle East 1937–1972: Observations Turbine Business," 8106, SAA.
[95] Feldenkirchen, *Siemens*: 358.

of the I. G. Central Committee, the inner circle of top executives of the managing board, indicating its strategic importance to the firm. Its leader, Heinrich Gattineau, had studied under one of Germany's most prolific India specialist, Karl Haushofer, at the University of Munich. The departments' activities included studies of foreign newspapers and government reports as well as frequent travels to the countries where I. G. conducted business.

Understanding nationalist movements around the world was a core part of the business of these departments. NW 7's leading managers visited those countries aspiring for self-determination and industrialization, including but not limited to India, to gather intelligence on how best to position the firm. For example, Max Ilgner, a member of I. G.'s board, traveled to Mexico in 1936. There, he pitched the potential contribution that the firm could make to local economic development to Mexican state and government officials and suggested joint ventures between Mexicans and Germans with a 60 percent Mexican share.[96] For India, it was Anton Reithinger, the head of the Economic Department, who developed a special expertise. He traveled widely on the subcontinent in 1937/1938.[97] In 1936, Reithinger had published a book, arguing that economic development around the world would increase foreign demand for German merchandise.[98] In India, he observed with delight that both British and Indian elites were favorable to India's economic development – the former to secure peace, the latter to achieve self-determination – so that Germans would not be forced to pick sides. Reithinger advocated strategic neutrality: not opposing British rule but capitalizing on "the Indians' wish to include other nations of the world in the development of their country." He also saw race as a major issue. Despite the problems that the Nazi regime had created for German business in India, he considered it a great advantage that "our people do not represent a 'superior/dominating people of gentlemen' [übergeordnetes Herrenvolk] but can rather act as friends on the same societal and personal level."[99] This advantage could be exploited even more, he argued, if I. G. Farben decided to end its cloaking arrangement with Havero and incorporate under Indian law as well as hire more Indian representatives in leading positions.[100]

[96] Report about Ilgner's visit to Mexico, December 15, 1936, GCD, roll 3185, NARA.
[97] Hayes, Industry and Ideology: 31.
[98] Reithinger, Gesicht. Hayes, Industry and Ideology: 160.
[99] Anton Reithinger, "East Asia Travel Reports 1937/38: Politics and Economics," 191/1/3, BA. For the trip see also, "Germany Aiming at Self-Sufficiency," Times of India, November 13, 1937: 22.
[100] Ibid.

Criss-crossing the country, Reithinger collected information that could help I. G.'s business there. He found that wherever Indian administrators or engineers took positions in the provincial, district, or municipal governments, they often broke with the preferences for British goods. "As soon as Indians moved into these positions, they bought, partly purely in opposition, in other countries." Reithinger reported having observed a switch to German goods in a city waterworks in Calcutta, at the local newspaper *Amrita Bazar Patrika*, and at the Bengal College. However, he cautioned that the situation in Bengal was possibly not representative of the whole country.[101] Better knowledge about regional differences was needed for strategizing based on nationalism.

It was exactly such regional variances that the new political departments at Siemens and I. G. explored in detail. Based on travel reports, dialogues with Indian visitors, and desk research, they learned to pay close attention to those regions of India which were known to be particularly supportive of India's fight for independence. Bengal had for long been fiercely anti-British, and several Bengali nationalists visited Germany or remained in close connection with German partners.[102] In addition to Bengal, Reithinger also found that in the United Provinces, Indians tried to exclude the British from economic transactions and actively sought out German, Japanese, and Italian alternatives. Less obvious at first glance was Reithinger's interest in the princely states and maharajahs, who in questions of economic development were almost completely independent. "In the provinces and progressive princely states new industrial centers are developing." Reithinger suggested to place observers both in the important princely states and near Congress governments, who could support the I. G. business and secure the trust of the ministers or princes.[103] For example, the state of Bhavnagar received more than 20 percent of its foreign goods from Germany in 1934. Several Indian maharajahs visited Germany in the 1930s to initiate commercial interactions. As early as August 1931, Siemens welcomed the Gaekwar of Baroda at its Berlin headquarters.[104] The meeting led Siemens' managers to conclude that the prince was firmly anti-British and keen on importing more German goods. Less than two years later, Siemens also welcomed the Maharajah of Rewa, who declared that

---

[101] Anton Reithinger, "East Asia Travel Reports 1937/38: Politics and Economics," 191/1/3, BA.

[102] "Indo-German Trade Relations: Sarkar Adumbrates 'scheme of Reciprocity' in Lunch Given at Berlin," *Bombay Chronicle*, September 20, 1936, copy in R 104777, PA.

[103] Anton Reithinger, "East Asia Travel Reports 1937/38: Politics and Economics," report #2: 15, 191/1/3, BA.

[104] "Visit Prince of Baroda," August 7, 1931, Organization Abroad 1945-65, SAA 8109.

he wanted to develop electricity in his state with the help of the German electrical company and that prior negotiations with Great Britain had failed because of the prince's fear of losing economic and political independence.[105]

The Olympic Games in Berlin in 1936 attracted more visitors, including the Maharajah of Mysore. A photograph of his arrival at the Tempelhof aerodrome circulated in the Indian press. In addition to sightseeing, he toured several German factories and met representatives of German industry and industry associations.[106] He was categorized as "German-friendly" and German managers were particularly excited about the fact that in Mysore, the prince relied on the support of a German advisor, Gustav H. Krumbiegel, who acted as his architectural consultant. Krumbiegel had left Germany in 1888 to work as an architect at Kew Gardens in Great Britain. He came to the princely state of Baroda in 1893 and since 1908 was active in Mysore.[107] Reithinger who met Krumbiegel during his India trip in 1937 reported that he was an older gentleman in good health and conscious of his German roots [deutschbewusst]. He was said to have extraordinary influence over the prince and "be a great asset for Germany."[108] The aforementioned Gaekwar of Baroda, who had been Siemens' guest in 1931, also returned to Berlin for the Olympics and was personally welcomed by Adolf Hitler.[109]

Regional differences helped target German strategy. Similarly relevant for political strategizing was the selection of industries. With India's industrial development advancing, machinery and chemicals were identified as the backbone of the German business with India. To better serve these two areas, some observers suggested to fully abandon the bazaar trade, in which at this point Japan clearly held the more competitive position. "Germany's strength is obviously not in the bazaar business, even though it has for long participated in it."[110] Instead, Germany

[105] "Negotiations with Maharadja of Rewa," several files, Organization Abroad 1945–65, SAA 8109.
[106] "Maharajah of Mysore in Berlin," Times of India, September 5, 1936: 16; "Late News: Maharaja of Mysore," Times of India, August 22, 1936: 13; Mirza M. Ismael, "Letter to Dr. Schneider," September 14, 1936, R 104777, PA. The German Orient Association welcomed the prince and proudly presented pictures of the encounter to Indian visitors afterwards. See, Natarajan, West of Suez: 64.
[107] Baweja, A Pre-history of Green Architecture: 28–29.
[108] See, Anton Reithinger, "East Asia Travel Reports 1937/38: Politics and Economics," report #2, 26, 191/1/3, BA.
[109] "Indian Affairs in London," Times of India, August 21, 1936: 19. On his trip see also, "Baroda Ruler for Olympics," Times of India, August 1, 1936: 14.
[110] Sen, Deutschland und die indische Wirtschaft: 89.

was well suited to focus on higher-value goods and business with the British-Indian Government. For the government business with the Indian Stores Department, the German Consul in Calcutta suggested to specifically support only the largest German manufacturers, rather than diverting attention to the many small businesses. He saw advantages in managing the tender process but also wanted to avoid price wars.[111] Finally, there was a push toward more advertisement for German products, for example, in the context of an industrial exhibition, which could communicate the importance of German high-quality products,[112] after decades of being known as a manufacturer of cheap bazaar goods (for details see Chapter 2).

German businesspeople sought out specifically those companies and industries that were perceived as being most influenced by Indian nationalism. They reasoned (based on prior experiences) that these were the ones most likely to buy German goods. Cotton goods in particular were often the target of nationalistically inspired boycotts. Consequently, spinning mills were inclined to source their machinery from non-British origins because their positive development in the 1930s was directly related to the national movement and the call for locally produced garments – a trend that Siemens took advantage of by targeting customers in this industry.[113] Similarly, the steel industry was considered crucial to India's industrial development and both Krupp and Siemens established close relationships with Tata's TISCO. Since 1931, Krupp and TISCO had been in close connection and representatives of TISCO visited Krupp in Germany in August 1931 and again in July 1935.[114] Siemens worked on a large project for TISCO in 1936 and 1937, for which the company sent a series of engineers to India.[115]

With their freshly honed political capabilities, German companies steadily increased their sales in India. With Siemens' sales growing from Rs.3 million (1928) to Rs.8 million (1938), demand was well established. However, Siemens did not realize profits during this time due to high operating costs and an overvalued Reichsmark after the British and the US had abandoned the gold standard in 1931 and 1933 respectively (see

[111] General Consulate Calcutta, "Letter to Foreign Office (Pilger)," August 29, 1935, Trade Relations between India and Germany, 1934, 123, R/245171, PA.
[112] Ganguly, "Speech on Indian Economy and Development of Indo-German Trade," November 13, 1934, R/245171 Trade Relations between India and Germany, 7–38, here: 37, PA.
[113] "Siemens India," March 31, 1932, 4286, SAA.
[114] "Memo on visit of Tata directors," July 19, 1935, Files on East India, 1933–1937, FAH 23-FAH 4 C 170, HAK.
[115] Franz Etzel, "Ein Ingenieur fliegt nach Indien," Mitteilungen VDE 19 (1937), 6, June 23, 1937: 1–7. Copy in: VVA Eso – Etzel, Franz, SAA.

Table 5.3 *Havero (for I. G. Farben) dyes and Siemens: sales and profits in India, 1926–1937 (in million rupees)*

Year	I. G. Farben (India) Dyes: Sales	I. G. Farben (India) Dyes: Profits (Total and % of Sales)	Siemens (India): Sales	Siemens (India): Profits and Losses (Total and % of Sales)
1926	19.08			
1927				
1928			2.97	
1929	19.32			
1930	19.84		4.26	−0.24 (−05.63%)
1931	26.17		3.39	−0.12 (−03.54%)
1932	25.51	0.22 (0.86%)	2.70	−0.12 (−04.44%)
1933	25.78	0.15 (0.58%)	2.92	−0.30 (−10.27%)
1934	27.81	0.27 (0.97%)	4.30	−0.19 (−04.42%)
1935	34.27	0.44 (1.28%)	4.67	−0.28 (−06.00%)
1936	30.51	0.36 (1.18%)	5.87	−0.33 (−05.62%)
1937	29.86	0.60 (2.01%)	8.69	−0.23 (−02.65%)
1938			8.16	−0.65 (−07.97%)

Source: For Siemens Economic Results Calcutta, 25/Lg/136; Annual Report 1931/2, 4886; Overseas-HR 1938, 8188; Results Overseas, 8150, all SAA. For I. G. Farben: Dyestuff Market British India 4/b/14/3/6; File of the Sales Community Dyestuffs, 330/1267; British India 1113; Sales Dyes 420, all BA.

Table 5.3). Siemens' other overseas locations similarly showed negative results until 1937, when global trade volume increased and the German Government's support scheme for exports improved the situation.[116]

It is therefore noteworthy that I. G. Farben's business in dyes not only went from Rs 19 million (1926) to close to Rs 30 million (1937) in sales but that the company also managed to realize net profits despite the difficult situation (see Table 5.3). This was partly due to a cartel deal that I. G. had entered with Swiss, French, and British dyestuff manufacturers in 1932. Such cartel agreements were typical for the interwar period, especially but not exclusively in Germany.[117] In January 1930, the German, Swiss (i.e., Swiss I. G. composed of Ciba, Sondoz, and Geigy), and French (Compagnie des Matières Colorantes, or Kuhlmann) dyestuff makers joined forces in an international cartel and negotiated with the British competitor Imperial Chemical Industries, or ICI, to join. ICI wanted the cartel to agree to a quota based

---

[116] Tooze, *Wages of Destruction*: 232–233. On Siemens see, Results Overseas, 8150, SAA.
[117] Fear, "Cartels"; Schroeter, "Cartels Revisited"; Fellman and Shanahan, *Regulating Competition*.

on the weight of dyestuffs sold by all makers within the British Empire. This was an unusual demand for ICI, since in other product lines the British manufacturer insisted on exclusive rights to the British Empire. However, in India the German competitors were so well established and there was less demand for some of the more sophisticated and profitable dyes that the British supplied. The continental cartel eventually agreed to the quota and thus granted ICI a complementary right to sell in Swiss and German markets beginning in 1932, where its more expensive dyes had a larger market.

The cartel was intended to last for the atypically long period of thirty-six years. It granted I. G. Farben a quota of 65.5 percent of world export sales and ICI 8.43 percent.[118] In 1933, two-thirds of the world's dye market (by value) was controlled by this cartel, which competed with US (19.6 percent), Russian (4.6 percent), and Japanese (3.7 percent) manufacturers, as well as some British and Dutch independents.[119] However, the implementation of the cartel was not without challenges. While the place of supply rules could easily be implemented in the mill business, I. G. Farben had less control over the bazaar business, which involved all cartel firms via large Indian merchants. It was therefore necessary to plan for local cartels. From 1931 onward, the firms of the cartel met weekly to discuss the implementation of the cartel agreements in India.[120] By 1938, they had agreed on rigid local conditions, including minimum net prices, terms of sales, the maximum number of local distributors, and the maximum commission to be granted to them (between 7.5 and 12 percent, depending on the product). However, making sure the theoretical guidelines were followed in the Indian bazaar segment remained difficult.[121]

With the cartel in place, India's importance as an export market for I. G. Farben rose. In 1920/1921, the companies of I. G. Farben had accounted for 34 percent of all dye imports to India. In 1929/1930 they supplied 70 percent of all dyes, making India I. G. Farben's fourth-largest foreign market with more than Rs 19 million in sales (US$6.86 million). At the same time, the British market share declined from 33 to 7.4 percent, a loss sometimes attributed to anti-British sentiments and boycotts in the country,[122] but also shaped by the implementation of the cartel rules. By 1938, India had risen to be I. G. Farben's largest foreign

[118] Coleman, *IG Farben and ICI*: 54. Plumpe, *I.G. Farbenindustrie AG*: 197–199, 455.
[119] "World Dye Production, Percentage of World Trade by the Cartel," 1933, 4/B/14/3/6, BA.
[120] "Havero's Dye Business in British India," February 1, 1938, R/8128/9967, BArch-B.
[121] Ibid.
[122] Reader, *I.C.I.*: Vol. 1: 439.

Table 5.4 *Havero (for I. G. Farben) net profits by department, in rupees, 1932–1937*

	Dyestuff	Photo	Pharma	Chemicals	Total
1932	131,377	23,913	79,667	(14,869)	220,088
1933	160,039	29,938	44,888	(84,681)	150,184
1934	272,185	45,313	22,943	(67,032)	273,408
1935	348,726	24,086	74,932	(5,732)	442,012
1936	316,620	21,227	50,527	(26,600)	361,773
1937	413,577	49,330	95,428	43,757	602,091
Average 1932–1937	273,754	32,301	61,397	(25,860)	341,593
Percentage of Total	80.14%	9.46%	17.97%	–7.57%	100.00%

For 1929–1931: Income-Tax for Havero; for 1932–1937: Havero Net Profits, both 330/1267, BA.

market with higher sales than even China and Britain.[123] The dominance was, however, limited to the market for dyestuffs, in which the German firms had the most experience.

Bolstered by political intelligence, the German companies in India expanded their business rather than retrenched in the late 1930s. I. G. Farben under the cover of Havero had a stronghold on the cartelized Indian dyestuff market but also realized profits in pharmaceuticals and photographic material (Agfa). In chemicals, it expanded its business but only temporarily broke even (see Table 5.4).

Siemens also expanded its activities and nurtured the business with turbines, power generators, and lamps.[124] It moved its Calcutta headquarters to the United India Building in Chittaranjan Avenue (see Figure 5.2); an address it shared with Agfa and Havero's pharmaceutical department.[125] Investments in further expansion and representative offices reflected the Germans' hope for a promising future.

Challenged by host- and home-country demands, the 1930s were the decade when German multinationals honed their political capabilities. Seeing a group of nations with their aspirations for self-determination and economic autarky, German businesspeople learned how to best engage nationalists and their agenda. In India, they invested in expansive and expensive propaganda, studied the fine-grained differences and

[123] Plumpe, *I.G. Farbenindustrie AG*: 197–199, 455.
[124] "Central Administration Overseas News," December 15, 1936, Sgr. Nr. 06825, 8156 and 9422; "Observations of turbine business," 8106; "Lamp Business in Overseas," 1937/8, 9486; "Remarkable Contracts of SSW in India," 68/Li/156, all SAA.
[125] "Central Administration Overseas News," October 1, 1936, Sgr. Nr. 06821, 9422, SAA. See also, "Six Story Building in Calcutta: Imposing Architecture," *Times of India*, August 31, 1933: 14.

Figure 5.2 Office building of Siemens (India) Limited in Calcutta, 1936. © Siemens Historical Institute.

dynamics of the Indian political environment, identified industries and regions prone to nationalism, and negotiated local cartel conditions. Much of this work was now done in organizational units dedicated to gathering and evaluating political intelligence. Over time, I. G. Farben's NW 7 developed into a major intelligence unit for political strategizing and published a series of reports on India, including studies on specific market conditions, for example, for dyes in India, a dossier on the development of the value of the Indian Rupee (1938), the historical development of India's emerging chemical industry (1942/1943), and various collections of clippings from Indian newspapers.[126] NW 7's total expenses grew from less than US$0.4 million in 1932 to US$2.8 million in 1943. German governmental agencies came to rely heavily on its reports, which drew on the experienced staff and I. G.'s sales network around the world. In 1937/1938, the Economic Department essentially turned into Germany's central agency for collecting and collating economic intelligence and a recognized collaborator of the Statistical Office,

---

[126] Copies of these reports: India General, 81/1, BA.

the Reichsbank, the Foreign Office, and the ministries of Economics, Agriculture, and Finance.[127]

While the imperial preference system raised discriminatory tariffs and the idea of an Indo-German Aryan community lost much of its credibility in the context of the Hitler regime, this did not put an end to German business in India. Rather than retrenching, German business expanded its activities in the Indian market and invested in political capabilities for managing both the home- and host-country political context. Seeds had been planted for a more systematic and longer-term strategy to do business in a volatile political world.

[127] Division of Investigation of Cartels and External Assets, *Report of the Investigation of IG Farbenindustrie AG*: 84.

Political capabilities, which the German companies with business in India developed over the course of the 1930s, were urgently needed both at home in Nazi Germany and in the Indian host country in the years leading up to World War II. Furthermore, political economy experts were at the forefront of planning for uncertain futures in both countries. Eventually, the outbreak of the war in 1939 provided a déjà vu moment for German business. It brought back the familiar challenges of expropriation and internment. Yet, strategic responses to them changed significantly compared to World War I, not least thanks to the political capabilities that multinationals had developed. What used to be ad hoc and short-term crisis management turned into long-term strategic planning, with an almost immediate emphasis on rebuilding the India business after the war.

In addition, veteran foreign business experts at Siemens and I. G. Farben experimented with a unified strategy for countries striving for independence. They took the unwelcome interruption during the war as an opportunity for reflection and explored how German business could position itself in a world of ambitious new nations. These ideas for "countries with strong nationalist movements," as one manager described the new category, were the culmination of decades of engagement with nations, their identities, and histories. In this broader strategy, German managers considered that nations did not evaluate their fate in isolation but rather imagined their future based on the experiences of other countries and the historical relationship between nations. Mental maps of nationalism reflected national ambitions and historical relationships of groups of countries, giving the debates about business in India a new outlook.

Crafting Indian Industrialization

By the late 1930s, the Congress Party had become more vocal and explicit in publicly expressing its business and trade aspirations. In India, "the independence movement led by the Congress Party became increasingly more vigilant, and the political demonstrations in the big industrial centers, such as Calcutta, Cawnpore, and others, were more numerous," reported Siemens (India) in its annual report for 1938/1939. "This development is naturally supported by the undeniable fact that the prestige of Great Britain is on a downward spiral."[1] This statement must be seen in the context of the long, unsuccessful negotiations over a new Indo-British trade agreement to replace the Ottawa Agreement, which had been voted down in 1936. It took three years to eventually reach a new agreement in March 1939.[2] In the meantime, the question of how India would pursue its goals of political independence and economic development was heatedly debated among all stakeholders, including German businesspeople who saw their business prospects inextricably intertwined with this movement.

In early 1938, the newly elected Congress President, the Bengali nationalist Subhas Chandra Bose, started the process of setting up a National Planning Committee to develop India's pathway to industrialization. The committee was inaugurated on December 17, 1938, and Bose appointed Jawaharlal Nehru as its first Chairman. In his presidential address in February 1938, Bose had sketched out a "scheme of industrial development" and pled for an "active foreign trade policy for India." Arguing against a new trade agreement with Britain, he explained that India "should not have any restrictive agreement with England such as would jeopardize its trade with the various non-empire countries which have been in several respects its best customers, or such would tend to weaken India's bargaining power *vis-à-vis* other countries."[3] Without explicitly mentioning Nazi Germany, he suggested a pragmatic approach, in which "we should not be influenced by the internal politics of any country or the form of its state. We shall find in every country men and women who will sympathize with Indian freedom, no matter what their own political views may be."[4] It did not take a stretch of the imagination to see the nod to Nazi Germany, to which Bose held close connections.

The Congress Party was a diverse organization with many different ideas and ideologies represented. One US expert described the movement as "a revolutionary omnibus containing the vast conglomeration of interests that saw reason to oppose British rule in India."[5] Thus, the early planning efforts were characterized by compromise. Bose advocated that small-scale cottage production and large-scale industrial factories should go together

[1] Annual Report Siemens (India) 1938/1939, August 8, 1939: 1–2, 8133/2, SAA.
[2] Chatterji, "Business and Politics in the 1930s."
[3] Bose, "Haripura Address": 49–50.
[4] Ibid., 56.
[5] Phillips Talbot, Manuscript "The Independence of India," March 18, 1947: 11; enclosed to letter from New Delhi, March 19, 1947, Phillips Talbot, "letters to Walter S. Rodgers," TS India T142, HIA.

in India's economic development, trying to bridge the gap between Gandhi's vision for the future of India and his own. He had earlier called on the Planning Committee to "carefully consider and decide which of the home industries could be revived despite the competition of modern factories and in which sphere large scale production should be encouraged."[6] A report by the German Consulate in Calcutta analyzed that Gandhi's influence in political matters was large but that as an economic politician "he does not have the same authority because the Congress is by and large significantly more progress-oriented and practical."[7] Bose's agenda was a case in point. He focused on developing what he called the "mother industries," that is, industries on which the development of other industries was dependent, such as power supply, machinery and machine tools, fuel, steel, heavy chemicals, and transport and communication.[8] In several of these industries, German manufacturers, such as Siemens (power supply, machinery, communication), Krupp (machinery and machine tools, steel), and I. G. Farben (heavy chemicals), were already important suppliers. Who was to say that there was no seat for them on the "omnibus"?

During the time of his presidency, the German-friendly Bose met with one of the leaders of the German business community in India, Oswald Urchs, and discussed Indo-German political and economic relations.[9] In a late-night meeting that lasted two-and-a-half hours, Bose argued that India's biggest concern was not the treatment of the Jews in Germany but rather Nazi Germany's approach to race, the way it questioned the roots of the Indo-Germanic race and instead insisted on the superiority of "Whites." In his opinion, this was one of the main reasons for the hostile press in India. When writing his report about the meeting for the Nazi Foreign Organization, Urchs concluded that, "[a] friendlier attitude of the Congress though can be of great economic advantage for us given the industrial plans under the Congress banner; and we need it desperately."[10] Urchs was hinting at the fact that only a few weeks earlier, Congress had discussed a boycott of German goods to

---

[6] Bose, "Haripura Address": 41.
[7] The report highlighted a few leading Congress politicians who were active in the development of an industrialization strategy, including the Dewan of Mysore, M. Visvesvaraya, and the industrial minister of Madras, V. V. Giri. German Consulate General Calcutta (Pausch), "Letter to Foreign Office Berlin," December 20, 1938, including report "India's Industrialization," India Various 1928–1942, 330–442, BA.
[8] Bose, "The National Planning Committee: Inauguration Speech at the First Meeting of the All-India National Planning Committee at Bombay on December 17, 1938." See also, "National Planning Committee Inaugurated: Objects Explained," *Times of India*, December 19, 1938: 5.
[9] Oswald Urchs, "Confidential report to [Nazi] Foreign Organization re Subhas Chandra Bose," December 24, 1938, 104777, PA.
[10] Ibid.

protest anti-Semitic laws in Germany.[11] Indian businessman Khwaja
Abdul Hamied reported that "business conditions in India are not too
good. I am trying my best to do all what is possible to increase the sales
of the articles manufactured by firms in Germany, whom I represent."
Hamied, who had received his PhD in Berlin in 1926, represented a few
German companies in India and was also the founder of the Indian pharmaceutical company Chemical, Industrial & Pharmaceutical Laboratories (Cipla). In his view, the main problem was misinformation about
Nazi Germany. "[T]he true position of affairs in Germany is not known
in this country. Very often it is misrepresented."[12]

As Congress' influence was rising, it became a more important force
in business. Members of the Congress Party had assumed office in
eight of the eleven Indian provinces in 1937. Under their leadership,
German companies were able to sell more German products and took
on infrastructure projects, which Congress now had to tackle "to show
the English that one is able to do so."[13] However, the beginnings of
Congress governments, while being advantageous for the direct competition with Britain, also brought new challenges. Among the biggest
problems of the Indian provinces were the limited financial resources
and the largely inelastic sources of revenue.[14] Ernst Deissmann, the
head of I.G.'s Legal Department, reported that the new political organization of India reflected in an increased need for money in the provinces. Deissmann's biggest concern was that India's financial needs
might manifest in discriminatory policies targeted at large foreign
corporations.[15]

The first battleground was taxation. According to the Government of
India Act of 1935, the Central Government had the right to taxation of
all incomes.[16] In the context of India's quest for independence and fiscal
autonomy, Havero's long-term Indian auditor and tax advisor, the highly
respected S. B. Billimoria, suggested to change the company's cloaked

[11] Podewils, "Telegram to Foreign Office," December 5, 1938, 104777, PA.
[12] K. A. Hamied, "Letter to Dr. von Hentig, Foreign Office," November 15, 1938, 104777, PA. On Hamied's business in and with Germany, see also Singh, "Khwaja Abdul Hamied." Vatsal, *Caring for Life*: 25–26.
[13] Dr v. Hentig, German Foreign Office, "Letter to Inspector General for the German Road Infrastructure," 24 February 1939, 104777, PA
[14] Markovits, "Indian Business": 487.
[15] Dr Deissmann, "Memorandum about the Founding of Agfa India Ltd.," 1938, 3, 330/1271, BA. Dr Ernst Deissmann was the head of I.G.'s Legal Department from 1935 to 1945. Before joining the multinational, he had managed the London office of the German Academic Exchange Service from 1930 to 1934 and was familiar with the legal environment of Great Britain and the British Empire.
[16] With the exception of agricultural income. See the historical chronology by Ambirajan, *Taxation*: 119.

organization. The "great Political [sic] changes in our Country ... make it very advisable that the Havero Company should at the earliest opportunity transfer their business in India to one or more Indian Companies."[17] All German companies in India had struggled over the previous few years with changes in India's legal environment, first and foremost increasing taxes, leading to a rush to Indianize.[18] Specifically, the Indian Companies Amendment Act of 1936 and the continuous changes of the Income Tax Act provided an important trigger for all German companies to reconsider their organizational structures and practices in India. The 1936 amendment (brought into law on January 1, 1937) included new provisions for "subsidiary companies."[19] It was the first law to officially recognize the "managing agency system" and introduced some checks and balances for how managing agents could act.[20] From the point of view of the German companies, the most crucial provisions were the extended publicity and bookkeeping rules, calling for profit and loss accounts of the holding companies, even if they were situated abroad.[21]

With the Indian provinces in dire need for financial resources, there were also a total of twenty-four amending acts to the Income Tax Act between 1922 and 1937 because income tax was one of the only ways that the provinces could increase their resource base.[22] The frequent changes proved to be a formidable challenge for foreign firms and kept a plethora of professional service providers (lawyers, accountants) in India busy.[23] The evolving Indian income tax, in its paragraph 42, gave the Indian authorities wide-ranging rights to tax foreigners.[24] While the letter of the law allowed taxation of any foreign exporter, the Government of India published instructions on how to apply it and clarified that the law targeted agencies in India that traded "in the country," not those trading

---

[17] S. B. Billimoria "Letter to W. E. Behrens," March 29, 1938, 330/1113, BA. The company Billimoria, founded in 1902, was Havero's tax advisor since 1926.

[18] For this rush to Indianize among the German companies in India, see Luitpold Schneider, "Letter to Dr. Weiss," March 9, 1939, 330/1117, BA

[19] Act. No. XXII of 1936. See, Central Legislature and Governor General of India, "Indian Companies (Amendment) Act, 1936." For analysis of the amendment also, Sen Gupta and Sen, *Indian Company Manual 1942*: 75.

[20] Varottil, "The Evolution of Corporate Law"; Misra, *Business, Race, and Politics*: 83–85. For a contemporary German perspective, see also "New Indian Company Law" [1938], Reorganization British India, 330/1112, BA.

[21] Sen Gupta and Sen, *Indian Company Manual 1942*: 223.

[22] For details, see Government of India Legislative Department, *Indian Income-Tax Act, 1922, as amended 1937*. Markovits, "Indian Business": 495–496. At the same time, it was also decided that for five years, part of the amount would stay with the Central Government to consolidate finance.

[23] Ambirajan, *Taxation*.

[24] Government of India Legislative Department, *Indian Income-Tax Act, 1922, as amended 1937*: 43.

merely "with the country." If there was no legal link between the Indian buyer and the foreigner, and if the buyer was himself liable for losses, the usual understanding was that it was trade "with the country." Yet, this determination laid with the Indian tax authorities.

In response to the dynamic legal and political situation, German companies made a deliberate effort to give their organizations a "more Indian look [Anstrich]."[25] While many German companies, such as Siemens and Krupp, were already registered as Indian companies, I. G. decided to replace its cloaking arrangement with Havero with three independent Indian companies, registered fully in India. These Indian companies would be taxed with not more than 15.63 percent income tax and 6.25 percent super tax flat rate, whereas a possible subsidiary of I. G. (one of the alternatives discussed) would run the risk of being progressively taxed with up to 43.75 percent super tax and would be forced to open its books. The three Indian companies – Agfa Photo Co., Ltd. (for photography products), Chemdyes, Ltd. (for chemicals and dyes) and Bayer Remedies, Ltd. (for pharmaceuticals) – were registered in December 1938 and took over all Havero activities on January 1, 1939.

Newly organized, the early months of 1939 were hopeful for several of the large German companies. The freshly restructured I. G. companies were well positioned to not only continue dominating the dyestuff market but also expand their market share in chemicals, pharmaceuticals, and photographic material. Similarly, Siemens proudly noted that "our organization is now in every respect ready for action."[26] Indian nationalists played into the German agenda by pushing for a revised foreign trade policy. The Federation of Indian Chambers of Commerce and Industry explicitly called for trade agreements with Germany, Italy, America, and Japan.[27]

To support the German companies in their efforts, several German businesspeople and the German Government together founded the Deutsche Indien Institut [German India Institute] in Bombay under the leadership of Georg Léon Leszczyński, with the goal of supporting economic and cultural cooperation between Germany and India. The institute was meant as a predecessor to a potential future German Chamber of Commerce in India.[28] It was officially founded in April 1938 and began its activities the following July.[29] Leszczyński, born 1896 in Berlin, had previously studied

---

[25] Dr Deissmann, "Memorandum about the Founding of Agfa India Ltd.," 1938, 3, Britisch-Indien VII, 330/1271, BA.
[26] Siemens (India), "Annual Report 1938/1939," August 8, 1939: 18, 8133/2, SAA.
[27] "India's Foreign Trade," Times of India, April 11, 1939: 8.
[28] Sauvage, "Letter to Waibel," December 2, 1938, 330/442, BA.
[29] Ibid.

oriental languages and law in Berlin and Munich and then worked as an interpreter at the German Legation in Kabul.[30] In 1929 and 1930, he was a journalist for the Associated Press of America and specialized in the countries of East Asia, which he visited frequently. From the mid-1930s he was in India for the Associated Press and the Deutsche Nachrichten-büro [German News Agency], the official news agency of Nazi Germany. While little is known about Leszczyński's political affiliations, he entertained some relationship with Vinayak Damodar Savarkar, a militant Hindu seeking collaboration with the totalitarian regimes in Europe.[31]

German politicians also became more actively involved in establishing relations with the Indian business elite. In the spring of 1939, the former German Minister of Economics and former President of the Reichsbank, Hjalmar Schacht, visited India and the *Times of India* speculated that he "will establish contacts with Indian business men and endeavor to commit them to some form of economic agreement with Germany."[32] Schacht arrived in Bombay in April 1939. He attended a cocktail party organized by J. R. D. Tata in his honor at the Hotel Taj Mahal, where he met the President of the Indian Chamber of Commerce, Mehta, and the President of the East India Cotton Association, Purshotamdas Thakurdas, as well as several mill owners, industrialists, and TISCO directors. Also among the invited guests were political figures, such as the Prime Ministers of the princely states of Hyderabad and Baroda, the Finance Minister of Jaipur, the Managing Director of the Imperial Bank of India, and the Governor of the Reserve Bank of India.[33] Schacht then toured Delhi, Lahore, Simla, Calcutta, Rangoon, Madras, Salem, and Bangalore. In South India, he was invited to a tea ceremony organized by C. Rajam, an industrialist of great standing, allowing him to socialize with the business leaders of the region.[34] Congress politician and member of the Legislative Assembly Satyamurti stressed in his speech to him that, "[n]ot just today, but also in the future, when India will be a free country, will India and Germany stay friends."[35] Schacht then went on to visit the princely state of Mysore, where he was invited to the Maharajah's

[30] Frankfurter Allgemeine Zeitung, "Georg L. Leszczyński": 30–31. "Peace Move in Afghanistan," 19 February 1929: 10.
[31] Casolari, "Hindutva's Foreign Tie-Up in the 1930s": 225.
[32] "Indian Foreign Trade," *Times of India*, April 11, 1939: 8.
[33] German General Consulate Bombay, "Letter to Foreign Office Berlin," April 18, 1939, 104777, PA. See also, "Dr. Schacht Arrives in Bombay," *Times of India*, April 11, 1939: 10.
[34] Schacht, *My First Seventy-Six Years*: 404.
[35] In German translation in: Dr Malik, "Note on the impression of Schacht's speech in Madras on the Indian press and the Indian leaders," June 12, 1939, 104777, PA; "Letter German Consulate General Calcutta to Foreign Office," June 19, 1939, 104777, PA

birthday party. Throughout his trip, Schacht refrained from commenting on the political situation in Nazi Germany and deflected journalists with humor and his insistence on being a tourist.

Schacht's "tourism" avoided a direct confrontation with Indian critics who closely observed Nazi Germany's military activities. After the Nazis occupied the Sudetenland in September 1938 and Czechoslovakia in March 1939, it became very difficult to do business in India. Both events were closely observed by the Indian media and triggered, once again, anti-German protests.[36] "[A]ll the newspapers (and especially the vernacular papers) drew the attention of the public in very big headlines to the grave situation in Europe (Czechoslovakian trouble) ... and the great danger of war," reported Havero already in May 1938.[37] In the fall of 1938, after the Sudeten Crisis and the transfer of the Sudetenland to the German Reich, I. G.'s Indian dyestuff department reported a "rush for goods" from the mills in response to the political situation. "[E]verybody is tense with apprehension" and there is an "acute state of nervousness prevailing among our mill friends."[38] The company attempted to deliver as promptly as possible "to counter-act the many and partly fantastic rumors in circulation as to our ability or otherwise to continue business and so as not to impair the old friendly relations."[39] In contrast to the mills, which were hording goods, the bazaar business was considered dull and "the unsettled international situation has had no stimulating effect on the market."[40] While the initial reaction to war rumors was mostly targeted at securing goods, in the following months anti-German sentiments also increased. In April 1939, the new locally-incorporated Chemdyes reported that the political tensions in Europe were used as propaganda against it. "Posters like 'Boycott German goods, otherwise you assist aggression and Nazism' and propaganda in Cinemas as well as Newspaper Campaigns influence our activities to a great deal. The customers are always reminded by English firms (ICI included) that in case of war preference of deliveries would be given to those firms who previously covered their demands with them."[41] In August 1939, Siemens similarly found that "our customers were publicly and officially warned not to hire German firms because of

---

[36] Siemens (India), "Annual Report 1938/1939," August 8, 1939: 5, 8133/2, SAA.
[37] Havero, "Weekly Minutes No. 535, Meeting on May 27, 1938," 8128–9782 (1 of 2), BArch-B. Underlined in the original.
[38] Havero, "Weekly Minutes No. 541, General Meeting on September 2, 1938," 8128–9782 (1 of 2), BArch-B.
[39] Ibid.
[40] Ibid.
[41] Chemdyes, "Excerpt of letter to Dr. W. Behrens," April 5, 1939, Chemdyes Ltd. Bombay, British India, 1938–1940, 330/1117, BA.

the danger of war."[42] Those that decided regardless for a contract with a German manufacturer demanded bank guarantees for their down payments, which made regular business very difficult.[43] There could be no more doubt that a military conflict was looming.

Heading into War

World War II began with the German invasion of Poland on September 1, 1939. Two days later Britain and France declared war on Germany. On September 16, 1939, the *Times of India* reported that about thirty firms in Bombay alone were under suspicion of being enemy firms and were put under the control of the Deputy Controller of Enemy Firms. These included the three newly formed companies of I. G. Farben (Agfa, Bayer Remedies, and Chemdyes), the Siemens (India) and Krupp (India) organizations, as well as several other German firms. On October 18, the Government of India announced that it had sequestrated Siemens, Krupp, and Bayer Remedies as enemy firms.[44] Agfa was also exposed as an enemy firm after a short delay.[45] However, no decision was yet taken regarding the more successfully cloaked Chemdyes.

Only three months later, Bayer Remedies officially closed shop and offered its "show cases with electric fittings for window display and museum purposes" for sale.[46] One of Bayer's shareholders speculated that the German nationality of the leading managers and the fact that one of them, Oswald Urchs, was suspicious as "Nazi politician" may have led the controller to his decision despite the cloaking structure that should have protected Bayer Remedies.[47] Bayer's remaining medicinal goods were sold at fixed prices through dealers and directly from the Bombay office of the German company.[48] Like Bayer Remedies, Siemens (India) was swiftly expropriated. Parts of it were sold piecemeal by the Custodian of Enemy Property. The Indian company Lakhiprasad Loknath & Co. first leased and then purchased the workshop of Siemens (India) in Calcutta, which was "considered to be one of the best electrical workshops in Calcutta."[49]

---

[42] Siemens (India), "Annual Report 1938/1939," August 8, 1939: 5, 8133.2, SAA.
[43] Ibid.
[44] "Enemy Firms Taken Over," *Times of India*, October 19, 1939: 12. See also, Consulate General of Switzerland, Bombay (Sonderegger), "Letter to Swiss Legation, Special Division, London," November 2, 1939, R/40601, PA.
[45] "Note British India," November 8, 1939, 9/K/1/2, BA.
[46] "Classified Ad," *Times of India*, December 23, 1939: 4.
[47] G. M. Fritze, "Letter to C. A. Caroe," December 23, 1939, 9/K/1/2, BA.
[48] "Bayer Medicines," *Times of India*, June 13, 1940: 5.
[49] "Classified Ad," *Times of India*, April 2, 1945; The Engineering Association of India, *Indian Engineering Industries*: 311.

However, not all German companies closed their doors immediately. To allow business to continue, some managers shifted responsibility to their Indian employees at the outbreak of the conflict. Krupp's manager gave his trusted auditor P. C. Hansotia, a Parsee, power of attorney for Krupp's business, until the company was formally expropriated.[50] Siemens (India) had a Swiss employee continue working with the Custodian until June 1940, when he was categorized as "German-friendly" and asked to leave the country.[51] Most of these arrangements to continue business during wartime were temporary.

One exception was the (successfully cloaked) Chemdyes, which came under the control of the Controller of Enemy Firms but was able to continue its business. The chemical department was managed by a Dutch citizen who had previously acted as head of the dyestuff department in Madras. Because several companies requested it, Chemdyes was granted permission to (partly) fulfill orders made before the war. "It is gathered that millowners and others will be able to get during the week supplies equivalent to about 25 per cent. of their orders."[52] For the rest of the year 1939, the Controller of Enemy Firms had a dedicated office at Chemdyes with a staff of four to five who approved transactions. The salaries of the controlling staff were paid by Chemdyes, not the Government of India. Most of the Chemdyes offices in other parts of the country were closed; except for the ones in Calcutta, Madras, and Karachi, which were managed by Indians but also needed approval by the Controller for every business transaction they undertook.[53] Despite these limitations, Chemdyes' profits increased significantly and beyond anyone's expectations because prices shot up after the outbreak of the war. The management of the chemical business, which had mostly incurred losses in the 1930s (see Table 5.4, page 154), had optimistically anticipated a net profit of Rs 600,000 for the year; the actual profit was closer to Rs 1.6 million[54]

In January 1940, Chemdyes' biggest competitor, the British company ICI, made an effort to convince the British-Indian authorities to expropriate Chemdyes, thus trying to eliminate a big competitor and potentially make its assets, employees, and customer information available to ICI. The director of ICI (India) traveled to Delhi himself and met with government representatives to ask them for a closer investigation of

[50] Report Steffens, "Kitco Bombay," January 30, 1947, 51/5059, WA, HAK.
[51] Siemens, "Report about Interned Employees in British India," undated [1940], 330/596, BA.
[52] "Enemy Firms in Bombay," *Times of India*, October 3, 1939: 5; "Chemdyes Limited: Marketing of Existing Stocks Allowed," *Times of India*, October 4, 1939: 12.
[53] "Note re Chemdyes Ltd.," January 11, 1940, 330/1117, BA.
[54] Ibid.

Chemdyes as a potential enemy firm. However, they informed him that no conclusive connection to Germany had been established so far. Subsequently, ICI reached out to Chemdyes' shareholders – most of them Dutch nationals – and proposed to buy their shares. However, I. G. Farben was able to convince its Dutch strawmen to hold on to their shares.[55]

It was only after the German occupation of the Netherlands in May 1940 that the British Indian Government eventually expropriated Chemdyes and declared the company an enemy firm. Just before sequestration of its property, Chemdyes had sold larger stocks to its various Indian dealers, with a gentlemen's agreement that the proceeds should be held available for future business.[56] In July, the Deputy Custodian of Enemy Property called for sealed tenders for the purchase of Chemdyes. He requested of any potential buyer to be "unconnected with any enemy dye industry and entirely independent of the existing management of Chemdyes," while at the same time being "technically competent to carry on … the business."[57] Thus, the company was offered exclusively to British or Indian competitors of the German company. In September, the Custodian announced that ICI (India) had purchased Chemdyes' remaining assets and liabilities.[58] Despite this outcome, I. G. Farben considered its cloaking of Chemdyes a success because it allowed the company to continue a very profitable business until mid-1940.

By October 1940, seventy-six German firms and forty-one Italian ones were expropriated and under control of the Custodian of Enemy Property. The head office of the Custodian, located in Bombay, had a staff of about seventy people at this time. Under the Custodian served two Deputy Custodians, one in Bombay and one in Calcutta, the two cities with the largest population of German businesspeople before the war (see Table 6.2). Two Assistant Custodians in Madras and Lahore, as well as several inspectors at major ports, completed the organization. The Custodian had the mandate to carry on the business of the sequestrated firms and recover any debts due to the enemy. The organization was financed by a 2 percent charge on all proceeds of the sale of enemy property.[59]

While the process of expropriating German assets took some time, German nationals residing in India were arrested almost immediately after the outbreak of the war. The very night that Britain and France declared war on Germany, on September 3, 1939, German nationals were interned as

[55] "Our Sales Organization Abroad Until the War," undated [after May 1940], Directorate Chemicals, 330/1088, BA.
[56] "Confiscation and Liquidation of I.G. (Buyback)," November 25, 1957, 381/065, BA.
[57] "Notice: Purchase of Assets of Chemdyes Limited," *Times of India*, July 22, 1940: 10.
[58] "Assets of Chemdyes," *Times of India*, September 3, 1940: 4; "Press Communique," September 2, 1940, published in: *The Calcutta Gazette*, October 3, 1940: 450.
[59] Special Correspondent, "Enemy Property," *Times of India*, October 25, 1940: 52.

enemy aliens once again, twenty-five years after the World War I internment.[60] In most parts of India, all male Germans were arrested, even if
they were Jews who had previously fled to India to escape persecution
in Germany. The only exception was the province of Calcutta, where
Jews remained free for the time being.[61] Approximately 900 men were
brought either directly to the camp at Ahmednagar, or via smaller camps,
such as Fort William in Calcutta.[62] In hindsight, Oswald Urchs, who was
also detained, remarked that "[t]he comfortable and secured life of these
people changed abruptly on the day of the internment."[63]

The first internment camp was situated once again in Ahmednagar.
Given the previous history of this camp during both the Boer War and
World War I, some Germans experienced a déjà vu upon arrival "at
the exact same spot where the old German prisoners of war were held
25 years ago."[64] While all Germans interned during World War I had
returned to Germany after the war, some later came back to India to
engage once more in business there. The most unfortunate individuals,
such as Sydney Schüder (born 1893) who came to India for Schering,
were interned twice at Ahmednagar, once during World War I and again
during World War II.[65] The Germans were brought to Ahmednagar by
train. Upon arrival, they had to walk from the train station to the camp
over a distance of approximately 8 kilometers (4.9 miles), which became
one of the often-reported events of the internment experience. Similar
to World War I, some internees again highlighted the embarrassment of
being supervised by "colored" (Sikh) soldiers. Otto Zimmer, the commercial attaché, stressed that "in the Indian context this [being supervised by Sikhs] is a massive humiliation for the Europeans."[66]

Unlike during World War I, German multinationals reacted swiftly to
the new internment situation. Both Siemens and I.G. Farben collected

[60] Overseas HR Department, "Report on Employees Abroad," undated, 8149, SAA.
[61] G. Schoberth, "Report about Living Conditions of Germans in Calcutta During the
First Nine Month of the War," November 5, 1940, 330/596, BA.
[62] Pazze, "Report," October 24, 1939, 330/596, BA; Schoberth, G., "Report about
Living Conditions of Germans in Calcutta During the First Nine Month of the War,"
November 5, 1940, 330/596, BA; Weingarten, "German Internees in the Far East,"
October 24, 1939, Office Waibel, 330/443, BA.
[63] Urchs, "Beobachtungen eines Lagerarztes": 181.
[64] Ibid.
[65] Schüder spent 1916 to 1920 in internment at Ahmednagar and was arrested again in
1939. Schüder, "Letter [recipient undisclosed]," November 17, 1939, Southeast Asia
Internees, 330/596, BA; Office Waibel, "List of internees in British India," July 3, 1941,
and enclosed list of all internees in British India who receive Orient Verein support,
German Internees in the Far East, 330/443, BA.
[66] Zimmer, "Report about the Events in Bombay Since Outbreak of the War," November
7, 1939, German Civil Internees in India, R/41819, PA.

information about their internees, stayed in close contact with their families, and shared all available eyewitness reports with them as well as with
other companies and the Foreign Office. First reports came from those
employees who were not German nationals, such as the Italian citizen
Peter Pazze of Chemdyes or the Swiss national Gustav Schoberth of
Siemens, who were able to return to Germany.[67]

As early as September 1939, German businesses back home coordinated their support activities in a "Special Committee for the Assistance
of Interned German Nationals in British India" in close cooperation with
the Foreign Office and the Nazi Party's Foreign Organization.[68] The Committee was an initiative of the German Orient Association, originally established in 1934 to support German business in the region, and headed by
Hermann Waibel, who had been a management board member of I. G.
Farben since 1928 and an expert for East Asian trade.[69] The committee's
first meeting was held on September 29, 1939 in Berlin and included representatives of I. G. Farben, Siemens, AEG, Krupp, Schering-Kahlbaum,
and Hansa India. They discussed a support scheme and planned for a letter
to be sent to all German firms with business in India to collect financial aid.
The letter highlighted that the scheme had nothing to do with charity but
rather would guarantee that the employees were available to reconstruct
German business in India after the war, highlighting the need for a long-
term strategy that could bridge politically turbulent times.[70]

While the affected companies in Germany debated possible support
schemes, businesspeople, who had experienced internment in India during World War I, lobbied for more engagement. C. W. Kuehns of the
Hamburg-based rubber company Phoenix addressed Hermann Waibel
directly. Reflecting on the entire quarter-century since the last internment he argued, "[i]t has been hard enough after the previous war to get
back onto foreign markets, and if we don't show our employees abroad
a warm heart, we later won't find anyone anymore who is willing to go
abroad to represent German interests."[71] To lobby for more systematic

[67] Pazze, "Report," October 24, 1939, 330/596, BA (Peter Pazze was born in Trieste
and worked since 1921 for Havero/I.G. Farben.) Schoberth, "Report about Living
Conditions of Germans in Calcutta during the First Nine Months of the War,"
November 5, 1940, 330/596, BA.
[68] "Note for files," January 10, 1944, Southeast Asia Internees, 330/596, BA; Orient
Verein, "Minutes of Orient Verein," September 29, 1939, Office Waibel, German
Internees in the Far East, 330/443, BA.
[69] Orient Verein, "Account Statement of the Orient Verein," 1939, R/61364, PA; For the
origins of the association see, "Trade Relations between India and Germany," 1934,
R/245171, 50–55, PA.
[70] Orient Verein, "Letter to German firms," September 30, 1939, R/41819, PA.
[71] C. W. Kuehns, "Letter to Waibel," September 13, 1939, 330/596, BA.

support, C. W. Kuehns, together with two other previous internees in India, Hans E. B. Kruse and C. Mensendieck, wrote an official letter to the Foreign Office appealing to the long-term strategy.

Again, as in 1914, after 25 years, German managers, engineers, chemists, and technicians are interned as prisoners of war in Ahmednagar. ... We all want that after the victorious war, patriotic, courageous young Germans go abroad again as commercial pioneers. How can we ever count on precious men to take this risk, if their home country cannot support them in times of need.[72]

Based on archival sources from different corporate and German Government archives, a database could be constructed with basic information on 361 of the World War II internees who worked for German companies in India, including details of their age, education, position in the company, marital status, and careers.[73] The total number of internees in Indian camps varied quite considerably, from c. 900 (at the first internment in September 1939) to 324 (according to the list of Swiss authorities in May 1940, after the temporary release of most Jews and missionaries) and 604 (according to a German Foreign Office report of August 1941, including a number of newly captured German sailors and the reinterned Jews and missionaries who had remained in India).[74]

---

[72] Mensendieck, C., Kruse, H. and Kuehns, C., "Letter to the Foreign Office Berlin," February 22, 1940, R/127689, PA. Hans E. B. Kruse went for Wiechers & Helm to Karachi in 1913 and spent five years in internment during World War I. Kruse, *Wagen*: 10–11.

[73] The data was collected based on Orient Verein and Waibel, "Letter to Foreign Office (Kundt)," October 7, 1939, and enclosed list of confirmed payments for support scheme with number of internees per firm, total: 102; Kaufmaennischer Ausschuss, "I. G. Farben employees in enemy countries," January 29, 1940, Office of the "Kaufmaennische Ausschuss" Berlin NW 7, Southeast Asia Internees, 330/596, BA; "List of confirmed payments for support scheme with number of internees per firm," [undated, c. February 1940], total: 232 internees, 330/596, BA; Orient Verein, "Letter to members of the Special Committee," April 3, 1941, and enclosed list of internees in British-India as identified by Foreign Office (May 14, 1940), total: 324, 330/596, BA; German Foreign Office, "Third Report about the Conditions of Germans in British-India and Ceylon," January 1941, total: 505 (September 1940), German Civil Internees in British India, R/14820, PA; Siemens HR Department, "Report 'Our Internees overseas'," 10 February 1940, and list of Siemens internees, January 15, 1941, total: 43, HR Statistics, 8149, SAA; Office Waibel, "List of internees in British India," July 3, 1941, and enclosed list of all internees in British India who receive Orient Verein support, total: 243, German Internees in the Far East, 330/443, BA; German Foreign Office, "Fourth Report about the Conditions of Germans in British-India and Ceylon," September 1941, total: 604 (August 11, 1941), German Civil Internees in British India, R/14821, PA.

[74] Paul Sauvage, "Letter [recipient undisclosed]," June 26, 1942, Office Waibel, German Internees in the Far East, 330/443, BA; German Foreign Office, "Fourth Report about the Conditions of Germans in British-India and Ceylon," September 1941, total: 604 (August 11, 1941), German Civil Internees in British India, R/14821, PA.

Information on age was available for 236 (65 percent) of the 361 internees with the average being 34.45 years. Marital status could be identified for 229 (63 percent). The group split evenly between husbands (111, 48.5 percent) and bachelors (118, 51.5 percent). The internees worked for a variety of German companies (see Table 6.1). The biggest employers were I. G. Farben (fifty-one internees), Siemens (thirty-six), and Krupp (fourteen).

Table 6.1 *Companies of German internees, 1939*

Company	Number of Internees	Percentage of Total
I. G. Farben	51	21.5
Siemens	36	15.2
Krupp	14	5.9
Polysius AG	12	5.1
AEG	10	4.2
Voith	8	3.4
Hansa India	6	2.5
Lohmann & Co.	6	2.5
Schering AG	6	2.5
Robert Bosch GmbH	5	2.1
Dr. C. Otto & Co. GmbH	4	1.7
MAN	4	1.7
Maschinenfabrik Sack GmbH	4	1.7
Carl Zeiss	3	1.3
Christian Poggensee	3	1.3
Daimler Benz	3	1.3
Damag AG	3	1.3
Deutsche Dampfschiff Ges. Hansa	3	1.3
Fritz Haeuser AG	3	1.3
Himalaja Expedition	3	1.3
Maschinenfabrik Buckau	3	1.3
Merck	3	1.3
Miag	3	1.3
Allianz	2	0.8
Auto-Union	2	0.8
Continental	2	0.8
Deutsche Akademie in Muenchen	2	0.8
Hugo Schneider AG	2	0.8
L. & C. Steinmueller	2	0.8
Lederfabrik Max Schneider	2	0.8
Maschinenfabrik Wagner-Doerries	2	0.8
Mannesmann	2	0.8
Tata Iron Steel	2	0.8
Bamag-Meguin	1	0.4
Beiersdorf	1	0.4

Table 6.1 (*cont.*)

Company	Number of Internees	Percentage of Total
Boehme Fettchemie	1	0.4
Bombay Talkies	1	0.4
C. F. Boehringer & Sohn GmbH	1	0.4
D.O.V. Eildienst	1	0.4
Deutsches Kali-Syndikat	1	0.4
Dr. Madaus & Co.	1	0.4
Elektrizitaetsgesellschaft Sanitas	1	0.4
F. H. Schule GmbH	1	0.4
Francke-Werke	1	0.4
H. C. Mueller & Co.	1	0.4
Hallesche Maschinenfabrik	1	0.4
Kistenmacher & Co.	1	0.4
Klein, Schanzlin & Becker AG	1	0.4
Maschinenbau & Bahnbedarf	1	0.4
Rheinmetall Borsig	1	0.4
Salge-Buehler GmbH	1	0.4
Schimmel & Co.	1	0.4
Stahlunion Export	1	0.4
Times of India	1	0.4
Total	237	100

Database by author.

Of the 236 internees for whom an educational background or position was given, the vast majority were salespeople (eighty-eight) and engineers (forty-eight) followed by technicians and mechanics (eighteen). Most German nationals resided in Bombay (ninety-three) and Calcutta (fifty-six) followed by Madras (seventeen), Jamshedpur (ten), where the Tata Iron and Steel Company (TISCO) was located, and Lahore (ten). While the concentration in the big commercial centers of India is not surprising, it is interesting to note that German businesspeople did not exclusively live in these areas but rather spread out over the vast Indian subcontinent, with one or two representatives of German firms present in many smaller cities in India (see Table 6.2).

For 183 internees (50.7 percent), the sources reveal when they first arrived in India. On average they had spent 3.78 years in the country prior to their internment. The veteran was the technician Otto Engelmann of I. G. Farben (born 1902) who first came to India in 1924. A total of forty-one businesspeople had arrived only a few months prior to being arrested. The internees also varied according to political leaning, which was reflected in

Table 6.2 *Last residence in India of German internees, 1939*

City	Number of Internees with Last Residence in This City
Bombay	93
Calcutta	56
Madras	17
Jamshedpur	10
Lahore	10
Dalmia Dadri	6
Delhi	5
Cawnpore	4
Ahmedabad	3
Ahmednagar	3
Bhadravati	3
Rangoon	3
Trichinopoly	3
Bangalore	2
Burnpur	2
Himalaya	2
Purwa Hiraman	2
Bhavnagar / Kathiawar	1
Bhopal	1
Chetak	1
Coimbatore	1
Curaru	1
Funalur	1
Karachi	1
Karur Taluk	1
Kevachi	1
Sagauli	1
Senares	1
Total	**235**

Database by author.

the structure of the internment camp. The camp was divided in A and B camp. At the A camp, prisoners paid Rs 3 (c. 23 British pence) daily for better food and accommodation.[75] Internally, the B camp was considered the "Nazi camp," with the argument that not paying any money to the British was a contribution to Germany's war efforts.[76]

[75] Schoberth, "Report about living conditions of Germans in Calcutta during the first nine month of the war," November 5, 1940, 330/596, BA; Osten, "Report," April 29, 1940, Southeast Asia Internees, 330/596, BA.
[76] Koppers, *Geheimnisse des Dschungels*: 198.

German women were not interned but had to live within much more moderate means. They started combining households to cut down on their living expenses.[77] They lived off their savings, some support money, and the earnings from selling furniture and household items.[78] The British-Indian intelligence bureau, jointly run by the India Office and the Government of India, suspected some of them of engaging in espionage and spreading propaganda. "[W]ith the internment of their men-folk, German women in this country are finding scope for intelligence work."[79] In particular Oswald Urchs' wife Therese was said to exercise control over other German women and collect information on the political leanings of their partners, which she reported back to her husband in internment.[80]

At the camp, a commission of British officials started interrogating each individual internee to determine their level of support for the Nazi government. As a consequence, between December 1939 and March 1940, approximately 600 Jews were released from internment.[81] The Jewish Relief Association, founded in 1934 in Bombay, had lobbied with the Government of India to free the Jewish internees and also provided them support during internment. By May 1940, the official list of the Swiss authorities counted 324 internees, of whom 220 had been identified by German companies as their employees.[82] Some observers speculated that the Commission's additional purpose was to identify which links German businesspeople had to Indian nationalist circles and how close these relationships were.[83] By the end of May and in early June, as the war intensified, the British authorities reinterned many of the formerly released and put women and children under house arrest. By September, the number of German nationals in Ahmednagar rose

---

[77] Orient Verein, "Letter (recipient undisclosed)," January 29, 1940, Office Waibel, German Internees in the Far East, 330/443, BA.

[78] Kopp, "Report Mrs. Kopp (Siemens), in letter by Foreign Office to Waibel," May 9, 1940, Southeast Asia Internees, 330/596, BA.

[79] Public and Judicial Dept., "Survey No. 30 of 1939 for the week ending 9th December, 1939," IOR/L/PJ/12 1913–1947: 184, APAC; on propaganda see also, "Survey No. 32 of 1939 for the week ending 30th December, 1939," IOR/L/PJ/12 1913–1947: 201, APAC.

[80] Public and Judicial Dept., "Survey No. 30 of 1939 for the week ending 9th December, 1939," 184, IOR/L/PJ/12 1913–1947, APAC.

[81] Schoberth, "Report about Living Conditions of Germans in Calcutta during the First Nine months of the War," November 5, 1940, 330/596, BA.

[82] P. Sauvage, "Letter [recipient undisclosed]," June 26, 1942, Office Waibel, German Internees in the Far East, 330–443, BA.

[83] "Anonymous report enclosed to letter Kuehns to Waibel," March 25, 1941, Southeast Asia Internees, 330/596, BA. Tucher, *Nationalism*: 113.

again to 505. In February 1941, German internees were transferred from Ahmednagar to the interim camp Deolali, 150 kilometers (93 miles) east of Bombay. The conditions in the much smaller camp Deolali were significantly worse than in Ahmednagar. As a consequence, the internees went on a hunger strike, which lasted 112 hours.[84] In October 1941, and in response to their protests and the complaints by Swiss and German authorities, the internees were transferred once more to the newly established central internment camp Dehra Dun, 200 kilometers (124 miles) northeast of New Delhi, near the Himalayas. In January 1942, approximately 2,000 internees from the Dutch East Indies joined the group at the Dehra Dun camp, increasing the overall number of prisoners approximately by a factor of five.

One interesting but so far underexplored aspect of the internment experience is the longer-term effect it had on collaborative business endeavors.[85] Almost all German businessmen in the region were forcefully brought together in Dehra Dun. This created a window of opportunity for creating networks which outlasted the war. The 300–400 German businessmen in India had close social ties as a comparatively small expat community. The internment experience reinforced those ties. Wives and children, who initially remained free, eventually started to share households to make ends meet and thus built very close relationships with each other, which continued into the post-war period. Interestingly, internment in India also created inter-generational ties beyond the group of people sharing the barracks at the same time. Internees from World War I, when hearing about the renewed internment in India, organized and lobbied for support with both German employers and the German authorities. They stressed the importance of ongoing company support especially in India, where skilled labor was scarce. Social connections persisted among the internees and their supporters. In this way, internment created a tight-knit community of businesspeople with experience and interest in India, which survived well into the post-war era (see Chapter 7).

Allies in Arms

While German businesspeople struggled with internment in India, political alliances between Germany and India experienced a revival during the

---

[84] Urchs, "Beobachtungen eines Lagerarztes": 188.
[85] For a first exploration see, Lubinski, Giacomin, and Schnitzer, "Internment."

war.[86] The above-mentioned Indian nationalist Subhas Bose, who was to play a crucial role in the Indo-German partnership, wrote about the outbreak of the war: "The much expected crisis had at last come. This was India's golden opportunity."[87] Similar to the high-flying expectations during World War I, he and other activists focused their energy once more on how to capitalize on the war to achieve their ultimate goal; Independence.

For the Germans, many of the motives for collaborating with Indian nationalists were the same as in World War I. The belief was that supporting uprisings in India might prove advantageous in the military conflict with Great Britain, which is why propaganda activities were considered crucial. More importantly though, German politicians and business leaders alike were also planning for a post-war future, thinking about possible ways to preserve goodwill with the Indian public, maintain relations with business partners and employees, and develop long-term strategies for the Indian market. The experience of World War I and the painful re-entry into the Indian market (see Chapter 4) had highlighted for them the importance of such activities.

The alliance with Subhas Bose formed the core of Germany's propaganda activities in India.[88] Bose was one of the most prominent Bengali nationalists and at the same time intimately familiar with Germany and its political landscape. After having received medical treatment in Vienna in 1933, he married his secretary, Austrian national Emilie Schenkl, and made repeated visits to Central Europe.[89] In Vienna, he co-founded the Indisch-Zentraleuropäische Gesellschaft [Indian Central-European Society] with the aim to foster India's economic development.[90] In 1938 and 1939, Bose acted as president of the Congress Party and supported autarky and self-governance for India, even if that meant a violent uprising against the British. In his speech at the opening of the annual session of the Congress Party in 1939, he articulated an ultimatum to Britain to concede all India's "national demands." He added that the time has come "for a major assault on British Imperialism."[91]

---

[86] For details on Indo-German relations during World War II, see Hauner, *India in Axis Strategy*.

[87] Bose, *The Indian Struggle (1935–1942)*: 28.

[88] For the extensive literature on Subhas Bose and his activities in Germany before and during World War II, see Bose, *His Majesty's Opponent*; Hayes, *Subhas Chandra Bose*; Hauner, *India in Axis Strategy*; Kuhlmann, *Subhas Chandra Bose*.

[89] Bose et al., *Letters to Emilie Schenkl*.

[90] Together with Otto Faltis, Pulverfabrik Skodawerke-Wetzler A.G. and Österreichische Dynamit Nobel Aktiengesellschaft. Otto Faltis, "Letter to Adolf Hitler," September 1, 1938, 104777, PA. For a review of the Society's activities see also, Faltis, "India."

[91] "Indian Ultimatum: President of Congress Threatens Sanctions," *The Western Morning News and Daily Gazette*, March 11, 1939: 9.

After Bose resigned from his Congress leadership in April 1939, following differences with Gandhi and other prominent politicians, he started engaging more actively for a collaboration with foreign powers. In India, he had been arrested by the British and was placed under house arrest because he had organized a mass protest in Calcutta, which violated an assembly law. After several months, he clandestinely escaped from Indian in 1940 and traveled to Berlin in 1941, where he reached out to the German Foreign Office.[92] Bose wrote a first memorandum about his plans for Indo-German cooperation in April 1941.[93] He argued that the Indian nation was hostile towards Great Britain and actively interested in contributing to its demise. Bose detailed different types of activities that could support this goal, including (radio) propaganda in India but also the establishment of a free Indian exile government, preferably situated in Berlin, and a variety of sabotage acts directed against Britain. Evaluating the proposal, the head of the political department of the Foreign Office, Ernst Woermann, concluded that while many of the ideas were indeed practical and deserved support, he would not want to officially make India's Independence one of Germany's goals and thus would restrain from accepting the Indian exile government. He was less concerned about Bose's request for financial support, which he agreed to grant "generously."[94]

That Bose's contributions to Germany's propaganda activities in India were invaluable was never in doubt for the German officials. Nazi propaganda was widespread in India just before and during World War II. The German Government organized radio broadcasts and published a newspaper in Hindi. Thanks to Bose's engagement, in 1942, the Germans had one hour of broadcast time in three Indian languages (Hindi, Bengali, and Mahrati) and were discussing extending airtime further.[95] A group of Indian activists in Berlin worked with Bose to prepare the propaganda material.[96]

Bose's propaganda skillfully built on earlier narratives of Indian and Aryan heritage, which he depicted as superior to British civilization,

---

[92] Bose's disappearance was widely reported in the British press. See, "Released Indian Leader Missing," *The Evening Telegraph*, January 27, 1941: 5; "Released Indian Leader Mystery," *Gloucestershire Echo*, January 27, 1941: 1; "Warrant for Arrest of Subhas Bose," *Aberdeen Press and Journal*, January 28, 1941: 1.

[93] "Memorandum Subhas Chandra Bose," Berlin, April 9, 1941, reprinted in: Auswärtiges Amt, *Akten zur deutschen auswärtigen Politik, Band XII.2*: #300, 414–417.

[94] "Notes by Head of the Political Department Woermann," Berlin, April 12, 1941, reprinted in: ibid., #323, 439–440.

[95] "Letter to the German Minister for Propaganda re Reinforcement of the German India Propaganda," August 19, 1942, R 55/20822, BArch-B.

[96] Kuhlmann, *Subhas Chandra Bose*: 168–179.

challenging Britain's claim for a "civilizing mission" in India. At the occasion of Indian Independence Day in 1943, Bose gave a speech in Berlin, in which he detailed his counter-history:

To offer some kind of moral justification for the British domination and exploitation of India, British propagandists have depicted India as a land where there is no unity, where the people are eternally fighting among themselves and where the strong hand of Britain is necessary to maintain order and ensure progress. But these presumptuous Britishers conveniently forget that long before their fore-fathers knew anything about administration or national unity – in fact, long before the Romans came to Britain to teach culture and civilization to uncivilized Britons – India had not only an advanced culture and civilization – but a modern Empire.[97]

Encouraging his listeners to adopt a longer-term view, Bose argued that "India is a country where the past has not been forgotten," and where history is measured not in decades "but in thousands of years."[98] The British newspaper *The Observer* commented on Bose that "[h]e broadcasts viciously, urging the Indians to rise up and throw out the British. Backed by the German station 'free India Radio' ... his line has included the suggestion that Germany should have a large say in the future of an India emancipated from British influence."[99] Indeed, Bose frequently stressed that India was ready to "link up India's fight for freedom with the struggle of the Tripartite Powers against our old enemy, Britain."[100]

In addition to propaganda, Bose also engaged in forming an army out of Indian prisoners-of-war previously captured in Africa and held in Germany. Repeatedly he tried to convince the Axis powers to officially declare their support for India's Independence movement. While it seemed, in 1941, that he would succeed in this quest, in the end the German and Italian Government opted against such a public declaration.[101] In late May 1942, Bose did achieve a more symbolic goal: meeting Adolf Hitler face-to-face (Figure 6.1), a meeting he had requested for quite

[97] Subhas Chandra Bose's Speech on the Occasion of the Independence Day on January 26, 1943 in Berlin, "Haus der Flieger," reprinted in *Azad Hind: Monthly for a Free India*, issue 1 and 2, 1943: 14–23, quote: 15. The speech was published in the journal *Azad Hind*, which was created to popularize the Indian nationalist viewpoint outside of India and published all articles in both German and English. For details see, Kuhlmann, *Subhas Chandra Bose*: 230–232.
[98] Subhas Chandra Bose's Speech on the Occasion of the Independence Day on January 26, 1943 in Berlin, "Haus der Flieger," reprinted in *Azad Hind: Monthly for a Free India*, issue 1 and 2, 1943: 14–23, quote: 15.
[99] Tom Harrisson, "Radio," *The Observer*, August 23, 1942. See also, R 55/20822, BArch-B.
[100] Subhas Chandra Bose's Speech on the Occasion of the Independence Day on January 26, 1943 in Berlin, "Haus der Flieger," reprinted in *Azad Hind: Monthly for a Free India*, issue 1 and 2, 1943: 14–23, quote: 21.
[101] Kuhlmann, *Subhas Chandra Bose*: 149–152.

Figure 6.1 Subhas Bose meeting Adolf Hitler, 1942. Image by Heinrich Hoffmann, May–June 1942, 146-1970-070-01, BArch-B.

some time.[102] While Bose considered his invitation by Hitler a success, he was also disappointed in the course of the conversation, which yielded no tangible results.

In early 1943, Bose left Germany on a submarine to Japanese-held Sumatra. In October, he was able to announce to an assembly of 50,000 Indians abroad that Free India had formed a provisional government, which was officially recognized by the Japanese Government. Shortly thereafter, Germany and Italy also acknowledged Free India, making these countries some of the first in the world to recognize an Independent India even before it officially achieved Independence.[103] However, Bose's efforts to lead an Indian army against the British were ultimately unsuccessful. In late 1944 and early 1945, the British Indian army fought back the Japanese attack on India, which was supported by Bose's army, while Bose himself tried to escape. According to most accounts, he died aged forty-eight in a plane crash in Formosa (now Taiwan) in August 1945.

Planning Frenzy

As the war took its course, both German and Indian businesspeople engaged in planning activities for an uncertain future. After dealing with supporting their employees in internment, German businesses turned towards planning a potential postwar reentry into India, when they hoped to, once again, count on Indian cooperation. When the war first broke out, British colonial intelligence reports noted that the German firms made every attempt to showcase their respect for their Indian employees, not only so that they would "regard the Nazi regime with favor and ... speak well of it among their friends, a fact which has propaganda value"[104]; but also to potentially use them for their India business again. In April 1940, the I. G. management even debated the possibility of voluntarily liquidating Chemdyes because it would allow the company to place qualified staff with Indian companies, rather than having the British competitor ICI take them over. This might leave a door open to people rejoining Chemdyes (or a successor company) after the war or at least would turn them into important contacts in Indian companies.[105]

[102] "To Put It Briefly," *The Western Daily Press and Bristol Mirror*, May 30, 1942: 1.
[103] Kuhlmann, *Subhas Chandra Bose*: 312–313.
[104] "D I B's reports on activities of Germans, Italians and Japanese in India," IOR/L/PJ/12/506, File 1080(A)/36: July 1939–February 1940, Survey No. 19, APAC. For an example see, "Bombay Firm Gives Notice to Staff: Thousand Persons Affected," *Times of India*, September 27, 1939: 13.
[105] "Note about the meeting on April 4, 1940," Chemdyes Ltd. Bombay, 330–1117, BA.

As the war continued and the active business in India dwindled, attention shifted to the task of strategizing for the future. Importantly, managers now more fully articulated a strategy of collaborating with nationalist movements that had been emerging for many years. Leading managers of both Siemens and I. G. induced from past experiences a strategy, now explicit, which targeted countries with strong aspirations for economic independence. Only months before the outbreak of the war, Max Ilgner, member of the board of directors of I. G. Farben, discussed this strategy in a speech and subsequent publication titled "Increasing [German] Exports via Intervention in the Industrialization of the World." He looked back at "the last seventy years in the world" and concluded that those countries which industrialized intensively increased both their purchasing power and imports significantly and for that reason should be supported in their development, which would ultimately profit Germany's own export business.[106] Again turning to evidence from the past, Ilgner observed that "Germany's exports to developing countries ... grew particularly swiftly over the past years, while those to old industrial countries even decreased."[107] Ilgner asserted this represented a "new and modern epoch of the world economy in the age of nationalization and industrialization," in which all nations "will in the long-run pressure for independence." To him it was important to develop a partnership relationship with them, instead of insisting on exploitation. "The highly developed and independent country, which actively contributes to the expansion of possibilities [of less-developed countries] as a partner, will anchor its general and economic influence in the strongest way."[108] In this, Ilgner's analysis resembled the contemporaneous arguments by Indian nationalist Sarkar, who argued that from the perspective of Asia, the world powers will in the future be divided into colonial and noncolonial nations, with Germany being the latter.[109] Both Sarkar and Ilgner expressed their strategic considerations in relation to a mental map of nationalism that very clearly stressed a line between colonizers and noncolonizers in the context of many nation-states seeking independence from colonial rule.

To achieve such partnerships, Ilgner advocated studying the different markets of the world. This was best done by having businesspeople

[106] Ilgner, *Exportsteigerung*: 8.
[107] Ibid., 9.
[108] Ibid., 10.
[109] Sarkar, *Sociology*: 35.

travel to and stay in these countries, with the dual goal of, on the one hand, gathering information and, on the other hand, acquiring the skill to accurately evaluate reports about these markets. Ilgner was a strong proponent of sharing available information among all German firms and the German Government for the sake of pursuing the interest of the nation, understood in a List'ian sense as a collection of productive powers. He also suggested educating local employees and supporting German cultural institutions abroad to familiarize the local population with the German language and customs.[110]

Like Ilgner, Wolfram Eitel, an experienced Siemens manager, also turned the unwelcome break in international business into an opportunity for reflection. He looked back to find clues for future strategies and observed that World War I had given a strong impulse to building local industries in several overseas countries.[111] In his memo of 1944, Eitel started outlining a strategy, in which he observed that both British and North American companies were too hesitant to support the building of national industries: "Their policy had always been to rather exploit them in a colonial sense." By contrast, Siemens made every effort to seize the opportunity that the expansion of national industries offered. While this had been an ad hoc strategy, for example when Siemens pursued the Shannon Project in newly independent Ireland immediately after World War I, individual projects and single-country plans were now synthesized into a multi-country strategy. For Eitel, this included continuous investment in industrial training, in which many overseas countries had a special interest. Grooming foreign engineers would increase competition but at the same time familiarize locals with German technology and business, which eventually would benefit German firms. His observations and plans for the future considered a larger strategy for dealing with all formerly dependent territories. Eitel tentatively labeled them markets "with strong nationalist movements," stressing the characteristic that these countries had in common.

Both Ilgner's and Eitel's elaborations suggest the emergence of a broader and more explicit business strategy for countries with aspirations for self-determination. In both of their plans, a mental map of nationalism became visible that foregrounds the historical similarities between nations and their future aspirations as seen from a German perspective. They built on the premise that nations with a history of political and economic dependency on a highly industrialized country had common needs and aspirations that the German companies could exploit more

---

[110] Ilgner, *Exportsteigerung*.
[111] Eitel, October 1944, Siemens Overseas, 8188, SAA.

fully if they developed a joint political strategy for these markets. A unified strategy, moreover, allowed the German multinationals to use activities in one country for public relations in another, exploiting the fact that
the different markets with strong nationalist movements observed each
other in their progress and place in the world. They saw and evaluated
each other as part of a larger landscape of nationalisms.

In India, too, strategizing for the future fit the Zeitgeist. As previously
seen, anticolonialism provided a wide umbrella for many different versions of India's economic future. Even within the Congress, competing views existed, loosely bound together by the rallying cry Swadeshi,
which since the early twentieth century had served as a short-cut for anti-
imperialism and expansion of indigenous industry. Yet, by which tactics
this dual goal was to be achieved, remained to be determined.

The followers of Gandhi understood self-sufficiency to mean rejecting
industrialization and instead supporting cottage industries at the village
level. By contrast, the camp around Jawaharlal Nehru envisioned a future
in which India was self-sufficient precisely because it developed India's own
industry and became independent of foreign imports. Both blamed British
colonialism for their plight: Gandhians for the way it had imposed foreign
economic ideas on India, Nehruvians for preventing Indian industrialization. The National Planning Committee outlined an Indian economy and
its sizeable public sector orchestrating resources for the nation. The emerging vision of India's economic future suggested the goal of self-sufficiency,
paradoxically with the means of external input.[112] Rather than closing India
off to the world, it supported an open-door policy – yet one with a strict
bouncer. World War II diverted attention away from these efforts for a brief
moment, not least because the massive protest movement "Quit India" led
to the arrest of many of the Congress leaders in 1942.

Yet, this moment allowed the Indian business elite to articulate their
version of India's economic future, while simultaneously making sure that
they offered an alternative to the more radical ideas in circulation within
the Congress.[113] In the Bombay Plan, formally titled "A Brief Memorandum Outlining a Plan of Economic Development" of 1944, the industrialists J. R. D. Tata, G. D. Birla, Sri Ram, and Kasturbhai Lalbhai,
together with three technocrats, A. D. Shroff, Ardeshir Dalal, and John
Matthai, laid out their development agenda for India. Unlike the earlier
efforts, this business version of the future advocated for private ownership
for most industries, while accepting a strong planning state.[114]

---

[112] Engerman, *The Price of Aid*: 25–27.
[113] Chibber, *Locked in Place*: 85–98.
[114] Thakurdas et al., *Memorandum*. See also, Kudaisya, *Tryst with Prosperity*.

More importantly for the Indo-German relationship, the Bombay Plan also suggested trade and the support of international partners for India's industrialization, which was presented as the most urgent development goal. "Nothing has more seriously hindered the development of India's industrial resources during the war than the absence of these basic industries."[115] It was on these basic industries, specifically power, metallurgy (especially steel), engineering, chemicals, armaments, transport, and cement, that "the whole economic development of the country depends"; they needed to "be developed as rapidly as possible."[116]

Swift industrialization, in this view, required not only heavy public spending but also collaboration with more industrialized countries. The authors of the Bombay Plan made an argument for both. Inspired by Keynesian economics and List's idea of productive powers, they posited that there was nothing wrong with "creating" money if it increased "the productive capacity of the nation."[117] Similarly, they considered it unavoidable that "India will be dependent almost entirely on foreign countries for the machinery and technical skill necessary."[118] The Bombay Plan was a widely debated and highly influential corrective to earlier plans, now clearly stressing the goal of industrialization by means of collaborating with more industrialized partners in the world economy.

The many different, parallel, and competing ideas for India's future accentuated the inherent uncertainty of the tumultuous political economy. German political capabilities had evolved the strategies for cloaking and internment from short-term crisis management to long-term strategic planning, with an almost immediate emphasis on rebuilding the India business after the war. Yet, the experimental ideas for a strategy targeted at countries "with strong nationalist movements" remained fluid. These formerly or currently dependent countries, Siemens' manager Eitel and I. G. Farben's manager Ilgner argued, had common goals, ambitions, and needs, which they planned to address with a unified strategy; one that only emerged slowly out of several decades of engagement with nationalisms around the globe.

Such a larger strategy for economic nationalism made sense because the countries in question did not evaluate their fate and future in isolation but rather looked at the global landscape of nationalisms and their

---

[115] Thakurdas et al., *Memorandum*: 9 (section 5).
[116] Ibid., 31–32 (section 42–43).
[117] Ibid., 55 (section 85).
[118] Ibid., 51 (section 78).

place in it. India certainly made plans and evaluated its options for a postcolonial period, which seemed imminent to the leaders of the Congress and the business elite. Competing imagined futures shaped the rhetoric of the final war years. By the end of the war and with the British announcing an interim government under Nehru in 1946, swift industrialization by means of public spending and international trade emerged as pillars of a plan for India's economic development.

7   Stability in a Wobbly World

"At the stroke of midnight hour, when the world sleeps, India will awake to life and freedom," declared Indian Prime Minister Jawaharlal Nehru on the eve of Independence in August 1947. Few events take on the weight of historical significance – the sense that a fundamentally new era is beginning – than the birth of an independent nation. Nehru made full use of the opportunity to mark the occasion as one that is about change. "A moment comes, which comes rarely in history, when we step out from the old to the new."[1]

Yet, the new beginning implied by Independence disguised the complex and often traumatic processes that characterized India's step onto the world stage. A host of unresolved problems awaited the former colony. The growing tensions between Hindus and Muslims culminated in the Partition of India into two states rather than one. Communal riots led to unbelievable horrors and some twelve million people were forced to flee their homes. Gandhi refused to celebrate Independence under these circumstances and instead criss-crossed the country trying to use his moral authority to end the bloodshed. In January 1948, after Gandhi had announced a fast to death to counter the violence, a young Hindu assassinated him in New Delhi. It was a tumultuous birth that the newly independent country experienced.[2]

Over 4,000 miles (6,400 kilometers) away, in West Germany, the world was not much calmer. With Germany's unconditional surrender on May 7, 1945, World War II had ended in Europe after six devastating years. But for years to come large swathes of Germany lay in ruins and millions of refugees roamed the country looking for new homes. The US journalist William Shirer, reporting from Berlin, described the material and psychological devastation he saw:

[1] "Tryst with Destiny," Speech delivered in the Constituent Assembly, New Delhi, August 14, 1947, on the eve of the attainment of Independence, in: Nehru, *Nehru's Speeches, Vol. 1*: 25–27, here: 25.
[2] Frankel, *India's Political Economy*.

How can you find words to convey truthfully and accurately the picture of a great capital destroyed almost beyond recognition; of a once mighty nation that has ceased to exist; of a conquering people who were so brutally arrogant ... and whom you now see poking about their ruins, broken, dazed, shivering, hungry human beings without will or purpose or direction.[3]

The parallels in the historical path India and Germany had taken were not lost on worldly observers. India expert Joseph Hunck, reporter for the German economic daily *Handelsblatt*, reflected that "the Federal Republic and India found themselves confronted with much the same problems to solve." After the devastating war, Germany "had to start from scratch on the reconstruction of the economy." India, "after years of economic enfeeblement, also found herself obliged to lay the foundation for a development which would banish hunger and poverty and raise the standard of living in accordance with a preconceived plan."[4] The hope that the end of war and colonial subjugation marked a new beginning was thus tempered by turmoil and turbulence that led both Germans and Indians to fall back on familiar relationships and tested patterns of economic interaction.

Stable Relationships in Cold War Turbulence

India celebrated its Independence at the very moment that the Cold War started to dominate global politics and economics. As political relationships around the world were reshuffled, the social networks between Germany and India were reformed based on interwar precedents and patterns. While politicians formulated novel ambitions to blend with ideologies of a reconfigured Cold War world, businesspeople in both countries instead opted for tried and trusted relationships.

In India, political ambitions focused on political independence and rapid industrial development. With the United States and the Soviet Union establishing themselves as two opposite poles in the international arena, most countries felt forced to pick a side. India took the fluidity of the period as an opportunity and opted for a policy of "non-alignment" in the belief that affiliating with either side was a threat to newly achieved Independence. "What does joining a bloc mean?", asked Nehru rhetorically in March 1948. "After all it can only mean one thing: give up your view about a particular question, adopt the other party's view on that question in order to please it."[5] Pragmatically, nonalignment also

---

[3] Entry "Berlin, November 4, 1945," in: Shirer, *End of a Berlin Diary*: 123.
[4] Hunck, *India's Silent Revolution*: 15.
[5] Prime Minister's statement March 8, 1948, in: Appadorai, *Select Documents on India's Foreign Policy*: vol. 1, 11.

allowed India to trade with and draw economic development aid from countries of both the Eastern and Western Blocs. The Polish economist Michał Kalecki described nonaligned nations as "the proverbial clever calves that could suckle two cows."[6]

India's rapid development strategy required imports from more industrialized countries, independent of their origin. But after freeing itself from the colonial yoke, India was simultaneously eager to avoid reliance on any one foreign country. In this context, collaborating with a politically weak but soon economically recovering West Germany was an attractive option. Business leader G. D. Birla forcefully argued that German knowledge should be made available to India. "Why should not India be allowed to recruit German technicians to help her in her industrialization? ... The war is over and Germany is completely crippled. There is, therefore, no military risk."[7] Few other industrialized countries were as thoroughly nonthreatening as Germany.

Germany, on the other hand, needed to rebuild its economy as well as re-establish itself as a player on global markets. To that end, Germany was not only investing in its export trade but also looking to improve its image abroad. It displayed both its industrial strength and the legitimacy of its business leaders after the Nazi years.[8] This also included a new interest in development aid (see Chapter 8), presenting post-war Germany as supportive of less industrialized nations, after having itself received support to reconstruct its war-struck economy after 1945.

Indeed, few economic relationships after World War II recovered as swiftly as the Indo-West German one. As early as July 1948, the Government of India signed its first Trade Agreement with the British and US occupation zones in West Germany.[9] Remarkably, it was India that, as the very first country in the world, officially ended the state of war with West Germany on January 1, 1950. This not only allowed political and economic cooperation to intensify but was also often recalled as proof for a special relationship.[10] Indians and West Germans were ready to get back to business.

As a first step, Indian buyers sought out German manufacturers for products long out of stock in India, just as they had done after World

---

[6] Quoted in: Engerman, *The Price of Aid*: 2.
[7] Birla, "An Industrial Mission": 423.
[8] For similar strategies employed in Germany, see Wiesen, *West German Industry*.
[9] The first trade agreement with East Germany dates from October 16, 1954. "Outstanding E. German Exhibits," *Times of India*, October 29, 1955: IX.
[10] Das Gupta, *Handel, Hilfe, Hallstein-Doktrin*: 81–84. Highlighted as special relationship, e.g. by Hunck, *India's Silent Revolution*: 14.

War I (see Chapter 4).[11] German multinationals with a pre-war presence in India also lost no time in reactivating their social networks. They did so by turning to former employees, either Germans who decided to remain in India or Indian pre-war staff. Both Bayer, one of the successor companies of the dismantled I. G. Farben, and Siemens sold their products through their respective agents as early as 1949.[12] Bayer was wooed by several of its former German employees who had remained in India after internment. They had joined hands with former Indian colleagues or Indian businesspeople of some standing and offered up these connections to Bayer as a conduit for redeveloping its presence on the subcontinent.[13]

Of the many offers made by former employees, Bayer opted to work with Joseph Wilde, formerly with Agfa in Calcutta, and his Indian collaborator Chowgule to sell its pharmaceuticals and chemicals on commission.[14] Wilde had been interned in India during the war. When it was his time to be returned to Germany in 1947, he escaped while being deported to Germany and went underground in Goa. Wilde, who had been one of the official Nazi Party members in the German community in India (see Chapter 5, page 145), may have wanted to avoid being questioned about his political affiliation. In Goa, he met the owners of the business house Chowgule, who had built their fortune in shipping and iron ore exporting.[15] Together they made for a compelling partnership. Wilde was a trusted and experienced manager and Chowgule had been able to acquire import licenses for pharmaceuticals from the Indian Government. Yet, after meeting with Vishwasrao D. Chowgule, a Bayer manager warned that "[h]e wants to be and remain the master of his own house in every respect. He is not willing to essentially sell us his name for a commission of 10%, foregoing any influence. As great as his interest in our representation is, as clearly as he is aware of its value,

[11] Friedr. Herder Abr. Sohn Solingen, "Letter to M. Allabux & Co. Bombay," October 19, 1948, and response December 3, 1948, Fi/22/3323, CASol.
[12] Press Information, "Fruitful Cooperation for 100 Years," November 10, 1967, 68/Li/156, SAA; "Participation in Foreign Agencies," October 19, 1961, 8109, SAA; "Bayer Remedies Limited, Bombay," 9/K/1/2, BA.
[13] "Historical Development of Bayer AG, Sales Pharma, Country Overview," 1953: 108–109, 1/6/6/18/1, BA.
[14] Chowgule received a commission of 10 percent for pharma products and 5 percent for chemicals. "Agency contract with Chowgule & Co. (Hind) Ltd. Bombay," March 17, 1949, 018/010/108, BA; "Classified Ad," *Times of India*, June 19, 1948: 8; "Letter Sales to Dr. Schramm," October 13, 1949, and accompanying reports "Fabrication in India," 9/K/1/2, BA.
[15] Tripathi and Jumani, *Concise Oxford History of Indian Business*: 171.

there is no longer any doubt today that he will never play the role of a straw man."[16] The collaboration, however, allowed Bayer to build on an existing organization and work with an Indian partner with established relations with the Indian Government. Chowgule, in return, invested in a swift expansion of its organization to Delhi, Calcutta, and Madras to sell Bayer's products widely in India and upon request hired several of I. G. Farben's German and Indian pre-war employees as a foundation for the partnership.[17]

Other Indian I. G. employees had earlier started their own companies. Already in 1940, some Indian I. G. employees had founded the Associated Research Laboratories (Arlab) Ltd. in Bhatgar, near Poona, which grew to about ninety employees in the post-Independence period. Bayer considered using Arlab as a base for its dyestuff manufacturing but failed to receive government permission for a collaboration with this company.[18] Given the many options it had, Bayer turned its attention elsewhere.

Similarly, using its existing network, Siemens started selling again via the Bombay Machinery & Tools Co., whose business was taken over by the Protos Engineering Co. Ltd. in July 1949.[19] Protos was a trademark that Siemens (India) had itself introduced to the Indian market shortly after its founding in 1925.[20] The German businessman Ferdinand Kurt Heller, who had been situated in Colombo before the war, used the name and opened Protos Engineering together with Georg Wilhelm, a former Siemens employee who he knew from the internment camp Dehra Dun. Together they approached two Indian businessmen, Harshad N. Kapadia and Mangharam C. Mansukhani.[21] The team of Protos also included the Siemens employee D. N. [David Nissim] Haskell, a Jewish-Indian engineer who had worked for Siemens since 1930, when he oversaw the erection of the Painganga Water Works in the Pen Valley, near Buldana.[22]

[16] Roehder, "Letter to Bayer," January 23, 1949, 302/0257, BA.
[17] "Historical Development of Bayer AG, Sales Pharma, Country Overview," 1953: 111, 1/6/6/18/1, BA.
[18] P. A. Narielwala, "Note," September 27, 1954; Borgwardt & Klebert, "Report about trip to India, February 8 to 25, 1955," March 3, 1955; Koehler, "Letter to Bayer," February 26, 1955, all in: 59/402, BA. Pochhammer, "Report of the General Consulate in Bombay," June 15, 1955, B 102/122085, BA-K.
[19] "Display Ad," Times of India, November 7, 1948: 16, and July 3, 1949: 9.
[20] "Classified Ads," Times of India, December 11, 1925: 9; February 17, 1930: 7, and February 27, 1930: 2.
[21] Dames-Willers, Ferdinand Kurt Heller (1900–1991): 26.
[22] A Correspondent, "New Water Work for Buldana," Times of India, June 10, 1930: 5. "Classified Ads," Times of India, January 23, 1949: 7; "Mr. D. N. Haskell: Late Managing Director of Protos Eng. Co. Ltd.," Times of India, March 14, 1957: 10.

Protos developed into an important trading company fully registered in India. It represented several German companies and many of its engineers were German nationals who had previously been interned with Heller.[23] Siemens used Protos first as a representative in India, then made a cloaked investment into Protos to create a dedicated Siemens Department.[24] Because Siemens did not yet have any local manufacturing, the expectation was that the Indian Government would not have allowed Siemens to open a pure sales company, but the collaboration with Protos provided the necessary cover. "The intention is to separate the Siemens Department from Protos and to set up an independent sales company as soon as the Indian authorities have given their approval."[25] After two wars and the Nazi regime, working with trusted middlemen and other forms of cloaking had become a familiar tactic for the German firms.

During the political turmoil in both India and Germany, the strategy to build on pre-war networks to re-establish business in India was the norm, not the exception. It promised some stability in a wobbly world. Many German businesspeople remained in India after the war. Some had started families in India, while others may have judged the business opportunities and their living conditions in India superior to the ones in defeated Germany. German internees were returned to Europe in December 1946 and January 1947, during a particularly harsh German winter. Most had no opportunity in the internment camp or during transport to signal their arrival to family members and make preparations for living arrangements. Finally, some wanted to avoid being questioned about their relationship to the Nazis. German internees returning from India were first transferred to the previous concentration camp Neuengamme, near Hamburg, in the British occupation zone. There, they were interrogated as potential Nazi sympathizers in over 130 questions about their political leanings. While most were cleared swiftly and sent home, selected individuals remained in custody for their political activities or

---

[23] Protos represented Gutehoffnungshütte, Maschinenfabrik Buckau R. Wolf A.G., KSB (Klein, Schanzlin & Becker), Werner und Pfleiderer, Deutz, Gesellschaft für Linde's Eismaschinen A.G., J. M. Voith and Haver & Boecker. On the German origin of its engineers see, "Dakota Crashes in Delhi," *Times of India*, May 10, 1953: 1. For networking during internment see also Dames-Willers, *Ferdinand Kurt Heller (1900–1991)*: 21, 25–26.

[24] "Classified Ad," *Times of India*, May 21, 1953: 12, and December 2, 1954: 8. Das Gupta argues that Siemens (India) de facto never ceased to exist because of the continuous work of the former Siemens employees. See, Das Gupta, "Divided Nations": 302.

[25] Wegner, "Note about meeting in Salzburg, September 28–29, 1961," October 19, 1961, Appendix 1, 8109, SAA.

close social relations with known Nazis.[26] Uncertainty loomed over the homecoming.

Whatever the individual motives, many Germans chose to remain in India after being freed from internment rather than returning to their homeland. Of the fourteen Krupp employees who were arrested at the outbreak of the war, six remained in India after internment and started working for Indian companies.[27] The leading manager, Otto-Zeno Steffens (born 1901), left India and then returned to take a position with Tata at Jamshedpur.[28] Another returnee, Stephen W. Popper, a British citizen who had received his education in Hamburg, had spent more than a decade in India before the war, until his German employer had encouraged him in the late 1930s to resign from his position because of his Jewish origin (see Chapter 5). He informed his former colleagues in Germany that he would open a company in Bombay for trading with Germany making use of his intimate knowledge of both national contexts.[29] The social networks created at the internment camp also did not dissolve after the internees' return. Many of them stayed in touch. Several internees collected each other's addresses and circulated their written memoirs of the internment experience after the war had ended.[30] Medical doctor Oswald Urchs was able to do a follow-up study on his camp malaria patients in the years 1954/1955, to analyze long-term problems.[31] The informal social network can only be exemplified. F. K. Heller, a successful businessman from Colombo and later managing director of Protos, one of the most influential German trading companies after the war, became acquainted with Georg Wilhelm, the later managing director of Siemens in India, and Ernst Fuhrmann, a project manager of Buckau-Wolf. These connections from internment provided the seed for many post-war activities in India (see the text that follows).[32]

---

[26] Tucher, *Nationalism*: 103–105. For two former Siemens employees who were not immediately released from Neuengamme, see "Note: Returnees from India," December 17, 1947, 8156, SAA.
[27] Otto Zeno Steffens, "Letter to Krupp," December 11, 1946, Personnel files, 1937–1947, 51/5036, WA, HAK.
[28] Otto-Zeno Steffens, "Letter to Hobrecker," May 20, 1947, 131/2668, WA, HAK. "German Technicians," *Times of India*, February 19, 1949: 6.
[29] Popper first came to India working for the German company Hugo Stinnes, and since 1929 held a managerial position with Havero and I. G. Farben. Stephen Popper, "Letter to Bayer Management," November 23, 1948, 329/524, BA.
[30] For example, Manuscript Hans Schäfer, Das Central Internment Camp Dehra Dun, ED 353, Repertorium Helbig, IfZ. Also made available online by relatives of former internees at: www.gaebler.info/2016/08/schaefer/.
[31] Urchs, "Zur Frage der Spätschäden."
[32] Dames-Willers, *Ferdinand Kurt Heller (1900–1991)*: 21, 25.

Other German India experts transitioned from business to politics or the press. The two former Siemens (India) employees, Ernst Kunisch (born 1896) and Walter Knips (born 1911), took positions as trade commissioners in Bombay and Islamabad, Pakistan, in 1952.[33] Here, they connected with a network of politicians equally shaped by great continuities. Several diplomats, who had been leading figures in colonial India, continued to work in similar roles. Wilhelm Melchers, who had served as the head of the "Orient-Referat" [Middle East Desk] of the German Foreign Office since 1939, became the second ambassador in New Delhi in 1957. Herbert Richter, who had been at the consulates general in Bombay and Calcutta in the 1930s, became counsellor at the New Delhi embassy from 1952 to 1958.[34] G. L. Leszczyński, the former head of the German India Institute, which was founded as a predecessor for a potential German chamber of commerce in India, stayed in India after internment. He first became a lecturer of German at the University of Agra (Meerut College) before taking a position as correspondent for the German Press Agency from 1951 to 1957 and for the Frankfurter Allgemeine Zeitung beginning in 1957.[35] While political systems and regulations changed, the network of India experts remained intact.

Building on these tried relations, trade between India and West Germany recovered exceptionally fast. In the immediate post-war years, India's imports from Germany stood at Rs 60 million; its exports to Germany at Rs 90 million, leaving India with an export surplus. Germany's war-shattered economy took in raw materials and foodstuffs in the first years after the trade agreement. Not least thanks to their pre-war social networks, Indians and German were back in business.

Experimenting with Public–Private Partnerships

During the interwar period, trade and industrialization had peacefully co-existed in India. With Independence, this balance changed. India prioritized state-led and carefully planned industrialization and did not disguise its focus on steel, machinery, cement, chemicals, and transport equipment. Indian economic planning was carried out in Soviet-inspired, so-called "Five-Year plans," developed and supervised by the Indian Planning Commission. During the period of the First Five-Year Plan (1951–1956), India's annual average export to Germany amounted to Rs 127 million, compared to imports from Germany of Rs 370 million. During the Second and Third Five-Year Plans, this trade deficit increased

---

[33] Lubinski, Giacomin, and Schnitzer, "Internment."
[34] See, Das Gupta, "Divided Nations": 301.
[35] Frankfurter Allgemeine Zeitung, "Georg L. Leszczyński."

Table 7.1 *Indo-German trade (in million rupees), 1951–1974*

	Import into India	% of India's Total Imports	Export from India	% of India's Total Exports	Balance of Trade
Annual average for the First Plan (1951–1956)	370	5.1	127	2.1	−243
Annual average for the Second Plan (1956–1961)	1095	11.2	173	2.8	−922
Annual average for the Third Plan (1961–1966)	1119	9.0	195	2.5	−924
Annual average for the Fourth Plan (1969–1974)	1368	7.0	488	2.7	−880

Source: J. K. Tandon, *Indo-German Economic Relations* (New Delhi: National, 1978), p. 10, based on Economic Survey, Government of India, New Delhi (various issues).

even further (see Table 7.1). In the second half of the 1950s, India's trade deficit with West Germany was highest among all trading partners, even higher than with Great Britain or the US. The main reason for this pattern was Germany's collaboration with the Indian Government in the strategically crucial steel industry.

Steel had been an area of focus for Indian development efforts for quite some time. It was thus not surprising that one of the earliest and most symbolic Indo-German projects of the immediate post-war period was a steel plant. A German consortium of companies erected and ran the plant in Rourkela in the state of Orissa. Although India already had two large private steel corporations, the TISCO and the Indian Iron and Steel Co. (IISCO), it was the Indian Government's declared ambition to establish public sector dominance over the steel industry through further investment.

To that end, a partnership with German companies was established. The process for forming the foreign partnership in steel became the model Indian officials used for future agreements in other industries. Rather than working with just one international partner, India invested in a total of three public steelworks, each supported by companies from a different country: The steel mill in Bhilai, Madhya Pradesh, was built with support by the Soviets, the one in Durgapur, West Bengal, with assistance from Great Britain, and the Rourkela plant became the project of the West Germans. The nearly simultaneous development of these three plants, their initially identical capacity targets, and the fact that all three were intended to transition to Indian management and Indian public ownership, led to continuous comparisons of these ventures in politics and press. Each of the three projects was also a "showpiece" representing the investing countries' approach to economic development. Timing and organizational setup invited for a public race to unveil the superior economic and social system.

Of the three projects, Rourkela was the first to take shape. As early as 1951 the Indian Government and the German steel manufacturer Krupp discussed the development of an Indian steel plant, while the negotiations with Russia dated to 1954. Krupp and its partner Demag signed a contract with the Indian Government on August 15, 1953, to advise the public Hindustan Steel (Private) Limited company in building a steel factory.[36] However, as was typical for many of these early public–private partnerships, financing the venture turned out to be challenging. After lengthy negotiations, the German Government decided to support the project with 50 million Deutschmark from the European Recovery Program, better known as the Marshall Plan, which had been granted to Germany for its own reconstruction after the war. Initially, Krupp-Demag was supposed to hold 20 percent ownership for a period of nine years, after which they would have the option of selling these shares. But, in November 1956, when the agreement was finalized, the German firms surrendered both their shareholding and directorships and instead operated as consultants and suppliers.[37] In addition, over 3,000 West German suppliers delivered products and services for the mega project.

For the German consortium companies an investment of this magnitude was a serious risk. German companies had just come out of a war in which most of their foreign assets had been expropriated. Yet, the German Government had previously established an insurance scheme to support business. The so-called "Hermes guarantees" insured German exporters or investors against political risks.[38] In the post-war period, the Hermes guarantees became a means of helping the struggling export industry back on its feet. Germany expanded the insurance's volume and coverage. By 1952, a total of 1.1 billion Deutschmark was Hermes insured and in 1957, this amount had risen to around 10 billion.[39] The Hermes coverage was crucial for setting up the Rourkela contract. However, it also tied the German Government into this development project.

---

[36] "Krupp Mitteilungen Nr. 1," February 1954, WA, HAK; Rajya Sabha (Council of States or upper house of the Parliament of India), Session 4, August 25, 1953, Part 2 (Other than Question and Answers), "Statement Regarding a New Steel Plant Project," 152–154, http://rsdebate.nic.in/handle/123456789/588267. See also, Gall, "Von der Entlassung": 528–534.

[37] "Krupps-DEMAG Directors to Resign from Rourkela Steel Plant Board," *Capital*, November 29, 1956; "German Investment to be Dispensed With," *The Statesman*, December 3, 1956. Copies in: Ministry of Economics, B/102/58481, BA-K.

[38] On the pre-war history of Hermes, see Weis, *Hermesbürgschaften*: 63–81.

[39] Hein, *Die Westdeutschen und die Dritte Welt*: 29.

Figure 7.1 (a) Inauguration and (b) panoramic view of Rourkela Steel Plant, Orissa, 1960s. WA 16c/220 H (a), dated January 12, 1960 and UF 2/5.8.99 (b), dated July 23, 1964. © Historical Archives Krupp, Essen.

As the building of the plant hit its first speed bumps, the German Government felt forced to intervene. Given Rourkela's status as a showpiece of Indo-German collaboration, Germany extended loans to suppliers and refinanced India's obligations in 1956, 1958, and 1959. It also provided additional loans as development aid. It was the aid for Rourkela that marked the entry of West Germany into development aid payments. Yet, because of the immense scale of this project, Germany developed the largest trade surplus with India of all Western countries and became an important voice in the negotiations about development aid for India (see Chapter 8).

The Rourkela steelworks began production in 1959 and was officially inaugurated on January 12, 1960 (see Figure 7.1). As was customary on such occasion, the equipment was decorated with flowers and lighted by candles for a religious celebration of the installation. About a similar ceremony at Bayer in 1960, one visitor reported,

In front of the main assembly, which was decorated with flowers and garlands, stood the image of a saint, lit by candles. After ancient ceremonies that have their origins in the Vedas, the holy books of the Hindus, the priest consecrated the machines, inviting protection and mercy from the gods. The plants were wetted with holy water and seeds, and symbols of fertility and wealth were thrown over motors, pipes, control boards and mixing drums.[40]

---

[40] Hans Brandt, Sales Pesticides, "Zwischen Himalaya und Kap Comorin," in: *Unser Werk* 1960, 83, BA.

As exotic as German observers found these ceremonies, the Rourkela project was a great opportunity for the German machinery and steel industry looking for new customers after the war. Moreover, it also sparked a domino effect, preparing the ground for further Indo-German collaborations. Politically, the German Government had great expectations for the Rourkela scheme, which gave it an opportunity to showcase the benefits of Germany's "social market economy," as an alternative to pure socialism and unfettered capitalism.

Throughout its existence, the Rourkela project was also an experiment. Immediately after the war, it came from a country with limited resources and little knowledge in running projects in less developed countries. This lack of experience with development projects resulted in serious challenges. By 1960, a German press article dubbed Rourkela, with reference to the infamous World War II-battle, "the Stalingrad of the German industry" because of the series of organizational and construction challenges it had faced.[41] While delays and logistical hiccups were not unusual for large steel projects, Rourkela was continuously and often unfavorably compared to the Soviet plant in Bhilai, which was completed almost simultaneously.[42] First, the resettlement of about 13,000 people, mostly Adivasi (the original inhabitants of Orissa), that was necessary for building Rourkela, ignited protests.[43] Second, logistical challenges delayed the erection of the plant. Most material was shipped from Germany to Calcutta but the harbor in Calcutta struggled to handle the large quantities, and shipments often arrived late or damaged (Figure 7.2). Labor unrests compounded the problem.

Third, the German consortium had over thirty firms deal independently with the Indian authorities, which had insisted on picking their own suppliers. The list of companies dealing directly with the Indian Government read like a Who's Who of German industry, including AEG, Brown, Boveri & Cie, Didier, Gutehoffnungshütte, Linde, Mannesmann-Meer, Sack Maschinenfabrik, and many more. By contrast, the Soviets negotiated with one voice.[44] Finally, there was negative press depicting the German workmen and their inappropriate behavior

---

[41] "Russen auf dem Dach," *Der Spiegel,* Issue 14, March 30, 1960: 22–34: 22.
[42] For details about the Rourkela project and the related social problems, see Unger, "Rourkela"; Das Gupta, *Handel, Hilfe, Hallstein-Doktrin*: 256–258. For the two steel plants as a front in the economic Cold War, see Engerman, *The Price of Aid*: 132–134. For the unfavorable comparison of Rourkela (and also, to a lesser extent, Durgapur) with Bhilai see, Eldridge, *The Politics of Foreign Aid in India.*
[43] Adivasi-Koordination, *Rourkela und die Folgen.*
[44] Knusel, *West German Aid to Developing Nations*: 85. For a complete list of the companies involved see Boeckmann, Harald, in conjunction with the Indian-Gemeinschaft Krupp-Demag GmbH, "Rourkela," Hamburg: Uebersee Verlag, 1959, DNBL, 26–27.

Figure 7.2 German goods at Calcutta harbor, 1956. Picture folder for the report by Chief Engineer A. Hezinger about his visit to Telco-India and Hindustan Motor Car in Calcutta from October 28 to November 24, 1956. © Mercedes-Benz Classic.

towards in particular Indian women.[45] These challenges created continuous public relations challenges. In the end, the plant was completed on time in February 1959 and before the Soviet one, a fact that the German authorities and the German press celebrated as a success.[46]

However, even after completing the building phase, criticism did not subside. Frequent complaints about technical deficiencies and mistakes created new image problems for German industry. The Germans, on the other hand, felt that the problem was with Indian unskilled labor and the lack of management by Hindustan Steel. However, educational initiatives were riddled with difficulties and slow to show results. Despite these issues, the German Government agreed to expand the steel plant

[45] "Rourkela," *Times of India*, May 13, 1960: 8; "Russen auf dem Dach," *Der Spiegel*, Issue 14, March 30, 1960: 22–34: 22; A. Raghavan "German Herrenvolk Refuse to Work with Indian Workmen," *Blitz*, Bombay, July 26, 1958, copies in: B/102/58481, BA-K. For an excellent study of the challenges and their development over time, see the detailed report by the head of the German social center at Rourkela, Sperling, *The Human Dimension of Technical Assistance*.
[46] "Sieg der Deutschen," *Der Spiegel*, Issue 3, January 9, 1966.

in 1962–1963, which gave the companies from the initial consortium and several additional suppliers a reason to expand their business with India. To avoid some of the earlier social and cultural issues, the German Government elected four experts to write a detailed report about the conditions at Rourkela, and subsequently engaged in a series of reform efforts. By 1965, the technical management was transferred to Indians, and the German personnel in Rourkela reduced to a total of forty experts. By 1975, Rourkela contributed about one-sixth of India's steel production.[47]

Rourkela put the post-war German steel industry back on the map. In hindsight, it was also often seen as "a costly but immensely valuable preliminary exercise" in development aid for the West German state.[48] However, the way the Rourkela project unfolded did not give German industry the impression that business in India was easy. When approached about a similar scheme, leaders of the German chemical industry, felt conflicted. Indo-German relations in chemistry looked back at a long history and many Indian chemists had received their training in Germany in the interwar period. The project the Government desired was instigated by one of them, Nagaraja Rao, an Indian chemist who had received his doctoral degree in Berlin prior to the war.[49] Rao had studied in Germany for three years and returned in 1946/1947, when he also visited Bayer's headquarters in Leverkusen.[50] He held a position as Industrial Adviser in the Ministry of Commerce and Industry and was keen on getting the three successor companies of I. G. Farben, which had been a major player in interwar India, to collaborate on a manufacturing project for chemical intermediates. The first request was for a survey of the Indian market. As was customary, the Indian Government also asked experts from the Italian Montecatini and from the British ICI but eventually decided in favor of the three successor companies of the pre-war I. G. Farben – Bayer, Hoechst, and BASF – who in June 1957 agreed to participate in a public venture for chemical intermediates.[51]

Yet the negotiations were anything but smooth. The years that had elapsed since the initiation of the steel project were marked by a dramatic decline in India's ability to finance such large initiatives because of a deterioration

[47] Unger, "Rourkela": 381–383.
[48] White, *German Aid*: 20.
[49] "Indische Chemievorhaben," *Handelsblatt*, February 4, 1959, copy in: Bayer, Political Economy Department, 82/1, BA; Schuell (Bayer), "Letter to Management," July 1, 1952, 329/524, BA.
[50] Dr Raab, "Report about India trip, April 30–May 27, 1952," 18, 329/524, BA.
[51] Dr Bongard, "Summary Report about Trip to Delhi, October 22–December 12, 1957," 59/402, BA.

in its foreign exchange balance (see Chapter 8). The Minister of Industry, Manubhai Shah, came to Bayer's headquarter in Leverkusen in 1958 and tried to negotiate a deferral of payments, for which he offered import licenses in exchange.[52] After almost two years of negotiations, the contract partners eventually agreed that India could receive loans from German credit institutions, guaranteed by the German chemical firms.[53] Bayer, BASF, and Hoechst, supported by the mechanical engineering company Uhde, would consult with the Indians and own a minority share of the newly founded "Hindustan Organic Chemicals Ltd." (HOC). The German partners coordinated their engagement in a separate contract and established an executive committee, in which each partner had one representative.[54]

Symbolically, the chemicals project was at least as important as the prior engagement for the public steel industry, and in many ways comparable. Reporting from an India trip in 1961, Bayer's representatives analyzed that for their Indian partners HOC "means the decisive step in their own chemical production and is comparable in its importance to the founding of Hindustan Steel (Priv.) Ltd.," which was responsible for Rourkela and the two other public steel companies.[55] The three German chemical firms expected the project to "improve their reputation in India" and positively affect their overall business.[56] While likely not profitable for quite some time, HOC was designed to open doors in India.

Emerging Indo-German Joint Ventures

The public–private collaborations in steel and chemicals also facilitated private Indo-German joint ventures. The Government of India actively encouraged Indians to establish partnerships with foreign industrialists as a crucial aspect of its development strategy. Reminiscent of the prewar Bombay Plan (see Chapter 6), the Industrial Policy Resolution of 1948 called for the state to develop industry but only suggested public control for a few selected sectors. Foreign investment, on the other hand, was actively encouraged, albeit only if it was advantageous to the

---

[52] Chika, "Letter to Bayer," 59/402, BA; "Discussion with Indian Industry Minister Shri Manubhai Shah," October 9, 1958, 302/230, BA.

[53] "Signing of Agreement, Intermediates Project," 1960, Engineering: Projects India, 59/402, BA.

[54] "Consortium Agreement," April/May 1961, Engineering: Projects India, 59/402, BA.

[55] Dr Bongard, "Summary of First India Trip of Consultants for Intermediates Project, October 26 to November 27, 1960," Appendix to letter January 3, 1961, Engineering: Projects India, 59/402, BA.

[56] Dr Erdmann, "Letter to German Foreign Office," September 12, 1957, B 102/122085, BA-K.

national interest and controlled by Indians. Building on this policy, Nehru's speech to the Lok Sabha (the lower house of parliament) on April 6, 1949, became the primary point of reference for collaborations. "Indian capital needs to be supplemented by foreign capital," Nehru proclaimed, because national savings would otherwise run out. Foreign capital investments would also make it easier to facilitate knowledge transfers. The goal was thus, "the utilization of foreign capital in a manner most advantageous to the country."[57] But Nehru also calmed nervous investors and promised no discrimination of foreign interests, no generic control of remittances, and fair compensation for any possible nationalization. While his statement previewed that majority ownership and control should transfer to Indians long-term, Nehru conceded possibilities for foreign control for a certain development phase as well as the option of employing non-Indian experts. "[E]ach case will be dealt with on its merits."[58] German industry certainly responded to this invite and took note of the preference for capital over consumer goods, which matched its capabilities very well.[59]

One of the earliest Indo-German joint ventures was the previously mentioned Protos Engineering Co., which F. K. Heller founded together with Georg Wilhelm and two Indian business partners. Protos had a diversified portfolio and provided its knowledge and connections in India as a service to German companies looking to enter the subcontinent. Protos prioritized those sectors which the Indian Government had marked as most urgent, specifically steel, engineering, sugar, and pharmaceuticals. Its co-founder, Heller, was well connected in the Indo-German business community and served as the first president of the newly established Indo-German Chamber of Commerce in Bombay beginning in 1956. It was the very first binational Chamber of Commerce in India. It was also the first German Chamber of Commerce in the country, after the earlier German India Institute never developed into a true chamber of commerce even though it had been established as a potential predecessor to such an organization (see Chapter 6). In 1958, the chamber had 144 Indian members and 178 German ones. To assure equality, the Articles of Association provided for Indian and German parity in the Standing Committee, and the office of president alternated annually between the two nationalities.[60]

---

[57] Nehru, "Statememt on Foreign Investments": 49.
[58] Ibid., 50.
[59] Arbeitsgemeinschaft Außenhandel der Wirtschaft des Vereinigten Wirtschaftsgebietes, "Letter to Administration Economy, Dr. Raemisch," May 4, 1949, B 102/2087/1, BA-K.
[60] "Dr. F. Bluecher's Good Wishes: Foundation Welcomed," *Times of India*, February 3, 1956: 12. See also, "Furthering Trade Relations between India and West Germany," *Times of India*, February 3, 1956: 12. Hunck, *India's Silent Revolution*: 57–58.

Heller and his Protos organization laid the groundwork and actively supported several Indo-German joint ventures over the following years.[61] Among the pioneering partnerships was German Remedies, a collaboration of seven large pharmaceutical manufacturers, including Boehringer, Nordmark, Schering, and Merck, for production in India. Protos also entered a joint venture with Klein, Schanzlin & Becker (KSB) for the establishment of a water pump factory in Pimpri near Pune and with engineering company Buckau-Wolf to build a sugar factory in India. In several cases, Protos held a 10 to 20 percent share of ownership in these companies and had a gentlemen's agreement with the German partner to vote together so that a formal minority participation, which the Indian Government preferred, effectively allowed for full control of the German partners.

Not all collaboration attempts were successful. As early as 1952, the Indian Government approached the German Consul in Bombay to discuss the possibility of establishing a raw film manufacturing facility in India.[62] In early 1953, Agfa India Limited was formed as sole distributor for Agfa's products in India. 75 percent of the shares were held by the Indian company Chika Limited.[63] Chika had been founded in 1951 and was formally an Indian company by design. One of Bayer's most trusted India experts, Wilhelm Winterhalder, was placed at Chika and oversaw the distribution of Bayer's products. Winterhalder had been with Bayer since 1923 and since 1926 was engaged as managing director for Havero and then Chemdyes in India. He reported that Chika had been adjusted to the political environment and argued that founding a company without Indian majority was principally wrong because it was obvious to him that "any foreign company would be discriminated against sooner or later."[64]

In ownership and management Chika was dominated by the Indian Ghia family, a business group originally from the textile trade. Maganlal Chunilal Ghia was a well-known Baroda industrialist, where he founded The New India Industries to manufacture specialty yarns in July 1942 and went public in 1945. The Chairman of the Board of New India was Ardeshir Darabshaw Shroff, one of the Directors of Tata Sons and a close friend of the Ghia family. A. D. Shroff was an eminent finance

---

[61] Dames-Willers, *Ferdinand Kurt Heller (1900–1991)*: 26–28. See also, "30 years Indo-German Chamber," *Times of India*, April 28, 1986: 18

[62] Agfa, "Raw Film Manufacturing Project," Appendix to "Letter to Bayer," April 4, 1959, 329/524, BA.

[63] Ibid.

[64] "Note about meeting on May 29, 1953, in Leverkusen," May 29, 1953, 329/524, BA. For Winterhalder's negotiations with the Indian Government, see also "Visit to New Delhi, May 13 to May 17, 1952," May 23, 1952, 329/524, BA.

expert, one of India's representatives at the United Nations' Bretton Woods Conference as well as one of the authors of the Bombay Plan.[65] After the death of M. C. Ghia, Shroff served as a mentor to his two sons, the brothers Bhupatrai M. and Damodar M. Ghia.

As the Ghia group became a new partner to Bayer, the German multinational considered ending its collaboration with Chowgule because Chowgule's goodwill with the government had allegedly been destroyed by tax irregularities. Joseph Wilde, who had first established this collaboration, was put in charge of the organization and technical service of Agfa India. However, as the collaboration with Chowgule soured, this Indian business family turned against its German partner. In April 1953, Bayer's Winterhalder was alarmed by the fact that Chowgule had petitioned the police not to extend Wilde's residence permit; a frequent challenge for commercially rather than technically educated Germans in India based on the assumption that the latter were mainly needed for advancing industrialization. Only with interference of the politically well-connected Ghias could Wilde's expulsion from India be avoided.[66]

In the spring of 1954, Agfa sent a technical mission to Bangalore to explore the potential of the raw film project.[67] However, the results were anything but satisfying. Agfa detailed that the Indian market for raw film was too small and that the losses of such a project would be significant.[68] Instead, Agfa suggested a much smaller pilot plant for photographic film and paper. Yet, the negative reaction to the proposed project left misgivings among members of the Indian Government, including with the powerful Minister of Commerce and Industry, T. T. Krishnamachari, a Madras-based businessman turned Congress politician. By 1955, Agfa abandoned the project and several of Bayer's India experts reported that the disappointed Indian Government had turned against them.[69] Bayer learned the hard way how all of its activities in India were judged according to its willingness to support India's nationalist goals.

[65] Dalal, *A.D. Shroff*: 21–27, 60–63.
[66] Winterhalder, "Letter to Mertens," April 2, 1953, 302/257, BA. The relationship with Chowgule was finally resolved in 1961.
[67] Dr. Prill, "Report about our India Trip May 21 to June 2, 1954," June 4, 1954, as well as Agfa, "Letter to R. J. Rego, Mysore Government" October 20, 1954, and Haberland, "Letter to R. J. Rego," August 24, 1954, all: 59/402, BA.
[68] Ibid.
[69] Winterhalder, "Letter to Koehler," September 30, 1954, and appendix; Prill, "Letter to Koehler," October 26, 1954, all: 59/402, BA. Parts of this Agfa project were eventually revitalized in the 1960s, when Agfa decided to participate in the New India Industries Ltd. and together with the Baroda-based company started the manufacturing of photo paper in Mulund, near Bombay. See, Bayer Annual Report 1962, BA.

Whereas the Rourkela experiment struggled with image problems and the Agfa project never went beyond the drawing board, other joint ventures celebrated successes. Among the most admired early Indo-German joint ventures were the investments in Indian transportation. Automobile manufacturing had been a top priority of the Indian Government for quite some time. Since the 1920s, the North American manufacturers General Motors and Ford assembled vehicles in India. Yet, under the new policies, the Indian Government insisted on a greater shift to local production, leading both companies to retreat from the Indian market. Following the established pattern, India approached the Secretary-General of the German Association of Automobile Industry, Wilhelm R. Vorwig, to counsel on the development of the local auto industry.[70]

For commercial vehicles, the German manufacturer Daimler-Benz (Mercedes) entered a joint venture with Tata Locomotive and Engineering Co. Ltd. (TELCO), which started with heavy diesel trucks.[71] Daimler-Benz made an investment of Rs 8 million and promised technical assistance for fifteen years. In line with Indian requirements, it proposed a five-year plan for gradually increasing the share of local production, until complete trucks could be manufactured in India. Only one year after entering into the agreement, TELCO and Daimler-Benz decided to double the production to meet soaring demand and Daimler-Benz made another Rs 8 million investment, raising its minority share to 12 percent. For their employees, they were able to rely on the former workers at General Motors and Ford who were already familiar with vehicle assembly.[72]

In early 1959, Mercedes' top management reported to the German Government that 45 percent of the value creation of this venture was done in India and that the work efficiency on the Indian factory floor was almost at par with Germany (for pictures of the plant, see Figure 7.3). The Mercedes executives also stated that they were relatively unconcerned about political risks because they had Hermes insurance, which would partly compensate them for politically motivated losses.[73] In the late 1950s, India was Daimler-Benz's most important individual market. By 1969, TELCO successfully produced vehicles without foreign

---

[70] Government of India Ministry of Commerce and Industry, *Tariff Commission Automobile 1953*; Vorwig and Government of India Ministry of Commerce and Industry, *Automobile Manufacture in India*. See also, Tetzlaff, "Revolution or Evolution?"

[71] "TELCO Concludes Pact with German Firm," *Times of India*, April 24, 1954: 4.

[72] "Tata Locomotive and Engineering Company Limited," *Times of India*, October 6, 1955: 4. Grunow-Osswald, *Internationalisierung*: 238, 274.

[73] Dr. Fremerey, "Note about Trip to Stuttgart on February 2, 1959," February 3, 1959, B 102/57925, BA-K.

Figure 7.3 Telco India, 1956. (a) Pre-assembly steering knuckles; (b) Vehicle assembly; (c) Paint shop; (d) Workers' dwellings. In: Picture folder for the report by Chief Engineer A. Hezinger about his visit to Telco-India and Hindustan Motor Car in Calcutta from October 28 to November 24, 1956. © Mercedes-Benz Classic.

assistance. Daimler-Benz's minority participation in TELCO, which later became Tata Motors, continued uninterruptedly until 2010.[74]

Unlike Rourkela, the Tata-Mercedes partnership was celebrated as a highlight of Indo-German cooperation[75] and initiated further business for German firms. In 1954, the German company Bosch invested in the Indian Motor Industry Company (MICO), which established itself as an important supplier for spark plugs and diesel injection pumps to the TELCO joint venture. MICO was founded in 1951 by the business family Saran. Raghunandan Saran, owner of a car assembly plant, collaborated with British Leyland Motors to start the company Ashok Leyland in 1954. He had already collaborated with Bosch before the war and now sold Bosch's products in India again.[76] Bosch, like many other German companies, relied on previous employees and partners to rebuild

[74] German Consulate in Calcutta, "Letter to Foreign Office," November 13, 1972, B 102/173584, BA-K; Grunow-Osswald, *Internationalisierung*: 215, 237–239.

[75] Analysis by K. B. Grautoff, Gildemeister AG, "Note on Private Investment in India," February 4, 1965, B 126/74987, BA-K.

[76] Roy, *A Business History of India*: 177. For details about the MICO collaboration, see Faust, *Spannungsfelder der Internationalisierung*.

its business in India after the war. MICO set up a new factory in Bangalore in 1953 and started producing spark plugs under Bosch license. Bosch initially began with a participation of 9 percent, then increased to 49 percent. Other investors included the Central Bank of India, ICICI (an institution formed in 1955 at the initiative of the World Bank, the Government of India and representatives of Indian industry to provide longer term project financing) and a group of Indian investors. By 1961, the German multinational boosted its ownership to 57.5 percent, claiming a majority for the German partner because of its strategic relevance to India's industrialization.[77]

While foreign majority ownership was not uncommon at this time, one crucial concern of India's political guard was the transfer of technical knowledge in joint ventures. Most of the partnerships therefore made sure to showcase their investment in the education of Indian labor. The Tata-Daimler-Benz joint venture initiated an apprentice school in India, modeled after the German three-year apprentice system, and also offered higher practical training for Indian engineers at the Daimler-Benz factory in Stuttgart, Germany.[78] Siemens similarly noted in 1959 that the company had trained a total of 400 Indian electrical engineers in its factories in Germany – one per week – since Siemens got back on the Indian market.[79] But these private sector initiatives did not stand alone. In his 1953 monograph "Deutschlands Rückkehr zum Weltmarkt" ["Germany's Comeback in the World Market"], Ludwig Erhard, then Federal Minister of Economics, stressed the great opportunities that India provided for Germany's export industry. However, he also insisted that technical support and collaboration were key for any long-term success in India.[80] This did not just refer to technical collaboration between Indian and German firms but explicitly included German state funding for the education of Indian talent. In this, Erhard pushed at an open door.

Education for Industrialization

Investments in education certainly had immediate practical relevance for India, but they were also of great symbolic significance. Indian nationalists had long condemned the lack of access to education during colonial times as immoral and had supported initiatives for students and interns

---

[77] Hermes Application Robert Bosch, May 30, 1962, B 126/74987, BA-K.
[78] A Special Correspondent, "Jamshedpur's Development as Industrial Centre," *Times of India*, June 29, 1957: A5; "Tata Locomotive and Engineering Company Limited: Speech of the Chairman," *Times of India*, August 13, 1957: 4.
[79] "Praise for Indian Engineers," *Times of India*, March 10, 1959: 10.
[80] Erhard, *Deutschlands Rückkehr*: 138–141.

to learn abroad (see Chapter 4). Educational schemes in Germany and Japan, as the two successful late developing countries of the world, were particularly intriguing for Indian observers. Germany became known in India for its focus on applied sciences and technical education. For Indian nationalists, their observations of German education were simultaneously a challenge of colonial rule and of British claims for a monopoly over industrial expertise.[81] Now, in Independent India, these theoretical considerations had to be turned into practical steps.

Since 1952, an Indo-German arrangement for industrial cooperation provided for the reception of Indian trainees and university students in Germany, picking up from pre-war continuities. The Indo-German Trade Agreement of 1955 included a provision that West Germany should make technical knowledge, scientific expertise, and training facilities available; without however including many details. Over time, West German technical assistance concentrated on specific projects, with the bulk of the funds going to two of them: the Indian Institute of Technology (IIT) in Madras and the prototype and training center in Okhla, near New Delhi.[82]

The IIT Madras was founded with technical assistance by the West German Government. Establishing an institute of higher education in engineering was first discussed during Nehru's visit to Germany in 1956 and eventually confirmed contractually in 1959. By that time, India already had an IIT in Kharagpur, near Calcutta, built with the support of the US, Great Britain, the Soviet Union, and UNESCO. For each of the following IITs, the Government of India arranged support from one international partner: the IIT Bombay was supported by the Soviets, the IIT Kanpur by the US, and the IIT Madras by the Germans. These four – Kanpur in the north, Madras in the south, Kharagpur in the east, and Bombay in the west – had originally been envisioned. A fifth followed due to the unexpected support by Great Britain, which financed the IIT in Delhi.[83] At the time of founding, in 1959, the IIT Madras was the largest educational project sponsored by the West German Government anywhere in the world. Germany provided Rs 17 million as well as twenty professors and four skilled craftsmen for a period of three to five years.[84] The instructors arrived in 1959, and by the late 1960s,

[81] Subramanian, *The Caste of Merit*: 63–65.
[82] Tandon, *Indo-German Economic Relations*: 13. Eldridge, *The Politics of Foreign Aid in India*: 14–15. Two other projects receiving West German aid were the Joint Advisory mixed farming project in Himachal Pradesh and a joint seismic survey during the years 1960 to 1963.
[83] Subramanian, *The Caste of Merit*: 71–72.
[84] Hunck, *India's Silent Revolution*: 70–71.

the staff still included twenty German professors and five experts.[85] Like the steel projects, all of the IITs also reflected the supporting country's socio-economical philosophy.

The relationship with Germany was key to the profile of the IIT Madras. "Where would you find the best instruction in German Technology, outside Germany?" asked an advertisement rhetorically. The answer: "In Madras – at the Indian Institute of Technology. Where are assembled some of the finest examples of German technological know-how and equipment to teach, train and guide tomorrow's engineers."[86] Among the different IITs, the IIT Madras was perceived as the most practical, steeped in the German approach to engineering as a hands-on and embodied skill. This was in stark contrast to the understanding of engineering in India at the time. In the colonial era, upper-caste Indians had been recruited into the engineering profession by elevating engineering to a science with a strong focus on mathematics, and by dismissing its practical character. After Independence, engineers were celebrated as supporting state-led nation-building, while those trained in practical workplace skills were mostly found on the lower rungs of society.[87] In this context, Humayun Kabir, union Minister for Scientific Research and Cultural Affairs, pointedly asked at the opening ceremony of the IIT Madras that the German experts "would help in raising the standard of the cultivation of manual skill of the students, which was almost neglected in their education."[88] Consequently, the curriculum was more focused on practical training, such as blacksmithing and woodworking, than other IITs. In 1961, a group of visiting professors from the Massachusetts Institute of Technology (MIT) noted that half of the first year and three months of the second year were entirely devoted to workshop training.[89] An IIT Madras advertisement exclaimed: "No ivory towers at IIT, Madras."[90] It was the practical orientation of German engineering that was most remarkable and most marketable about the German IIT.

West Germany cheerfully supported this narrative of hands-on, hardworking German craftsmen because it demonstrated technical prowess and, in the words of historian Corinna Unger, helped Germany claim,

[85] Subramanian, *The Caste of Merit*: 107.
[86] "Advertisement for the IIT Madras," *Times of India*, November 23, 1969: 21.
[87] For the development of the engineering profession during the colonial period, see Ramnath, *Birth of an Indian Profession*. Subramanian, *The Caste of Merit*.
[88] "Technical Studies: Institute Opened in City," *The Hindu (Madras)*, August 1, 1959, quoted in: Subramanian, *The Caste of Merit*: 109.
[89] Bassett, "Aligning India in the Cold War Era": 797.
[90] "Advertisement for the IIT Madras," *Times of India*, November 23, 1969: 21.

"a spot among the former colonial powers in the postcolonial scramble for markets and influence."[91] West Germany's own recent history gave it some experience knowledge on how to rebuild an economy after crisis. As Nehru observed, "Germany was a defeated country with no capital left, you might say, everything was in deficit."[92] Reminiscent of Friedrich List's arguments for late developing countries, which had for long been popular in India, he pointed to German education as the strongest tool for recovery.

[T]he real wealth of the country is not the fine buildings, the fine factories and all that. It is the men and women of training and their capacity to work hard. … [O]bviously what I mean by training is modern scientific, technological training. Germany had it.[93]

The recollections of an Indian student of the IIT Madras who did an internship in Germany highlight the deep impression that Germany's recovery after the war made on development aspirations of many Indians. He remembered about his workplace that "it was a factory which had been absolutely flattened at the end of the Second World War. … So, they had built it back brick by brick and then a lot of people, handicapped people, with one arm missing, one leg missing … they brought this thing back, and the kind of pride it took."[94] Successfully rebuilding an economy in distress was a skill that India hoped to emulate from post-war Germany.

The focus on training and economic concerns, moreover, fashioned a variety of technical assistance that appeared nonpolitical. Despite its undeniable role in Cold War diplomacy, the IIT Madras foregrounded the practical results of education. The second project, a prototype and training center, had a similar ambition but specifically focused on small firms. Gandhi's supporters had for long advocated for the cottage industries in the countryside. Their ideals shared some elements with the German "Mittelstand" ideology, a politically powerful rhetoric in post-war Germany, under the Mittelstand enthusiast, Finance Minister Ludwig Erhard.[95]

---

[91] Unger, "Industrialization vs. Agrarian Reform": 62.
[92] Nehru, "Maintain Individuality for Creativity and Progress."
[93] Ibid.
[94] The interview was part of an historical-anthropological study about engineering education in India. The name of the interviewee was anonymized. Quoted in: Subramanian, *The Caste of Merit*: 136.
[95] Berghoff and Köhler, *Varieties of Family Business*: 131–136; 154–160. Berghoff, "The End of Family Business?." Lubinski, "Die Sparkassen und das Geschäft mit dem Mittelstand."

The idea for the prototype center was first discussed in the spring of 1957, during the India visit of the German foreign minister Heinrich von Bretano. It was contractually confirmed as the "Indo-German Prototype Production and Training Centre for Small Scale Industries" in an agreement of October 25, 1958. The Okhla workshop, located south of New Delhi, was designed to impart practical knowledge to workmen required for small-scale industry as well as to specialists to be attached to small industry service institutes. Topics included modern work techniques and machinery knowledge (learned on German machines) but also industrial costing for small-scale industry. In addition, the workshop developed new machines and equipment and executed jobs ordered by small industry. The German Government dedicated Rs 5 million for the equipment of the workshop and assigned twenty-three German experts to teach there. The Indian Government matched these funds.[96] At the inauguration ceremony for the workshop Nehru praised the initiative as "far more important than big factories and steel mills" and as the "basis for industrialisation."[97] Echoing Rourkela one more time, Okhla was the first of a series of prototype workshops that opened during the 1960s, supported by several Western powers and Japan.[98]

Especially in education, Germany had for long served as an exemplar. The idea that Germany as a late-developing country had mastered similar challenges that India was facing suggested that it could provide lessons of some value. As early as the late nineteenth century, Indian education reformers observed German educational institutions with curiosity, and the continuous flow of Indian interns and students to Germany but also German educators to India dated back to the interwar and even pre-World War I period (see Chapters 1 and 4). Germany continued to serve as a model for India's development path. And newly interpreting development pathways should shape how Germans and Indians thought about each other for years to come.

---

[96] "Agreement between India and the Federal Republic of Germany Regarding the Establishment of a Prototype Production and Training Centre for Small Scale Industry," Indian Treaty Series 12 (1958), accessed online: www.commonlii.org/in/other/treaties/INTSer/1958/12.html. See also, Unger, *Entwicklungspfade in Indien*: 175–176. Preuß and Deutsche Gesellschaft für Internationale Zusammenarbeit GmbH, *'Ohne Toleranz funktioniert nichts': Indisch-deutsche Technische Zusammenarbeit*: 17–19. Hunck, *India's Silent Revolution*: 72–74. "German Aid For Project: Prototype Workshop," *Times of India*, July 1, 1957: 7.
[97] "People Must Learn New Skills Fast," *Times of India*, March 3, 1961: 7.
[98] "Steps for Development of Small Industries," *Times of India*, July 15, 1959: 8.

8   Reimagining the World in Stages

The primary development goal of the years 1956 to 1961, the span of the Second Five-Year Plan, was rapid industrialization. India invested heavily in imports from abroad, including from Germany, which turned into one of its most important trading partners. Yet, only months after the start of the plan, India plunged into a foreign exchange crisis that lasted more than two years. The shortage challenged many of the elaborate plans and opened an era of chronic lack of exchange. This trial pushed India towards closer ties with the West, especially with the United States. Western aid provided a solution to the acute problem; yet it also came at a cost. Donor countries expanded their repertoire of policy demands toward India, and new institutions, like the Aid India Consortium, a multilateral development cooperation, provided the organizational base for both coordinated aid and coordinated demands.

This process was reinforced by a fundamental change in the underlying mental map of nationalism. In the donor countries, the idea of "countries in development" rather than nations striving for self-determination suggested a policy direction focused on a predetermined path to growth. The strategy of most Western governments as well as that developed by multinationals took inspiration from social scientists' newly created abstractions (such as stage models and GDP comparisons) that provided new interpretations of the changing world around them. Grappling with the relationship between nations was less a matter of interpreting ideas derived from politics and ideologies and more an exercise of mastering "development science." In this framework, nation-states with a unique history and identity increasingly turned into building blocks of a worldview that prioritized countries' development stage over its unique national features.

While top-level strategy of German multinationals turned towards increasingly abstract and universal models of the world, strategy on the ground in India was shaped not by predictable categories but by one-off and specific negotiations with Indian officials. India was not a passive recipient of Western policies. It responded to the political price tag of aid with a strategy of continuously radicalizing enforcement of its licensing regime, which disciplined and restricted multinationals. In India, ambitious development policy took a back seat to covert haggling between individual multinationals and Indian officials, raising first and foremost the unpredictability of doing business in India. The powerful abstractions that henceforth shaped development policy and multinational strategy revealed a country's stage of growth and previewed how targeted policy could advance its trajectory. Yet, this insight came at the expense of concealing the relationship between historically developed nations. The mental map populated by diverse nation-states was reframed in stark black and white – rich vs. poor countries – and their past rehistoricized as one stage on a path towards Western-style prosperity.

The Stages that Rule the World

India's Second Five-Year Plan had focused on the public sector and outlined a series of costly investments in heavy industry, including the construction of a trio of steel mills (see Chapter 7). The foreign exchange crisis of 1956 called these plans into question and provided an opening for its political opponents, especially those who wished for closer ties with the West.[1] The ambitious agenda would have been difficult to finance under the best of circumstances. Indian planners suggested that some of the necessary resources would come from sterling balances or foreign loans; yet the majority was to be found within the Indian economy.[2] In July 1958, India's burn rate climbed up to about US$10 million per week. Foreign exchange reserves nosedived, and experts assumed they would be wiped out before the end of the year.[3]

India's first reaction to the crisis was to defer many projects of the plan to reduce the demand for imports. The second step was to look for aid from abroad. As the Soviet Union's capacity to provide foreign exchange was limited, India turned to the West for budget relief, first and foremost to the United States. There, India's urgent need happened to blend with the ideas of a group of scholars and politicians, making the case for development assistance in a Cold War world of nations.

Particularly influential became the work of two Massachusetts Institute of Technology (MIT) scholars, economist Max Millikan and economic

---

[1] Engerman, *The Price of Aid*: 159–189.
[2] Mahalanobis, *The Approach of Operational Research to Planning in India*: 107.
[3] India Consortium (English). Washington, DC : World Bank Group. http://documents .worldbank.org/curated/en/164191468034447809/India-Consortium; similarly also, Engerman, *The Price of Aid*: 161–165.

historian Walt Rostow, who argued for long-term development support as a measure against communist influences. Working at the MIT Center for International Studies, funded by the Ford and Rockefeller foundations, they studied how underdeveloped countries evolved and how the United States could optimally support their development. Some of their results circulated among US policymakers since the mid-1950s and were eventually published as a proposal "for an effective US foreign policy." Its ultimate goal was "to promote the evolution of a world in which threats to … our way of life are less likely to arise."[4] In a very optimistic, if not utopian, vision, Rostow and Millikan saw development aid as the most promising tool to have "the industrialized and underdeveloped areas ultimately emerge from the present revolutionary phase of history as members of a common, harmonious world community"[5] – a community that was free of communist influences and celebrated America's way of life.

For Rostow, these ideas were only a brief preview of his magnum opus *The Stages of Economic Growth*, which was published a few years later with the expressive subtitle "A Non-Communist Manifesto."[6] In it, Rostow elaborated on the looming threat that poverty and colonialism may lure people in less-developed countries toward communism. To make his case for sprawling development aid, Rostow created an evolutionary model of five stages of growth that economies go through: traditional society, preconditions for take-off, take-off, the drive to maturity, and the age of high mass-consumption. His rationale was that supporting nations in their quest for reaching this final stage would not only combat global poverty but also provide the best protection against communism.[7] To the delight of any Cold War warrior, Rostow's argument drained global relations between nations of unwieldly ideological and historical differences and rendered them manageable based on what was cast as a set of technical development problems that could be solved.

As a part-time policymaker with government experience, Rostow's pitch was rhetorically elegant and politically powerful.[8] His evolutionary perspective was outlined clearly and accessibly, with strong quotable topic sentences that served politicians as sound bites. The metaphor of a "take off" became a staple of development theory and political debate. It was this engine of growth that made the end stage of "high mass-consumption" achievable to all nations. "[S]ectoral optimum positions

---

[4] Millikan and Rostow, *A Proposal*: title and 3.
[5] Ibid., 143.
[6] Rostow, *The Stages of Economic Growth*.
[7] Ibid., 4–16.
[8] For biographical information see, Milne, *America's Rasputin*.

are determined on the side of demand, by the levels of income and of population, and by the character of tastes; on the side of supply, by the state of technology and the quality of entrepreneurship, as the latter determines the proportion of technically available and potentially profitable innovations actually incorporated in the capital stock."[9] As a big equalizer, Rostow's world was focused on measurable input and output factors abstracting from culture, history, and national identity.

The success of *Stages of Economic Growth* did not depend on the originality of the argument but rather on its ability to integrate different existing schools of thought. The scheme was comforting to many because it was a modernized version of existing growth narratives, such as List's idea of late-developing nations and Marx' depiction of class struggle. It also served as a justification for many steps taken in the past. Even colonialism, in Rostow's elaborations, served a purpose. "Colonies were often established ... to fill a vacuum; that is, to organize a traditional society incapable of self-organization (or unwilling to organize itself) for modern import and export activity, including production for export."[10] To some extent, this mirrored the narrative of the "civilizing mission," used to justify colonialism (see Chapter 4). However, while Rostow did not fundamentally challenge the colonial logic, he translated the notion of superiority based on race into one based on economic strength and turned it into an ephemeral phenomenon. With the right support, all nations could ultimately reach the nirvana of high mass consumption.

Rostow's path to modernization strongly influenced development policy and remnants of it can be detected until today.[11] Importantly, his abstraction from the diverse experiences of many developing countries toward a universal model gave order to data that was being gathered around this time. Economists had started collecting economic information on different countries of the world and standardized their presentation in national income accounts. These global abstractions, including Gross Domestic Product and Gross National Income but also Rostow's stage model, informed a swiftly changing discourse on development aid.[12] This paradigmatic shift in researching global poverty went hand in hand with a belief that state action could do much to alleviate it. Both national governments and international organizations were among the pioneers in collecting and analyzing the newly available data.

---

[9] Rostow, *The Stages of Economic Growth*: 13.
[10] Ibid., 109.
[11] Rist, *The History of Development*: 103.
[12] Speich Chassé, *Die Erfindung des Bruttosozialprodukts*; Speich, "The Use of Global Abstractions."

What these imaginaries of development had in common was that they created a fresh, all-encompassing drawing of a world in development. To this map, economists applied a limited number of policies to foster growth. Rostow's *Stages of Economic Growth* fits this mold because no nation was excluded from the "marvelous fresco of humanity marching towards greater happiness"[13] and Rostow's ideas for fostering development were universally applicable. It was a world of economic uplift.

Rostow meant his framework to serve as a guide for resource allocation. Supporting countries in their progression through the stages of growth had the advantage of suggesting that with the optimally focused aid payments, these countries could "take off" towards a self-sustained process of economic development, effectively becoming independent of future aid. In the long run, this would turn the countries receiving US aid into valuable trading partners.[14] And, by suggesting a prominent role for the United States, he relieved former colonizing countries from shouldering the burden by themselves. Consequently, Rostow was also one of the early proponents for multilateral rather than bilateral aid.[15]

Indian politicians took the same position but for different reasons. A collective action by several possible lenders, they hoped, would make them less dependent on the mighty United States and, at the same time, allow them to capitalize on America's sway over its allies. In September 1957, Nehru reported that Finance Minister T. T. Krishnamachari had left for a badly needed fundraising trip. For Nehru, the club of donors was rather limited. "I do not think there is any hope or chance of our getting substantial help from the United Kingdom. The United States is the only country, apart perhaps from Western Germany, which can help us substantially."[16] Nehru was right to consider West German money a complement to US payments, despite the Germans' relative inexperience with development aid.

At the time that India was looking for support from abroad, West Germany's official policy for developing countries was still at a nascent stage. As West Germany reappeared as a trading partner on the world stage, development aid was primarily used as a tool for increasing exports. The first aid payments financed short-term orders in Germany and were meant to develop longer-term partnerships. However, the German

[13] Rist, *The History of Development*: 98.
[14] Pearce, *Rostow, Kennedy, and the Rhetoric of Foreign Aid*: 65–67.
[15] Millikan and Rostow, *A Proposal*: 65.
[16] Nehru, "SWJN2, 39: 109–111": 109, 110.

political apparatus had no ministry officially responsible for development aid yet. One observer succinctly summarized the situation as "something of a mess."[17] The first official budget for development aid – a modest amount of 500,000 Deutschmark – had come from funds of the Marshall Plan and was allocated to the Ministry of Economics in 1953 because the Marshall funds were meant for Germany's economic recovery. They were a form of development aid that Germany had received from the US and now passed on to other countries. Three years later, the German parliament approved 50 million Deutschmark for development aid, which were integrated into the budget of the Foreign Office, indicating the importance of aid for foreign relations. Especially the US requested its German ally to participate more actively and also financially in the global fight against communism. Although somewhat grudgingly, German politicians had to accept that they could no longer play the role of a country in need itself.[18] It was time to develop a policy for supporting less-developed nations.

However, burden sharing did not mean that the Germans thought of themselves as identical to their Western allies. To the contrary. In a world of crumbling empires, Germany's identity as a nation imbued distinct advantages. Leaning on the pre-war experiences in India, German politicians showcased their image as (alleged) noncolonialists. Asked about his take on colonialism, Vice Chancellor Franz Blücher, during his trip to India in January 1956, declared how happy he was that Germany's relations "are not at all troubled by this question"[19] – a statement that made it onto the title page of the *Times of India*. In the previous April 1955, twenty-nine newly emerging nations of the Global South convened in the Asia-Africa Conference in Bandung, Indonesia. The often-cited "spirit of Bandung" connected these nations in their opposition to colonialism and prepared the ground for collaborations.[20] In a later reflection, Blücher deduced that "[t]he Federal Republic has a good starting position for cooperation with the developing countries in so far as it is not burdened by the odor of colonial relations of domination."[21]

---

[17] White, *German Aid*: 11.
[18] Dr Drechsler, "Economic Support for Developing Countries," September 5, 1956, Part 2 of 2, B 102/13758, BA-K.
[19] V. N. Bhushan Rao, "India, Vital Force for Peace, Says Dr. Bluecher," *Times of India*, January 22, 1956: 1. See also, Das Gupta, *Handel, Hilfe, Hallstein-Doktrin*: 128. Kleinschmidt and Ziegler, "Deutsche Wirtschaftsinteressen."
[20] Lee, *Making a World after Empire*.
[21] Blücher, "Elaboration about Under-Developed Areas, II," September 10, 1956, N/1080/306, vol. 1, BA-K.

Most experts on all sides of the political spectrum agreed that Germany had advantages because it appeared to be a non-colonial country, and that these could be leverage for Germany's export industry. Reflecting on Blücher's trip, a representative of the Indo-German Institute in Stuttgart stressed that "the German businessperson benefits from the fact that the Federal Republic cannot be suspected of being a colonial power."[22] Similarly, a German association supporting international interns found that many Indians came to Germany because it "is considered a non-imperialist and anti-colonial power."[23] No white paper of development policy in these years failed to make this argument. The Foreign Office argued that "the underdeveloped states have an overly sensitive national feeling, and experience has shown that they are suspicious of all measures taken by the West." However, and to Germany's advantage, "the Federal Republic is undoubtedly one of the least suspicious states in this regard."[24] A paper by the Ministry of Economics suggested that Germany is "largely unsuspicious in the eyes of these countries [developing countries] after 2 lost wars and after the loss of any political power."[25] The impression was that Bonn had no legacy sphere of interest in the developing world and seemed conveniently too weak to build one with neocolonial methods.

Historical arguments mattered to this positioning, especially in India. The German Consul observed that in India latent sympathies for Germany still existed "from the – otherwise forgotten – times of common struggle against England."[26] Other observers shared his impression that while Indian politicians avoided the direct memory of political collaboration between Nazi Germany and India and "do not appreciate being reminded," Indians looked at Germany fondly because of their history of joint struggle.[27]

This status as an (allegedly) non-colonial country also shaped German reflections about alliances in both business and politics. As the chemical company Bayer pondered revitalizing its India business, it quickly rejected the idea of collaborating with British partners. "In view of the general negative attitude of the Indian authorities towards further British

[22] "Note about Speech by Dr. Isberg," February 1, 1956, N/1080/143, BA-K.
[23] Burmeister, "Letter to Dr. Grosser," April 13, 1956, B/102/57923, BA-K.
[24] Foreign Office, "Cooperation with Underdeveloped Countries," April 24, 1956, B/102/13758, Part 2, BA-K.
[25] Dr Hasselblatt (in representation), "Economic Support for Developing Countries," September 6, 1956, B 102/13758, Part 2, BA-K.
[26] Dr Roehreke, "Possible Motives of Nehru-Visit," July 6, 1956, B/122/501, Part 2, BA-K.
[27] Von Scherpenberg, "Letter to Foreign Office," June 6, 1951, B/102/2089, BA-K.

influence, cooperation with English companies is ruled out."[28] Instead, contributions from Switzerland seemed more attractive because of this country's conveniently neutral political position.[29] Similar considerations shaped the debate about development policy in the two German ministries involved, the Foreign Office and the Economic Ministry. Where in the world was the value added of a uniquely German participation the greatest? "[T]he main focus of German economic aid would have to be in those countries which seem suspicious of the economic aid of the colonial mother countries, especially England and France, because of the anti-colonial resentment that now exists."[30] Or, as suggested in a different policy document, German aid should avoid close cooperation with other Western European countries, except for the "less exposed countries such as Switzerland and Sweden."[31] A related concern were neocolonial power plays. The United States' activities were seen as adjacent to colonialism in many less developed countries. As Rostow himself remarked, the United States "has come to be regarded increasingly in the uncommitted areas of the world as a power at best neurotic and at worst aggressive, … and with a game of international power diplomacy."[32] Indeed, German administrators found that the same countries with a colonial past were "also critical of American economic aid."[33] The optimal geopolitical game for Germany was "a partnership of equals encumbered by no totalitarian, colonial or monopoly claims to rule."[34] For Germany's pioneering development experts, drafting policy in a decolonizing world required a close look at nations' historical relationship and trajectories.

Yet, these deeper political layers of development imaginaries competed with the dogmatic straitjacket of German foreign policy, the Hallstein Doctrine. Preventing other countries from acknowledging East Germany as an independent state was the primary objective of Germany's foreign relations, often at the expense of other goals. Whenever it became likely that a state or region would enter diplomatic relations with East

---

[28] Reischel, "India: German Participation in Chemical Industry," September 3, 1956, B/102/122085, BA-K.

[29] Indeed, the Swiss Government and Swiss companies utilized their image as a neutral nation in negotiations with the Indian Government. See, Donzé, "The Advantage of Being Swiss."

[30] Foreign Office, "Cooperation with Underdeveloped Countries," April 24, 1956, B/102/13758, Part 2, BA-K.

[31] Dr Hasselblatt (in representation), "Economic Support for Developing Countries," September 6, 1956, B/102/13758, Part 2, BA-K.

[32] Millikan and Rostow, A Proposal: 6.

[33] Foreign Office, "Cooperation with Underdeveloped Countries," April 24, 1956, B/102/13758, Part 2, BA-K.

[34] Ministry of Economics, "Economic Cooperation with Developing Countries," September 18, 1956, B/102/13758, Part 1 of 2, BA-K.

Germany, West Germany gave special attention to this country, including in its development aid. However, many of these measures appeared ad-hoc and erratic, not least because the political responsibilities for development aid were heavily dispersed within Germany's bureaucracy.[35]

Against the background of the Hallstein Doctrine, block-free India, which was more than once on the verge of acknowledging East Germany, developed into one of the biggest recipients of German aid.[36] It also became a veritable laboratory for German development projects. Most initiatives were first tested in India and lessons later transferred to other developing nations. However, while Germany carefully crafted its image as a non-political benefactor, its development aid was anything but neutral. Around the same time that India negotiated for Western aid, Germany insisted on a return of its pre-war assets, which had been expropriated as enemy property in India during the war. The Indian Custodian of Enemy Property held approximately Rs 29.6 million of German pre-war assets, among them more than Rs 12 million from sequestrated goods of I. G. Farben.[37] In 1951, the Government of India maintained the stance that it would not return these possessions.[38] However, after a series of negotiations, India released these assets in batches, first for use of approved re-investment in India only and later for remittances up to a threshold of Rs 5,000.[39] In most Western countries, governments never returned assets to the former enemy aliens. However, in "developing countries" – a category that only started to become relevant in policy making – the German Government insisted on reimbursement, often in unveiled exchange for development aid.[40] While business leaders, like Ernst von Siemens, celebrated the Indian Government for its "fair" approach,[41] it quickly

---

[35] Hein, *Die Westdeutschen und die Dritte Welt*; Bohnet, *Geschichte der deutschen Entwicklungspolitik*; Das Gupta, *Handel, Hilfe, Hallstein-Doktrin*.

[36] Voigt, *Die Indienpolitik der DDR*; Das Gupta, *Handel, Hilfe, Hallstein-Doktrin*.

[37] German Consulate Bombay, "Letter to I.G. Farbenindustrie in Abwicklung," July 13, 1957, 9-K-1-2, BA. Rajya Sabha (Council of States or upper house of the Parliament of India), Session 50, November 26, 1964, Part 1 (Questions and Answers), "Assets of German Nationals," 1231–1234, here: 1231.

[38] Das Gupta, *Handel, Hilfe, Hallstein-Doktrin*: 51.

[39] "Rs. 47.37-Crore Bonn Credit: Pact Signed," *Times of India*, November 27, 1963: 1; Deutscher Bundestag, "Reparationsschädengesetz," 04/1456 of August 13, 1963; Rajya Sabha (Council of States or upper house of the Parliament of India), Session 50, November 26, 1964, Part 1 (Questions and Answers), "Assets of German Nationals," 1231–1234, http://rsdebate.nic.in/handle/123456789/535662; ibid. Session 37, March 26, 1962, Part 1 (Questions and Answers), "Release of the Frozen Assets of German Nationals," 1162–1163, http://rsdebate.nic.in/handle/123456789/554900.

[40] Damm, *Die Bundesrepublik Deutschland und die Entwicklungsländer*: 114.

[41] "Der Name Siemens bedarf hier keiner Einführung," *Siemens-Mitteilungen*, 1, 1968, 68/ Li/156, SAA.

became obvious that returning the pre-war assets was a requirement for further development aid. "It would be incomprehensible to the German public and parliament if German funds on a large scale were devoted [to India], before the old, expropriated assets had been returned."[42] It would not be the last demand on Indian policy in exchange for aid.

The Politics of Aid for India

While German administrators debated the most effective form of aid to support their own political agenda, Germany's post-war allies, especially the US, had different ambitions. Rostow's development stages gave some urgency to focused investments to push countries along their path. Thus, the US urged Germany to become more involved. It was in response to India's currency exchange crisis that the five non-communist countries that traded most with India – the United States, West Germany, Britain, Canada, and Japan – met under the leadership of the International Bank for Reconstruction and Development (IBRD, later World Bank) in 1958. Indian politicians had actively supported this multilateral donor conference because they interpreted it as a way to organize aid that made them less dependent on any one country, while at the same time leveraging US sway over its allies for more aid. The members of what later came to be known as the Aid India Consortium (AIC) engaged in a rescue operation and provided US$350 million for the period from October 1958 to March 1959 to help India overcome its exchange crisis.[43]

Germany participated in this rescue mission by postponing payments due on Rourkela credits, which had already been granted before the meeting, as well as with some additional aid payments.[44] However, decision-makers on development policy in Germany debated the pros and cons of bilateral vs. multilateral aid for several years. Bilateral aid had the advantage that the contribution could take Germany's specific relationship to the receiving country into account. By contrast, a uniquely German position, based on Germany's history and role in the world, became imperceptible in the context of the AIC.[45] Foreign Minister von Bretano described the dilemma: "We must ensure that valuable bilateral links are

[42] Vialon, "Letter to Chancellor: German Assets in India," July 2, 1959, 136/7285, BA-K.
[43] India Consortium (English). Washington, DC: World Bank Group. http://documents .worldbank.org/curated/en/164191468034447809/India-Consortium; Akita, "The Aid-India Consortium."
[44] Das Gupta, *Handel, Hilfe, Hallstein-Doktrin*: 171–172.
[45] "The Economic Cooperation of West Germany with the Developing Countries," August 30, 1957, B/102/13758, Part 1 of 2, BA-K.

not sacrificed to multilateral agreements."[46] Still in 1958, shortly after the emergency help for India, the President of the Bundesbank, Karl Blessing, advocated for multilateral aid, while Ludwig Erhard, then Minister of Economics, made the contrasting case for bilateral agreements.[47] The best one could hope for was defining specific areas for each type of aid.

Paradoxically, not even the AIC was a forum for multilateral aid in the true sense. As the historian David Engerman points out, it was "more like an extended coffee klatsch at a fancy private club."[48] Whenever the amount of aid had been established, India initiated bilateral negotiations with each lender. This was important because next to the amount of aid, the conditions also mattered. The US regularly pledged the highest amount on moderate terms. However, they offered it in the form of project aid, with India receiving the loans gradually as projects became completed. In addition, the money was restricted to purchases in the US. By comparison, the credit conditions offered by Germany and Great Britain were stiffer with interest rates of around 6 percent. Most of the German aid was dedicated to refinancing or extending Rourkela. However, whatever was not for the steel works came as untied aid and was made available to the Indian budget immediately. India's trade deficit with West Germany was so large that Germany did not feel the need to insist on use of the funds exclusively in Germany. As a gesture, giving India the option of spending the money on the most fitting or cheapest suppliers was certainly good politics and required less bureaucratic hassle.[49] But even the untied aid was not without strings. All countries of the AIC had what was tactfully described as policy "recommendations" for India, which were pushed even more forcefully. As the donor countries met more regularly, evergreens on the wish list were a stronger focus on promoting agriculture, more attention to the private sector, expanding exports and foreign direct investment (FDI), and reducing the overall speed and ambition of industrialization.[50]

Starting with the third meeting in September 1960, the AIC became a more permanent institution. Previously, the IBRD had sent three financial experts – Hermann Josef Abs of Germany, Oliver Franks of Great Britain, and Allan Sproul of the US – on a fact-finding mission to India.

---

[46] Federal German Government Bulletin of July 13, 1955, quoted in: Weis, *Hermesbürgschaften*: 30.
[47] "Department Meeting September 8, 1958 about West German Support to Developing Countries and Regions," September 8, 1958, B/102/13759, Part 1 of 2, BA-K.
[48] Engerman, *The Price of Aid*: 182.
[49] Dr Allardt, Bonn, "Letter to German Embassy, New Delhi," March 22, 1962, B/12/1295, PA; On this debate see also, Das Gupta, *Handel, Hilfe, Hallstein-Doktrin*.
[50] Engerman, *The Price of Aid*.

"The Three Wise Men" recommended a long-term aid commitment to India, earlier communication of future pledges to allow for better planning, as well as a stronger focus on non-tied aid, that is, aid that gives the recipient the freedom to procure goods and services from anywhere. The AIC members shifted from emergency relief towards development policy. They focused on the upcoming Third Five-Year Plan slated for April 1961. At the exact same time, West Germany reorganized its administration for development aid. An Inter-Ministerial Committee for Questions of Development Policy was set up in 1960. In the aftermath of the 1961 election, Germany created for the first time a dedicated Ministry for Economic Cooperation.[51] The new German Minister for Economic Cooperation had his work cut out for him. In the AIC meetings that followed, Germany continued to be the second largest lender after the United States; but also under immense pressure by them. US policy makers weaponized public opinion and the American ambassador in Delhi publicly declared that West Germany would be responsible if the AIC meeting were to fail.[52] The memory of this meeting and the accompanying resentments lingered in the reorganized German administration.

The following year, the Germans were on their guard to avoid a repetition of this experience. It was unacceptable to their freshly minted policy to grant money to India this generously, if archrival Pakistan received significantly less.[53] To make matters worse, several German businesses with operations in India urged that, like the US and Great Britain, financial aid should be tied to purchases at home, to guarantee fair competition between Western businesses.[54] Initially, the German development experts in Bonn rejected this idea. A change of this policy would ruin "the quality advantage of our aid over that of other lenders" and therefore also its "particular political effectiveness."[55] Yet, less than a month later, Germany informed India that it was considering tying its aid to a buy-German requirement. India reacted immediately and pled its case for "free money," arguing that it had already planned for Germany's immediately available funds – to no avail.[56]

[51] Bohnet, *Geschichte der deutschen Entwicklungspolitik*.
[52] Krapf, "Aufzeichnung: Politische Bedeutung der Finanzhilfe der Bundesrepublik für Indien" January 9, 1962, in: Pautsch, *Akten zur Auswärtigen Politik 1962*: 91–94.
[53] Duckwitz, "Telegram No. 18," January 22, 1962, B/12/1295, PA.
[54] Duckwitz, "Letter to Foreign Office," January 24, 1962, and "Telegram No. 56," February 26, 1962; both: B/12/1295, PA.
[55] Dr Allardt, Bonn, "Letter to German Embassy, New Delhi," March 22, 1962, B/12/1295, PA.
[56] Duckwitz, "Telegram No. 109," April 16, 1962, B/12/1295, PA; On India's response, Heyden, "Telex No. 168," May 23, 1962. See also, Das Gupta, *Handel, Hilfe, Hallstein-Doktrin*: 258–259.

The disappointment in India was huge, not least because India had hoped to use the German exemplar to sway other lenders to similar actions. While the first German tranche for India's Third Five-Year Plan had come as untied money, the second one was given on a project-related basis. One victim of this change was the collaboration between the Indian Government and the German chemical industry. As German aid could no longer be spent to pay cash for machines and equipment, as originally intended, the HOC project was once again delayed.[57] In the meantime, not wanting to hold industrialization, India had also granted licenses for chemical intermediates to other manufacturers, making the market more competitive. The German chemical firms soured on the project, which became increasingly more expensive. In 1963, six years after the initial proposal, Bayer and its partners decided to once and for all abandon the HOC project, much to the disapproval of Indian policy-makers.[58] And goodwill with the Indian Government was an asset class that was rising in value.

Navigating the License Raj

India's turn to the West during the exchange crisis changed the policy regime for doing business in India. Already with Independence, India had laid out a general framework for collaborations with foreign investors. Majority of ownership and control of joint ventures should ultimately transition to Indians; yet there was some flexibility in the implementation. Consequently, foreign capital moved relatively freely. In hindsight, a German observer summarized that in the post-Independence period the "majority claim was not enforced ... and was hardly taken seriously by most foreign investors."[59] In 1951, the Industries (Development and Regulation) Act increased control over private industry. To orchestrate the rare resources, India established a Licensing Committee in 1952, which controlled every phase of the manufacturing process through licenses. While the licensing system was not new – it had first been established in World War II – it became increasingly more restrictive for foreign firms.[60] Licenses were issued exclusively by the Government.

---

[57] Dr Bongard, "Note Intermediates Project India/Financing," September 20, 1962, 302/0234, BA.

[58] Holzrichter, "India Project," 369/133, BA; Dr. Bongard, "Note Intermediates Project/Meeting with Mr. Venkateswaran on March 28, 1963," 302/0234, BA; "Note Intermediates Project/Meeting at Indian Embassy Brussels," August 7, 1963, 302/0234, BA.

[59] Dr S. Krueger, "Study about Equity Participation," May 4, 1971, 59/402, BA.

[60] Desai, "Evolution of Import Control."

224 Reimagining the World in Stages

The evaluation of proposals was done on a case-by-case basis, which meant it was hard to predict, changed with the political priorities of the day, and incentivized corruption. The decisive criteria were evaluative, in particular the question if the proposal had a positive impact on India's national well-being, usually interpreted as successfully transferring technical know-how (but how much and in what timeframe) or improving the currency exchange situation through import substitution or exports (but to what extent). Multinationals regularly dealt with surprises in the licensing system.

Slowly and steadily, as India's most active trading partners pushed for Indian concessions in exchange for AIC aid, India tightened the rules for engagement. The Industrial Policy Resolution of 1956 divided industries into priority groups, with some being the exclusive responsibility of the state, while in others private sector contributions were welcomed. The Industrial Development Procedure Committee, established in 1963, required the "letter of intent" as a first step towards a license and distinguished key from non-key industries. Since 1965, the Government took openly discriminatory measures against foreign majority firms. Indian companies and Indian capital were given preference in the "delicensing procedure," that is, the critical review of existing licenses and restrictions on new ones. It became more challenging, as one German entrepreneur described it, to navigate "the constantly changing kaleidoscope of the Indian planned economy."[61] Frequent changes continuously reconfigured the rules of the game.

Below the level of the national policy kaleidoscope, different foreign companies made different choices. When the Reserve Bank of India surveyed all foreign collaborations in 1964, it found that Great Britain accounted for 56 percent of all agreements in subsidiaries, compared to 41 percent of all minority participations and 34 percent of purely technical collaborations. The United States participated in all three types almost evenly with 17 percent of all agreements in subsidiaries, 19 percent minority participation and 18 percent technical collaborations. West Germany, by contrast, displayed a clear preference for minority participation (17 percent) and technical collaborations (15 percent), whereas it accounted for only 5 percent of the agreements in subsidiaries.[62]

Both Siemens and Bayer initially avoided the licensing regime by using middlemen, but eventually started developing new strategies for managing it. Building on its earlier collaboration with Protos, Siemens founded

[61] K. B. Grautoff, Gildemeister AG, "Note on Private Investment in India," February 4, 1965, B/126/74987, BA-K.
[62] Reserve Bank of India, *Foreign Collaboration in Indian Industry 1968*.

the Siemens Engineering & Manufacturing Co. of India Private Ltd. in 1957 and turned it into a public company in 1961.[63] Even before this official re-emergence on the Indian market, Siemens had started building electrical equipment in a factory in Worli, near Bombay. It also collaborated with Bharat Bijlee Ltd., a company that produced specialty motors for industry and transformers, and the Cable Corporation of India, which made insulated cables, since the late 1950s.[64] Both manufactured under Siemens' license and Siemens India distributed their products. Siemens also expanded its manufacturing with a switchgear factory in Andheri, near Bombay. To best leverage the opportunities that presented itself in India, Siemens collaborated with the storied Khatau business group, founded in 1874, and businessman Dharamsey Mulraj Khatau. D. M. Khatau served as Chairman of the Board of Siemens India and regularly visited Siemens in Germany.[65]

Strategically, Siemens positioned itself to respond to India's articulated national goals. The focus on what Subhas Bose had earlier called the "mother industries" and what the authors of the Bombay Plan highlighted as "basic industries" (see Chapter 6) was still shaping the agenda, and West Germany was a reasonable source of these products. Accordingly, Siemens advertised, "the basic prerequisite for India's expanding industry is an ample supply of electric power."[66] The company highlighted its experience in this area and pointed to successfully completed projects, such as the Pathri power station in Uttar Pradesh. It then promised continuous collaboration in the future: "[T]he House of Siemens is placing its experience in the field of electrical engineering at the disposal of India."[67] Siemens was granted the right to increase its ownership from a minority to a 51 percent majority in 1964.[68] In 1967, the Government gave permission to return to the pre-war name, Siemens (India) Ltd.[69]

The German chemical industry similarly showcased the complementarity of its skills with India's development goals. Importantly, it also established strong partnerships with local Indian business families; first Chowgule (see previous chapter) and shortly thereafter also the Ghia

---

[63] Siemens Press Information, "Fruitful Cooperation for 100 Years," November 10, 1967, and "ZA Circular No. 302," both 68/Li/156, SAA.

[64] For a brief history of the Cable Corporation of India, see "The Birth and Growth of CCI," *Times of India*, April 19, 1980: 12.

[65] Siemens, "Siemens – Your Partner in India"; Siemens Press Information, "Fruitful Cooperation for 100 Years," November 10, 1967; "ZA-Monthly Report January/February," 1964, all: 68/Li/156, SAA.

[66] "Classified Ad," *Times of India*, March 30, 1956: A3.

[67] Ibid.

[68] Siemens, "ZA Monthly Report January/February," 1964, 68/Li/156, SAA.

[69] Siemens, "ZA Monthly Report Oktober 1967," 68/Li/156, SAA.

Group. Bhupatrai M. Ghia and his brother Damodar M. Ghia, who had previously collaborated with Bayer in the Agfa and HOC projects, belonged to a traditional Hindu joint family, an extended family arrangement which focuses on intergenerational continuity and unity. For corporate diplomacy, the relationship with the Ghia family was invaluable. B. M. Ghia was not just a respected businessman but also a close friend of A. D. Shroff, the financial expert of the Tata conglomerate, who had represented Indian interests at Bretton Woods and was one the authors of the Bombay Plan.[70] As Ghia's mentor, Shroff guided him in his dealings with Bayer but also represented Bayer's interests with the Indian Government. It was Shroff who personally submitted an application for manufacturing dyes in India with German input in exchange for a royalty payment.[71] A new company, Colour-Chem, entered the market for dyes and started production in February 1959 (see Figure 8.1).[72] It was set up as a collaboration between the Ghia brothers and their company Chika and two of the I. G. Farben successor companies, Bayer and Hoechst, who together held a minority of 30 percent.

In collaboration with the Ghia-owned company Chika, Bayer also established the Bayer Agrochem Private Limited in 1958 for the market for pesticides and some pharmaceuticals.[73] In this company, Bayer held a majority share of 56.25 percent from the start, while the Ghia Group owned the remaining 43.75 percent.[74] The business in pesticides was particularly lucrative in the context of the AIC-lenders and the World Bank pushing for more investment in agriculture and India pursuing what came to be known as the "Green Revolution." Over the following two decades, India invested in new technologies to foster an agricultural "take off" and reduce food shortages. Bayer's agrochemicals were a great fit for this swiftly expanding market.[75]

In 1960, based on continuously growing sales numbers, Bayer combined its sales and manufacturing activities in said Bayer Agrochem, despite Ghia's initial protest that it would demote him to "an Indian

---

[70] Central Commercial Office, "Letter to Haberland," June 16, 1953, 329/524, BA.
[71] Bayer, "Minutes of the Meetings Held in Leverkusen on July 7 and July 9, 1953, Concerning India," 302/257, BA; Loehr, "Letter to Haberland and others," March 2, 1960, 369/134, BA.
[72] Annual Reports 1958 and 1959, Bayer Annual Reports, BA.
[73] Bayer, "History of Pesticides Division, part II: India" 1/6/6/39, BA; Bayer, "Note Bayer India Ltd.," October 11, 1966, 302/236, BA.
[74] Dr Hansen, "Letter to Haberland and others," July 21, 1960, 59/402, BA.
[75] On this period, see Frankel, *India's Green Revolution*. For Bayer also Verg, Plumpe, and Schultheis, *Meilensteine*: 457.

Figure 8.1 Colour-Chem, Bombay, 1963. Filling liquid dye into barrels. Dated February 1, 1963; id: 0-25035, BA. © Bayer AG, Archives Leverkusen.

figurehead for the then predominantly European interests."[76] Yet, Ghia eventually gave his blessing and Bayer managed to consolidate. Agrochem was exceptional in the Indian context. Of 310 applications for Indo-foreign collaborations between 1957 and 1960, only twenty-three permitted the foreign partner to hold a majority, reported one Bayer manager after a visit to India.[77] However, Bayer operated in a priority industry and had social capital thanks to Ghia's network. It could also leverage its contributions to the HOC project, while it was still being pursued, which made it time sensitive to utilize the goodwill created with the HOC project.[78] Riding this wave, Bayer also negotiated a diversification into rubber chemicals which India approved because it

[76] Gierlichs and Knauff, "Note about Meeting with Mr. Ghia on July 28, 1960," August 1, 1960, 369/133, BA.
[77] Werner Gebauer, "India: Visit Bayer Agrochem from March 27 to April 3, 1960," 363/36, BA.
[78] Bayer, "Cost Estimate Bayer Agrochem," August 17, 1961, 302/233, BA.

wanted to avoid any dependence on the British ICI, until then the only provider of such products.[79] In every individual negotiation with Indian officials, there were good reasons to cut the new Agrochem some slack. And Bayer was committed to "defend our majority stake in this company tooth and nail."[80]

One goal with Agrochem was to consolidate Bayer's interests in India. This was motivated by the Indian Government's policy for export promotion and by considerations for political bargaining power. "It must be our goal to create 'a multi-footer' in India so that exports of one product can be used to import raw materials for other products." This became increasingly important in the context of export requirements. Finally, it was clear to the decision-makers that more engagement for Indian industrialization in a variety of business lines would increase their bargaining position with the government, an experience they had also made in other countries on their way to development. "The experiences made in other countries speak in favor of organizing the various investment projects together in one company as early as possible," reported a Bayer manager in 1960.[81]

Over time, it became more obvious to Bayer that the licensing system was not just a nuisance but could also be used to pre-empt competitors from entering the market.[82] During the 1960s, Bayer learned to strategically apply for licenses to guarantee its position in the market.[83] However, this focus on diversification posed a dilemma because India's political kaleidoscope, on paper, rejected not just foreign influence but increasingly also the concentration of economic power. "However, we should allow ourselves to be pushed to the extreme in this regard and then, if there are any further production plans, start a second similar company, if necessary with another Indian group."[84] Bayer was confident in its ability to lobby the Indian Government for support for its plans.

In pharmaceuticals, Bayer moved all of its business from Chowgule to Bayer Agrochem in 1963, combining it organizationally with the business with pesticides and rubbers.[85] In the context of this consolidation,

[79] Dr Ehmann, "Report about Meetings Held on Rubber Project wiht Indian Ministry of Commerce and Industry," November 24, 1961, 369/133, BA.

[80] Dr Knauff, "Note: Manufacturing in India," December 4, 1961, 369/133, BA.

[81] Silcher, "Letter to Dr. Knauff," May 16, 1960, 363–36, BA.

[82] See also the example of Unilever, Jones, *Renewing Unilever*: 171.

[83] Dr Friedrich, "Report about India Trip from November 9 to December 5, 1969," January 26, 1970, 369/137, BA. For this strategy see also, Roy, *A Business History of India*: 174.

[84] Dr Knauff, "Note: Manufacturing in India," December 4, 1961, 369/133, BA.

[85] Contract Bayer with Chowgule, November 10 and 21, 1953, and end of contract, 19/140, BA.

it renamed the business Bayer (India) Limited.[86] Similar to Siemens, the Bayer name was well introduced in India because of the earlier work of Bayer (before World War I) and Bayer Remedies (1938–39), and the frequent use of the Bayer name and logo in advertisements. The new Bayer India signed a collaboration agreement with Bayer Germany in late 1963, which was approved by the Indian Government. This agreement, which initially seemed less than spectacular, came with a long-term influential clause. As part of the approval process, Indian officials confirmed Bayer's majority stake for a duration of twenty years.[87] It required a look far into the future to envision a transition to Indian control.

After the ink was dry on this agreement, Bayer indeed held on to its majority and also insisted on five out of nine seats on the Board, despite political pressure to the contrary. The Indian partners started with 43.75 percent at founding and increased this percentage slightly to 47.275 percent in 1975 and 49 percent in 1981, with an increasing part of this Indian ownership placed on public markets. The fact that Bayer never agreed to give up its majority was a general strategy of the multinational. It insisted both in Asia (Japan, Turkey) and Latin America (Mexico, Brazil, Argentina, and Peru) on at least ownership parity; in 70 percent of its subsidiaries abroad Bayer held a clear majority.[88]

Governance for the business with dyes in India was less amenable but not for lack of trying. Bayer's attempts to increase its share in Colour-Chem failed due to objections by the Indian Government.[89] Instead, Bayer and Hoechst opted for a gentlemen's agreement with their Indian partners, which guaranteed that the two German firms would remain the only technical consultant and shared the right to appoint the general plant manager.[90] If by means of majority ownership or trusted stakeholder, both Bayer and Siemens pursued a control strategy in India, in clear contradiction to Indian national policy.

Despite the frequent remixing of the political kaleidoscope, Siemens and Bayer navigated the policy landscape well until at least the mid-1960s. Nehru's death in May 1964 and the brief tenure of his successor, Lal Bahadur Shastri, who passed away unexpectedly in January 1966, once again transformed the political scene. In addition, the foreign exchange crisis, which had temporarily seemed under control, reared

[86] Dr Knauff, "Letter to Bayer Management," March 20, 1963, 59/402, BA.
[87] Bayer Board, "Excerpt Minutes," November 4, 1963, 302/234, BA.
[88] Bayer Annual Reports, 1958 to 1994, BA. See also, Kleedehn, Rückkehr auf den Weltmarkt: 342.
[89] Dr Bongard, "Note India," August 10, 1966, 318/33, BA.
[90] Dr Bongard, "Note Colour-Chem Limited, Bombay," October 6, 1966, 302/236, BA.

its ugly head again. Reserves decreased dramatically by almost 40 percent in 1964. When Indira Gandhi, Nehru's daughter, was elected the third Prime Minister in the decade, India found itself in crisis again. Under the pressure of its foreign aid sponsors, Indira Gandhi agreed to devalue the Rupee in June 1966, which was a repeatedly made suggestion by the AIC countries. Yet, despite this colossal and politically controversial concession, aid payments by the AIC members were less generous than expected and cost Indira Gandhi's Congress Party political capital. Left-leaning forces in India saw the culprit for the economic challenges in foreign intervention and in the concentration of power in monopoly companies. The anti-monopoly sentiment eventually resulted in the Monopolies and Restrictive Trade Practices Commission of 1969, which forced companies to seek approval for any expansion or diversification if they had assets over a stipulated level.

This was bad news for Siemens and Bayer, which were both in the process of expanding their business in India. Bayer built a new facility in Thane, near Bombay, with an investment of Rs 66 million, which started production in 1967.[91] Siemens similarly inaugurated its new factory in the city of Kalwa, also in the Thane district, in 1966 (see Figure 8.2).[92] Both companies thus opted for location in the Bombay area, which was the center of industry in India. "Bombay in 1938 was a town of under a million. There were still coconut groves and fishermen in the north of the island. Today, it has seven million people, and the factories run for nearly forty miles," remembered a Unilever executive in the 1970s. "Around Bombay, all through Western Maharashtra, there has been extensive industrialization."[93] In 1974, the Bombay/Poona area was home to 165 out of 415 Indo-German joint ventures (40 percent), followed by Delhi (15 percent), Calcutta (11 percent), Gujarat (7 percent), Bangalore (7 percent), Madras (5 percent) and Uttar Pradesh (4 percent).[94]

Yet, building these plants was difficult due to the new and continuously expanding red tape. In the case of Bayer, the abandonment of the HOC project only a few years earlier meant that the company had lost much goodwill.[95] The Indian Government demanded unequivocally that

[91] Bayer Press Information, "Chemical Plant in Bombay Completed," March 11, 1970, 9/L, BA.
[92] Siemens, "Siemens Mitteilungen," issue 4, April 1966: 18, 68/Li/156.
[93] "Mr. Zinkin's Report on India," undated [c. 1970s], UNI/BD/SC/3/518.
[94] Schoettle, German Consulate Bombay "Letter to Foreign Office," April 26, 1975, B 102/173584, BA-K.
[95] Dr Friedrich, "Letters [Recipient Unknown]," October 28, 1963, and undated, 369/134, BA.

Figure 8.2 Siemens Kalwa Works, 1967 and 1970. Siemens Kalwa Works, 1967 and Motor Production at Kalwa, 1970 © Siemens Historical Institute.

all equipment that could theoretically be made in India had to be sourced there, but the opinions on what could be purchased locally diverged. Bayer's manager Dr Friedrich complained that "the terms quality and usability are irrelevant for the Indians. In addition, the devices manufactured in India are many times more expensive than our imported quality products."[96] The easy way out – importing from home – was no longer an option.

Consequently, German project managers were forced to roam the country to explore the growing Indian industry – with some success. "In fact, we were surprised at what industry has opened up here."[97] A Unilever manager described similar changes. "[O]ne sees tube wells everywhere, every village is electrified ... In every town there are workshops and small factories. Virtually none of this existed thirty years ago."[98] However, many of the companies were very small, as Bayer managers tried to demonstrate with their photographs (see Figure 8.3).

These tiny shops were unable to meet the country's growing needs. Thus, there was very little competition and local prices were regularly 30 to 40 percent above import prices. After lengthy negotiations, the Government conceded to allow some imports, yet only for those products, for which local manufacturers sent a letter of regret, confirming that they could not provide them in the required quality.[99] This created additional delays, pushed the German manufacturers to exaggerate the technical sophistication of the equipment they needed, and created new dependencies on the local industry and Indian partners.

Despite these challenges, Bayer India broke even for the first time in 1969. Given this positive result and the further tightening of the licensing policy in 1970, Bayer reconsidered its dogmatic stance on its majority ownership. Since the amendment to the "Foreign Exchange Regulation Act" (1965), foreign companies were no longer allowed to represent other companies (both foreign and Indian) without prior approval by the Reserve Bank. Bayer India, for example, was only granted the right to carry out indent transactions, that is, collecting purchase orders in exchange for commission, for Bayer until a cut-off date in 1972. It was forbidden from representing any Indian company or from selling the products of its own subsidiary, Colour-Chem. The government exercised a plan to dismantle foreign majorities with the license regime as its main weapon.

Furthermore, depending on their classification, the Indian Government imposed export requirements on private companies to mitigate the

96 Ibid.
97 Ibid.
98 "Mr. Zinkin's Report on India," undated [c. 1970s], UNI/BD/SC/3/518.
99 Dr Friedrich, "Letters [Recipient Unknown]," October 28, 1963, and undated, 369/134, BA.

Figure 8.3 Indian electrical workshop, Calcutta, 1963. "Engineering: Projects India, 1953–1985," 59-402, BA. © Bayer AG, Archives Leverkusen.

critical exchange situation. In 1970, to further curb foreign influence, royalty rates were limited to a maximum of 5 percent, with averages of 2–3 percent. The duration of collaboration agreements, which was originally set at up to twenty years and had already been reduced to ten years a few years earlier, was limited to five years. One of the most disturbing changes was the 1970 Indian patent law, which only recognized process but not product innovation. This was particularly challenging for Bayer's work in the pharmaceutical industry. Some Indian firms reverse-engineered well-established pharmaceutical products based on patent descriptions and sold them successfully in India.[100] Having just passed the break-even point, life was getting harder in India, even for those German multinationals that capitalized on their contributions to India's development efforts.

---

[100] Patent Department, "Letter to Prof. Hansen, Patent Law in India," 302/1013, BA. See also, Roy, *A Business History of India*: 183; Zaman and Khanna, "The Cost and Evolution of Quality at Cipla."

The Mixed Legacy of FERA

While India's licensing system was hard to manage and often unpredictable, the process of disciplining multinationals remained slow and uneven. Many companies used their bargaining power in their negotiations with the government. In fact, for several multinationals the licensing system, which had originally been perceived as restrictive and unpredictable, turned out to protect the most established players. "Business learnt to play by the rules of the game"[101]

Initially, the focus was on foreign majority ownership, which was only relevant to a small subset of German companies. In a detailed study of 1971, a Bayer expert found that of all Indo-foreign joint ventures, British companies held an average of 81 percent of ownership and their US counterparts even 84 percent. Both ranked above the average of 78.5 percent. By comparison, West German companies held significantly smaller shares of on average 58.6 percent, one of the lowest means together with Sweden (53.8 percent).[102] In the chemical industry, which was considered one of the priority areas for Indian industrialization, the Germans entertained a total of fifteen joint ventures. Ten of them had minority participation of the German partners. The former I. G. companies BASF and Hoechst, with a long history in India, held parity in their ventures. The Century Enca Ltd. had a foreign majority, but it was split between two collaborators, the German Glanzstoff and the Dutch Akzo. No German chemical firm had as persistently defended its majority as Bayer (see Table 8.1).

As the only true majority owner, Bayer considered reducing its share. However, having experienced the case-by-case evaluations by the Indian Government in the past, the Germans hoped for concessions in exchange. One manager remarked that,

[d]ue to the individual and often pragmatic treatment of each case by the Indian authorities, which does not allow a prediction of the reaction of the authorities in advance, it is proposed to enter into consultative, non-binding discussions about the reduction of the majority in stages up to the final phase of 50% in exchange for reciprocating rewards.[103]

"How much can we get for it?", was often the guiding question for these negotiations. Bayer and Siemens also looked to other developing

---

[101] Roy, *A Business History of India*: 194. For the example of Unilever's successful negotiations with the Indian Government over price controls, see Jones, *Renewing Unilever*: 171–172.

[102] Dr S. Krueger, "Study about Equity Participation," May 4, 1971, 59/402, BA.

[103] Meyerheim, "Letter to Bayer Management," June 9, 1971, quote: page 4, 59/402, BA.

Table 8.1 *Participation of German chemical firms in Indian joint ventures, 1971*

Indian Company	German Ownership (%)	German Partner(s)
1. Bayer (India) Ltd. Bombay	57.4	Bayer
2. Century Enca Ltd. Bombay	51	22.5% Glanzstoff 28.5% Akzo (Dutch)
3. BASF India Ltd. Bombay	50	BASF
4. Hoechst Pharmaceuticals Ltd. Bombay	50	Hoechst
5. Hoechst Dyes & Chemicals Ltd. Bombay	50	Hoechst
6. Dr. Beck & Co. (India) Ltd. Bombay	49	Dr. Beck
7. German Remedies Pvt. Ltd. Bombay (*)	49	9.7% Boehringer 9.9% Bauer & Cie. 9.7% Nordmark-Werke GmbH 9.8% Schering AG 9.9% Chemiewerk Homburg
8. Boehringer-Knoll Ltd. Bombay	48	Boehringer
9. Franco-Indian Manufacturing Co. Ltd. Bombay	41	Hoechst (via 82% in Hoechst Pharmaceuticals)
10. PIL (Polyolefins Industries Ltd.) Bombay	33.3	Hoechst
11. Colour-Chem Ltd., Bombay	32.8	Bayer (16.4%) Hoechst (16.4%)
12. The New India Industries Ltd. Baroda	25.7	Agfa Gevaert
13. Leukoplast (India) Pvt. Ltd.	24.775	Beiersdorf
14. Indian Organic Chemicals Ltd. Bombay	12.5	CW Hüls
15. Dr. Paul Lohmann India Ltd. Calcutta	10	Lohmann

Note: * Information about German Remedies from 1963 based on Boehringer Hermes Application, B 126-70213, BA-K; about Beiersdorf, Reckendrees, Beiersdorf: 175; all others: Dr S. Krueger, "Study about Equity Participation," May 4, 1971, Engineering: Projects India, 59–402, BA.

countries for inspiration, most notably to the important markets of Argentina and Brazil.[104] Yet the planned negotiations were delayed by the 1971 war between India and Pakistan. Because of the war, the United States temporarily ceased their aid payments to India, thus exacerbating

[104] Dr Hansen, "Letter to Schmitz, Sales Pharma," June 29, 1959, 405/61, BA.

the Indian exchange situation. West Germany took a different stance and continued supporting India. Thus, for Bayer and other multinationals the war was a double-edged sword. On the one hand, they expected certain advantages as an Indo-German venture thanks to the continuing development aid. On the other hand, they feared that the US position would push India closer to the Soviet camp and lead to more socialist policies.[105] Observing rather than acting seemed like the best course of action.

In 1973, in the wake of the first global oil price shock, India passed the Foreign Exchange Regulation Act (FERA), which became law on January 1, 1974. It made it mandatory for firms to reduce foreign ownership to less than 40 percent. A law of the same name had already existed since 1947 and regulated foreign firms in their operations in India and their employment of foreigners. The law was meant to limit the outflow of exchange and at the same time was a political peace offering to the political left. As a radical proposal to combat foreign interference, the Indian and international press marked it as a major milestone in Indian policy. Hermann Josef Abs, the influential German banker and previous member of the group of Wiseman that the World Bank had sent to India, visited the country again in January 1973 to explore the changes for foreign investors. Reporting on his unofficial meetings with political and business leaders he went as far as to say that he "would advise a firm which has not invested in India against going there."[106]

However, while FERA initially seemed draconian, its implementation was less dramatic than it first appeared. Multinationals were able to negotiate the time to reduce ownership. The law also left room for exceptions, for example for companies in core areas of Indian industrialization, for strong exporters as well as for those firms that introduced sophisticated technology to India. A Bayer representative who happened to be in India in September and October 1973 reported from his conversations with the different authorities that there was no reason to be concerned. As an insurance policy, Bayer founded a new company, Jagat Chemicals, which was set up with fully Indian ownership.[107] Like other German multinationals, Bayer guaranteed its influence over Jagat by selecting a German manager and by working with a trusted steward, S. V. Rangaswamy, who became both Chairman and majority owner. Rangaswamy had represented Bayer's interests in

[105] Bayer India, "Letter to Bayer: Outlook 1972" Late December 1971, 59/402, BA.
[106] As reported to Unilever's Overseas Committee by Maurice Zinkin, "Dr. Abs' Visit to India," January 18, 1973, UNI/BD/SC/3/518, UAC.
[107] Dr Krueger, "Letter to Bayer Management," October 19, 1973, 59/402, BA.

Karnataka (previously Mysore) for over twenty-five years and was also a collaborator of Chika.[108] Bayer also agreed to slowly reduce its ownership in Bayer India from over 57 percent to 51 percent over the next five years, which was a sign of goodwill but still did not comply with FERA.[109]

Over the next four years, the economic situation in India worsened. Inflation and increasing debts intensified India's dependence on foreign aid. The Government reduced credit lines for companies in India, which created problems for many, including Bayer, to run their regular business.[110] In June 1975, Indira Gandhi declared a state of emergency, which lasted until March 1977. During the Emergency, constitutional rights were suspended. Gandhi had the authority to rule by decree, and several of her political opponents were imprisoned.[111]

After the Emergency, many of the rules for foreign business were enforced even more rigorously. During the 1977 election, Indira Gandhi's Congress Party suffered a devastating defeat by the Janata Party, and Morarji Desai became the first non-Congress Prime Minister of India. He appointed the radical trade union activist George Fernandes, who had been in active political resistance to the Emergency, as Minister for Industries. Originally from Goa with Portuguese roots, Fernandes was known for his colorful and impulsive personality. The German ambassador in India, Dirk Oncken, described him as "somehow belong[ing] to two worlds, one Western and one Indian." He was seen as intelligent and likable but also polarizing in his behavior.[112] In his new position, Fernandes became responsible for supervising foreign multinationals. For many Anglo-American firms, this was when, in the words of historian Tirthankar Roy, "the room to negotiate was taken away, and compliance with FERA was ensured."[113] The Chairman of Hindustan Lever, the Indian subsidiary of Unilever, T. Thomas reported that Fernandes "is a bit of terror to big business."[114]

Shortly after his appointment, Fernandes clashed with the US multinationals Coca-Cola and IBM and eventually triggered their departure from India. A total of over fifty companies decided to end their operations in

[108] Kollo, "Information on S. V. Rangaswamy, Chairman of Jagat," June 10, 1981, 302/1013, BA.
[109] Dr Krueger, "Study of Decrease of Bayer's Participation in Bayer India Limited," September 14, 1973, 59/402, BA.
[110] Dr Krueger, "Report about Situation in India and BIL, October 1974," November 4, 1974, 59/402, BA.
[111] Frankel, *India's Political Economy*.
[112] Oncken, German Embassy New Delhi "Letter to Foreign Office," June 19, 1979, B 213/12504, BA-K.
[113] Roy, *A Business History of India*: 196.
[114] T. Thomas, Chairman of Hindustan Lever, "Letter to J. Louden, Unilever," July 19, 1977, UNI/BD/SC/3/518, UAC.

India in 1977/1978.[115] Fernandes also put pressure on Hindustan Lever, asking it to divest to a 40 percent shareholding. Hindustan Lever reduced its equity from 65.5 percent to 51 percent in 1979 but then bargained for keeping a majority, a request eventually granted by a new government in 1981. It also invested in a very prominent research laboratory.[116] But the compromise left clear marks on the multinational's strategy. Unilever made the concessions to export 10 percent of its production and diversify into "core" areas of Indian industrialization, for example detergent chemicals and cement. Unilever's Overseas Committee expressed the worry that these "heavy investments would be destroying the yield of the company"; however, they were judged for the "benefit they would bring to the company as a whole. At least we were being seen to be innovative and protecting our business thereby."[117] However, Hindustan Lever, as one of the few foreign-controlled consumer goods companies in India, remained a target for criticism.[118]

German business executives experienced Fernandes' tenure differently. First, full majority ownership was overall rare among the German companies in India. Investments by many mid-size German companies and a general risk avoidance had led to minority participation as the common form of engagement in India, which was one of the reasons for the more collaborative attitude of the Indian Government. Second, even the few German multinationals that were majority or parity owners quickly relaxed their concerns. Shortly after his appointment, Fernandes spoke at the annual assembly of the Indo-German Chamber of Commerce and stressed that German industry had no need to worry. He explained that India would continue to need foreign investment and that German capital was welcome. When celebrating the excellent collaboration with German companies, Fernandes specifically mentioned Siemens, Bosch, and Bayer – all three majority owners of their Indian subsidiaries. He clearly meant to reassure those German businesses most worried about FERA and took the time to explain that IBM's and Coca-Cola's products were neither sophisticated nor highly needed in India.[119] Analyzing Fernandes' visit, Bayer's Political

[115] Nayak, *Multinationals in India*: 36.
[116] "Meeting of the Special Committee Held at Unilever House," August 14, 1979, with Overseas Committee; "HLL and FERA – A Status Note"; and "Proposed Strategy with Regard to FERA," all UNI/BD/SC/3/518, UAC.
[117] Overseas Committee Annual Estimate 1979: India, UNI/BD/SC/3/518, UAC. See also, Aldous and Roy, "Reassessing FERA." Choudhury and Khanna, "Charting Dynamic Trajectories." Jones, *Renewing Unilever*: 172–174.
[118] Encarnation, *Dislodging Multinationals*: 111–112, 165.
[119] Forstmann, "Note Fears of Deterioration of Investment Climate in India/Conversation with George Fernandes on September 15, 1977," September 16, 1977, 302/1013, BA.

Economy Department was happy to learn about his "surprisingly positive attitude towards German foreign investment in India." For Fernandes, the author posited, German joint ventures, unlike their British
and US counterparts, did not pursue political goals or tried to exert
influence in India.[120]

Moreover, it became known in the business community that Fernandes
entertained close social ties to the German trade union movement. Fernandes is "very friendly with the Socialist trade-union leaders in West
Germany, etc." reported Hindustan Lever's Chairman T. Thomas.[121]
During the Emergency, while Fernandes and his family had to go underground, he received financial assistance from West Germany. Fernandes,
then Chairman of the Indian Socialist Party, approached European
socialist leaders for support, including Willy Brandt, the chairman of the
Social Democratic Party of Germany and German Chancellor from 1969
to 1974. At Fernandes' arrest in India, Willy Brandt, together with the
Swedish Olof Palme, and the Austrian Bruno Kreisky, wrote to Indira
Gandhi and demanded fair treatment for Fernandes.[122] The backing of
these activists also influenced public opinion against Gandhi's emergency policy. Bayer's conclusion that "without Willy Brandt Fernandes
would no longer be alive" was certainly exaggerated, but Fernandes had
a soft spot for Germany and kept close relations with the German trade
unions throughout his life.[123]

In this new context, Bayer and Siemens, together with other German majority owners, defended their shares, despite the more rigorously
enforced rules for foreign business. Siemens' biggest challenge was not
its majority share but an accusation that it had paid a bribe of 25 million
Deutschmark to Fernandes to acquire approvals for a wide-ranging collaboration with the largest Indian public engineering firm, Bharat Heavy
Electricals Ltd., or BHEL.[124] Indian journalists feared that the goodwill
Fernandes enjoyed in West Germany may be "exploited for expanding
interests of multinational firms in this country."[125] The BHEL agreement
was fodder for many heated debates, with one Indian parliamentarian

---

[120] Political Economy Department, "India: Investment Climate," October 13, 1977,
302/1013, BA.
[121] T. Thomas, "Letter to J. Louden, Unilever," July 19, 1977, UNI/BD/SC/3/518, UAC.
[122] Vivekanandan, *Global Visions of Olof Palme, Bruno Kreisky and Willy Brandt*: 75–76,
150–151, 236.
[123] Political Economy Department, "India: Investment Climate," October 13, 1977,
302/1013, BA. See also, Budhwar, *A Diplomat Reveals*: 16–18.
[124] For this accusation see, "Indien: Wahnwitziger Betrag," Spiegel 42 (1978), October
15, 1978.
[125] John, K. C. "Siemens Expansion May Hit Indigenous Electronic Units," *Times of India*,
July 5, 1978: 1.

branding it as the work of traitors who had no commitment to the concept of self-reliance.[126]

Bayer was less in the crosshairs and confidently claimed that "the FERA laws have so far been flexibly enforced by every Indian government and Bayer is not currently at risk to be forced to lower its 51% majority share."[127] Bayer's main competitor, the British ICI, did not own a majority but held on to parity ownership. However, the Indian Government owned 9 percent of ICI itself and also had the option of buying it out in case of a sale.[128] Despite this governance compromise, ICI, unlike Bayer, showed little interest in expanding its presence in India under the new political regime.

Both Siemens and Bayer navigated the FERA era with support of their Indian allies. Since 1955, Bayer had a political liaison officer in New Delhi to represent its interests, which was seen as a necessary expense. "Most of the other major chemical companies in the world already have an agent in Delhi who looks after their interests with the Indian government."[129] The managing director of Bayer India from 1973 to 1977, von Drigalski, remembered that the experts for Indian Government relations built not just on local but even on intergenerational expertise. "For orientation in the Udjok Bhavan [Udyog Bhawan] and the arranging of appointments with officials, one needs experts stationed in Delhi, so-called liaison officers, without whom no larger company can do. Ours was called Mr. Lal. He had already taken over the job from his father."[130] And Lal was not the only expert for India's complex political economy. Siemens held on to its majority, not least by leveraging its partnership with the important public company BHEL and with George Fernandes.[131] Bayer's business continued to benefit from the fruitful collaboration with the Ghia Group. B. M. Ghia became a champion for the German chemical firm and also integrated Bayer's managers into his social circles. Von Drigalski developed a personal friendship with the Ghia family and reported from the

[126] Special Correspondent, "BHEL-Siemens Technical Pact Move Defended," *Times of India*, March 22, 1979: 5.
[127] Kollo, "Information on S. V. Rangaswamy, Chairman of Jagat," June 10, 1981, 302/1013, BA.
[128] Roy, *A Business History of India*: 199.
[129] Borgwardt & Klebert, "Report about trip to India, February 8 to 25, 1955," March 3, 1955, B 59/402, BA-K.
[130] von Drigalski, *Stationen eines langen Weges*: 156.
[131] K. C. Khanna, "Lessons Not to be Forgotten: Implications of BHEL-Siemens Deal," *Times of India*, December 18, 1979: 8. For details about the collaboration see, Oncken, German Embassy New Delhi, "Letter to Foreign Office," February 21, 1979, and June 19, 1979, B 213/12504, BA-K.

Table 8.2 *Bayer India Limited and Siemens India Limited: sales and pre-tax profits (in million rupees), 1968–1986*

	Bayer			Siemens		
	Sales	Pre-tax Profit	% Profits of Sales	Sales	Pre-tax Profits	% Profits of Sales
1968				197	7.6	3.9
1969	58	4.1	7.1	242	22.1	9.1
1970	74	10.6	14.3	321	34.5	10.7
1971	105	16.1	15.3	385	40.8	10.6
1972	132	23.2	17.5	437	45.8	10.5
1973	161	30.9	19.2	537	81.7	15.2
1974	218	46.6	21.3	708	106.0	15.0
1975	253	49.5	19.5	733	92.9	12.7
1976	298	40.5	13.6	761	101.1	13.3
1977	358	38.9	10.9	712	n/a	n/a
1978	444	54.6	12.3	939	78.9	8.4
1979	498	48.2	9.7	1,255	96.5	7.7
1980	533	21.1	4.0	1,050	128.4	12.2
1981	447	13.2	2.9	1,201	164.0	13.7
1982	660	62.3	9.4	1,438	170.0	11.8
1983	735	54.1	7.4	1,390	154.0	11.1
1984	821	66.6	8.1	1,379	104.0	7.5
1985	922	83.0	9.0	1,735	154.0	8.9
1986	1,014	90.1	8.9	1,984	188.0	9.5

Bayer India Limited, Bombay, Annual Reports, 1969–1986, 9/L, BA; Siemens India Limited, Times of India reporting, 1968–1987.

lavish parties he and his wife attended, which "had something courtly about them" and which were crucial for him as a source of political information.[132]

For both of these German multinationals, sales and profits grew over the following decades (see Table 8.2). In the 1970s, Bayer's pre-tax profits grew from Rs 4 million in 1969 to Rs 48 million in 1979, although sales numbers were still relatively modest. In the early 1980s, labor unrests and lockouts resulted in a loss of production at Bayer, while prices of raw materials increased, and foreign rivals successfully imported cheaper pesticides than what Bayer produced locally. Yet the slump was temporary. In the mid-1980s, Bayer realized profits of Rs 90 million and sales of over Rs 1 billion. Throughout the 1970s and 1980s, pesticides made up the lion's share of the business with over 50 percent of sales in

[132] von Drigalski, *Stationen eines langen Weges*: 161.

the conducive context of the Indian Green Revolution. Pharma and rubber chemicals together accounted for the remainders.[133]

Siemens India had pre-tax profits of Rs 90 million in the mid-1970s. Its performance dipped in 1977/1978, after the BHEL publicity crisis and severe strikes (which also affected Unilever and ICI)[134], but then recovered swiftly. Siemens hit the milestone of Rs 1 billion in sales in 1979 and realized pre-tax profits of between 7 and 13 percent of sales in the 1980s.

Supported by a slowly starting liberalization process in the 1980s, both Bayer and Siemens continued to expand their business in India. Nationalism mattered for the business these German firms did in India. However, the way stakeholders looked at and made sense of nations had fundamentally change from previous decades. The political avalanche of decolonization gave a new urgency to economic development. Postcolonial nationalism was still focused on political self-determination but included in it the twin brother of economic development.[135] Rostow's stage model advocated a worldview in which nations pursued nothing but economic development, supported by the planning optimism and state-led development policy of the 1950s. It was now a task for governments to strategize about development tactics. Together, these changes in the way nations were conceptualized amounted to a major turning point in history. As early as 1958, Gunnar Myrdal summarized that,

> [T]he emergence in underdeveloped countries of this common urge to economic development as a major political purpose, and the definition of economic development as a rise in the level of living of the common people, the agreement that economic development is a task for government, and that government must prepare and enforce a general economic plan, containing a system of purposefully applied controls and impulses to get development started and to keep it going – all this amounts to something entirely new in history.[136]

The idea that countries evolved along predictable stages of growth – eloquently argued by Rostow and others – and that public development aid could propel them along this trajectory were new to contemporaries.

But the process of comparing nations' development progress was rooted in and dependent on new global abstractions, such as the calculation of national incomes or Rostow's stage model, which made it possible to compare fundamentally heterogeneous nations. It was this family of global abstractions that unveiled global inequality in a new way.

---

[133] Bayer India Limited, Bombay, Annual Reports, 1969–1986, 9/L, BA.
[134] Overseas Committee, "Annual Estimate 1977: India," UNI/BD/SC/3/518, UAC.
[135] Myrdal, *Rich Lands and Poor*. 7.
[136] Ibid., 82.

As governments and development experts re-imagined the world of nations, they introduced a new mental map and a new vocabulary to describe it. The idea of "developing countries" highlighted the statistically measurable economic strength of nations and how it could be improved.

However, it did so at the cost of other characteristics, which had previously been meaningful. The category "developing country" is fundamentally different from that of "colonial country," which highlights the dominance of a colonizer over its dependent territories, or "countries with strong nationalist movements" (see Chapter 5), which highlights the agency and resistance of a nation vis-à-vis others. All of these descriptors abstract from reality, like any map abstracts from the concrete conditions of the territory it describes. Yet, each of them shows the world through a different lens. The new mental map that emerged in the second half of the twentieth century focused on the process of development and highlighted its repeatable patterns. At the same time, it abstracted from concrete nations and concrete companies within them. What was once a world of national identities that companies studied, with concrete relationships, histories, and aspirations, developed into a world of countries at different stages of development. Few summarized this as succinctly as Gunnar Myrdal in his book title, *Rich Lands and Poor*. It was a world reduced to wealth and poverty.

This reframing also changed international business strategy. It deemphasized the historical relationship between nations, which had previously influenced decisions. The idea of a stage model for economic development robbed nations of their historical relationships in favor of a predictable and universal pattern of development, which was free of business diplomacy. At both Siemens and Bayer, world regions and comparative tables replaced the narrative accounts about individual foreign markets, which had previously been common. In 1952, Siemens' organizational structure had still grouped Great Britain and Ireland together with India, Indonesia, and the Far East, whereas the Benelux countries and France were classified together with former African colonies; and Brazil belonged in a separate category with Portugal and Spain.[137] The history of colonialism characterized how companies made sense of countries and clusters of nations. Similarly, Bayer's annual reports in the 1950s and 1960s listed countries by order of importance for their business, and, for each country, provided a narrative account of objectives and progress.[138] Over time, both companies reorganized and clustered foreign markets into world regions and used overview tables with cumulative results and

---

[137] Organizational Plan, Organization Business Abroad 1945–65, 8109, SAA.
[138] Bayer Annual Reports, BA.

maps to describe them.[139] This transition was reinforced by the increase in organizational size and the move from functional to multidivisional organizational structures, which many German multinationals undertook in the early 1970s.[140]

Yet, as the mental map of nationalism became more universally applicable, it also became less useful as a sensemaking device within any one specific country. For German multinationals in India this move toward a more abstract mental map of nationalism, paradoxically, resulted in a strategy composed of heavily localized tactics. First, the lack of predictability of political negotiations in India led to actions with the explicit goal of circumventing regulations. Second, multinationals engaged in lobbying efforts and nurtured political relationships. Third, businesspeople explored the options for (and content of) possible one-off agreements.

Importantly, even without a history of colonialism in India – and partly because of this difference to British rivals – German business built on a strong legacy in the subcontinent and stressed its historic commitment to India. Whereas strategy scholars argue that a previous colonial relationship reduces administrative distance and thereby facilitates cross-border business,[141] large German multinationals of the likes of Bayer and Siemens not only looked back at a long, storied history in India, but also actively mobilized their past and the historical relationship between Germany and India. History marketing stressed past achievements, joint ambitions, and the two nations' complementarities in their capabilities and aspirations. "The House of Siemens having more than 90 years of experience ... took an active part in the realization of the first [Five-Year] plan" or "After one hundred years in India, shouldn't an electrical company be able to provide all the electrical equipment its clients need? ... Ask us."[142] These ads spotlighted the long history of selected German companies in India.

Having a believable claim to assisting India on the path to growth was important for German companies because it gave them bargaining power in local negotiations. But the Indo-German bilateral relationship lost in importance as abstract ideas of developing countries and their

---

[139] Siemens Central Administration Foreign Business, Organization July 1962, 8109, SAA. Bayer Annual Reports, BA. Similarly also at Daimler-Benz. See, Annual Report 1980 and 1995. www.daimler.com/investors/reports-news/.
[140] McKenna, *The World's Newest Profession*: 165–191.
[141] P. Ghemawat, "World 3.0: Global Prosperity and How to Achieve It," Boston, MA: Harvard Business Review Press, 2011, 54–59. See also, Lundan and Jones, "Commonwealth Effect."
[142] Siemens ads, in: Times of India, 30 March 1956: A3 and Financial Express Special issue, 1970, B 213/6807, BA-K.

predetermined development path changed how stakeholders envisioned global markets. Even the rhetoric of the noncolonial, nonthreatening Western partner that Germany had for long nurtured, was of a different era, when the socio-historical bilateral relationship between both nations shaped the mental map of nationalism. What was once seen as a world of nations with unique histories, identities, and aspirations turned into a pattern of development that was perceived to unfold in much the same way across the globe.

Conclusion: Rehistoricizing Nations

The reopening of the country to foreign investment in the 1991 industrial policy also meant that the ghost of the East India Company was finally laid to rest. These structural reforms and the reforms of the external sector signaled a major change in India's perception towards foreign investment and marked a paradigm shift in India's economic thinking. In many ways, this marked a major shift from economic nationalism India practiced thus far towards economic liberalism that understood the value of freeing the markets from state control.[1]

(Prabhash Ranjan, 2019)

India, today, reflects the complex relationship between nationalism and globalization at play in this book. The country's liberalization in 1991 was widely considered a move to greater international integration that would entail a softening of Indian economic nationalism – that, as Prabhash Ranjan put it in the quotation above, "the ghost of the East India Company was finally laid to rest." India's political history over the last three decades, however, has been marked by soaring rather than softening nationalism. Rising nationalism has gone hand in hand with greater, not lesser, international integration. Foreign direct investments and trade have grown significantly, and Indian workers have been increasingly important in many regions of the global economy from Silicon Valley to the Persian Gulf.

Indeed, the recent wave of nationalist movements – the United States, United Kingdom, France, Denmark, Russia, Turkey, and China to name just a few – has surprised many scholars and intellectuals who expected the globalization of the last few decades to displace a sense of national affiliation. Not too long ago, American economist Robert Reich predicted:

---

[1] Ranjan, *India and Bilateral Investment Treaties*: 106–107.

There will no longer be national economies ... Each nation's primary political task will be to cope with the centrifugal forces of the global economy which tear at the ties binding citizens together ... As borders become ever more meaningless in economic terms, those citizens best positioned to thrive in the world market are tempted to slip the bonds of national allegiance.[2]

The common wisdom is thus often to diagnose surging nationalist movements as reactionary responses against global integration. As sociologist Anthony Giddens posits, "[T]he revival of local nationalisms, and an accentuating of local identities, are directly bound up with globalizing influences, to which they stand in opposition."[3] While there is a kernel of truth to this interpretation, it fails to account for the complex ways in which globalization and economic nationalism have developed hand in hand over the long run.

Navigating Nationalism has highlighted the deep limits of treating nations and nationalism simplistically as barriers to international integration or as political risks in international strategy. As Sebastian Conrad has noted about global integration since the late nineteenth century, "the interconnectedness of the world ... did not lead to national affiliations becoming diluted, as some contemporaries (and some later historians) believed, but in fact helped to make the idea of the nation more established across the globe."[4] The globally integrated world has been one in which nations and nationalism have mattered more, not less.

To better integrate nations into our understanding of international business history and strategy, *Navigating Nationalism* has argued that we need to move beyond a transactional view of international business steeped in the assumption that nationalism introduces political risks and increases transaction costs, towards a relational view in which multinationals are understood as integral players in an evolving geopolitical landscape comprised of national communities. Such a view considers how multinationals navigate two sets of relationships that characterize nations: the relationships that define the nation as an "imagined community" with a collective past and an aspirational future and the relationships that define the nation in relation to other nations which together comprise the world of nations.[5] These relationships allow us to consider the ways in which the economics of international business are inseparable from the politics and ideology of the global economy.

---

[2] Reich, *The Work of Nations*: 3.
[3] Giddens, *Beyond Left and Right*: 5.
[4] Conrad, *Globalisation and the Nation*: 380.
[5] Anderson, Imagined Communities.

The Business of Nation Formation

Taking nations seriously in international business history, I have shown, involves treating them as more than formal countries or as groups of policymakers or stakeholders. It involves understanding and analyzing them as imagined communities. Such a view requires a temporal perspective that takes into account not just the present uses of international trade and investment but its aspirational purposes – the projected futures that are important to the identity of the imagined community. Hence, multinationals like Siemens and Bayer could effectively expand their presence in India despite the growing protectionism of the 1960s and 1970s, by positioning themselves as providers of the electrical goods needed for a future modern economy and of the fertilizers for an aspired Green Revolution in India.

Along with projected futures, national histories are equally important to the temporal nature of national identity and hence to multinational strategy. German multinationals were able to position themselves in India by evoking a sense of common historical experience with Indian nationalists that emphasized a common historical foe in Great Britain. Such a view requires moving beyond a limited sense of history as a legacy or as path dependency to an appreciation of history as an interpretation of the past in the present. History works to characterize meanings of actors and actions in the present. German multinationals in the interwar period successfully recognized how Indian nationalist histories were beginning to offer opportunities to present their own histories as essential complements to the historical and future-oriented imaginations that made the Indian nation.

In short, German business navigated Indian nationalism most effectively when they recognized the historical qualities of nationalism – the ways in which trade and investment were infused with particular hopes for the future and deeply shaped by interpretations of the past. This semantic nature of nationhood demanded that strategic attention be devoted to the political and ideological meanings of Indian nationalism and how a multinational's business and economic relationships could be positioned in relationship to these meanings. Investments in such meaning-making capabilities – such as I. G. Farben's and Siemens' development of business intelligence units and the attempts by individual managers to recast Indo-German history – address how important it was as an aspect of strategizing.

Treating nations as communities with imagined futures and interpreted pasts also brings greater focus to List's notion of national "productive powers" as an important aspect of global strategy. Rather than seeing international business as based in economic exchange focused typically on national consumption, List's concept of "productive powers" draws attention to the culture and capabilities of a nation based in its aspirations and its past, and the particular worth it ascribes to the importance of these goods in light of political and cultural as well as economic value. Hence the importance of large-scale power plants in post-Independence India extended well beyond its economic importance to the value of establishing India as a modern country.

Recognizing these aspects of nations in turn expands our understanding of the range of multinational tactics and activities required for skillful internationalization. As we have seen, German multinationals engaged in a wide-ranging set of activities integral to their strategy for capitalizing on rising nationalist sentiment in India. These included investments in educational programs, community and stakeholder engagement on firm boards and in governance, new historical narratives to showcase similarities or complementarities with other nations, and the development of intelligence to track nationalist politics and craft effective political responses. The nature of these activities extended well beyond what some scholars have called non-market strategy. In fact, politics and political rhetoric were anything but non-market; they were crucial for making the market.

Mapping Nationalism

Nations identify themselves not only based on the imagined historical and aspirational relationships among their members but also in relationship to other nations. Nations, I have emphasized, are not isolated communities but rather have formed and evolved as part of a global process in which one nation positions itself in relation to other nations. Identifying others as friends or foes or clustering groups of nations in ways that form an imagined global topography – what I have called mental maps of nationalism – shape the relational and perceptual assumptions in which international business operates.

Navigating Nationalism has argued that in the century between 1880 and 1980, Indo-German business relations evolved to be perceived on the landscape of three powerful and very different mental maps. The first distinguished the "civilized" nations of the West as a group that held allegedly justifiable authority over the "uncivilized" nations of the rest. In this context, German multinationals were considered essentially like British ones and German multinational strategy typically aped that of their British counterparts. The second mental map began to form (with a few experimental predecessors) in the wake of the Treaty of Versailles and increasingly cast Germany as a victim of British imperial tendencies, despite Germany's own history as a colonizer. The emerging mental map allowed for a strategic realignment in which German multinationals increasingly positioned themselves as outsiders to colonialism. Rhetorically and in social practices, they shared culture and history in common with their Indian counterparts. While this mental map continued into the post-war era, it was gradually displaced in the 1960s and 1970s by a mental map that categorized countries based on their stage of development on a path to prosperity. Some German firms continued to do good business in India but claims to a special relationship between the two countries began to fade in the context of the Cold War and the collaboration of Western nations in multilateral development organizations.

Navigating Nationalism thus involved not just a bilateral relationship between home and host nation, but a grasp of the global landscape of national relationships, rivalries, and friendships that were perceived to constitute the world. As we have seen, savvy multinationals not only increasingly invested in capabilities to understand these relationships but also to shape them in ways that valorized their products and services and delegitimized their rivals.[6] Since the nature of mental maps shifted over time as their underlying narrative logic changed, effective multinational strategy required the sophistication to understand these shifts and identify the latitude that a particular mental map afforded for the use of particular tactics. For instance, the emergence of the interwar mental map that allowed German multinationals to cast themselves against their British rivals as outsiders to colonialism allowed more direct nation-to-nation strategizing than the Cold War era mental map that saw all nations along a linear path of development.

Recognizing how mental maps of nationalism shape international business allows a more robust way to analyze strategy in the international economy, even today. The nationalist resurgence that has gripped a number of nations over the last few years raises questions about the emerging mental map that will shape global business in the years to come. Hobsbawm, ever prescient, distinguished contemporary nationalism from the liberation-oriented mid-twentieth-century wave. Earlier nationalisms were "unificatory as well as emancipatory" whereas the most recent forms are characterized by "rejections of modern modes of political organization, both national and supranational. Time and again they seem to be reactions of weakness and fear, attempts to erect barricades to keep at bay the forces of the modern world."[7] A competing

---

[6] For details on this process, see also Lubinski and Wadhwani, "Geopolitical Jockeying."
[7] Hobsbawm, *Nations and Nationalism*: 164.

mental map might be seen in the growing tensions between the United States and China and the emergence (or re-emergence) of an East versus West, steeped in a history of the "great divergence" that presently attracts much scholarly attention.[8] Such a mental map might paint competing visions of national economies, with some based in Western Enlightenment concepts of individual economic rationality and others rooted in Eastern conceptions and cosmology. One lesson from this book is that the mental maps that emerge will not be based on the nature of economic trade and investment as it may actually be in the present. They will be about how it is perceived to be in the future based on historical trajectories of the past; "imaginaries of the future are a crucial element of capitalist development," especially in a world of nations.[9]

Fundamentally, then, navigating nationalism effectively will require historical skill. Given the nature of nations as historically constituted entities, multinational strategies become meaningful in a historical framework. Strategists capable of understanding and acting upon the historical qualities of nations and in the context of the evolving historical relationship between nations will be better positioned to capitalize on the evolving mental maps of nationalism we are experiencing today. As in the past, the emerging nationalism today will not represent the end of globalization but rather a strategic shift in how nations and multinationals relate to each other in a globally integrated world.

[8] Pomeranz, *Great Divergence*. Austin, Dávila, and Jones, "The Alternative Business History." Jones, "The Great Divergence and the Great Convergence."

[9] Beckert, *Imagined Futures*: 6.

Appendices

Appendix 1: British and German Trade to British India

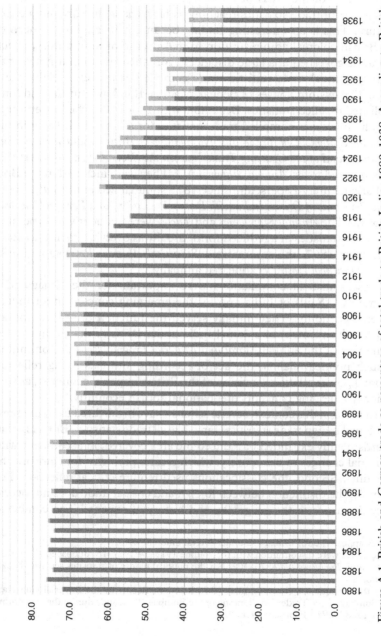

Figure A.1 British and German trade as percentage of total trade to British India, 1880–1938. According to British Indian statistics, in the period 1880 to 1938, British trade accounts for between 76.2 percent of total trade to British India (in 1881) and 29.9 percent (in 1938). German trade was non-existent in 1880 and again in 1919, in the context of World War I and trading with the enemy legislation. It reached its peak of 9.7 percent in 1937. Annual Statement (several volumes).

Appendix 2: Comment on Trade Statistics for British India

India is one of the areas of the world for which historians have a systematic set of trade statistics reaching as far back as the early nineteenth century. This is an interesting finding because it highlights the need of the British colonial administration to make sense of the territory, which had to be governed at a large distance. From the early to mid-nineteenth century, annual trade statistics were compiled at the level of the provinces. The custom houses of Bengal, Madras, Bombay, Burma, and Sind published detailed statistics. Beginning with 1866/1867, the Government of India moreover compiled trade statistics for all of British India in the *"Annual Statement of Trade and Navigation of British India with Foreign Countries, and of the Coasting Trade between the Several Presidencies* (in this book referred to as: *Annual Statement*)."[1] They were included in the British Parliamentary Papers, and since 1875 summarized in the *Tables relating to the Trade of British India with British Possessions and Foreign Countries* (*Tables*).[2] The *Annual Statements* and *Tables* were frequently incorporated into other statistics in a reduced form, usually as overview tables. In addition, since 1867, the summarized *Statistical Abstract Relating to British India* (*Statistical Abstract*) appeared annually.

These statistical compilations were important for the "imaginative geography" (Said) of India and for the emerging concept of an Indian national economy. They initially served the function of showcasing an alleged advancement of colonial India under British rule, as showcased in the title of the annual *Moral and Material Progress Report*. Committed to such political claims, the act of recording and classifying reflected colonial power relations, a vision of the British imperial economy, as well as newly emerging concepts of a national Indian economy.[3]

Produced in this context, several scholars have highlighted the limitations of colonial Indian trade statistics. First, like all trade statistics, British Indian records silently expanded or reduced the area covered, in accordance with territorial changes of the country, which creates problems for comparisons over time. Second, the classifications used require critical reflection. For example, the distinction between foreign and coastal trade does not necessarily do justice to the geography and history of regions.[4] The combined

---

[1] They appeared until 1950/1952 under several different titles.

[2] The *Tables* were discontinued with the volume 1913–14/1917–18, published in 1920.

[3] Goswami, *Producing India*: 73–102. For the political nature of statistics see also Tooze, *Statistics*.

[4] For this critique see also, "Bombay (British India): Report by the Imperial Consulate in Bombay about Trade and Shipping of the Bombay Presidency during the accounting year 1908," *DHA* February 1910, 226.

import trade of the five provinces of Bengal, Bombay, Sind, Madras, and Burma was known as "foreign," whereas the trade between the provinces and between them and non-British ports (in French or Portuguese territories of India) was classified as "coastal." Third, scholars have pointed to the problem of overland trade that during certain periods surpassed 10 percent of the sea-borne trade in value but remained excluded.[5] In sum, the colonial economy of India was conceptually divided in a domestic and a foreign trade part, with statistics clearly spotlighting the latter.

Throughout the twentieth century, stakeholders also criticized that the statistics were not reliable for determining the origin of foreign goods. It was frequently a default assumption that "foreign" goods were likely British. Statistics often did not distinguish country of origin of foreign goods from their last port of shipment. Thanks to the excellent export organization, many goods came through Britain but other routes were also popular before World War I, as described in Chapter 1. Given the depth and accessibility of the Indian numbers, parallel statistics are often available but rarely used. For example, German and Indian trade statistics regularly showed great discrepancies and contemporaries called them out. The complaints about misclassified goods and unreliable data were frequent until at least the late 1930s (for details see, Chapters 2 and 4.) In 1936, the economic magazine *Capital* reported that, "[t]he exceptional divergence in the statistics of the two countries [Germany and India] is a matter of fundamental economic significance in view of foreign trade accounts serving as a foundation to commercial policy."[6]

These shortcomings can be explained by the fact that the statistics were compiled to record long-distance trade between India and Great Britain for a specific purpose: to show the effective governance of a distant colony. Arjun Appadurai argues that "statistics were generated in amounts that far defeated any unified bureaucratic purpose. ... [N]umbers gradually became more importantly part of the illusion of bureaucratic control and a key to a colonial imaginary in which countable abstractions ... created the sense of a controllable indigenous reality."[7] Their declared purpose was to show the "extent of the market for the products of the UK among the common population of India."[8] Therefore, it was the distinction between articles of Indian and foreign (effectively British) origin

[5] Sugihara, "Notes."
[6] A German Correspondent, "Indo-German Trade – Conflicting Official Figures," *Capital*, 20 February 1936, copy in: R/8128/9127, BArch-B.
[7] Appadurai, "Numbers in the Colonial Imagination": 117.
[8] Proceedings of the Revenue Department, NWP, November 1875, no 9, 3, APAC; quoted in: Goswami, *Producing India*: 81.

that was of greatest relevance. Only slowly over time, as several chapters in this book have shown, did the rivalry between Western countries become reflected in these statistics.

Appendix 3: Imports from Germany into India

Table A.1 *Chief imports from Germany into India, 1913/14 (with percentage of Germany's trade in the total import trade of India)*

Product	% GER of Total
Synthetic indigo	88.7
Aniline dye	79.7
Alizarin dye	69.1
Metals: aluminum	48.2
Cutlery	43.4
Metals: steel	36.4
Metals: copper, wrought	35.5
Toys and requisites for games	26.2
Liquors – ale, beer, and porter	24.1
Hardware	18.3
Haberdashery and millinery	17.4
Paper and pasteboard	17.3
Glass and glassware	14.7
Chemicals	12.4
Cement	10.7
Salt	10.6
Metals: iron or steel	10.3
Apparel	9.1
Instruments	8.4

Department of Statistics, India, "Memorandum and Statistical Tables Relating to the Trade of India with Germany and Austria-Hungary," Second Issue, Calcutta: Superintendent Government Printing, India 1914: 4.

Bibliography

Many Indian cities, such as Kolkata (previously Calcutta), Mumbai (Bombay) and Bengaluru (Bangalore), today use names that reflect the Indigenous pronunciation of their original moniker. Throughout the book, I follow the official name usage, e.g., employing Calcutta when speaking about the city prior to 2001 and Kolkata thereafter.

Archives

Acronym	Archives and Collections
APAC	Asia, Pacific, and African Collections (APAC), British Library, London, UK
BA	Bayer AG, Corporate History & Archives, Leverkusen, Germany
BArch-B	Federal Archives of Germany [Bundesarchiv], Berlin, Germany
BArch-K	Federal Archives of Germany [Bundesarchiv], Koblenz, Germany
CAMuc.	City Archives Munich, Munich, Germany
CASol.	City Archives Solingen [Stadtarchiv Solingen], Solingen, Germany
EMI	EMI Archive Trust, Hayes, Middlesex, UK
ERC	Early Record Catalogues Collection, British Library, London, UK
HAK	Alfried Krupp von Bohlen und Halbach-Stiftung, Historical Archives Krupp [Historisches Archiv Krupp], Essen, Germany
HIA	Hoover Institute Archives, Stanford, CA, USA
IfZ	Institut für Zeitgeschichte (IfZ), Munich, Germany
LOC	Library of Congress, Manuscript Division, Washington, DC, USA
MBC	Mercedes Benz AG, Mercedes-Benz Classic, Germany
NAI	National Archives of India, Delhi, India
NARA	National Archives and Records Administration, College Park, Maryland, USA
PA	Foreign Office of Germany [Politisches Archiv des Auswärtigen Amts], Berlin, Germany
SAA	Siemens AG, Siemens Historical Institute, Corporate Archives [Siemens Aktenarchiv, SAA], accessed in Munich, now Berlin, Germany
UAC	Unilever Archives, Port Sunlight, UK
UAM	University Archives Munich, Munich, Germany
WBSA	West Bengal State Archives, Kolkata, India
	Online Collections
ESB Online	Electricity Supply Board Archives, Online Collection, Dublin, Ireland, www.esb.ie/who-we-are/our-history/esb-archive
WBG Online	World Bank Group Archives, www.worldbank.org/archive

Libraries (with Unique Holdings)

BSB	Bavarian State Library Munich [Bayerische Staatsbibliothek München], Munich, Germany
Stabi	Berlin State and University Library [Staats- und Universitätsbibliothek Berlin], Berlin, Germany
BL	British Library, London, UK
CSAS	Centre of South Asian Studies, Cambridge University, South Asian Newspapers on Microfilm
DNBL	German National Library [Deutsche Nationalbibliothek], Leipzig, Germany
SUB	Göttingen State and University Library [Staats- und Universitätsbibliothek Göttingen], Göttingen, Germany
NLI	National Library of India, Kolkata, India
ZBW	ZBW Leibniz Information Centre for Economics [Leibniz-Informationszentrum Wirtschaft], Kiel, Germany

Newspapers and Magazines (with Access Information)

Aberdeen Press and Journal, The British Newspaper Archive, LOC

Amrita Bazar Patrika, NLI

Azad Hind: Monthly for a Free India, SUB

Bombay Chronicle, CSAS

Bombay Sentinel, CSAS

Deutsches Handels-Archiv (DHA), Stabi

Die Sprechmaschine, Stabi

Dundee Courier, The British Newspaper Archive, LOC

Filmindia, The Museum of Modern Art Library, New York, Media History Digital Library, archive.org

Gloucestershire Echo, The British Newspaper Archive, LOC

Hardware and Metal [Toronto and Montreal], Canadian Trade Journals Collection, archive.org

Indo-German Commercial Review (since September 1923: *Industrial Review for India*; since January 1925: *Industrial and Trade Review for India*; since October 1925: *Industrial and Trade Review for Asia*), Stabi

Industrie- und Handelszeitung, Stabi

Los Angeles Herald, California Digital Newspaper Collection, LOC

Manchester Guardian, ProQuest Historical Newspaper, BL

Phonographische Zeitschrift, Stabi

Talking Machine News, BL

Talking Machine World, LOC

The Calcutta Gazette, West Bengal Public Library, archive.org

The Evening Telegraph, BL

The New York Times, LOC

The Observer, ProQuest Historical Newspaper, BL

The Scotsman, The British Newspaper Archive, LOC

The Singapore Free Press and Mercantile Advertiser, LOC

The Times, London, BL
The Times of India, Mumbai, India, ProQuest Historical Newspaper, SUB
The Western Daily Press and Bristol Mirror, The British Newspaper Archive, LOC
The Western Morning News and Daily Gazette, The British Newspaper Archive, LOC
Zeitschrift für Instrumentenbau, Stabi

Published Works

Aalders, Gerard, and Cees Wiebes. *The Art of Cloaking Ownership: The Secret Collaboration and Protection of the German War Industry by the Neutrals: The Case of Sweden*. Amsterdam: Amsterdam University Press, 1996.

Abdelal, Rawi. *National Purpose in the World Economy: Post-Soviet States in Comparative Perspective*. Ithaca, NY: Cornell University Press, 2001.

Abelshauser, Werner, Wolfgang von Hippel, Jeffrey Allan Johnson, and Raymond G. Stokes. *German Industry and Global Enterprise: BASF – The History of a Company*. Cambridge, UK: Cambridge University Press, 2004.

Adivasi-Koordination. *Rourkela und die Folgen: 50 Jahre industrieller Aufbau und soziale Verantwortung in der deutsch-indischen Zusammenarbeit*. Heidelberg: Draupadi Verlag, 2007.

Ahuja, Ravi. "Lost Engagements? Traces of South Asian Soldiers in German Captivity, 1915–18." In *When the War Began We Heard of Several Kings: South Asian Prisoners in World War I Germany*, edited by Franziska Roy, Heike Liebau, and Ravi Ahuja, 131–166. New Delhi: Orient Blackswan, 2011.

Akita, Shigeru. "The Aid-India Consortium, the World Bank, and the International Order of Asia, 1958–1968." *Asian Review of World Histories* 2, no. 2 (2014): 217–248.

Akita, Shigeru. "Introduction: From Imperial History to Global History." In *Gentlemanly Capitalism, Imperialism, and Global History*, edited by Shigeru Akita, 1–16. Basingstoke and New York: Palgrave Macmillan, 2002.

Akita, Shigeru, and Nicholas White, eds. *The International Order of Asia in the 1930s and 1950s*. Farnham, UK, and Burlington, VT: Ashgate, 2010.

Aldous, Michael, and Tirthankar Roy. "Reassessing FERA: Examining British Firms' Strategic Responses to 'Indianisation'." *Business History* 63, no. 1 (2021): 18–37.

Ambirajan, S. *The Taxation of Corporate Income in India*. Bombay: Asia Publishing House, 1965.

Andersen, Steen. "Building for the Shah: Market Entry, Political Reality and Risks on the Iranian Market, 1933–1939." *Enterprise & Society* 9, no. 4 (2008): 637–669.

"Escape from 'Safehaven': The Case of Christiani & Nielsen's Blacklisting in 1944." *Business History* 51, no. 5 (2009): 691–711.

Anderson, Benedict. *Imagined Communities: Reflections on the Origin and Spread of Nationalism*. London: Verso, 1983.

Appadorai, Angadipuram, ed. *Select Documents on India's Foreign Policy and Relations, 1947–1972*. 2 vols. Delhi and New York: Oxford University Press, 1982.

Appadurai, Arjun. "Numbers in the Colonial Imagination." In *Modernity at Large: Cultural Dimensions of Globalization*, edited by Arjun Appadurai, 114–135. Minneapolis and London: University of Minnesota Press, 1996.

Arnold, David. *Everyday Technology: Machines and the Making of India's Modernity*. Chicago: University of Chicago Press, 2013.

Aurobindo, Sri. "The Aims of the Nationalist Party [Speech Delivered in Nagpur 30 Jan. 1908]." In *The Complete Works of Sri Aurobindo: Vol. 6 and 7: Bande Mataram Political Writings and Speeches 1890–1908*, edited by Sri Aurobindo Ashram Trust, 846–854. Pondicherry: Sri Aurobindo Ashram Press, 2002 [1908].

"National Education [Speech Delivered in Girgaum, Bombay, 15 Jan. 1908]." In *The Complete Works of Sri Aurobindo: Vol. 6 and 7: Bande Mataram Political Writings and Speeches 1890–1908*, edited by Sri Aurobindo Ashram Trust, 810–817. Pondicherry: Sri Aurobindo Ashram Press, 2002 [1908].

Austin, Gareth, Carlos Dávila, and Geoffrey G. Jones. "The Alternative Business History: Business in Emerging Markets." *Business History Review* 91, no. 3 (2017): 537–569.

Auswärtiges Amt. *Akten zur deutschen auswärtigen Politik 1918–1945, Serie D: 1937–1941, Band XII.2 Die Kriegsjahre, 5. Band, 2. Halbband, 6. April bis 22. Juni 1941*. Göttingen: Vandenhoeck & Ruprecht, 1969.

Bajohr, Frank. *"Aryanisation" in Hamburg: The Economic Exclusion of Jews and the Confiscation of their Property in Nazi Germany*. New York: Berghahn Books, 2002.

Ballantyne, Tony. *Orientalism and Race: Aryanism in the British Empire*. Basingstoke: Palgrave Macmillan, 2002.

Bandyopadhyay, Bholanath. *The Political Ideas of Benoy Kumar Sarkar*. Calcutta: K. P. Bagchi & Co., 1984.

Banerjea, Pramathanath. *Fiscal Policy in India*. Calcutta: Macmillan and Company, 1922.

Barooah, Nirode Kumar. *Chatto: The Life and Times of an Indian Anti-Imperialist in Europe*. New Delhi and New York: Oxford University Press, 2004.

Germany and the Indians between the Wars. Norderstedt: Books on Demand, 2018.

India and the Official Germany, 1886–1914. Frankfurt am Main: Peter Lang, 1977.

Bartlett, Christopher, and Sumantra Ghoshal. *Managing across Borders: The Transnational Solution*. Boston, MA: Harvard Business School Press, 1989.

Bassett, Ross Knox. "Aligning India in the Cold War Era: Indian Technical Elites, the Indian Institute of Technology at Kanpur, and Computing in India and the United States." *Technology and Culture* 50, no. 4 (2009): 783–810.

The Technological Indian. Cambridge, MA: Harvard University Press, 2016.

Bäumler, Ernst. *Farben, Formeln, Forscher: Hoechst und die Geschichte der industriellen Chemie in Deutschland*. Munich: Piper, 1989.

Baweja, Vandana. A Pre-History of Green Architecture: Otto Koenigsberger and Tropical Architecture, from Princely Mysore to Post-Colonial London. University of Michigan: Unpublished PhD thesis, 2008.

Bayer. *Geschichte und Entwicklung der Farbenfabriken vorm. Friedr. Bayer & Co. Elberfeld in den ersten 50 Jahren.* Munich: Meisenbach Riffarth & Co., 1918.

Baynes, Norman Hepburn. *The Speeches of Adolf Hitler, April 1922–August 1939.* London and New York: Oxford University Press, 1942.

Beckert, Jens. *Imagined Futures: Fictional Expectations and Capitalist Dynamics.* Cambridge, MA: Harvard University Press, 2016.

Bell, Duncan. *The Idea of Greater Britain: Empire and the Future of World Order, 1860–1900.* Princeton, NJ: Princeton University Press, 2007.

Bentwich, Norman. "International Law as Applied by England During the War." *American Journal of International Law* 9, no. 2 (1915): 352–371.

Berghoff, Hartmut. "The End of Family Business? The Mittelstand and German Capitalism in Transition, 1949–2000." *Business History Review* 80, no. 2 (2006): 263–295.

Berghoff, Hartmut, and Ingo Köhler. *Varieties of Family Business: Germany and the United States, Past and Present.* Frankfurt am Main: Campus Verlag, 2021.

Bernhardi, Friedrich von. *Deutschland und der naechste Krieg.* Stuttgart and Berlin: J. G. Cotta, 1912.

Germany and the Next War. London: Edward Arnold, 1914 [Original in German: 1912].

Bhattacharyya, Amit. *Swadeshi Enterprise in Bengal.* Calcutta: Mita Bhattacharyya, 1986.

Swadeshi Enterprise in Bengal, 1921–47. Kolkata: Setu Prakashani, 2007.

Bidwell, Robin Leonard. *Currency Conversion Tables: A Hundred Years of Change.* London: Rex Collings Ltd., 1970.

Birla, G. D. "An Industrial Mission [A Speech Delivered at a Party Given by Sir Abdul Halim Ghaznavi in 1945]." In *The Path to Prosperity: A Collection of the Speeches & Writings of G. D. Birla,* edited by Parasnath Sinha, 414–426. Allahabad: The Leader Press, 1950.

Boddewyn, Jean J., and Thomas L. Brewer. "International-Business Political Behavior: New Theoretical Directions." *Academy of Management Review* 19, no. 1 (1994): 119–143.

Bohnet, Michael. *Geschichte der deutschen Entwicklungspolitik: Strategien, Innenansichten, Erfolge, Misserfolge, Zeitzeugen, Herausforderungen.* Munich: UVK Verlag, 2019.

Boon, Marten, and Ben Wubs. "Property, Control and Room for Manoeuvre: Royal Dutch Shell and Nazi Germany, 1933–1945." *Business History* 62, no. 3 (2020): 468–487.

Bose, Subhas Chandra. "The Haripura Address: Presedential Address at the 51st Session of the Indian National Congress held at Haripura." In *Subhas Chandra Bose: Pioneer of Indian Planning,* edited by Planning Commission, 23–61. New Delhi: Government of India, 1997 [1938].

The Indian Struggle (1935–1942). Calcutta: Chuckervertty, Chatterjee & Company Ltd., 1952.

"The National Planning Committee: Inauguration Speech at the First Meeting of the All-India National Planning Committee at Bombay on December 17, 1938." In *Subhas Chandra Bose: Pioneer of Indian Planning,* edited by Planning Commission, 87–91. New Delhi: Government of India, 1997 [1938].

His Majesty's Opponent: Subhas Chandra Bose and India's Struggle against Empire. Cambridge, MA: Belknap Press of Harvard University Press, 2011.

Bose, Subhas Chandra, Emilie Schenkl, Sisir Kumar Bose, and Sugata Bose, eds. *Letters to Emilie Schenkl, 1934–1942, Netaji Collected Works,* vol. 7. Delhi: Oxford University Press, 1994.

Böttinger, Henry Theodor von. Durch "360 Längen-Grade" <Rund d'rum 'Rum>: Tagebuchblätter über meine Reise um die Welt 11. Dezember 1888 bis 1. Juni 1889. Elberfeld: [Unknown], 1889.

Breuilly, John. "Introduction: Concepts, Approaches, Theories." In *Oxford Handbook of the History of Nationalism,* edited by John Breuilly. Oxford: Oxford University Press, 2013: 1–18.

Bucheli, Marcelo, and Stephanie Decker. "Expropriations of Foreign Property and Political Alliances: A Business Historical Approach." *Enterprise & Society* 22, no. 1 (2021): 247–284.

Bucheli, Marcelo, and Min-Young Kim. "Attacked from Both Sides: A Dynamic Model of Multinational Corporations' Strategies for Protection of Their Property Rights." *Global Strategy Journal* 5, no. 1 (2015): 1–26.

"Political Institutional Change, Obsolescing Legitimacy, and Multinational Corporations." *Management International Review* 52, no. 6 (2012): 847–877.

Bucheli, Marcelo, and Erica Salvaj. "Political Connections, the Liability of Foreignness, and Legitimacy: A Business Historical Analysis of Multinationals' Strategies in Chile." *Global Strategy Journal* 8, no. 3 (2018): 399–420.

"Reputation and Political Legitimacy ITT in Chile, 1927–1972." *Business History Review* 87, no. 4 (2013): 729–756.

Budhwar, Prem K. *A Diplomat Reveals.* New Delhi: Dorling Kindersley (India), 2007.

Bühlmann, Elisabeth. *La Ligne Siemens: La Construction du Télégraphe Indo-Européen, 1867–1870.* Bern: Peter Lang, 1999.

Campbell, Henry. *The Law of Trading with the Enemy in British India, Together With all Ordinances and Statutes, Proclamations, Orders of Council, Notifications, Press Communiques, Etcetera, Connected Therewith.* Calcutta: Butterworth & Co. (India), Ltd., 1916.

Casolari, Marzia. "Hindutva's Foreign Tie-Up in the 1930s: Archival Evidence." *Economic and Political Weekly* 35, no. 4 (2000): 218–228.

Casson, Mark, and Teresa da Silva Lopes. "Foreign Direct Investment in High-Risk Environments: An Historical Perspective." *Business History* 55, no. 3 (2013): 375–404.

Central Legislature and Governor General of India. "The Indian Companies (Amendment) Act, 1936." *In A Collection of the Acts of the Indian Legislature for the Year 1936.* Delhi: Manager of Publications, 1937.

Chandra, Bholanath. "A Voice for the Commerce and Manufactures of India." *Mookerjee's Journal* 12 March (1873): 77–121.

Chandra, Bipan. *Nationalism and Colonialism in Modern India.* New Delhi: Orient Longman, 1984.

Chapman, Emmett A., and United States. Bureau of Foreign and Domestic Commerce. *India as a Market for American Goods.* Washington DC: Government Printing Office, 1925.

Chatterjee, Atul Chandra. *Notes on the Industries of the United Provinces.* Allahabad: F. Luker, Superintendent, Government Press, 1908.

Chatterji, B. "Business and Politics in the 1930s: Lancashire and the Making of the Indo-British Trade Agreement, 1939." *Modern Asian Studies* 15, no. 3 (1981): 527–573.

Chibber, Vivek. *Locked in Place: State-Building and Late Industrialization in India.* Princeton, NJ: Princeton University Press, 2006.

Choudhury, Prithwiraj, and Tarun Khanna. "Charting Dynamic Trajectories: Multinational Enterprises in India." *Business History Review* 88, no. 1 (2014): 133–169.

Coleman, Kim. *IG Farben and ICI, 1925–53: Strategies for Growth and Survival.* Basingstoke: Palgrave Macmillan, 2006.

Commercial Intelligence Department. *Prices and Wages in India, 24th issue.* Calcutta: Office of the Superintendent of Government Printing, India, 1907.

Conrad, Sebastian. *Globalisation and the Nation in Imperial Germany.* Cambridge: Cambridge University Press, 2010.

Cotton, Charles William Egerton. *Handbook of Commercial Information for India.* Calcutta: Government of India, Central Publication Branch, 1919.

Cox, Howard. *The Global Cigarette: Origins and Evolution of British American Tobacco, 1880–1945.* New York: Oxford University Press, 2000.

Crane, George T. "Economic Nationalism: Bringing the Nation Back In." *Millennium* 27, no. 1 (1998): 55–75.

Curtis, Lionel, and Great Britain. Parliament. Joint Select Committee on the Government of India Bill. *Papers Relating to the Application of the Principle of Dyarchy to the Government of India.* Oxford: Clarendon Press, 1920.

Da Silva Lopes, Teresa, Mark Casson, and Geoffrey Jones. "Organizational Innovation in the Multinational Enterprise: Internalization Theory and Business History." *Journal of International Business Studies* 50 (2019): 1338–1358.

Da Silva Lopes, Teresa, Carlos Gabriel Guimarães, Alexandre Saes, and Luiz Fernando Saraiva. "The 'Disguised' Foreign Investor: Brands, Trademarks and the British Expatriate Entrepreneur in Brazil." *Business History* 60, no. 8 (2018): 1171–1195.

Da Silva Lopes, Teresa, and Shin Tomita. "Trademarks as 'Global Merchants of Skill': The Dynamics of the Japanese Match Industry, c1860–c1930." *Business History Review* (Forthcoming).

Dalal, Sucheta. *A.D. Shroff: Titan of Finance and Free Enterprise.* New Delhi and New York: Viking, 2000.

Dames-Willers, Klaus. *Ferdinand Kurt Heller (1900–1991): A Short Biography of the Exciting Life of a Staunch German Humanitarian, a Courageous Visionary and One of Trade and Industry's Daring Pioneers.* Mumbai: Indo-German Chamber of Commerce, 2016.

Damm, Ulrich. *Die Bundesrepublik Deutschland und die Entwicklungsländer: Versuch einer Darstellung der politischen Beziehungen der Bundesrepublik Deutschland zu den Entwicklungsländern unter besonderer Berücksichtigung der Entwicklungshilfe.* Coburg: Hans Biehl, 1965.

Das Gupta, Amit. "Divided Nations: India and Germany." In *India in the World, 1947–1991: National and Transnational Perspectives*, edited by Andreas Hilger and Corinna Unger, 300–325. Frankfurt am Main: Peter Lang, 2012.

Handel, Hilfe, Hallstein-Doktrin: Die bundesdeutsche Suedasienpolitik unter Adenauer und Erhard 1949 bis 1966. Husum: Matthiesen, 2004.

Das, Santanu. *India, Empire, and First World War Culture: Writings, Images, and Songs.* Cambridge: Cambridge University Press, 2018.

Dasgupta, Ajit K. *A History of Indian Economic Thought.* London and New York: Routledge, 1993.

Dasgupta, Jnanendra Chandra. Studien über 2-Chloranthrachinon-3-carbonsäure. Berlin: Ebering, 1913.

Decker, Stephanie. "Building up Goodwill: British Business, Development and Economic Nationalism in Ghana and Nigeria, 1945–1977." *Enterprise & Society* 9, no. 4 (2008): 602–613.

"Corporate Legitimacy and Advertising. British Multinationals and the Rhetoric of Development from the 1950s to the 1970s." *Business History Review* 81, no. 1 (2007): 59–86.

"Corporate Political Activity in Less Developed Countries: The Volta River Project in Ghana, 1958–66." *Business History* 53, no. 7 (2011): 993–1017.

Dejung, Christof. *Commodity Trading, Globalization and the Colonial World: Spinning the Web of the Global Market.* New York: Routledge, 2018.

Dejung, Christof, and Andreas Zangger. "British Wartime Protectionism and Swiss Trading Firms in Asia during the First World War." *Past & Present* 207, no. 1 (2010): 181–213.

Department of Commerce and Henry D. Baker. *Special Consular Report No. 72: British India with Notes on Ceylon, Afghanistan and Tibet.* Washington DC: Government Printing Office, 1915.

Department of Commerce and Labor. *Special Consular Reports No. 55: Foreign Trade in Musical Instruments.* Washington DC: Government Printing Office, 1912.

Department of Overseas Trade, and Thomas M. Ainscough. General Review of the Conditions and Prospects of British Trade in India, During the Fiscal Year 1919–20 and 1920–21, Revised to October 1921. London: His Majesty's Stationery Office, 1921.

Report on the Conditions and Prospects of British Trade in India, 1926–27. London: His Majesty's Stationery Office, 1927.

Trade of India: Report on the Conditions and Prospects of British Trade in India, at the close of the War. London: His Majesty's Stationery Office, 1919.

Desai, Ashok V. "Evolution of Import Control." *Economic and Political Weekly* 5, no. 29/31 (1970): 1271–1278.

Deutscher Wirtschaftsdienst. *Britisch Indien: Aussenhandel und Absatzmoeglichkeiten.* Berlin: Deutscher Wirtschaftsdienst, 1925.

Division of Investigation of Cartels and External Assets. *Report of the Investigation of IG Farbenindustrie AG.* Washington DC: War Department/Government Printing Office, 1945.

Domosh, Mona. *American Commodities in an Age of Empire.* New York: Routledge, 2006.

Donzé, Pierre-Yves. "The Advantage of Being Swiss: Nestlé and Political Risk in Asia during the Early Cold War, 1945–1970." *Business History Review* 94, no. 2 (2020): 373–397.

Donzé, Pierre-Yves, and Takafumi Kurosawa. "Nestlé Coping with Japanese Nationalism: Political Risk and the Strategy of a Foreign Multinational Enterprise in Japan, 1913–45." *Business History* 55, no. 8 (2013): 1318–1338.

Drummond, Ian M. *Imperial Economic Policy 1917–1939.* Toronto: University of Toronto Press, 1974.

Dunning, John H. "Reappraising the Eclectic Paradigm in the Age of Alliance Capitalism." *Journal of International Business Studies* 26, no. 3 (1995): 461–493.

Dunning, John H., and Sarianna M. Lundan. *Multinational Enterprises and the Global Economy.* Cheltenham, UK and Northampton, MA: Edward Elgar, 2008.

Dutt, Romesh Chunder. *The Economic History of India.* London: K. Paul, Trench, Trübner & Co., Ltd., 1902.

East India (Sedition Committee). *Report of Committee Appointed to Investigate Revolutionary Conspiracies in India With Two Resolutions by the Government of India.* London: His Majesty's Stationery Office, 1918.

Egorova, Yulia. *Jews and India: Perceptions and Image.* Abingdon and New York: Routledge, 2006.

Eichengreen, Barry, and Douglas A. Irwin. "Trade Blocs, Currency Blocs and the Reorientation of World Trade in the 1930s." *Journal of International Economics* 38, no. 1 (1995): 1–24.

Eldridge, Philip J. *The Politics of Foreign Aid in India.* London: Weidenfeld and Nicolson, 1969.

Encarnation, Dennis J. *Dislodging Multinationals: India's Strategy in Comparative Perspective.* Ithaca, NY: Cornell University Press, 1989.

Engel, Alexander. *Farben der Globalisierung: Die Entstehung moderner Märkte für Farbstoffe 1500–1900.* Frankfurt am Main and New York: Campus, 2009.

Engerman, David C. *The Price of Aid: The Economic Cold War in India.* Cambridge, MA: Harvard University Press, 2018.

Epkenhans, Tim. "Geld darf keine Rolle spielen: 2. Teil: Das Dokument." *Archivum Ottomanicum* 19 (2001): 120–163.

Erhard, Ludwig. *Deutschlands Rückkehr zum Weltmarkt.* Düsseldorf: ECON, 1953.

Faltis, Otto. "India and Austria." *The Modern Review* 59, no. 2 (1936 February): 205–207.

Farrell, Gerry. *Indian Music and the West.* Oxford and New York: Oxford University Press, 1997.

Faust, Julian. *Spannungsfelder der Internationalisierung: Deutsche Unternehmen und Außenwirtschaftspolitik in Indien von 1947 bis zum Ende der 1970er Jahre.* Baden-Baden: Nomos, 2021.

Fear, Jeffrey. "Cartels." In *The Oxford Handbook of Business History,* edited by Geoffrey Jones and Jonathan Zeitlin, 268–292. Oxford: Oxford University Press, 2008.

Feldenkirchen, Wilfried. "Big Business in Interwar Germany: Organizational Innovation at Vereinigte Stahlwerke, IG Farben, and Siemens." *Business History Review* 61, no. 3 (1987): 417–451.

Siemens, 1918–1945. Columbus: Ohio State University Press, 1999.

Werner von Siemens: Inventor and International Entrepreneur. Columbus: Ohio State University Press, 1994.

Fellman, Susanna, and Martin Shanahan. *Regulating Competition: Cartel Registers in the Twentieth-Century World.* Abingdon and New York: Routledge, 2016.

Fischer-Tiné, Harald. *Der Gurukul Kangri oder die Erziehung der Arya-Nation: Kolonialismus, Hindureform und 'nationale Bildung' in Britisch-Indien (1897–1922).* Heidelberg: Ergon, 2003.

Fitzgerald, Robert. *The Rise of the Global Company: Multinationals and the Making of the Modern World.* Cambridge: Cambridge University Press, 2015.

Forbes, Neil. *Doing Business with the Nazis: Britain's Economic and Financial Relations with Germany, 1931–1939.* London and Portland, OR: Frank Cass, 2000.

"Multinational Enterprise, 'Corporate Responsibility' and the Nazi Dictatorship: The Case of Unilever and Germany in the 1930s." *Contemporary European History* 16, no. 2 (2007): 149–167.

Forbes, Neil, Takafumi Kurosawa, and Ben Wubs, eds. *Multinational Enterprise, Political Risk and Organizational Change: From Total War to Cold War.* New York: Routledge, 2019.

Framke, Maria. *Delhi - Rom - Berlin: Die indische Wahrnehmung von Faschismus und Nationalsozialismus 1922–1939.* Darmstadt: wbg Academic, 2013.

Frankel, Francine R. *India's Political Economy: The Gradual Revolution (1947–2004).* Oxford: Oxford University Press, 2006.

India's Green Revolution: Economic Gains and Political Costs. Princeton, NJ: Princeton University Press, 1971.

Frankfurter Allgemeine Zeitung. "Georg L. Leszczyński." In *Sie redigieren und schreiben die Frankfurter Allgemeine, Zeitung für Deutschland,* edited by Frankfurter Allgemeine Zeitung, 30–31. Frankfurt am Main: Selbstverlag Frankfurter Allgemeine Zeitung, 1960.

Fraser, Thomas Grant. "Germany and Indian Revolution, 1914–18." *Journal of Contemporary History* 12, no. 2 (1977): 255–272.

The Intrigues of German Government and the Ghadr Party against British Rule in India, 1914–1918. University of London, unpublished PhD thesis (1974).

Gackenholz, Hermann. *Das Diktat von Versailles und seine Auswirkungen.* Leipzig: Reclam, 1934.

Gaisberg, Frederick William. *The Music Goes Round.* New York: The Macmillan Company, 1942.

Music on Record. London: Robert Hale Ltd., 1946.

Gajjar, Tribhuvandas Kalyandas. "Welcome Address." In *The Industrial Conference Held at Surat, December 1907: Full Text of Papers Read at and Submitted to it,* edited by The Industrial Conference, 1–21. Madras, 1907.

Gall, Lothar. "Von der Entlassung Alfried Krupp von Bohlen und Halbachs bis zur Errichtung seiner Stiftung 1951 bis 1967/68." In *Krupp im 20. Jahrhundert: Die Geschichte des Unternehmens vom Ersten Weltkrieg bis zur Gründung der Stiftung,* edited by Lothar Gall, 473–589. Berlin: Siedler, 2002.

Gallagher, John, and Ronald Robinson. "The Imperialism of Free Trade." *Economic History Review* 6 (1953): 1–15.

Ganachari, Aravind. *Indians in the First World War.* New Delhi: SAGE, 2020.

Gao, Cheng, Tiona Zuzul, Geoffrey G. Jones, and Tarun Khanna. "Overcoming Institutional Voids: A Reputation-Based View of Long-Run Survival." *Strategic Management Journal* 38, no. 11 (2017): 2147–2167.

Gauba, Khalid Latif. *The Rebel Minister: The Story of the Rise and Fall of Lala Harkishen Lal*. Lahore: Premier Publishing House, 1938.

Germana, Nicholas A. *The Orient of Europe: The Mythical Image of India and Competing Images of German National Identity*. Newcastle upon Tyne: Cambridge Scholars Publishing, 2009.

Geyer, Michael, and Charles Bright. "World History in a Global Age." *American Historical Review* 100, no. 4 (1995): 1034–1060.

Ghemawat, Pankaj. *The Laws of Globalization and Business Applications*. Cambridge, UK: Cambridge University Press, 2017.

Redefining Global Strategy: Crossing Borders in a World Where Differences Still Matter. Boston, MA: Harvard Business School Press, 2007.

Ghemawat, Pankaj, and Geoffrey G. Jones. "Globalization in Historical Perspective." In *The Laws of Globalization and Business Applications*, edited by Pankaj Ghemawat, 56–81. Cambridge, UK: Cambridge University Press, 2017.

Giddens, Anthony. *Beyond Left and Right: The Future of Radical Politics*. Cambridge, UK: Polity Press, 1994.

Gilpin, Robert. *Global Political Economy*. Princeton, NJ: Princeton University Press, 2001.

The Political Economy of International Relations. Princeton, NJ: Princeton University Press, 1987.

Gordon, A. D. D. *Businessmen and Politics: Rising Nationalism and a Modernising Economy in Bombay, 1918–1933*. New Delhi: Manohar, 1978.

Gossman, Lionel. *The Passion of Max von Oppenheim: Archaeology and Intrigue in the Middle East from Wilhelm II to Hitler*. Cambridge, UK: Open Book Publishers, 2013.

Goswami, Manu. *Producing India: From Colonial Economy to National Space*. Chicago and London: University of Chicago Press, 2004.

"Rethinking the Modular Nation Form: Toward a Sociohistorical Conception of Nationalism." *Comparative Studies in Society and History* 44, no. 4 (2002): 770–799.

Gould, Peter, and Rodney White. *Mental Maps*. Harmondsworth: Penguin Books, 1974.

Government of Great Britain. *Trade of the British Empire and Foreign Competition. Despatch from Mr. Chamberlain to the Governors of Colonies and the High Commissioner of Cyprus and the Replies Thereto. Presented to both Houses of Parliament by Command of Her Majesty*. London: Eyre and Spottiswoode, 1897.

Government of India. *A Collection of the Acts of the Indian Legislature for the Year 1934*. New Delhi: Government of India Press, 1934.

Dispatch No. 91, dated March 14, 1901, reprinted in: Report of the Bombay Chamber of Commerce for the year 1901. Bombay: Government of India, 1902.

The Gazette of India Extraordinary: Imperial Economic Conference, Ottawa, 1932: Report of the Indian Delegation. Simla: Government of India, 1932.

Government of India, Department of Finance and Commerce. *Annual Statement of the Sea-Borne Trade and Navigation of British India with the British Empire and Foreign Countries.* Calcutta: Superintendent Government Printing, India, several volumes.

Government of India Legislative Department. *The Indian Income-Tax Act, 1922 (XI of 1922), As Modified Up to the 15th November 1937.* New Delhi: Government of India Press, 1937.

Legislation and Orders Relating to the War. Delhi: Superintendent Government Printing, India, 1915.

Government of India Ministry of Commerce and Industry. *Report of the Tariff Commission on the Automobile Industry.* New Delhi: Government of India Publications, 1953.

Great Britain India Office. *Statistical Abstract Relating to British India from 1892/3 to 1901/02, Compiled from Official Records and Papers Presented to Parliament.* London: Great Britain India Office, 1903.

Great Britain War Office. *Statistics of the Military Effort of the British Empire during the Great War, 1914–1920.* London: His Majesty's Stationery Office, 1922.

Great Britain War Office, John Frederick Maurice, and Maurice Harold Grant. *History of the War in South Africa, 1899–1902.* London: Hurst and Blackett limited, 1906.

Great Britain. Foreign Office. *Handbook of Commercial Treaties, etc., with Foreign Powers.* London: His Majesty's Stationery Office, 1931.

Grimmer-Solem, Erik. *Learning Empire: Globalization and the German Quest for World Status, 1875–1919.* Cambridge and New York: Cambridge University Press, 2019.

Gross, Stephen G. *Export Empire: German Soft Power in Southeastern Europe, 1890–1945.* Cambridge and New York: Cambridge University Press, 2015.

Grunow-Osswald, *Elfriede Die Internationalisierung eines Konzerns: Daimler-Benz 1890–1997.* Vaihingen: IPA Verlag, 2006.

Gutmann, Alfred. *25 Jahre Lindstroem: 1904–1929.* Berlin: Carl Lindstroem A.G., 1929.

Hamied, Kwaja Abdul. *An Autobiography: A Life to Remember.* Bombay: Lalvani Pub. House, 1972.

Hanisch, Marc. "Curt Prüfer - Orientalist, Dragoman und Oppenheims 'man on the spot'." In *Erster Weltkrieg und Dschihad: Die Deutschen und die Revolutionierung des Orients,* edited by Wilfried Loth and Marc Hanisch, 167–191. Munich: Oldenbourg, 2014.

"Max Freiherr von Oppenheim und die Revolutionierung der islamischen Welt als anti-imperiale Befreiung von oben." In *Erster Weltkrieg und Dschihad: Die Deutschen und die Revolutionierung des Orients,* edited by Wilfried Loth and Marc Hanisch, 13–38. Munich: Oldenbourg, 2014.

Der Orient der Deutschen: Max von Oppenheim und die Konstituierung eines außenpolitischen Orients in der deutschen Nahostpolitik. Berlin: De Gruyter, 2021.

Hansen, Per H. *Danish Modern Furniture, 1930–2016: The Rise, Decline and Re-Emergence of a Cultural Market Category.* Odense: University Press of Southern Denmark, 2018.

"Networks, Narratives, and New Markets: The Rise and Decline of Danish Modern Furniture Design, 1930–1970." *Business History Review* 80, no. 3 (2006): 449–483.

Har Dayal, Lala. *Forty-Four Months in Germany and Turkey, February 1915 to October 1918: A Record of Personal Impressions.* London: P. S. King & Son, Ltd., 1920.

Hauner, Milan. *India in Axis Strategy: Germany, Japan, and Indian Nationalists in the Second World War.* Stuttgart: Klett-Cotta, 1981.

Haushofer, Karl. "Der Ost-Eurasiatische Zukunftsblock." *Zeitschrift für Geopolitik* 2 (1925): 81–87.

Hayes, Peter. *Industry and Ideology: IG Farben in the Nazi Era.* Cambridge and New York: Cambridge University Press, 1987.

Hayes, Romain. *Subhas Chandra Bose in Nazi Germany: Politics, Intelligence and Propaganda, 1941–43.* New York: Columbia University Press, 2011.

Headrick, Daniel R. *The Tentacles of Progress: Technology Transfer in the Age of Imperialism, 1850–1940.* New York: Oxford University Press, 1988.

  The Tools of Empire. Technology and European Imperialism in the Nineteenth Century. New York: Oxford University Press, 1981.

Hein, Bastian. *Die Westdeutschen und die Dritte Welt: Entwicklungspolitik und Entwicklungsdienste zwischen Reform und Revolte 1959–1974.* Munich: R. Oldenbourg Verlag, 2006.

Helleiner, Eric. "Economic Nationalism as a Challenge to Economic Liberalism? Lessons from the 19th Century." *International Studies Quarterly* 46 (2002): 307–329.

Helleiner, Eric, and Andreas Pickel, eds. *Economic Nationalism in a Globalizing World.* Ithaca, NY: Cornell University Press, 2005.

Henderson, W. O. *Friedrich List: Economist and Visionary, 1789–1846.* London and Totowa, NJ: F. Cass, 1983.

Henisz, Witold J. *Corporate Diplomacy: Building Reputations and Relationships with External Stakeholders.* Sheffield: Greenleaf Publishing Limited, 2014.

Henisz, Witold J., and Bennet A. Zelner. "Strategy and Competition in the Market and Nonmarket Arenas." *Academy of Management Perspectives* 26, no. 3 (2012): 40–51.

Henrikson, Alan K. "The Geographical 'Mental Maps' of American Foreign Policy Makers." *International Political Science Review* 1, no. 4 (1980): 495–530.

Higgins, David M. *Brands, Geographical Origin, and the Global Economy: A History from the Nineteenth Century to the Present.* Cambridge: Cambridge University Press, 2018.

Higgins, David, and Geofrrey Tweedale. "Asset or Liability? Trade Marks in the Sheffield Cutlery and Tool Trades." *Business History* 37, no. 3 (1995): 1–27.

Hitler, Adolf. *Mein Kampf [English Translation by Ralph Manheim 1943].* Boston, MA: Houghton Mifflin Company, 1943 [Original: 1925].

Hobsbawm, Eric J. *Nations and Nationalism Since 1780: Programme, Myth, Reality.* Cambridge: Cambridge University Press, 1992.

Hodgson, Geoffrey M. *How Economics Forgot History: The Problem of Historical Specificity in Social Science.* London and New York: Routledge, 2001.

Hodgson, James Goodwin. *Economic Nationalism.* New York: H. W. Wilson, 1933.

Hoffman, Ross J. S. *Great Britain and the German Trade Rivalry, 1875–1914.* New York: Russell & Russell, 1964.

Hoffmann, Wiebke. *Auswandern und Zurückkehren: Kaufmannsfamilien zwischen Bremen und Übersee: eine Mikrostudie, 1860–1930.* Münster: Waxmann, 2009.

Holmén, Janne. "Changing Mental Maps of the Baltic Sea and Mediterranean Regions." *Journal of Cultural Geography* 35, no. 2 (2018/05/04 2018): 230–250.

Huberich, Charles Henry. *The Law Relating to Trading With the Enemy.* New York: Baker, Voorhis & Company, 1918.

Hunck, Joseph M. *India's Silent Revolution: A Survey of Indo-German Cooperation.* Düsseldorf: Verlag Handelsblatt, 1958.

Ilgner, Max. *Exportsteigerung durch Einschaltung in die Industrialisierung der Welt.* Jena: Gustav Fischer, 1938.

Ince, Onur Ulas. "Friedrich List and the Imperial Origins of the National Economy." *New Political Economy* 21, no. 4 (2016/07/03 2016): 380–400.

India Census Commissioner. *General Report of the Census of India, 1901. Presented to both Houses of Parliament by Command of His Majesty.* London: Darling & Son, 1904.

India Fiscal Commission. *Report of the Indian Fiscal Commission 1921–22.* Simla: Superintendent Government Central Press, 1922.

Indian Industrial Commission. *Indian Industrial Commission Report 1916–1918.* Calcutta: Superintendent Governemt Printing India, 1918.

Minutes of Evidence 1916–1917, Vol. II, Bengal and Central Provinces. Calcutta: Superintendent Government Printing India, 1918.

Indian National Party. *British Rule in India; Condemned by the British Themselves.* London: Indian National Party, 1915.

Indian Tariff Board. *Report of the Indian Tariff Board Regarding the Grant of Supplementary Protection to the Steel Industry.* Calcutta: Government of India, 1925.

International Committee of the Red Cross, and F. Thormeyer. Reports on British prison-camps in India and Burma, visited by the International Red cross committee in February, March and April, 1917. London: T.F. Unwin Ltd., 1917.

Izawa, Ryo. "Municipalisation, War, Tax and Nationalisation: Imperial Continental Gas Association in an Era of Turmoil, 1824–1987." In *Multinational Enterprise, Political Risk and Organizational Change: From Total War to Cold War*, edited by Neil Forbes, Takafumi Kurosawa, and Ben Wubs, 55–68. New York: Routledge, 2019.

Jacobsen, Hans Adolf. *Nationalsozialistische Aussenpolitik, 1933–1938.* Frankfurt am Main: A. Metzner, 1968.

Jebb, Richard. *Studies in Colonial Nationalism.* London: E. Arnold, 1905.

Johnson, Jeffrey Allan, and Roy M. Macleod. "The War the Victors Lost: The Dilemmas of Chemical Disarmament, 1919–1926." In *Frontline and Factory: Comparative Perspectives on the Chemical Industry at War, 1914–1924*, edited by Roy M. Macleod and Jeffrey Allan Johnson, 221–245. Dordrecht: Springer, 2006.

Jones, Charles A. *International Business in the Nineteenth Century: The Rise and Fall of a Cosmopolitan Bourgeoisie.* New York: New York University Press, 1987.

Jones, Geoffrey. *Renewing Unilever: Transformation and Tradition.* Oxford: Oxford University Press, 2005.

"The End of Nationality? Global Firms and 'Borderless Worlds'." *Zeitschrift für Unternehmensgeschichte* 51, no. 2 (2006): 149–166.

"The Gramophone Company: An Anglo-American Multinational, 1898–1931." *Business History Review* 59, no. 1 (1985): 76–100.

"The Great Divergence and the Great Convergence." In *The Routledge Companion to the Makers of Global Business*, edited by Teresa Da Silva Lopes, Christina Lubinski and Heidi J. S. Tworek, 578–592. Abingdon and New York: Routledge, 2020.

"Learning to Live with Governments: Unilever in India and Turkey, 1950–1980." *Entreprises et Histoire* 49, no. 4 (2007): 78–101.

Multinationals and Global Capitalism: From the Nineteenth to the Twenty-First Century. Oxford and New York: Oxford University Press, 2005.

"Origins and Development of Global Business." In *The Routledge Companion to the Makers of Global Business*, edited by Teresa Da Silva Lopes, Christina Lubinski, and Heidi J. S. Tworek, 17–34. Abingdon and New York: Routledge, 2020.

Jones, Geoffrey G., and Rachael Comunale. "Business, Governments and Political Risk in South Asia and Latin America since 1970." *Australian Economic History Review* 58, no. 3 (2018): 233–264.

Jones, Geoffrey G., and Christina Lubinski. "Managing Political Risk in Global Business: Beiersdorf 1914–1990." *Enterprise & Society* 13, no. 1 (2012): 85–119.

Jones, Geoffrey G., and Simon Mowatt. "National Image as a Competitive Disadvantage: The Case of the New Zealand Organic Food Industry." *Business History* 58, no. 8 (2016): 1262–1288.

Kautsky, Karl, ed. *Die deutschen Dokumente zum Kriegsausbruch 1914. Herausgegeben von Max Montgelas and Walter Schuecking, 5 Bd.* Berlin: Deutsche Verlagsgesellschaft für Politik und Geschichte, 1919.

Kaye, John William. *The Administration of the East India Company*. London: R. Bentley, 1853.

Keenan, John Lawrence, and Lenore Sorsby. *A Steel Man in India*. New York: Duell, 1943.

Kerly, Duncan Mackenzie, Sir. *The Law of Merchandise Marks and the Criminal Law of False Marking, With a Chapter on Warranty of Trade Marks and a Collection of Statutes, General Orders and Forms*. London: Sweet & Maxwell, 1909.

Keynes, John Maynard. *The Economic Consequences of the Peace*. London: Macmillan, 1919.

Kinnear, Michael S. *The Gramophone Company's First Indian Recordings, 1899–1908*. Bombay: Popular Prakashan, 1994.

Sangeet Ratna, The Jewel of Music: A Bio-Discography of Khan Sahib Abdul Karim Khan, Victoria, Australia, 2003.

Nicole Records: A Discography of the 'Nicole Record' with a History of Nicole Frères, Limited, The Nicole Record Company, Limited and Associated Companies, Victoria, Australia, 2001.

"Odeon in India." *International Talking Machine Review* 77 (1990): 2260–2270.

Kipping, Matthias, R. Daniel Wadhwani, and Marcelo Bucheli. "Analyzing and Interpreting Historical Sources: A Basic Methodology." In *Organizations in Time: History, Theory, Methods*, edited by Marcelo Bucheli and R. Daniel Wadhwani, 305–329. Oxford: Oxford University Press, 2014.

Kittler, Friedrich A. *Gramophone, Film, Typewriter*. Stanford, CA: Stanford University Press, 1999.

272 Bibliography

Kleedehn, Patrick. *Die Rückkehr auf den Weltmarkt: Die Internationalisierung der Bayer AG Leverkusen nach dem Zweiten Weltkrieg*. Stuttgart: Franz Steiner Verlag, 2007.

Kleinschmidt, Christian, and Dieter Ziegler. "Deutsche Wirtschaftsinteressen zwischen Entwicklungshilfe und Dekolonisierung: eine Einleitung." In *Dekolonisierungsgewinner: Deutsche Aussenpolitik und Aussenwirtschaftsbeziehungen im Zeitalter des Kalten Krieges*, edited by Christian Kleinschmidt and Dieter Ziegler, 1–18. Berlin: De Gruyter, 2018.

Knoke, Josef Wilhelm. *Zwischen Weltwirtschaft und Wissenschaft: Der Unternehmer und Wirtschaftsbürger Henry Theodor von Böttinger (1848–1920)*. Essen: Klartext, 2019.

Knusel, Jack L. *West German Aid to Developing Nations*. New York: Praeger, 1968.

Kobrak, Christopher. "Politics, Corporate Governance, and the Dynamics of German Managerial Innovation: Schering AG between the Wars." *Enterprise & Society* 3, no. 3 (2002): 429–461.

Kobrak, Christopher, and Per. H. Hansen, eds. *European Business, Dictatorship, and Political Risk, 1920–1945*. New York: Berghahn Books, 2004.

Kobrak, Christopher, and Jana Wüstenhagen. "International Investment and Nazi Politics: The Cloaking of German Assets Abroad: 1936–1945." *Business History* 48, no. 3 (2006): 399–427.

Kochhar, Rajesh. "Tribhuvandas Kalyandas Gajjar (1863–1920): The Pioneering Industrial Chemist of Western India." *Current Science* 104, no. 8 (2013): 1093–1097.

Kocka, Jürgen. "The Entrepreneur, the Family, and Capitalism: Examples from the Early Phase of German Industrialization." In *Industrial Culture and Bourgeois Society: Business, Labor, and Bureaucracy in Modern Germany, 1800–1918*, edited by Jürgen Kocka, 103–138. New York: Berghahn Books, 1999.

Köhler, Ingo. *The Aryanization of Private Banks in the Third Reich*. Cambridge: Cambridge University Press, 2016.

König, Wolfgang. *Sir William Siemens 1823–1883*. Munich: C. H. Beck, 2020.

Koop, Volker. *Hitlers fünfte Kolonne: Die Auslands-Organisation der NSDAP*. Berlin: Be.bra, 2009.

Koppers, Wilhelm. *Geheimnisse des Dschungels: Eine Forschungsreise zu den Primitivstaemmen Zentral-Indiens 1938/39*. Lucerne: Josef Stocker, 1947.

Krampf, Arie. *The Israeli Path to Neoliberalism: The State, Continuity and Change*. London, New York: Routledge, 2018.

Kreutzmüller, Christoph. "Augen im Sturm? Ausländische Zeitungsberichte über die Judenverfolgung in Berlin 1918–1938." *Zeitschrift für Geschichtswissenschaft* 62, no. 1 (2014): 25–48.

Kruse, Hellmut. *Wagen und Winnen. Ein hanseatisches Kaufmannsleben im 20. Jahrhundert*. Hamburg: Die Hanse/EVA, 2006.

Kudaisya, Medha M. *Tryst with Prosperity: Indian Business and the Bombay Plan of 1944*. New York: Penguin, 2018.

Kuhlmann, Jan. *Subhas Chandra Bose und die Indienpolitik der Achsenmächte*. Berlin: Verlag Hans Schiler, 2003.

Kuhn, Ernst. *Der Einfluss des arischen Indiens auf die Nachbarländer im Süden und Osten*. Munich: C. Wolf & Sohn, 1903.

Kulke, Eckehard. *The Parsees in India: A Minority as Agent of Social Change.* Munich: Weltforum Verlag, 1974.

Kurosawa, Takafumi. "Breaking through the Double Blockade: Inter-Atlantic Wartime Communications at Roche." *Jahrbuch für Wirtschaftsgeschichte* 56, no. 1 (2015): 227–256.

Kurosawa, Takafumi, Neil Forbes, and Ben Wubs. "Political Risks and Nationalism." In *The Routledge Companion to the Makers of Global Business,* edited by Teresa Da Silva Lopes, Christina Lubinski and Heidi J. S. Tworek, 485–501. Abingdon and New York: Routledge, 2020.

Lee, Christopher J. *Making a World after Empire: The Bandung Moment and Its Political Afterlives.* Athens: Ohio University Press, 2010.

Lethbridge, Roper. *India and Imperial Preferences: With Statistical Tables.* New York, Bombay and Calcutta: Logmans, Green & Co., 1907.

Levi-Faur, David. "Friedrich List and the Political Economy of the Nation-State." *Review of International Political Economy* 4, no. 1 (1997): 154–178.

Lewis, Martin W., and Kären E. Wigen. *The Myth of Continents: A Critique of Metageography.* Berkeley, Los Angeles and London: University of California Press, 1997.

Liebau, Heike. "Berlin Indian Independence Committee." In *1914–1918-Online. International Encyclopedia of the First World War,* edited by Ute Daniel, Peter Gatrell, Oliver Janz, Heather Jones, Jennifer Keene, Alan Kramer, and Bill Nasson: issued by Freie Universität Berlin, Berlin 2015-03-27. DOI: 10.15463/ie1418.10588., 2015.

List, Friedrich. *The National System of Political Economy, translated from German by Sampson S. Lloyd.* London: Longmans, Green, and Co., 1885 [1841].

The Natural System of Political Economy, translated by *W. O. Henderson.* London and Totowa, NJ: F. Cass, 1983 [1837].

Outlines of American Political Economy. Philadelphia: Samuel Parker, 1827.

Lohmann, Heinrich Carl. *Die Ausfuhr Solinger Stahlwaren nach Britisch-Indien, Burma und Ceylon.* Würzburg: Mayr, 1934.

Loth, Wilfried, and Marc Hanisch, eds. *Erster Weltkrieg und Dschihad: Die Deutschen und die Revolutionierung des Orients.* Munich: Oldenbourg, 2014.

Lubinski, Christina. "Dynamische Fähigkeiten: Die Sparkassen und das Geschäft mit dem Mittelstand." In *Die Entstehung der modernen Sparkasse: Von der "Ersparnisanstalt" zum marktorientierten Unternehmen (1950er bis 1980er Jahre),* edited by Günther Schulz, 137–164. Stuttgart: S-Communication Services, 2022.

"From 'History as Told' to 'History as Experienced': Contextualizing the Uses of the Past." *Organization Studies* 39, no. 12 (2018): 1785–1809.

"Global Trade and Indian Politics: The German Dye Business in India before 1947." *Business History Review* 89, no. 3 (2015): 503–530.

"Liability of Foreignness in Historical Context: German Business in Preindependence India (1880–1940)." *Enterprise & Society* 15, no. 4 (2014): 722–758.

Lubinski, Christina, Valeria Giacomin, and Klara Schnitzer. "Internment as a Business Challenge: Political Risk Management and German Multinationals in Colonial India (1914–1947)." *Business History* 63, no. 1 (2021): 72–97.

Lubinski, Christina, and R. Daniel Wadhwani. "Geopolitical Jockeying: Economic Nationalism and Multinational Strategy in Historical Perspective." *Strategic Management Journal* 41, no. 3 (2020): 400–421.

Lundan, Sarianna M., and Geoffrey Jones. "The 'Commonwealth Effect' and the Process of Internationalisation." *World Economy* 24, no. 1 (2001): 99–118.

Luo, Yadong. "Toward a Cooperative View of MNC-Host Government Relations: Building Blocks and Performance Implications." *Journal of International Business Studies* 32, no. 3 (2001): 401–419.

Lynch, Kevin. *The Image of the City.* Cambridge MA: MIT Press, 1960.

Magee, Gary B., and Andrew S. Thompson. *Empire and Globalisation: Networks of People, Goods and Capital in the British World, c. 1850–1914.* Cambridge and New York: Cambridge University Press, 2010.

Mahalanobis, Prasanta Chandra. *The Approach of Operational Research to Planning in India.* Bombay: Asia Publishing House, 1963.

Malaviya, Madan Mohan. *A Criticism of Montagu-Chelmsford Proposals of Indian Constitutional Reform.* Allahabad: C. Y. Chintamani, 1918.

Manela, Erez. *The Wilsonian Moment: Self-Determination and the International Origins of Anticolonial Nationalism.* Oxford and New York: Oxford University Press, 2007.

Manikumar, K. A. *A Colonial Economy in the Great Depression, Madras (1929–1937).* Chennai: Orient Longman, 2003.

Manjapra, Kris. *Age of Entanglement: German and Indian Intellectuals across Empire.* Cambridge, MA: Harvard University Press, 2014.

"The Anticolonial Laboratory: Indian Nationalist Diaspora in German-Speaking Europe." In *The Bauhaus in Calcutta: An Encounter of Cosmopolitan Avant-Gardes,* edited by Regina Bittner and Kathrin Rhomberg, 151–171. Ostfildern: Hatje Cantz Verlag, 2013.

"Transnational Approaches to Global History: A View from the Study of German-Indian Entanglement." *German History* 32, no. 2 (2014): 274–293.

Mann, Michael. "Touchbearers Upon the Path of Progress: Britain's Ideology of a 'Moral and Material Progress' in India." In *Colonialism as Civilizing Mission: Cultural Ideology in British India,* edited by Harald Fischer-Tiné and Michael Mann, 1–26. London: Anthem Press, 2004.

Markovits, Claude. *Indian Business and Nationalist Politics, 1931–1939: The Indigenous Capitalist Class and the Rise of the Congress Party.* Cambridge: Cambridge University Press, 1985.

"Indian Business and the Congress Provincial Governments 1937–39." *Modern Asian Studies* 15, no. 3 (1981): 487–526.

Martland, Peter. "Gaisberg, Frederick William (1873–1951)." *In Oxford Dictionary of National Biography.* Oxford: Oxford University Press, 2004.

Recording History: The British Record Industry, 1888–1931. Lanham, MD: Scarecrow Press, 2013.

Since Records Began: EMI, the First 100 Years. London: Batsford, 1997.

McDonough, Frank. *Neville Chamberlain, Appeasement, and the British Road to War.* Manchester: Manchester University Press, 1998.

McKale, Donald M. *The Swastika Outside Germany.* Kent, OH: Kent State University Press, 1977.

McKenna, Christopher D. *The World's Newest Profession: Management Consulting in the Twentieth Century*. Cambridge: Cambridge University Press, 2006.

Mehta, Makrand. "Science versus Technology: The Early Years of the Kala Bhavan, Baroda, 1890–1896." *Indian Journal of History of Science* 27, no. 2 (1992): 145–170.

Miller, Rory M. "Staffing and Management in British MNEs in Argentina and Chile, 1930–1970." In *The Impact of Globalization on Argentina and Chile: Business Enterprises and Entrepreneurship*, edited by Geoffrey Jones and Andrea Lluch, 152–181. Cheltenham: Edward Elgar, 2015.

Millikan, Max E., and Walt W. Rostow. *A Proposal: Key to an Effective Foreign Policy*. New York: Harper and Brothers, 1957.

Milne, David. *America's Rasputin: Walt Rostow and the Vietnam War*. New York: Hill and Wang, 2001.

Mintzberg, Henry, and James A. Waters. "Of Strategies, Deliberate and Emergent." *Strategic Management Journal* 6, no. 3 (1985): 257–272.

Misra, Maria. *Business, Race, and Politics in British India, c.1850–1960*. Oxford: Clarendon Press, 1999.

Mittal, Satish Chandra. *Freedom Movement in Punjab, 1905–29*. Delhi: Concept Pub. Co., 1977.

Modig, Hans. *Swedish Match Interests in British India During the Interwar Years*. Stockholm: LiberFörlag, 1979.

Mollan, Simon, and Kevin D. Tennent. "International Taxation and Corporate Strategy: Evidence from British Overseas Business, circa 1900–1965." *Business History* 57, no. 7 (2015): 1054–1081.

Moore, Jerrold Northrop. *A Voice in Time: The Gramophone of Fred Gaisberg, 1873–1951*. London: Hamilton, 1976.

Mordhorst, Mads. "Arla and Danish National Identity: Business History as Cultural History." *Business History* 56, no. 1 (2014): 116–133.

Morrow, John H. Jr. *The Great War: An Imperial History*. London and New York: Routledge, 2004.

Murphy, Mahon. *Colonial Captivity during the First World War: Internment and the Fall of the German Empire, 1914–1919*. Cambridge: Cambridge University Press, 2017.

Musolino, Dario. "The Mental Maps of Italian Entrepreneurs: A Quali-Quantitative Approach." *Journal of Cultural Geography* 35, no. 2 (2018/05/04 2018): 251–273.

Myrdal, Gunnar. *Rich Lands and Poor: The Road to World Prosperity*. New York: Harper & Brothers, 1958.

Nakano, Takeshi. "Alfred Marshall's Economic Nationalism." *Nations and Nationalism* 13, no. 1 (2007): 57–76.

Natarajan, S. *West of Suez*. Bombay: Nalanda Publications, 1938.

Nayak, Amar K. J. R. *Multinationals in India: FDI and Complementation Strategy in a Developing Country*. Basingstoke: Palgrave Macmillan, 2008.

Nehru, Jawaharlal. *Jawaharlal Nehru's Speeches, Vol. 1, Sept. 1946–May 1949*. New Delhi: Government of India. Ministry of information and broadcasting. The publications division, 1967 [1949].

"Letter Nehru to Vijaya Lakshmi Pandit, 17 Sept. 1957." In *Selected Works of Jawaharlal Nehru, 1 August–31 October 1957, Second Series, Volume 39*, edited by Mushirul Hasan, 109–111. New Delhi: Jawaharlal Nehru Memorial Fund, 1984 [1957].

"Maintain Individuality for Creativity and Progress: Speech at a Civic Reception, Trivandrum, April 24, 1958." In *Selected Works of Jawaharlal Nehru, Second Series, Volume Forty Two (1 April–30 June 1958)*, edited by Aditya Mukherjee and Mridula Mukherjee, 26–38. New Delhi: Jawaharlal Nehru Memorial Fund, 2010 [1958].

"Statement on Foreign Investments, April 6, 1949." In *Selected Works of Jawaharlal Nehru, Second Series, Volume Ten*, edited by S. Gopal, 49–51. New Delhi: Jawaharlal Nehru Memorial Fund, 1990 [1949].

Neuman, Daniel M. *The Life of Music in North India: The Organization of an Artistic Tradition*. Chicago: University of Chicago Press, 1990.

Oberhaus, Salvador. "Zum wilden Aufstande entflammen": Die deutsche Propagandastrategie für den Orient im Ersten Weltkrieg am Beispiel Ägypten. Saarbrücken: VDM Verlag, 2007.

Oberholzer-Gee, Felix, and Dennis A. Yao. "Integrated Strategy: Residual Market and Exchange Imperfections as the Foundation of Sustainable Competitive Advantage." *Strategy Science* 3, no. 2 (2018): 463–480.

Osterhammel, Jürgen. "Nationalism and Globalization." In *The Oxford Handbook of the History of Nationalism*, edited by John Breuilly, 694–712. Oxford: Oxford University Press, 2013.

Osterheld, Joachim. "British Policy towards German Speaking Emigrants in India 1939–45." In *Jewish Exile in India 1933–1945*, edited by Anil Bhatti and Johannes H. Voight, 25–44. New Delhi: Manohar, 1999.

Panayi, Panikos. "German Business Interests in Britain During the First World War." *Business History* 32, no. 2 (1990): 244–258.

ed. *Germans as Minorities during the First World War: Global Comparative Perspective*. Burlington, VT: Ashgate, 2014.

The Germans in India: Elite European Migrants in the British Empire. Manchester: Manchester University Press, 2017.

Prisoners of Britain: German Civilian and Combatant Internees During the First World War. Manchester: Manchester University Press, 2012.

Pautsch, Ilse Dorothee. *Akten zur Auswärtigen Politik der Bundesrepublik Deutschland: Band I: 1. Januar bis 31. März 1962*. Munich: R. Oldenbourg Verlag, 2010.

Payn, Howard. *The Merchandise Marks Act 1887, with special reference to the importation sections and the customs regulations and orders made thereunder*. London: Stevens, 1888.

Pearce, Kimber Charles. *Rostow, Kennedy, and the Rhetoric of Foreign Aid*. East Lansing: Michigan State University Press, 2001.

Pedersen, Morten. *Internationalisation and Strategic Control: An Industrial History*. Abingdon and New York: Routledge, 2021.

Pickel, Andreas. "False Oppositions: Reconceptualizing Economic Nationalism in a Globalized World." In *Economic Nationalism in a Globalizing World*, edited by Eric Helleiner and Andreas Pickel, 1–20. Ithaca, NY: Cornell University Press, 2005.

Pillai, A. Raman. "Das B. T. [Berliner Tageblatt] und Indien." *Der Tagesspiegel* 250 (1918).

Das Judentum und die gegenwärtige Weltlage Hildburghausen: Reprint of Politisch-Anthropologische Monatsschrift 20, issue 5–7, 1921.

Deutschland-Indiens Hoffnung: Rede. Göttingen: Carl Spielmeyer, 1914.

"Indien und die europaeische Krise." *Westermanns Monatshefte* December (1914).

Plumpe, Gottfried. *Die I.G. Farbenindustrie AG: Wirtschaft, Technik und Politik 1904–1945.* Berlin: Duncker & Humblot, 1990.

Pomeranz, Kenneth. *The Great Divergence: China, Europe, and the Making of the Modern World Economy.* Princeton, NJ: Princeton University Press, 2000.

Preuß, Sabine, and Deutsche Gesellschaft für Internationale Zusammenarbeit GmbH. *'Ohne Toleranz funktioniert nichts': Indisch-deutsche Technische Zusammenarbeit: Berufsbildung, Hochschule, ländlicher Entwicklung (1958–2010), Reportagen, Interviews, Porträts.* Frankfurt am Main: Brandes & Apsel, 2013.

Probst, Hans Georg. *Unter indischer Sonne: 19 Monate englischer Kriegsgefangenschaft in Ahmednagar.* Herborn: Oranienverlag, 1917.

Proctor, Tammy M. *Civilians in a World at War, 1914–1918.* New York: New York University Press, 2010.

Pryke, Sam. "Economic Nationalism: Theory, History and Prospects." *Global Policy* 3, no. 3 (2012): 281–291.

Raianu, Mircea. *Tata: The Global Corporation That Built Indian Capitalism.* Cambridge, MA: Harvard University Press, 2021.

Raina, Dhruv, and S. Irfan Habib. "Technical Institutes in Colonial India Kala Bhavan, Baroda (1890–1990)." *Economic and Political Weekly* 26, no. 46 (1991): 2619–2621.

Ramnath, Aparajith. *The Birth of an Indian Profession: Engineers, Industry, and the State, 1900–47.* New Delhi: Oxford University Press, 2017.

Ranade, Mahadev Govind. *Essays on Indian Economics: A Collection of Essays and Speeches.* Madras: G. A. Natesan & Co., 1906 [1898].

Ranjan, Prabhash. *India and Bilateral Investment Treaties: Refusal, Acceptance, Backlash.* Oxford and New Delhi: Oxford University Press, 2019.

Ray Choudhury, Ranabir. *Early Calcutta Advertisements, 1875–1925 [A Selection from the Statesman].* Bombay: Nachiketa Publications, 1992.

Ray, Rajat Kanta. "The Bazaar: Changing Structural Characteristics of the Indigenous Section of the Indian Economy before and after the Great Depression." *The Indian Economic & Social History Review* 25, no. 3 (1988): 263–318.

Reader, W. J. *Imperial Chemical Industries: A History.* London: Oxford University Press, 1970.

Reckendrees, Alfred. *Beiersdorf: The Company Behind the Brands Nivea, Tesa, Hansaplast & Co.* Munich: Beck, 2018.

"Business as a Means of Foreign Policy or Politics as a Means of Production? The German Government and the Creation of Friedrich Flick's Upper Silesian Industrial Empire (1921–1935)." *Enterprise & Society* 14, no. 1 (2013): 99–143.

Reich, Robert. *The Work of Nations: Preparing Ourselves for 21st-Century Capitalism.* New York: Vintage Books, 1992.

Reinert, Erik S. "German Economics as Development Economics: From the Thirty Years' War to World War II." In *The Origins of Development Economics: How Schools of Economic Thought Have Addressed Development,* edited by Jomo K. S. and Erik S. Reinert, 48–68. London and New York: Zed Books, 2005.

Reithinger, Anton. *Das wirtschaftliche Gesicht Europas.* Stuttgart and Berlin: Deutsche Verlags-Anstalt, 1936.

Reserve Bank of India. *Foreign Collaboration in Indian Industry: Survey Report.* Bombay: Reserve Bank of India, 1968.

Rist, Gilbert. *The History of Development: From Western Origins to Global Faith.* New York: Zed Books, 1997.

Rius-Ulldemolins, Joaquim. "Barcelona and SEAT, a History of Lost Opportunity: Corporate Marketing, Nation Branding, and Consumer Nationalism in the Automotive Industry." *Enterprise & Society* 16, no. 4 (2015): 811–846.

Roland, Joan G. *The Jewish Communities of India: Identity in a Colonial Era.* New Brunswick, NJ: Transaction, 1998.

Rostow, Walt W. *The Stages of Economic Growth: A Non-Communist Manifesto.* Cambridge: Cambridge University Press, 1990 [1960].

Rothermund, Dietmar. *An Economic History of India: From Pre-Colonial Times to 1991.* London and New York: Routledge, 1993.

Roy, Tirthankar. *A Business History of India: Enterprise and the Emergence of Capitalism from 1700.* Cambridge: Cambridge University Press, 2018.

The Economic History of India, 1857–1947. New Delhi: Oxford University Press, 2006.

Ryland, Shane. "Edwin Montagu in India, 1917–1918: Politics of the Montagu-Chelmsford report." *South Asia: Journal of South Asian Studies* 3, no. 1 (1973/08/01 1973): 79–92.

Said, Edward W. *Orientalism.* New York: Vintage Books, 1979.

Sampath, Vikram. *'My Name is Gauhar Jan!' The Life and Times of a Musician.* New Delhi: Rupa Publications, 2010.

Sarkar, Benoy Kumar. "The Hitler-State: A Landmark in the Political, Economic and Social Remaking of the German People (part I)." *The Insurance and Finance Review* 4, no. 8 (1933): 466–474.

"The Hitler-State: A Landmark in the Political, Economic and Social Remaking of the German People (part II)." *The Insurance and Finance Review* 4, no. 9 (1933): 515–525.

The Political Philosophies since 1905. Madras: B. G. Paul & Co., 1928.

The Politics of Boundaries and Tendencies in International Relations. Calcutta: N. M. Ray Chowdhury, 1926.

The Sociology of Races, Cultures and Human Progress: Studies in the Relations between Asia and Eur-America. Calcutta: Chuckervetty, Chatterjee & Co., 1939.

Sarkar, Sumit. *The Swadeshi Movement in Bengal, 1903–1908.* New Delhi: People's Pub. House, 1973.

Schacht, Hjalmar. *My First Seventy-Six Years: The Autobiography of Hjalmar Schacht.* Translated by Diana Pyke. London: Alan Wingate, 1955.

Schickert, Adolf. *Die Ausfuhr und das Ausfuhrgeschäft nach Britisch-Indien.* Gelnhausen: Kalbfleisch, 1929.

Schroeder, Leopold von. *Mysterium und Mimus im Rigveda.* Leipzig: H. Haessel, 1908.

Schröter, Harm G. "Cartelization and Decartelization in Europe, 1870–1995: Rise and Decline of an Economic Institution." *Journal of European Economic History* 25, no. 1 (1996): 129–153.

"Cartels Revisited: An Overview on Fresh Questions, New Methods, and Surprising Results." *Revue Economique* 64, no. 6 (2013): 989–1010.

Schröter, Harm G. "Continuity and Change: German Multinationals Since 1850." In *The Rise of Multinationals in Continental Europe*, edited by Geoffrey Jones and Harm G.Schröter, 28–48. Aldershot: Edward Elgar, 1993.

Scott, John D. *Siemens Brothers, 1858–1958: An Essay in the History of Industry*. London: Weidenfeld and Nicolson, 1958.

Sen Gupta, Nares C., and Kanti C. Sen. *Indian Company Manual: A Practical Handbook for Lawyers and Businessmen*. third ed. Calcutta: N. M. Raychowdhury Co. Ltd., 1942.

Sen, Sudhir. *Deutschland und die indische Wirtschaft*. Stuttgart: F. Enke, 1937.

Shaffer, Ernest N. *Ein Emigrant entdeckt Indien*. Munich: Verlag Information und Wissen, 1971.

Shirer, William L. *End of a Berlin Diary*. New York: Popular Library, 1961 [1947].

Shulman, Stephen. "Nationalist Sources of International Economic Integration." *International Studies Quarterly* 44, no. 3 (2000): 365–390.

Sidki Darendeli, Izzet, and T. L. Hill. "Uncovering the Complex Relationships between Political Risk and MNE Firm Legitimacy: Insights from Libya." *Journal of International Business Studies* 47, no. 1 (2016): 68–92.

Sieferle, Rolf Peter. "Indien und die Arier in der Rassentheorie." *Zeitschrift für Kulturaustausch* 37, no. 3 (1987): 444–467.

Singh, Harkishan. "Khwaja Abdul Hamied (1898–1972) – Pioneer Scientist Industrialist." *Indian Journal of History of Science* 45, no. 4 (2010): 533–558.

Sinha, Mrinalini. "Britishness, Clubbability, and the Colonial Public Sphere: The Genealogy of an Imperial Institution in Colonial India." *Journal of British Studies* 40, no. 4 (2001): 489–521.

Sinha, Vineeta. "Sarkar, Benoy Kumar (1887–1949)." In *The Blackwell Encyclopedia of Sociology*, edited by George Ritzer, 4006–4009. London: Blackwell, 2006.

Six, Clemens. "Challenging the Grammar of Difference: Benoy Kumar Sarkar, Global Mobility and Anti-Imperialism Around the First World War." *European Review of History: Revue européenne d'histoire* 25, no. 3–4 (2018): 431–449.

Sluyterman, Keetie. "Decolonisation and the Organisation of the International Workforce: Dutch Multinationals in Indonesia, 1945–1967." *Business History* 62, no. 7 (2020): 1182–1201.

Smith, Andrew. "The Winds of Change and the End of the Comprador System in the Hongkong and Shanghai Banking Corporation." *Business History* 58, no. 2 (2016): 179–206.

Smith, Andrew, and Daniel Simeone. "Learning to Use the Past: The Development of a Rhetorical History Strategy by the London Headquarters of the Hudson's Bay Company." *Management & Organizational History* 12, no. 4 (2017): 334–356.

Smith, Anthony D. *Nationalism*. Oxford: Oxford University Press, 2010.

Smith, Vincent Arthur. *The Early History of India, From 600 B. C. to the Muhammadan Conquest*. Oxford: Clarendon Press, 1908.

Speich Chassé, Daniel. *Die Erfindung des Bruttosozialprodukts: Globale Ungleichheit in der Wissensgeschichte der Ökonomie*. Göttingen: Vandenhoeck & Ruprecht, 2013.

Speich, Daniel. "The Use of Global Abstractions: National Income Accounting in the Period of Imperial Decline." *Journal of Global History* 6, no. 1 (2011): 7–28.

Spengler, Oswald. *Neubau des Deutschen Reiches*. Munich: Beck, 1924.

Sperling, Jan Bodo. *The Human Dimension of Technical Assistance: The German Experience at Rourkela, India*. Ithaca, NY: Cornell University Press, 1969.

Statistisches Reichsamt Germany. *Statistisches Jahrbuch für das Deutsche Reich*. Berlin: Hobbing, several volumes.

Stevens, Charles E., and Oded Shenkar. "The Liability of Home: Institutional Friction and Firm Disadvantage Abroad." In *Institutional Theory in International Business and Management*, edited by Laszlo Tihanyi, Timothy M. Devinney, and Torben Pedersen, 127–148. Bingley: Emerald Group Publishing Limited, 2012.

Stevens, Charles E., En Xie, and Mike W. Peng. "Toward a Legitimacy-Based View of Political Risk: The Case of Google and Yahoo in China." *Strategic Management Journal* 37, no. 5 (2016): 945–963.

Strachan, Hew. "The First World War as a Global War." *First World War Studies* 1, no. 1: 3–14.

Strother, French. *Fighting Germany's Spies*. Garden City, NY: Doubleday, Page, 1918.

Subramanian, Ajantha. *The Caste of Merit: Engineering Education in India*. Cambridge, MA: Harvard University Press, 2019.

Suddaby, Roy, Diego Coraiola, Charles Harvey, and William Foster. "History and the Micro-Foundations of Dynamic Capabilities." *Strategic Management Journal* 41, no. 3 (2020): 530–556.

Sugihara, Kaoru. "Notes on the Trade Statistics of British India." *Newsletter Osaka University, Faculty of Economics* 6 (www.ier.hit-u.ac.jp/COE/Japanese/Newsletter/No.6.english/SUGI.html) (1997).

Szöllösi-Janze, Margit. "Losing the War but Gaining Ground: The German Chemical Industry during World War I." In *The German Chemical Industry in the Twentieth Century*, edited by John E. Lesch, 91–121. Dordrecht: Kluwer, 2000.

Tamir, Yael. *Liberal Nationalism*. Princeton, NJ: Princeton University Press, 1993.

Tammen, Helmuth. *Die I. G. Farbenindustrie Aktiengesellschaft (1925–1933): ein Chemiekonzern in der Weimarer Republik*. Berlin: H. Tammen, 1978.

Tandon, J. K. *Indo-German Economic Relations*. New Delhi: National, 1978.

Teece, David J. "A Dynamic Capabilities-Based Entrepreneurial Theory of the Multinational Enterprise." *Journal of International Business Studies* 45, no. 1 (2014): 8–37.

Tetzlaff, Stefan. "Revolution or Evolution? The Making of the Automobile Sector as a Key Industry in Mid-Twentieth Century India." In *Cars, Automobility and Development in Asia: Wheels of Change*, edited by Arve Hansen and Kenneth Bo Nielsen, 62–79. London and New York: Routledge, 2017.

Thakurdas, Purshotamdas, J. R. D. Tata, G. D. Birla, Ardeshir Dalal, Shri Ram, Kasturbhai Lalbhai, A. D. Shroff, and John Matthai. *Memorandum Outlining a Plan of Economic Development for India, Part One*. London: Penguin Books, 1944.

The Engineering Association of India. *Indian Engineering Industries*. Calcutta: J. N. Ghosh, 1953.

The Times of India. *Directory of Bombay (City & Presidency), Karachie-Poona-Ahmedabad*. Bombay: The Times of India Office, 1932.

Tietke, Mathias. *Yoga im Nationalsozialismus: Konzepte, Kontraste, Konsequenzen.* Kiel: Ludwig, 2011.

Tomlinson, B. R. "Britain and the Indian Currency Crisis, 1930–2." *Economic History Review* 32, no. 1 (1979): 88–99.

Tooze, J. Adam. *Statistics and the German state, 1900–1945: The Making of Modern Economic Knowledge.* Cambridge and New York: Cambridge University Press, 2001.

The Wages of Destruction: The Making and Breaking of the Nazi Economy. New York: Viking, 2007.

Trautmann, Thomas R. *Aryans and British India.* Berkeley: University of California Press, 1997.

Travis, Anthony S. *The Rainbow Makers: The Origins of the Synthetic Dyestuffs Industry in Western Europe.* Bethlehem and London: Lehigh University Press, 1993.

Trentmann, Frank. *Free Trade Nation: Commerce, Consumption, and Civil Society in Modern Britain.* Oxford and New York: Oxford University Press, 2008.

Tripathi, Dwijendra, and Jyoti Jumani. *The Concise Oxford History of Indian Business.* New Delhi, Oxford, and New York: Oxford University Press, 2007.

Trivedi, Lisa. *Clothing Gandhi's Nation: Homespun and Modern India.* Bloomington: Indiana University Press, 2007.

Tucher, Paul H. von. *Nationalism, Case and Crisis in Missions: German Missions in British India, 1939–1946.* Erlangen: P. Tucher, 1980.

Tworek, Heidi. *News from Germany: The Competition to Control World Communications, 1900–1945.* Cambridge, MA: Harvard University Press, 2019.

Unger, Corinna. *Entwicklungspfade in Indien: Eine internationale Geschichte, 1947–1980.* Göttingen: Wallstein, 2015.

"Export und Entwicklung: Westliche Wirtschaftsinteressen in Indian im Kontext der Dekolonisation und des Kalten Krieges." *Jahrbuch für Wirtschaftsgeschichte/Economic History Yearbook* 53, no. 1 (2012): 69–86.

"Industrialization vs. Agrarian Reform: West German Modernization Policies in India in the 1950s and 1960s." *Journal of Modern European History* 8, no. 1 (2010): 47–65.

"Rourkela, ein 'Stahlwerk im Dschungel': Industrialisierung, Modernisierung und Entwicklungshilfe im Kontext von Dekolonisation und Kaltem Krieg (1950–1970)." *Archiv für Sozialgeschichte* 48 (2008): 367–388.

United States. *United States Congressional Serial Set, No. 2685.* Washington DC: Government Printing Office, 1890.

United States Census Bureau. *Statistical Abstract of the United States: 1901.* Washington DC: Government Printing Office, 1902.

United States Tariff Commission. *Census of Dyes and Other Synthetic Organic Chemicals 1921.* Washington DC: Government Printing Office, 1922.

Cutlery Products: A General Survey of the Industries of the United States, Germany, and the United Kingdom, and of International Trade, with Particular Reference to Factors Essential to Tariff Considerations. Washington DC: Government Printing Office, 1938.

Urchs, Oswald. "Beobachtungen eines Lagerarztes über psycho-neurotische Reaktionen während einer über sieben Jahre dauernden Internierung in Britisch-Indien." *Psyche* 11, no. 2 (1948): 181–210.

"Zur Frage der Spätschäden nach Kriegs-Malaria." *Muenchner Medizinische Wochenschrift* 100, no. 18 (1958): 710–713.

van der Eng, Pierre. "Managing Political Imperatives in War Time: Strategic Responses of Philips in Australia, 1939–1945." *Business History* 59, no. 5 (2017): 645–666.

"Turning Adversity into Opportunity: Philips in Australia, 1945–1980." *Enterprise & Society* 19, no. 1 (2018): 179–207.

Varottil, Umakanth. "The Evolution of Corporate Law in Post-Colonial India: From Transplant to Autochthony." *American University International Law Review* 31, no. 2 (2016): 253–325.

Vatsal, Tulsi. *Caring for Life: The Cipla Story since 1935.* Mumbai: The Shoestring Publisher, 2020.

Verg, Erik, Gottfried Plumpe, and Heinz Schultheis. *Meilensteine: 125 Jahre Bayer, 1863–1988.* Leverkusen: Bayer, 1988.

Vernede, R. E. *An Ignorant in India.* Edinburgh and London: William Blackwood and Sons, 1911.

Vivekanandan, B. *Global Visions of Olof Palme, Bruno Kreisky and Willy Brandt: International Peace and Security, Co-operation, and Development.* Cham: Palgrave Macmillan, 2016.

Voigt, Johannes H. *Die Indienpolitik der DDR: Von den Anfängen bis zur Anerkennung (1952–1972).* Cologne: Böhlau, 2008.

"Hitler und Indien." *Vierteljahrshefte für Zeitgeschichte* 19, no. 1 (1971): 33–63.

von Daniels, Adam Edler. *Vollständige Abschilderung der Schwert- und Messer-Fabriken: fort sonstigen Stahl-Manufacturen in Sohlingen.* Düsseldorf: I. G. Boegeman, 1802.

von Drigalski, Dierk. *Al andar se hace camino: Stationen eines langen Weges.* Berlin: epubli GmbH, 2011.

von Papen, Franz. *Memoirs.* Translated by Brian Connell. London: André Deutsch, 1922.

Vorwig, Wilhelm R., and Government of India Ministry of Commerce and Industry. *Automobile Manufacture in India.* New Delhi: Government of India Publications, 1953.

Warren, Algernon. *Commercial Travelling: Its Features, Past and Present.* London: T. Fisher Unwin, 1904.

Webster, Anthony. *The Twilight of the East India Company. The Evolution of Anglo-Asian Commerce and Politics, 1790–1860.* Woodbridge and Rochester, NY: Boydell & Brewer, 2009.

Weiher, Sigfrid von. *Die englischen Siemens-Werke und das Siemens-Überseegeschäft in der zweiten Hälfte des 19. Jahrhunderts.* Berlin: Duncker & Humblot, 1990.

Weis, Wolfgang. *Hermesbürgschaften, ein Instrument deutscher Aussenpolitik?: Eine Fallstudie zum Verhältnis von Aussenpolitik und Aussenwirtschaftspolitik.* Munich: tuduv-Verlags-Gesellschaft, 1990.

White, John. *German Aid: A Survey of the Sources, Policy and Structure of German Aid.* London: The Overseas Development Institute Ltd., 1965.

White, Nicholas. "Surviving Sukarno: British Business in Post-Colonial Indonesia, 1950–67." *Modern Asian Studies* 46, no. 5 (2012): 1277–1315.

Wiesen, S. Jonathan. *West German Industry and the Challenge of the Nazi Past 1945–55.* Chapel Hill: University of North Carolina Press, 2001.

Wilkins, Mira. "European and North American Multinationals, 1870–1914: Comparisons and Contrasts." *Business History* 30, no. 1 (1988): 8–45.

ed. *The Growth of Multinationals.* Aldershot: Edward Elgar, 1991.

The History of Foreign Investment in the United States to 1914. Cambridge, MA: Harvard University Press, 1989.

"Multinationals and Dictatorship. Europe in the 1930s and early 1940s." In *European Business, Dictatorship, and Political Risk, 1920–1945*, edited by Christopher Kobrak and Per. H. Hansen, 22–38. New York: Berghahn Books, 2004.

Wolpert, Stanley A. *Tilak and Gokhale: Revolution and Reform in the Making of Modern India.* Berkeley: University of California Press, 1962.

Woods, Philip. "The Montagu-Chelmsford Reforms (1919): A Re-assessment." *South Asia: Journal of South Asian Studies* 17, no. 1 (1994): 25–42.

Wubs, Ben. *International Business and National War Interests: Unilever between Reich and Empire, 1939–45.* London and New York: Routledge, 2008.

"Unilever's Struggle for Control: An Anglo-Dutch Multinational under German Occupation." *Zeitschrift für Unternehmensgeschichte* 52, no. 1 (2007): 57–84.

Yarbrough, Beth V., and Robert M. Yarbrough. *The World Economy: Trade and Finance.* Mason, OH: Thomson/South-Western, 2006.

Zachariah, Benjamin. "Transfers, Formations, Transformations? Some Programmatic Notes on Facism in India, c. 1922–1938." In *Cultural Transfers in Dispute: Representations in Asia, Europe, and the Arab World Since the Middle Ages*, edited by Jörg Feuchter, Friedhelm Hoffmann, and Bee Yun, 167–192. Frankfurt am Main and New York: Campus, 2011.

Zaheer, Srilata. "Overcoming the Liability of Foreignness." *Academy of Management Journal* 38, no. 2 (1995): 341–363.

Zaman, Muhammad H., and Tarun Khanna. "The Cost and Evolution of Quality at Cipla Ltd., 1935–2016." *Business History Review* 95, no. 2 (2021): 249–274.

Zantop, Susanne. *Colonial Fantasies: Conquest, Family, and Nation in Precolonial Germany, 1770–1870.* Durham, NC, and London: Duke University Press, 1997.

Zöllner, Hans-Bernd. Birma zwischen *"Unabhängigkeit zuerst, Unabhängigkeit zuletzt:" Die birmanische Unabhängigkeitsbewegungen und ihre Sicht der zeitgenössischen Welt am Beispiel der birmanisch-deutschen Beziehungen zwischen 1920 und 1948.* Münster: LIT, 2000.

Index

Printed in the United States
by Baker & Taylor Publisher Services